ERP

Tools, Techniques, and Applications for Integrating the Supply Chain

The St. Lucie Press/APICS Series on Resource Management

ERP

Tools, Techniques, and Applications for Integrating the Supply Chain

by

Carol A. Ptak
CFPIM, CIRM, Jonah

with

Eli Schragenheim

The St. Lucie Press/APICS Series on Resource Management

S^t_L

St. Lucie Press
Boca Raton • London
New York • Washington, D.C.

APICS®
THE EDUCATIONAL SOCIETY
FOR RESOURCE MANAGEMENT
Alexandria, Virginia

Library of Congress Cataloging-in-Publication Data

Ptak, Carol A.
  ERP: tools, techniques, and applications for integrating the supply chain /
Carol A. Ptak, Eli Schragenheim.
        p.   cm. -- (St. Lucie Press / APICS series on resource management)
      Includes bibliographical references and index.
      ISBN 1-57444-270-8 (alk. paper)
      1. Production management. 2. Management information systems.
    3. Business logistics.   4. Theory of contraints (Management)
    I. Schragenheim, Eli.   II. Title.   III. Series.
    TS155.P798   1999
    658.5—dc21

                                                                                99-31615
                                                                                CIP

No claim to original U.S. Government works
International Standard Book Number 1-57444-270-8
Library of Congress Card Number   99-31615
Printed in the United States of America   2 3 4 5 6 7 8 9 0
Printed on acid-free paper

Dedication

Many friends supported, encouraged, and aided the writing of this book. One person in particular continues to be my best friend, inspiration, and source of strength. Over 20 years ago we made the promise to share good times and bad, richer and poorer, in sickness and in health. Little did we know what adventures those promises would bring during the subsequent 2 decades. Looking back, we have been there and done that and more. Your quiet strong faith always helped pull me through those really hard times and continues to inspire me to become a better person. Your great sense of humor made the bad times seem more like the good times. This book is dedicated to my very best friend and husband, Jim.

"We are what we repeatedly do. Excellence, then, is not an act, but a habit."

Aristotle

Contents

Section III: ERP Selection and Implementation

Section IV: Application

Eli Schragenheim

Foreword

In this book there is something of real value for everyone in industry and service businesses. The focus is on manufacturing and supply chains, but nonmanufacturing people in logistics services will find lots of help. It's to the point, easy reading, nontechnical, and lightened with appropriate humor.

All of the basic techniques are explained adequately to understand their functions, but are presented in the context of what they do well when used properly and what limitations they have. Theory is subordinated to practice. The theme throughout the book is how to implement modern computer-based systems successfully in the real world. It is not a book to read cover-to-cover at leisure and put aside in a bookcase. It's a reference to keep very handy and use while working to avoid expensive pitfalls.

George W. Plossl, CFPIM

Preface

The myriad three letter acronyms that have evolved over the years can be overwhelming and confusing for the normal practitioner. Every company is asking its personnel to do more with less and to leverage technology to increase productivity. Software suppliers and experts in each of the various tools will attempt to convince this overwhelmed and incredibly busy potential customer that theirs is the one and only true path to success. Somehow through this endless number of choices the successful practitioner must find the right road to follow for his/her company to achieve a lasting success with a positive return on investment. *ERP: Tools, Techniques, and Applications for Integrating the Supply Chain* provides a clear road map through this confusing morass. This book is written in a readily understood form with many real life examples from a variety of industries and applications to illustrate key points.

A computerized case study is attached to this book. MICSS, Management Interactive Case Study Simulator, provides a learning-from-experience platform. The version of MICSS included here was specifically designed for managers of manufacturing organizations in the enterprise resource planning (ERP) era. The computerized case study lets the reader manage a small company in a fluctuating market with unreliable suppliers and fairly good integrated information system. The challenge is to learn to control the dynamics of this virtual company by utilizing the relevant information. Through this educational simulation some crucial management issues in handling an ERP package are revealed. An analysis showing how to "win" the game and maneuver the organization to financial success is provided.

The purpose of this book is to introduce the tools and techniques of ERP, discuss the application of these to different types of enterprises, and provide the reader with the opportunity to try the concepts on a computer simulator. Competition today is forcing companies to integrate tightly with their customers and suppliers and reduce the time requirement to flex the supply chain. The demand for products is getting higher in variety and shorter in lead-time. Only through a tight integration — from the customer's customer to the supplier's supplier — can a company hope to successfully compete.

Before any company can be linked effectively into a world-class agile supply chain, their own internal processes must be world class. Like the old saying, a chain is only as strong as its weakest link. Many companies are attempting to link with suppliers and customers only to find that the relationship unravels due to the lack of basic controls in their own business. ERP is a way to effectively plan and manage all the resources of an enterprise. This book is intended to provide the road map for successful selection, implementation, and utilization of ERP for a variety of industries to improve overall competitiveness.

The Author and Simulation Team

Carol A. Ptak, CFPIM, CIRM, Jonah, is a leading trainer, educator, and consultant for integrating organizational performance. She specializes in production and inventory management, operations, and organizational assessment. Ptak has built up an expansive breadth of experience in manufacturing operations. She has successfully managed small and large divisions in a variety of industries that resulted in focused factory start-ups that incorporated outsourced manufacturing facilities  and processes, turn-around efforts, innovation of foolproof material, and production control systems. She also has managed ERP system implementations, high-performance work teams, and improved research and development logistics. A highly accomplished author, lecturer, and trainer, Ptak has combined a solid academic base with 20 years of pragmatic experience.

She holds an MBA from Rochester Institute of Technology, and is a frequent educator and trainer for universities and international APICS conferences, including the World Symposium in South Africa. Ptak is the author of numerous articles and the book *MRP and Beyond*. She is certified through APICS at the fellow level (CFPIM) and was certified in Integrated Resource Management (CIRM) with the first group internationally. Prior to her election as APICS president, she served on the Society's board of directors as president-elect, executive vice president, vice president SIGs, the SIG committee for small manufacturers (SM SIG), 1995 TEAM committee, and the 1996 international conference committee. Ptak is a member of the Seattle and Commencement Bay APICS chapters, and is committed to manufacturing excellence through education. She is now employed as part of the Worldwide ERP Solutions team by IBM.

The Simulation Team

Eli Schragenheim is the Development, Research and Education Manager of MBE and is a world expert in the Theory of Constraints (TOC) management system, as well as other cutting-edge management technologies. He is a frequent speaker at international conferences and is the author of several landmark papers. Schragenheim has developed a wide range of educational tools for management and these are in daily use throughout the world.

MICSS is produced by MBE Simulation Ltd. This company is a merger of two companies with a great deal of experience in management, education, and information systems. Elyakim Management Systems Ltd. started the development of MICSS (1992) and then merged with BCO Solutions Ltd., a company specializing in the implementation of sophisticated information systems, to form MBE Simulations Ltd.

Acknowledgments

This book would not have been written without a whole lot of help from many friends. I would like to acknowledge some special contributions.

- **Michael Clark, CPIM** — The person who started this book with his crazy note of an idea. Your unflagging belief, encouragement, inspiration, and nagging were critical to the completion of this book.
- **George W. Plossl, CFPIM** — Always my hero as a gentleman, a scholar, and an inspiration to push the field of enterprise management forward, yet not forget the basic requirements of success. You are truly the heritage of the field, clearly seeing from where we have come and yet possessing a clear vision of where we are going.
- **Richard Ling, CFPIM** — Thank you so much for sharing your lifetime of experience including the history of our profession and passion in sales and operations planning and demand management. This work would not have been complete without it.
- **Keith Launchbury, CFPIM, CIRM** — For all the work on the ERM checklist. Getting an opportunity to work with you always provides an opportunity to learn.
- **Eli Goldratt** — For our spirited discussions on the next generation for ERP and V, A, T, I organizations. Your brilliant insights are always an inspiration and learning experience for me.
- **Lisa Scheinkopf, CPIM, Jonah** — For sharing the TOC cost accounting measures and encouraging me to pursue my Jonah education.
- **Toshiyuki Okai, Sanyo North America** — Thank you for the lessons in Japanese.

- **Arnie Kennedy, CFPIM, CIRM** — Thank you for the walk through the history of ERP.
- **Bill Kuzmich** — For the detailed insights into the process industry requirements.
- **Jerry Bapst, CFPIM, CIRM** — For the definitions and experience in the remanufacturing industry.

and last, but most of all

- **William F. Latham, CFPIM, CIRM** — My good twin. Having you as the technical reviewer on this second book was the calm in this storm. You have been a good friend through all kinds of weather and all around good guy. I am honored that you count me in your close circle of friends.

MICSS Program

License for the Use of the MICSS Program

MBE Simulations Ltd. grants the purchaser of this book, *ERP: Tools, Techniques, and Applications for Integrating the Supply Chain* by Carol A. Ptak, the license to **one installation** of the enclosed MICSS program on a PC computer or a notebook. Installation of the MICSS program on a network is not allowed. You will need a CD drive to work with MICSS.

The use of MICSS (Management Interactive Case Study System) is limited to personal learning only. Any commercial use of the software is strictly forbidden.

All copyrights in the MICSS program shall at all times remain the property of MBE Simulations Ltd. The user is not allowed to introduce any modifications to the software or to the label on the diskette. The user may not reverse engineer, decompile, list, or print the software.

MBE Simulations Ltd. does not and cannot warrant the performance of or the results that may be obtained by use of the software. MBE Simulations Ltd. hereby specifically disclaims any and all express and implied warranties with respect to the software.

Under no circumstances shall MBE Simulations Ltd. be liable to the user or any other person for any special, incidental, or consequential damages, including, without limitation, lost profit or lost data, loss of other programs, or otherwise, and whether arising out of breach of warranty, breach of contract, tort (including negligence) or otherwise, even if advised of such damage or if such damage could have been reasonably foreseen, except only in case of personal injury where applicable law requires such liability.

Installation of MICSS with the ERPBOOK Scenario

For Microsoft® Windows 95 and up:

1. Insert the CD into the CD drive.
2. Click on "Start," then click on "Run"
3. Type "X:\setup" and click on "OK" where X is the CD drive.
4. Follow the instructions.
5. To call MICSS, put the CD in the drive and click on the MICSS icon.

The Characteristics of the Full Version of MICSS (Management Interactive Case Study Simulator)

The current version of MICSS, along the ERPBOOK scenario, was carefully chosen to satisfy the needs of this book. However, the enclosed program is just a limited version of a management education tool called MICSS (Management Interactive Case Study Simulation). The main objective of the full version is to provide a learning platform for real-world managers through workshops and self-learning.

With its additional capabilities, MICSS is designed for a variety of workshops. The topics include *Management in the ERP Era, Integrated Resource Management, Inventory Management, Production Activity Control,* and *The Theory of Constraints Challenge.* The length of a typical workshop is between 2 and 3 days. In such a workshop the participants initially face a case study to run for a year. Typically, the first run is not too successful, which opens the mind to new ideas about the system, the policies, the processes, and the integrative thinking that is needed. With the aid of the instructor, the participant learns to verbalize the cause and effect in the virtual environment. This understanding leads the way to come up with better policies, focused information needs, and a superior control system to guide management in making the best of an uncertain environment.

The full version of MICSS includes a wide variety of different scenarios: more products, more machines, more materials, different routings with intermediate products, the option to buy more machines, activating a second shift, and advertising and outsourcing of components.

Universities, management training centers, consultants, and educators, who would like to consider the possibility of using MICSS, are invited to write to *mbe@mbe-simulations.com.*

How to Use This Book

Busy business professionals are constantly looking for a set of tools that can help them achieve their goals. *ERP: Tools, Technique, and Applications for Integrating the Supply Chain* provides many of the conceptual tools and their application for enterprise planning, management, and execution. The author, an experienced manufacturing and distribution professional, speaks the language of the manufacturing business in a variety of industries. Time and other resources are in critical short supply. ERP enhances the productivity of these critical resources. Most books on the subject of an integrated enterprise planning system are so complex that the businessperson feels overwhelmed and shies away from the ideas. These tools and techniques are then left only to the production and inventory control professional. *ERP: Tools, Technique, and Applications for Integrating the Supply Chain* describes, from the perspective of the business manager, steps and concepts, in a step-by-step fashion that can be clearly understood to be successful.

In addition, a computerized simulation tool has been provided. This allows the reader to first understand the concepts of ERP and then practice the implementation in "virtual reality" before attempting the implementation in real life. Please refer to the section on the details of MICSS for more information about this exciting opportunity to put your new knowledge to the test.

This book was designed to be used over and over, and can be read cover to cover to gain an understanding of the evolution of the tools. In addition, the book also can be used as a quick look-up reference to obtain insight on a particular subject. Additional resources included at the end of each chapter and the complete index provide an easy road map to the desired subject.

ERP: Tools, Technique, and Applications for Integrating the Supply Chain is written by a proven author who has been there and has learned by failure and success in a variety of industries. These valuable lessons learned are blended into the examples used. This book provides the tools for you to lay the cornerstone to a sturdy foundation for the future and avoid pitfalls commonly encountered during the selection and implementation of an integrated ERP system.

Introduction

The evolution of computer power has been closely followed by the power of planning tools for the manufacturing enterprise. In the mid 1960s, the first use of the computer for planning material was introduced and was aptly named MRP for material requirements planning. During the decades that followed, the production and inventory control professional further developed this tool and began to use MRP to not only control material but to plan and manage capacity as well. This tool of closed loop MRP was used to assure that the master plan was realistic in terms of not only materials but also capacity. As the computer resource continued to add more power, the idea came to integrate the material and capacity resource plan with the financial resources of the company. MRPII, Manufacturing Resource Planning, then evolved as the next logical step in the integrated planning process. According to APICS, The Educational Society for Resource Management, "MRPII is a method for the effective planning of all resources of a manufacturing company." As computers continued to grow more powerful in processing and smaller in size, ERP (Enterprise Resource Planning) was evolved.

Now the computer can be utilized for even more complex but routine tasks for managing the business. ERP is distinguished from MRPII in the use of relational databases, fourth-generation languages, integrated computer-aided engineering tools such as product data managers (PDM), and open-system portability to integrate systems such as advanced planning and scheduling (APS), finite scheduling systems, and manufacturing execution systems (MES).

Successful implementation of any integrated management system is dependent on some key actions. First, understanding your customers' needs and expectations and their impact on your operation is essential to establishing a meaningful planning system. An effective demand management and sales and operations planning process is essential for the integrated enterprise. Once this process has been well established, APS tools that are part of a fully integrated ERP system provide excellent "what if" scenarios for the manager to determine the most beneficial mix of orders and customers.

Every company must have the same focus to stay in business — providing a quality product or service for a customer at a profit. Equally important is to understand the material flow process. The cost of material now exceeds the cost of labor in most companies today. Developing a meaningful planning system for a process that is not well understood is nearly impossible. In any successful company, the output of every process must fulfill the needs of the receiving customer. The customer can be the next work area in the factory, the next process step in the service industry, or the final outside paying customer. Ordinarily, one of the customer's highest priorities is timely delivery of usable material. One method to accomplish this is having large piles of inventory at each link of the supply chain to buffer demand changes, supply unreliability and overall process variability. The demand for agility throughout the supply chain no longer allows this to be a viable option. Customers are demanding higher product variety and shorter lead times.

A better method is to control the process of material delivery and minimize variability throughout the supply chain by sharing the information about the requirements from the customer's customer to the supplier's supplier. These supplier partnerships have proven to reduce cost of material for the customer. ERP is a critical link in that integrated chain. Without an integrated planning and control system, the information that will be passed to suppliers and customers is suspect in quality and usability. The typical cost of material in a manufacturing company averages 60 to 70% of the total cost of goods sold. Even a small reduction can have a big impact on company profitability. A nimble supply chain is essential as a competitive tool as we move into the next millennium. A successful ERP implementation is a critical link of that chain.

Successful implementation of these incredibly sophisticated tools requires education about the control system requirements and expected results. Equally important, a thorough understanding of the overall business strategy and material process flow will result in the best application of the tools. A common understanding of this essential knowledge provides the means for successful communication among implementation team members and the final users. This education must be provided for anyone involved with the management of internal plant resources or the external suppliers or customers. Many ERP implementations fail because this education is neglected.

There is a general lack of understanding of how the ERP system can be used to benefit the company and move it closer to its goals. Communication fails because there is not a common understanding of the terms used in the system and the desired objectives. People for whom the system should benefit do not have a clear picture of what the results should look like. A clear, communicated vision is critical for overall maximum competitiveness. However, expecting people to change to a system they do not understand is unrealistic. Purchasing a technical solution does not solve the problem. You can purchase the finest set of golf clubs. However, unless you go for lessons and practice for hours, you will never play with the professionals. The best Stradivarius violin does not make a virtuoso. The same is true for an ERP system implementation. Unless you learn how to fully utilize the potential power, you will have a very expensive inventory control system.

ENTERPRISE
MANAGEMENT

1 History of ERP

In the beginning, there was inventory, and it was good! Companies could afford to keep inventory on hand to satisfy customer demand. The normal policy in purchasing was to keep a little of everything on order all the time just to make sure that it never ran out. We were in the age of reorder point systems where the assumption was that the customer would continue to order what they had before and the future would look very much like the past. In most industries this was a good assumption. If a part was not needed before, there was no need to order it now. Product life cycles were measured in years. If a little extra was ordered, it was not a big issue since it could be used up before it became obsolete. Inventory was an asset not only on the balance sheet but also in the mind of the average manager. Warehouses, automated storage/retrieval systems, and carousel systems were designed, developed, and installed to manage, sort, and retrieve inventory. The techniques of the day focused on the most efficient manner of managing these large volumes of inventory.

Requirements Generation to MRP

Silently the need to order only what was really needed crept in on the horizon. No longer could a company afford to order some of everything. Orders had to be based on what was being sold. What was already in inventory or committed to arrive on a purchase order offset this requirement. Forecasting these requirements was impossible and the tried and true reorder point system to effectively manage those purchased parts failed miserably. With the invention of the computer an epiphany in materials management occurred.

3

According to Dick Ling, CFPIM, in the 1950s at an IBM Plant in Pough-keepsie, NY the first requirement generation software was written.

APICS, the Educational Society for Resource Management, was founded in 1957 as the American Production and Inventory Control Society. This professional organization was begun by a handful of visionaries who felt there was a need for education, training, and the formalization of the best methods used to manage the two most critical resources in an enterprise — inventory and direct labor. A dictionary of terms and their meaning was tangible evidence of this organization's role in the new industry. This standard allowed systems to quickly evolve and improve in functionality.

This was followed in the early 1960s by a bill of material processor written on a 1400 disk computer in Milwaukee. In 1967 IBM helped bring to market the first management operating systems (MOS), including PICK. IBM continued to bring field developed programs to plan and manage inventory to the general market. By this time, the 360 model computer was on the scene and the first MRP (material requirements planning) systems continued to develop in functionality. By the early 1970s the words "material requirements planning" were in common use. In 1975 Joseph Orlicky from IBM wrote the classic work, *MRP: The New Way of Life in Production and Inventory Management*. This work documented the state-of-the-art at the time, including Dr. Orlicky's own experience developing and implementing MRP systems as a Director of Production Control for a major farm machinery manufacturer. APICS began the "MRP Crusade" to bring the required body of knowledge to support and adequately utilize this new tool to the manufacturing enterprise.

Little did we realize the impact that the computer would have on material planning and enterprise management. From the manual planning and huge posting card decks, this new-fangled computer system promised to automatically plan, build, and purchase requirements based on the items to be shipped, the current inventory, and the expected arrivals. The posting originally done on the manual input/output cards was replaced by transactions directly made in the computer and documented on pick lists. The amount in inventory was visible to everyone with a computer without having to go to the card deck and look it up. MRP, or "little MRP," represented a huge step forward in the planning process. For the first time, based on a schedule of what was going to be produced which was supported by a list of materials that were needed for that finished item, the computer could calculate the total need and compare it to what was already on hand or committed to arrive. This comparison could suggest an activity to place an order, cancel orders that were already placed, or simply move the timing of these existing orders. As George Plossl, one of the fathers of MRP, says so eloquently, "MRP calculates what I need, compares it to what I have, and calculates what I need to go get and when." This is the real significance of MRP. For the first time the material planning function could answer the question of WHEN. Rather than being reactive and waiting until the shortage occurred, the planner could be proactive and time phase orders, including releasing orders with multiple deliveries. These larger orders with multiple delivery dates typically can provide a significant cost advantage for the company due to favorable vendor pricing.

Before MRP, only the very high-dollar parts could have this much control because of the amount of time that it took to analyze activity and plan replenishment. All calculations before the advent of the computer were done by hand or on a rudimentary adding machine or slide rule. A small change caused the planner to recalculate the whole plan every time. Clearly there was not enough time in the day to accomplish this for every part used by the company. However, any production person knows the importance of every last part, no matter how small or inexpensive. Even those low-dollar items that look so unimportant on the planner's schedule can stop a very valuable and expensive shipment. The Murphy's law of planning states that these shortages will always be identified at the last possible minute on the most critical shipment. Approved substitution lists to allow the product to still ship as scheduled when the right parts weren't there were the norm. Tracking the real "as-built" condition of the final product was a paperwork blizzard. Even with only relatively few shortages, attempting to work around missing parts is a huge source of aggravation for production personnel. In addition, missing parts contribute to quality problems and decreased productivity. The quality problems come from starting and stopping the manufacturing process. This also leads to difficulty communicating the exact level of completion. Additional time is required to complete the product because the job must be put aside due to the shortage, found when the missing part arrives, and then taken to the next level of completion. Sufficient work in process has to be staged on the shop floor to provide possible work in the event that a shortage is discovered. The ability of the planning system to schedule all the parts at the same time so that production can be started and run efficiently was a tremendous step forward for productivity and quality. Now, orders could be completed from beginning to end without incurring all the inefficiencies of repeated starting and stopping.

Some simplifying assumptions were needed to allow the computers of the day to make the required calculations. One of these assumptions was that orders should be started at the last possible date to provide for minimal inventory while still serving the customer's need on time. This process is known as backward scheduling. Therefore, all orders were scheduled backwards from the desired completion date to calculate the required start date. In project management language, all operations were placed on the critical path. This meant that the earliest date the operation could start was the same as the latest date the operation could start. There was no slack time in the schedule. The downside of this assumption was that if there was any hiccup in the execution of the plan, the order would most likely be late to the customer since there was no recovery time in the schedule. If one part needed for the finished part was going to be late, there was no automatic way to know the impact on the other needed parts. Slack was built into the schedule through conservative lead times. Even with these simplifying assumptions, the benefits far outweighed the costs and more companies began to embrace the tools and techniques of MRP.

During the 1960s and 1970s, MRP and the accompanying tools and techniques were beginning to be well understood and began to show benefits for the manufacturing operations that implemented it well. The MRP crusade was born. Companies were able to gain control over their material purchases and order only what was needed and when. Productivity and quality improved in the companies who effectively implemented these tools. The inventory asset was significantly reduced. Cash flow dramatically improved as a result. This provided a tremendous competitive advantage. As more companies began to use this critical tool, the level of sophistication in the use of the tools also increased.

Closing the MRP Loop

As more people learned how to utilize this material planning methodology, they quickly realized something very important was missing. Not only did you need all the parts to get the job done, you also must have sufficient capacity to get the job done. The idea of closing the loop with a capacity plan was introduced and closed loop MRP or "big MRP" was born. During this same time the computers were increasing in power and decreasing in price. The computing capacity to do the extra mathematical computations was affordable and available. Some may question which came first, the computer power or the recognized need. This pattern continued to repeat itself many times. The fact remained that the recognition of the need was there and the computational power was available to accomplish the calculations.

Now, not only could the materials be calculated, but also, based on those material plan priorities, a capacity plan could be calculated. Defined paths for the production process were required in addition to the list of materials needed for each of the finished parts. These paths defined upon which machines the parts would be built so that capacity and load could be planned and scheduled. Many options existed in how to set up capacity planning. If there was a desire to manage capacity at a single machine, then this single machine had to be an individual workcenter. If the level of visibility was only at a group level, then this group of machines could be planned as a capacity center.

Another critical assumption needed to complete the computations on the computers of the day was that infinite capacity existed at each of these workcenters to satisfy this calculated demand when it was required. This is a very common drawback in the use of these tools still today. Every practitioner knew that infinite capacity was not an accurate reflection of reality. But, for the first time, reports were available where the overload conditions could be identified and proactively resolved for each workcenter. The problem was visible on a proactive basis planned into the future. This allowed the preparation of plans and options to address the overload situation rather than only reacting when the problems arose. In reality, lead times were typically long enough to allow workcenters to smooth out unbalanced workloads in the short term and still support the overall required completion of the work order. Closed loop MRP represented an enormous step forward in the material and capacity planning process. The practitioners of the day continued to get more sophisticated in the use of these computer tools.

Manufacturing Resource Planning (MRPII)

Once again the technology improved simultaneously with the realization that as every piece of inventory moved, finances moved as well. If a part was received at the factory, not only should the inventory on hand go up but also there should be a corresponding increase in the raw material inventory asset on the financial books. This is balanced by an increase in the liability level in the accounts payable account. As a group of parts moves to the shop floor to build the finished product, the raw material asset should go down and the work in process asset should go up. The labor and overhead charges from the shop floor personnel also are added to the work in process asset account with an offset to the accounts payable account. When the finished part completes its path through the shop, the work in process asset account goes down and the finished goods asset account goes up. As the finished product is sold, the finished good asset account goes down and the accounts receivable asset account goes up. At every step of the way, as the inventory moves, financial accounting moves with it — in duplicate — with balanced credits and debits. The power and affordability of available technology was now able to track this inventory movement and financial activity. Ollie Wight named this integrated system MRPII (Manufacturing Resource Planning).

MRPII does not mean that MRP was not done correctly the first time or that it is Part 2 in a series of sequels. It does mean that it is a significant evolution of this critical planning tool. MRPII closed the loop not only with the financial accounting system but also with the financial management system. Now all the resources of a manufacturing company could be planned and controlled.

In 1985, Dick Ling and others brought sales and operations planning to the management toolbox. Now a company had a front-end planning tool that used information from the detailed planning and control system to manage demand at the operational level. During this time, few computer tools were commercially available to complete these calculations. The sales and operations planning process was accomplished offline in a manual process and reviewed on a monthly basis. The demand management process continues to be a challenge even today. This process is further detailed in Chapter 3.

Within the commercially available systems of the day, production activity control data collection systems collected time and material from the shop floor to compare these actual costs against the expected costs. The APICS dictionary defines MRPII as "a method for the effective planning of all resources of a manufacturing company." For the first time a company could have an integrated business system that provided visibility of the requirements of material and capacity driven from a desired operations plan, allowed input of detailed activities, translated all this activity to a financial statement, and suggested actions to address those items that were not in balance with the desired plan. MRPII was in reality a closed loop communication system. Companies quickly realized that to be competitive there was a requirement for this centralized communication system.

Good information leads to good decisions. The advances in computer tools allowed these decisions to be made more quickly as the information became more accessible. Once again, integrated information systems provided a competitive advantage. Industry "best practices" were developed and standardized so that the target and process for successful implementations were well known. The early pioneers of MRPII, including Ollie Wight and many others, developed the "proven path." These lessons were learned the hard way by the early pioneers. They now could be shared so that others could be spared the pain and agony of trial and error. A checklist was developed to assess the quality of an implementation based on best practices of successful companies. This was known as *The Oliver Wight ABCD Checklist for Operational Excellence.* This document is still published by the Ollie Wight organization. This little book describes in detail the behaviors and expected business practices required to accomplish the best return on investment from a MRPII implementation. The *ABCD Checklist* is a succinct summary of the journey to success.

Just in Time (JIT)

The next major shift during the late 1980s and early 1990s was that "time to market" was getting increasingly shorter. The first to market with a product made the most long-term profit. Lead times expected by the market continued to shorten and customers were no longer satisfied with the service level that was considered world class only a few years earlier. Customers were demanding to have their products delivered when, where, and how they wanted them. Companies began to develop and embrace the philosophies of Just in Time (JIT) and supplier partnerships as a way to remain competitive. During the same time frame, the cost of goods sold was shifting drastically from labor to purchased materials. The Association for Manufacturing Excellence (AME) was formed to address the need for the development of new tools and techniques. APICS shifted from the "MRP Crusade" to the "Zero Inventory Crusade."

To bring some perspective to this shift, during the 1940s and 1950s it was not uncommon for a company to have 40 to 60% of the cost of goods sold contributed by labor costs. Given this fact, it was no wonder companies automated and focused on the productivity of labor. Labor was the driving force for profitability. This was the major focus of the planning systems: get the material to the operation and never allow that operation to run out of work. It was better to have extra inventory than allow the operation to run out of work.

Beginning in the 1990s the focus shifted to material becoming the driving force for profitability. Many companies found that material had grown to 60 to 70% of their cost of goods sold while the labor cost declined to 10 to 20%. Major improvement in labor productivity only yielded small improvement in the overall company's profits. To improve the overall financial performance of the enterprise, the focus of the planning system logically shifted to effectively planning material and optimizing material utilization. Investment in improvements in material utilization could result in big returns. Carrying extra inventory was no longer a competitive business practice.

At the same time, the response lead times expected by the market continued to shorten and customers were no longer satisfied with the service level that was considered world class only a few years earlier. Customers were demanding to have their products delivered when, where, and how they wanted them. Companies began to develop and embrace the philosophies of JIT and supplier partnerships as a way to remain competitive. Competitiveness and profitability was now something that not only the production department focused upon, rather the whole enterprise had to be focused on this goal. All enterprise resources had to be aligned to those goals and integrated in their approach to reach the corporate objectives. No longer could departments launch things over the wall to the next department. Integrated resource management was the focus for a competitive company.

Enterprise Resource Planning (ERP)

Empowerment of employees was needed to provide the agility that was required to compete in the market. But, how can the employees make good decisions without good information? Companies needed a single management system that would be the repository of data and provide valuable information on demand. No longer was it tolerable to submit a request to the Information Technology (IT) department (or MIS department) and wait 9 man-months of programming time to get this critical information. Information was quickly needed at the decision makers' fingertips, which then could be used to make good business decisions.

The cost of technology continued to plummet and the advent of the personal computer revolutionized once again the face of business management systems. Quickly the large inflexible mainframes were being replaced by new client-server technology. The power of these small personal computers exceeded the power of the large mainframes that were routine only a few years earlier. It was now possible to run a fully integrated MRPII system on a small personal computer. The cost of systems now made this integrated solution available to even the smallest companies. Not only did small companies utilize this novel approach to computing, the largest companies also began to move quickly from the centralized mainframe system to these agile client-server systems. A whole new breed of software companies came to the forefront to handle this next stage of evolution and ERP; enterprise resource management was now on the scene.

The changing pace of technology had once again leveraged forward the planning and control systems in recognition of a real business need. In addition, unlike previous evolutions, the ERP software companies opened the door for these critical business systems to be implemented in companies that were not manufacturing companies. ERP is far more than just MRPII running on a client-server architecture. ERP includes in its breadth all the resource planning for the enterprise including product design, information warehousing, material planning, capacity planning, and communications system, to name just a few. These critical business issues affect not only manufacturing companies but also all companies that desire to achieve competitiveness by best utilizing their assets, including information. The rapid sales growth of ERP systems to nonmanufacturing companies reinforces this point.

Understanding the history and evolution of ERP is essential to understanding its current application and its future. ERP is not just MRPII with a new name. ERP is the next logical sophistication level in an evolutionary series of computer tools that began in the 1950s. The functionality has grown very similar to rings on a tree. Each layer is built on the fundamentals and principles developed in the previous layer (Figure 1.1).

As the power and sophistication of the computer continues to grow, the continued development of tools and techniques to collect data, provide information, and to better manage the enterprise can be expected in support of the goal of profitability and growth.

Supply Chain Management

Also important to remember is that under the covers of the most sophisticated enterprise planning system today is the same elegantly simple mathematical model introduced in the first MRP system. This model of "what do I need, what do I have, what do I need to get and when" is the backbone of the integrated supply chain. Requirements are taken from the customer or internally developed forecasts. These requirements are compared to what is on hand. Finally, a calculation of what is needed is completed including an offset of the estimated lead time to determine when that item is required from the supplier. This process of "what is needed, what is available, what is required and when" is accomplished by each link of the supply chain. New advances in technology allow these calculations to be completed very quickly

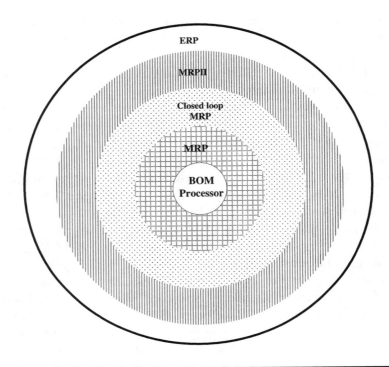

Figure 1.1   ERP growth rings.

and instantly communicated electronically all along the supply chain. Care must be taken that technology does not totally replace an effective demand management process. Without intelligent demand management, the risk of excess inventory is still very real. In addition, another barrier to full automation of requirements communication is not a technological constraint but rather the confidence that the calculated requirements are accurate. This accuracy is not dependent on the mathematical computations of the computer. The accuracy is dependent on the quality of the data input into the system. This is an issue that cannot be addressed simply by the purchase of a new computer program. This phenomenon has been plaguing software implementations since the invention of the computer.

Summary

Just because you may have purchased the latest word processing software product, you will not instantly become Ernest Hemingway. Similarly, past history has shown that the great majority of attempted MRP, MRPII, or ERP implementations will fail. Understanding the history of the tool can help the practitioner avoid the pitfalls of the past and enhance the probability of success for the future. Although no two companies are the same, standard tools and techniques are available that are similar to the varied tools in a toolbox. Each tool and its application must be well understood before the best selection can be made for the job at hand. Different situations and industries mandate the use of different tools. Too many times when the only tool that you know how to use is a hammer, all the challenges look like nails! This book provides the understanding of the various ERP tools and techniques, their application to different industries, and how ERP can be integrated throughout the supply chain. The pitfalls to avoid and secrets for a successful implementation are identified to best utilize this critical enterprise communications tool to increase overall enterprise profitability and growth now and in the future.

General ERP Resources

http://www.erpsupersite.com/, Website with hot links and updates for ERP.
http://www.erpworld.org, the "how to" conference for mid-sized companies interested in ERP.
Ollie Wight Organization, *http://www.ollie.com.*
Association for Manufacturing Excellence enables members' companies to achieve excellence and competitive advantage. This is accomplished through education, documentation, research, and experience sharing. AME membership provides a forum for all functions of manufacturing enterprises. AME, 380 West Palatine Road, Wheeling, IL 60090-5863, phone (847) 520-3282, fax (847) 520-0163.
APICS, The Educational Society for Resource Management, 5301 Shawnee Road, Alexandria, VA 22312, phone (703) 354-8851, fax (703) 354-8106, Customer Service: 800-444-2742, *http://www.apics.org.*
ABCD checklist, APICS # 03282.

2 The Theory of Constraints and ERP

Eli Schragenheim

Management Philosophies and Information Technology

Executives and managers use different language than information system people and, therefore, there is often a lack of understanding of both the managerial needs and the capabilities of the information system to supply that need. Executives look to satisfy their customer needs, for competitive edge, and for great financial results. The environment that managers operate in is never well defined. The rules for achieving these goals are never clear-cut. One may dictate a policy that a salesman should not give price reductions over 5%, but suppose he gives a reduction of 5.015% on a large sale to a big and important client. Did the salesman disobey the policy? It is doubtful whether many executives will pay attention to that breech of policy. Five percent is not perceived as something very precise. For all practical purposes, 5.015% is the same as 5%. However, a computer program is very literal and will scream at the unlawful action. The computer world has a basic difficulty of dealing with fuzzy rules, which is often the norm in an organization. While there is some fuzziness in areas like Artificial Intelligence, fuzzy rules and logic are very problematic in information systems. What is natural for a real-world manager becomes painful for an information system professional.

The different use and meaning of terminology are causing many problems in the communication between management and the information system professionals. Mutual dissatisfaction is quite common. The technical difficulties cause many misunderstandings. Executives and managers are aware that they need the information system, but complain if it does not fully

15

support their needs. Many information system people feel that management doesn't know what they want, that they constantly change their mind, and eventually are dissatisfied with what they themselves have asked for.

The different mentality between executives and information system professionals has caused the two areas to develop in different directions. The ERP information system may provide the bridge for better mutual understanding as it touches a basic element in management that really needs support. Information technology (IT) has developed in huge steps. This development is based on the technology itself. There are no clear links between the development of IT and the development of management thinking and practices. However, in the past 20 years management thinking has been vastly advanced as well. New management philosophies emerged. Some of them lost their initial popularity, but even for those the kernel of their ideas are now rooted in the minds of many managers. Take total quality management (TQM) as an example. It is not considered today as highly as it was during the 1980s. But, be aware that "quality" is now much more important than it was in the 1960s. It is also common knowledge that quality assurance should be done throughout the process and carried out by the operators themselves.

ERP can provide a link between the new management philosophies and the information system technology. The real value of ERP to organizations lies in the term "enterprise." From a top management view, the idea of ERP is much greater than the technology to provide an efficient client-server environment and a common database, both of which support improved accuracy and fast availability of information. For top management, the new ERP packages may provide a tool to unite the various functions within the organization into a whole effective organization striving to achieve the common goal with the same level of resources.

Isn't this objective what all the new management philosophies are telling us? Treat the whole organization as one system. Solve the problems on the interfaces, achieve true teamwork and cooperation, partnering and focus on the customers' needs. All these terms describe the vision of system thinking. System thinking is a necessary condition for successful supply chain management.

The vast majority of the software companies tend not to develop their packages around specific management approaches. At most they adopt some "best practices" for various areas. The concept that lies behind most packages is that they can serve any sound management approach. The parameterization of the current packages tries to back up that basic concept. However, this managerial support is, at best, only partial and is the result of understanding and misunderstanding of the new management ideas. There is always the option to add specific functions to the ERP system, but this also will serve only as an intermediate solution. Eventually, the competition between different ERP packages will be based on giving added value to managing the organization. Such an added value has to be based on specific management concepts that link the various functions into one system striving to get more of the organization's goal than thought possible.

This chapter concentrates on one particular new management approach and its impact on the integration information system. With proper understanding of the managerial ideas behind such a management philosophy, the needs from an ERP system become clearer, and many significant benefits can be realized.

The Basics of Theory of Constraints (TOC)

The Theory of Constraint (TOC) is a management philosophy, developed in the early 1980s that is still gaining popularity. TOC has defined itself as a whole system approach more than any other management philosophy. The potential impact of TOC on IT in general and ERP in particular is quite considerable. It reveals one very relevant point: the management philosophy is material to the information system.

The impact of TOC on ERP can be classified in three main areas:

1. Specific TOC techniques that should be part of ERP.
2. Defining the requirements from the ERP according to the TOC generic thinking.
3. Managing the actual implementation project of ERP according to the TOC project management methodology.

The TOC developed out of an information system called OPT (optimized production technology) developed in the late 1970s and early 1980s. This is one of the oldest finite-capacity schedulers for manufacturing organization and it is still available. The special case of OPT is that its developers found that the underlining principles of the software conflict with some managerial norms. The developers were aware that such a conflict is devastating to the proper implementation of this new management approach. The new management approach was born by Dr. Eli Goldratt who also led the development of OPT.

The "OPT Thoughtware" paved the way to the much more generic and far reaching Theory of Constraints. Three basic principles constitute the core of TOC:

1. An organization has a goal to achieve.
2. An organization is more than the sum of its parts.
3. The performance of an organization is constrained by very few variables.

The second basic principle expresses the system thinking approach. There should be a synergy between the various parts of the organization, otherwise there is no value in staying together within one organization. Behind this synergy lies the need to synchronize many different resources and activities in order to create value in the eyes of a customer. The synchronization of the various parts generates many dependencies within the organization. This is the key to understand the third basic principle. It is not feasible to manage so many dependencies and variables such that the products and services will achieve customer satisfaction while utilizing many resources to their maximum potential level.

The third principle leads to the following definition: TOC defines a constraint as anything that limits the performance of the whole organization vs. its goal. The essence of the third principle is that only a few constraints can be active at a time. This recognition has a huge impact on the way organizations should be managed.

Out of the three basic principles and by applying common sense logic, Dr. Goldratt developed the five focusing steps of TOC.

1. **Identify** the system's constraints.
2. Decide how to **exploit** the system's constraints.
3. **Subordinate** everything else to the above decisions.
4. **Elevate** the system's constraints.
5. Go back to Step 1, but do not allow **inertia** to cause a system constraint.

The ramifications of those simple looking steps are huge. Besides these direct ramifications, TOC has developed a set of tools called the "Thinking Processes" that assist management in the diagnosis of core problems and developing workable solutions. Some of the ramifications of TOC will be described below. For a serious overview of TOC, there are now quite a number of books that concentrate on TOC. Dr. Goldratt's books (*The Goal,*

The Haystack Syndrome, It's Not Luck, and *Critical Chain*) are certainly mandatory reading. Many other books on TOC, including *Management Dilemmas: The Theory of Constraints Approach to Problem Identification and Solutions* from the author of this chapter, give either a wide scope overview of the approach or more depth into a specific subject.

Specific TOC Techniques

Four specific TOC techniques are described below: a shop floor planning method, a control system, a multiproject planning and control method, and a TOC management accounting approach. All of these methods lend themselves to programming.

TOC has emerged from the shop floor. It is not surprising that the first TOC technique was directed at the shop floor. The Drum-Buffer-Rope (DBR) methodology is a shop-floor planning scheme that has replaced the OPT method on how to schedule the resources. Later, a control methodology was developed called Buffer Management to complement the planning mechanism. In the 1990s, a parallel effort called the Critical Chain, is being carried out to develop a TOC methodology for project management. This methodology was expanded to project management the TOC way. The most important of all is the unique way TOC is treating the global financial measurement and its impact on management accounting.

All those techniques can and should be part of any ERP package. Very few TOC modules are currently available in the market, with varying degrees of fit to the specific methodologies. Following are the basics of the methodologies.

The Drum–Buffer–Rope (DBR) Technique

What Should Dictate the Pace of Production?

TOC is looking for the weakest link in the chain. Let's first look only at the internal chain: the sequence of operations using internal resources that are required to turn raw materials into finished products. Later, external variables, like market demand and availability of materials, should be considered as well. The weakest link of the internal chain defines the maximum possible output with the current resource availability. The reader might argue that many manufacturing floors resemble a net rather than a chain. When we speak about the weakest link in a net, we may find that in a net more than one weakest link might be found — each of these links imposes a practical limit to the output of the whole system.

However, only very few "weakest links" can be found in any net. In the shop floor the links are actually resources. Only very few resources, usually just one, put a true limit to the production pace. That means that any realistic planning should focus on the resource that lacks the most capacity. All the rest of the system has excess capacity that helps to keep the planning of the critical resource intact.

When the market demand is lower than the capacity of the critical resource, then the pace of the whole system should be fully dictated by the market demand. When the demand approaches the limit imposed by the most loaded resource, that particular resource, in turn, becomes a capacity constraint resource (CCR). It is the balance between the demand and the CCR that dictates the actual pace of the system.

Sensible planning of the shop floor must adhere to both the market demand and the capacity of the CCR. This planning of the output of the system is called the Drum. The name is taken from a great story in the *The Goal*, Dr. Goldratt's first and most famous book. The name implies something that sets the "rhythm" for the whole system. Hence, the combination of the market demand and the limit imposed on the system by the CCR, leads to realistic planning of the CCR and its output.

The Drum must be protected from Murphy's law. Theoretically, all the other parts of the system have enough flexibility to support the Drum because of their excess capacity. However, temporary peaks of load and incidental delays may interfere and waste the precious capacity of the CCR or simply cause a shipment to miss the due date. In order to protect the CCR and the commitments to the market, a protection mechanism must be established. This is called a "Buffer." The TOC notion of a buffer is somewhat different than its common use. Buffer, according to TOC, is designed to protect ONLY the critical areas, the areas that control the performance of the whole system. In TOC terminology, they are the physical **constraints** of the system.

In a make-to-order environment the buffer is expressed in **time** units and is called time-buffer. Releasing the materials enough ahead of time of the planning for the CCR and/or delivery dates provides the necessary protection against uncertainty (Murphy). Once the materials are released they should flow as fast as possible in order to reduce the chance of missing the schedule of the CCR or delivery to the customer. The time-buffer is used to schedule the release of materials and to properly schedule the CCR. As the time-buffer takes into account the possible occurrences of delays, it should be longer than the average lead-time between the material release and the protected area. Hence, most of the material will arrive to the protected area some time before the actual use of it. Thus, some inventory is likely to pile up at that area. Note that this is different than a planned level of stock. It is not an inventory buffer. The protection is dependent on the time allowed for a batch of parts to go through a sequence of operations, maybe several levels in the bill of material (BOM). As the time estimate contains "safety time," some in-process inventory is accumulated in the queue of the CCR.

In order to support the proper flexibility of the nonconstraint resources — no material is allowed to be released to the floor prior to the time determined by Drum minus the Buffer time. This is called the "Rope," a mechanism that guards that no materials will be released before the scheduled time (which already considers the amount of uncertainty). Implementing the Rope means to knowingly under utilize the resources that are nonconstraints (having excess capacity). TOC logic points out that there is no point to fully utilize resources that have excess capacity.

In the DBR methodology, buffers are also used at assembly points where parts that go through a CCR are assembled with parts that don't go through a CCR. These buffers actually protect the delivery dates by allowing the Rope to schedule the appropriate time for those items that are assembled with CCR parts. The items that go directly to the CCR and/or the shipping area (meaning no CCR operations for that product) are scheduled by the Rope using the shipping buffer or the CCR buffer. Material constraints only exist in rare cases. Most of the time we expect that proper planning of the purchasing side will not allow stock-outs to choke the CCR or the commitments to the market.

The main point in describing the DBR methodology is to demonstrate that it is very different from the vast majority of the advanced planning and scheduling (APS) modules. It is certainly the simplest APS in the market. This characteristic of TOC is one of its greatest assets. In a complex environment, and with a lot of uncertainty around, only simple processes can really work. The position of TOC regarding "optimization" is that the system can be optimized only up to the natural "noise" of uncertainty. As the level of uncertainty is fairly high in the vast majority of the organization, not much good can be achieved from over-sophisticated algorithms. Please note that this conclusion arrived at by Dr. Goldratt is the result of his developing the OPT package, certainly one of the more complex algorithms for finite-capacity scheduling.

What is the impact of DBR on the information system? Certainly a production manager who believes DBR is the right planning scheme would like the ERP package to support the DBR logic. In itself it is not too hard to maneuver MRP to imitate DBR. The real difficulty is to integrate Buffer Management with the DBR planning within an MRP software module. The other difficulty is to sustain the understanding of how such a simple mechanism is able to produce a realistic schedule and at the same time draw the maximum capacity from the system when the market demand calls for it. DBR actually provides a protection mechanism against fluctuations (and Murphy's law).

DBR makes a clear distinction between planning and execution, and actually plans only a part of the whole system, leaving the other part to react to whatever is happening on the floor. DBR may schedule few resources that are CCR's and it always schedules the material release, where the schedule means "never before time." True DBR does NOT schedule the nonconstraints, not because it cannot do finite-capacity scheduling, but because this is the wrong thing to do, as uncertainty is bound to disrupt all the planning. The right way to plan is to schedule in detail only the material release and the CCR's activities. Planning that is protected by the "buffer" has a very good chance of being correctly executed.

DBR is usually targeted at "make-to-order" environments. It can work also in "make-to-stock" with some minor modifications. The basic logic for the master production schedule is that the default planning is simply the list of the firm orders due-dates. One can, of course, insert additional requirements based on forecast, but there should be a very valid reason for that. Unless it is evident that a load peak is expected and there is not enough capacity on the CCR to fulfill all the demand at the peak time, only then would a DBR production manager allow producing for forecast. In typical "make-to-stock" environments, the customer's lead-time is much shorter than the production lead-time. It forces the planning to be based on stock, but even in that case fast response is of utmost importance and can be achieved only when production is focused on the immediate and certain needs. Being pushed to do things that currently have no clear demand causes the nonconstraints to lose their excess capacity and thus lose their ability to react fast to new demand or changing priorities.

Buffer Management — A Control Mechanism

TOC uses time-buffers as protection mechanism against common variations of uncertainty. But, buffers are not enough. There is a need to identify problematic situations and respond with corrective actions. Buffer

Management is a true control mechanism. The point of controlling the execution is not to gather data for comparison between the actual state and the planning. Such a mechanism processes huge amounts of data and the ability of the manager to draw a clear conclusion are diminished. An effective control should provide a reactive mechanism to handle uncertainty by monitoring information that points to a threatening situation then taking corrective action accordingly. If an order was supposed to be processed on Wednesday and was actually processed on Friday, this is probably only one small detail that adds nothing to the execution of the planning. If it is very important that every order be shipped on time then, in the vast majority of the cases, it should be completed a significant amount of time before the actual date. When most of "safety time" has been exhausted, only then is there a need for worry.

The kernel idea behind the Buffer Management is to monitor the cases when the protection mechanism is nearly exhausted. Buffer Management looks at the areas protected by a buffer and focuses on those incidents where most of the buffer has been used, and then gives the "almost late" orders high priority, which can be translated as expediting. Of course, expediting should be done only sparingly, otherwise it has no value.

Let's illustrate the Buffer Management activity. Suppose an order is due on February 28. The materials are released on February 14, assuming an average lead-time of a week and a maximum of 2 weeks considering the uncertainty. When should the production manager's attention be attracted to that order? Certainly February 21 is too early to react. On the other hand the production manager should not let the order sit unnoticed until the due-date itself. If something has happened, such as a human mistake, a temporary peak of load somewhere, or any other reason for delay, there should be some attention at a time when it is not too late to take action and expedite the order.

The Buffer Management methodology speaks of three "zones" of the buffer. The earliest zone is where we don't really expect the order to show up at the protected area. This is the "ignore" zone. The next one, called "the monitor zone," calls attention to but no reaction as there is still enough time to expedite and it might not be needed. The most important zone is the "emergency zone." Here, there is a need to react, otherwise the order will be late.

In the above example, we have a buffer of 10 days that includes all the operations from material release to the shipment without implementing CCR. This maximum lead-time estimation of 10 days is divided into three parts. The first 4 days are certainly the "ignore" part. After all, there are several operations to be done. The next 3 days are the "monitor" zone. Most of the orders will be completed by that time. If an order is not completed within both previous zones, it should be located and expedited.

The time-buffer that is attached to the DBR planning methodology includes the net processing time. In a manufacturing environment the net processing time is a very small part of the actual lead-time. As a matter of fact, the time-buffer is a careful estimation of a fairly long lead-time to move the part from one protected area (the stockroom) to another protected area. The difference between the time-buffer and the lead-time in the MRP methodology is that MRP lead-time is defined for every level in the BOM, while the TOC buffer is defined from the material release area to the CCR or the shipping dock. On top of that, Buffer Management suggests a practical way to control the smooth execution of the plan by concentrating only on the exceptions, those orders that penetrate into the "emergency zone" or the "red-line." Note that every operation in the shop floor is directed at one buffer, at the CCR, shipping, or assembly. Hence, the buffers encompass the entire floor.

Buffer Management would have gained a lot from a computerized program. As a matter of fact, it should have been fairly easy to come up with such a program. Search for the orders in the emergency zone, explode the bill of that order, and identify the resources where it might reside. In a shop floor that has online data retrieval, the exact location and work order ID can be immediately traced. In other cases, the work orders should be identified and looked after. As a matter of fact, in a fully MES computerized shop floor, the foremen each day can get a sorted list of all the waiting orders with their relative penetration into the buffer they feed. Thus, it is possible to know in advance the needs of the constraint(s) and to be able to organize the load much more effectively even when no formal sequencing is done for this workcenter.

Buffer Management as a control mechanism yields one more significant value. With all the need for data accuracy, the data regarding setup and processing times are too dynamic to be measured properly. Any change in the engineering might change the timing. Many *in situ* improvements are done. Setup and processing times are very difficult to measure accurately because the operators are reluctant to be measured so precisely. Standard times cannot be accurate by definition, hence, we have to live with less-than-perfect data accuracy on the shop floor. When we take into consideration the need to maintain a certain amount of excess capacity (protective capacity) and the devastating nature of uncertainty, we realize that when product-mix changes and/or market demand go up, the timely performance of the shop floor might be threatened.

What happens when a nonconstraint is losing its protective capacity? It turns out to be an interactive constraint. Managing interactive constraints is very difficult with constant threats on the satisfactory performance of the organization. If we know in advance, we could look at various ways to reduce the pressure. Buffer Management is capable of giving an advanced warning that the protection mechanism is losing its effectiveness. When too many orders penetrate the emergency zone, there is a clear sign of a system under pressure. The identity of the new "troublemaker" can be revealed as the workcenter that holds more orders that have penetrated into the emergency zone than any other. The data regarding which workcenter is holding those orders are collected and processed as a Pareto Chart.

As a true control mechanism, Buffer Management is relying on a different set of data than the one used for planning. Hence, it can point out a "troublemaker" that hardly looks this way when the capacity data are analyzed. Thus, Buffer Management can point out inconsistent data and send us to check the accuracy of those data items that seem both relevant and are suspected of being inaccurate.

Project Management — The TOC Way

More and more companies find out that in addition to their production or service operations, they are also in project management. Some companies have their main line of operations organized as projects (multiproject environments), and their operation is distinct from regular production. Some ERP companies have project management-oriented modules.

TOC has some clear messages regarding management of multiproject organizations. It starts with some new insights regarding the management of a single project, but then the approach evolves to deal with the bigger picture of handling multiprojects. In what way is managing multiprojects different than managing a manufacturing organization? A project is conceived as something unique, meaning it is one of a kind. This is not perfectly true, but we also know in manufacturing that for some job-shops every order is unique. Dr. Goldratt made the following observation, "if the net processing time on one unit, meaning all the time a resource is actually working on the unit, is less than 1 hour, this is certainly manufacturing. If the processing time is more than 100 hours, it is certainly a project." Is the relative length of a project vs. a fully customized order the only difference between managing a project environment and managing a job-shop? Additional effects that are inherent in project management and clarify the distinction are

1. The level of uncertainty in project management is much higher than in a job-shop.
2. In project management it is the people who are the main resources and it is the human factor that dominates the length of an operation of a task.
3. Managing the human capacity is much more complex than managing the capacity of machines.

Highlighted here are only the main points TOC makes regarding multi-project management and what impact they may have on the ERP software. First, let's start with managing a single project. The true challenge is how to manage the uncertainty. The same logic as in manufacturing also applies here: let's protect the weakest area only. What is the weakest area in projects? The Critical Path — the sequence of operations that dictates the length of the project. TOC has suggested one important insight to the critical path. The critical path is usually defined assuming infinite capacity, very much like the basic MRP module. Once resource contention is taken into consideration, the real sequence of operations that dictates the length of the project is called the Critical Chain. This is covered in more detail in Chapter 18.

How do we protect the critical chain from the huge amount of uncertainty? First of all we have to protect the due date of the whole project. A Project Buffer is installed at the end of the critical chain. Then, we must protect the critical chain from all other operations that merge into it at some point. Whenever a sequence of operations is integrated into the critical chain, a Feeding Buffer is put in, thus pushing that sequence backward in time.

Of course, the duty of the buffers is to account for the uncertainty. That means that the time estimation for the individual tasks should NOT include "safety time" but be based on a 50% chance of meeting that time. This approach certainly carries a cultural paradigm shift which should be handled and considered. The bigger problem is to manage a multiproject environment. A common example is the R&D department of a large manufacturing organization. In such an environment usually many different projects are running concurrently. There is a constant pressure on the human resources. When the global priorities are not clearly set, the common phenomenon is "multitasking," meaning people who switch back and forth between different tasks for different projects. This behavior increases the perception of uncertainty and inflates the time estimates given by the experts for the duration of the individual tasks. Parkinson law sees to it that all the time assigned to a task will be used. We can see how every project gets longer and longer and the competition on the resources become fierce, even though no resource is a true bottleneck.

The challenge of managing the resources of a multiproject environment should be addressed by ERP vendors. It is certainly a crucial part in the enterprise resource management. To meet the challenge, TOC proposes three components to the solution:

1. **The Drum concept.** The idea is to stagger the release of new projects based on assessments regarding the availability of a critical resource. Please note that the critical resource is not a bottleneck. It cannot be fully utilized, otherwise it will take forever to complete the projects. But, it is a resource that is causing a lot of competition between projects and there is a real need to reduce that amount of resource contention.
2. **The Buffer concept.** Insert a structured protection mechanism only on the critical areas.
3. **Buffer Management.** Process the actual data on how those buffers are actually used ("consumed" is the TOC term for it) and derive a decision support system based on that information.

The relevancy of multiproject management to the ERP packages is not in doubt. The links to the bigger system need to be installed. The internal clients of a multiproject department may be production or marketing. On the other hand, the purchasing and finance parts need to be inline with whatever happens in that department. The vision of the enterprise cannot be complete without including the management of multiprojects when they apply.

Throughput and Constraints Accounting

All ERP packages have a management accounting module. After all, the goal of so many organizations is to make money. All the not-for-profit organizations have cash as their scarce resource. Hence, there is a real need for some algorithm that would tie operational processes and decisions to money.

Traditional cost accounting has been under constant attack since the 1980s. Dr. Goldratt became famous, or infamous if you wish, when he stated that "cost accounting is enemy No. 1 of productivity." From a different angle, a new approach called Activity-Based Costing (ABC) made similar accusations towards the traditional cost accounting. Management accounting is an area for which the ERP system needs to define the concepts upon which it should operate. One cannot define the huge difference between the traditional way, the ABC way and the TOC way, just by parameters. It has to be very different software modules. Just to give a clue to the difference, TOC claims that the term "the cost of a product unit" is a mathematical phantom without any substance of its own. Please note that this is a generic claim, it is not important how the product-unit cost was calculated, it is wrong as such. What do people understand when they are told that "every unit of this widget is costing us $21?" The straightforward interpretation is that, if the company produces one additional unit of the widget, additional expenses of $21 will be incurred.

This is usually not true. The cost of a unit of product includes two parts: true variable expenses that actually occur when one unit is produced, and relatively fixed expenses that do not change per one unit, but may change with larger quantities. Hence, when an additional unit is produced, all we know is the amount of variable costs that took place. However, when large quantities or long-term decisions are involved, the true costs may be higher than just those that vary with every unit.

So, how should we treat all the "fixed costs?" The traditional cost accounting looks for a key to allocate those costs to the products and services. ABC tries to model the actual activities that are derived by producing a product or a service. Those activities consume capacity of resources for which the organization pays. Hence, the cost of producing one additional unit should include the relative cost of the activities actually performed.

TOC claims that there is a flaw in this logic. The cost of maintaining a resource is fixed per the capacity limit of that resource. If the organization chooses not to utilize all the potential capacity of that resource, the cost is still incurred. Hence, when an additional unit is produced, all the activities that were done by resources that have excess capacity are free — the organization doesn't pay for those activities.

A management accounting approach called "marginal costing" already made this claim in part. The idea is to look ONLY for the true variable costs per unit. That approach is considered to be very short-term because of the negative effect of when the costs seem relatively low there is a tendency to quote lower prices. The result is that the fixed costs are not fully covered and the organization suffers a loss.

The TOC approach may remind people of the marginal costing method, but the similarity is very superficial. TOC objects to any allocation of fixed costs, but is not going to ignore them. Moreover, TOC is **system oriented** and by that a different logic emerges. TOC looks for the marginal costs for the whole system rather than the marginal costs associated directly with the decision at hand. TOC does NOT recommend reducing the selling price, instead it encourages market segmentation so that different pricing can be used.

TOC defines three global financial measurements:

- **Throughput** (T): The rate at which the organization generates money
- **Inventory/Investment** (I): All the money the system invests in purchasing things the system intends to sell
- **Operating Expenses** (OE): All the money the system spends in turning inventory into throughput

The definition of throughput means the difference between the revenues and the truly variable costs. This notion is similar to the "contribution" definition that considers only the marginal costs. However, TOC doesn't treat "direct labor" as truly variable costs.

How does TOC use the measurements for decision making? First of all it puts a lot of emphasis on the **T** measurements because many daily decisions impact only the **T** leaving the **OE** and **I** at the same level. For instance, an emergency order for 100 units has been received from an important client. All the materials are available. The decision considered is to change priorities and add one more setup, but not to do any overtime due to the additional order. How might such a decision be analyzed? As nobody is hired or fired and no overtime or emergency shipment from a supplier is needed, no change in the total OE is incurred. There will no significant change in the **I**. Some raw material inventory is going into production and then goes out to a client — the average level of **I** is kept the same.

The decision only affects the level of **T**. However, it is not certain that the additional **T** for the whole organization will be equal to the **T** generated by the order itself. This is because the order may cause the loss of **T** of something else. It may happen when an internal constraint is active. In that case, accepting the order for 100 units means rejecting (quoting a price or delivery date that is not acceptable to the client) another order in the near future because of lack of capacity on the constraint. In order to calculate the true level of Δ**T**, the difference in the total **T** for the whole organization, the impact of the order on other orders needs to be evaluated. The same thing may happen if the order was given a reduction in price, which causes the reduction of the price to other clients as well. In such a case the global change in the **T** level needs to be evaluated.

This emphasis on the global system as a whole makes the TOC management accounting very different from marginal costing. What happens when the additional order has to be partially processed using overtime? In such a case, when there is a direct link between the order and the overtime, the additional costs are to be calculated for the decision itself: **ΔOE**. The TOC decision rule is: **ΔT** − **ΔOE** needs to be positive. This difference represents the additional profit, what is going directly to the bottom line.

The internal constraints of the organization have a major impact in evaluating the **ΔT** for any decision. In certain cases where there is only one clear physical constraint in the organization, and the decision considered isn't going to cause another resource to become a constraint, it is possible to calculate a priority rule among the products. For each product we can calculate the **T** per product unit divided by the time the constraint needs to invest to generate that throughput. What we get is **T/CU** — throughput per constraint-unit for every product. Certainly we like to load the constraint with those products that yield more **T** for every unit of the constraint. This can and should be the basis for devising the best product mix.

Please note that the **T** per product unit is NOT the profit per unit. Also, note that the priority rule of **T/CU** is applicable only when the two basic assumptions are valid: there is one and only one active internal constraint and the decision considered does not alter that.

TOC management accounting can be computerized and be a part of an ERP package. It can be handled also by maneuvering the existing management accounting module to produce **T, I,** and **OE**. It is not convenient or straightforward, but it can be done. The ramifications for the decision makers are very large. The TOC cost measurements are further detailed in Chapter 9. For ERP users, this may be the toughest decision concerning TOC. There can be no full TOC implementation if **T, I,** and **OE** are not properly considered.

Defining the Requirements for ERP According to the TOC Generic Thinking

The impact of TOC on ERP goes beyond the specific techniques that may or may not be a part of the package. TOC thinking defines a "well-behaved" organization. It further supplies tools to examine the benefits and hazards that may materialize from implementing ERP. In particular, every module and every feature within the package can be examined with these tools.

The process that defines the requirements from the chosen package is of utmost importance. This definition is as crucial to the implementation as it is to the choice of package. What might be devastating in this process is the tendency to add more and more requirements because people think they might be needed. The immediate negative effect will be a long and shaky implementation. But, the real devastating effect will come later, when the use of the huge system will not yield benefits. Instead of supporting the organization to achieve more of its goal, a lot of time and efforts will be dedicated in maintaining the information system and making it work. The users of the ERP will be confronted with huge amount of data — most of that data have no relevancy to any decision that needs to be considered. There is a lot of similarity between a software package and a shop floor. When the shop floor is full of work-in-progress (WIP), the priorities become so complex as to be nonexistent, lead-times are long, quality problems occur all the time, and the organization fails to achieve its potential. Every feature that is not really needed is causing damage because it needs to be maintained and from time-to-time people actually try to use the module just because it is there. They spend time with it and the organization does not get any added value. The key strategy for ERP success is to understand the organization's goal and how the technology can be used as a tool to help the enterprise achieve its goal.

The TOC tools for examining the added value of any new idea can be effective for constructing the main set of features that are needed to support the organization to achieve its goal. Is it too pretentious an objective to strive for? For any organization there are just a few key processes that handle the core business. All the other processes support the key processes on a certain aspect. The linkages between the processes can be clearly defined and, thus, the integrative information needs can be clarified. Whenever a new plant is designed, there is a structured planning process to ensure no redundant machinery is purchased and no missing machines or tools will be identified when the plant is supposed to start producing. The process of determining the requirements from an ERP package is much more difficult. It needs an overall review of the key processes and it needs good understanding of the current practices of translating forecasted market demands to materials, capacity, and logistics. One also needs to comprehend the role of information in the decision making and to be able to point out what information items are needed. While software engines that search for the data and then present it to the executive are pretty common, the question arises whether the database has all that is needed and whether it contains too much that is not needed.

A TOC–ERP implementation will result in a LEAN–ERP. The main characteristic of such an implementation is that it is targeted at what is crucial for the success of the organization. Certainly it should contain much of the techniques described above, even by using the current packages with the right "twist" to it. It still will be an enterprise resource planning system, though. The integrative aspect of the ERP implementation is the most dominant factor of all. However, every module would contain only what is really needed for managing the organization as a whole.

TOC speaks on "exploitation of constraints" and "subordination to constraints" as necessary elements for properly managing the daily activities of the organization. These two terms have very strong impact on the role of the information system within the organization. Exploitation means ensuring that the weakest links in the organization are fully utilized and do what is the most profitable to the organization as a whole. Subordination means to design the processes throughout the organization so every process supports the exploitation scheme in the best way possible. As a matter of fact, under the subordination concept every process has a clear objective that can be translated into measurements and that support the exploitation scheme. Let's look at some examples for exploitation and subordination and the impact of these on the requirements of the information system.

Suppose a company is limited by having only two real good sales agents. There isn't a problem in obtaining more sales agents, but their average output is far less than that of the two experienced and capable agents. The exploitation means planning carefully the missions for these agents. The plan should achieve two objectives: (1) to cause them to work as much as they can, and (2) to choose those missions that have better chance to materialize while still needing the special qualities of the two. The subordination processes that should support the above scheme would enable collecting enough information for assessing the chances of the leads. More information should provide the possible size of sale, the location of the leads, and the transportation means. All this information must be presented in a manner easily transformed to a schedule. The entire planning of the sales force missions should start with planning the activities of the two senior salespersons (the constraint of the organization) and only then assigning missions to the other salespersons. In such an organization the sales module is by far the most important module of the ERP. Of course, other modules are needed to ensure meeting the customer requirements, but their particular features are less crucial than those that handle the constraint of the organization.

Another example is when a certain type of machinery is constraining the organization from expanding its market. Suppose that 20 different extruders are the capacity constraint of the organization. Now, every extruder has it's own capabilities. They are not identical machines. Certain materials can go through only two or three specific extruders while others can go though any extruder, but with different timing. The exploitation of the group of extruders should be able to come up with a schedule for the group (the Drum, mentioned above) that squeezes as much throughput as it can produce. Of course, we assume that only "almost certain" demand is being produced, otherwise the extruders would not be the limiting factor (meaning the constraint of the organization). In order to evaluate the alternative scheduling options for that group, advanced planning system (APS) is certainly needed here. The APS should look almost solely to the extruders to produce the best utilization that is in line with the market demand. The subordination processes should be focused on two objectives: (1) to ensure the smooth execution of the Drum, the schedule for the extruders, and (2) to maintain fast flow of the material from the extruders until completion.

It is possible to cause almost any ERP package to perform a good approximation of the exploitation and subordination processes. Sometimes it may involve forcing the software module to act differently than what it was designed to do. Of course, when it comes to the constraints of the whole organization, there are significant differences between approximating the exploitation and providing the best exploitation scheme.

In addition to managing the daily transactions and operations, the ERP package is expected to provide the necessary data for decision support. Here the impact of TOC can be huge. TOC is basically a decision support management approach. The huge amount of data is contrary, even damaging, to an active management support. The TOC management accounting system is focused on that end. From other angles TOC provides analysis tools to define the control information that points to real problems hidden somewhere in the organization.

For instance, TOC analysis can be very effective in defining the necessary data elements concerning the clients of the organization. To be effective we need to define the smallest set of data that will likely be needed in the future to support a decision or action. Do we need all the transaction details for that? Is every tiny delay in payment crucial for evaluating whether to continue selling to that client? Remember, where a huge amount of data are stored, "Murphy" can have a feast!

And the last point: it takes a really good pilot to fly a modern aircraft. Isn't it common sense that when the organization embarks on the implementation of a brand new information system, the managerial capabilities must be updated? The whole point in implementing ERP is to provide the local, mid-level, and senior managers with an access to integrative information that wasn't easily accessible before that. Do we assume all of the managers are well aware of the meaning of the integrative information that they haven't used so far? Suppose every salesperson in the company knows how to look at the capacity requirements planning (CRP) reports and is well aware how the CRP profile impacts the chance that the sale that is about to be signed will be completed on time. The question is: will this impact the salesperson decision? TOC leads managers to think beyond the immediate area of responsibility and causes them to see real value in doing that.

Managing the Implementation Project

Implementing ERP in a company is a quite complex project. A company going into such a project should be aware that project management tools are absolutely needed for proper management of the project. Unfortunately, too many implementations of ERP are not organized according to the project management body of knowledge. When a WBS (work breakdown structure) is not well prepared, the organization is bound to face unpleasant surprises. The WBS for an ERP implementation has to contain far more than the technical tasks. It should include educating all the users and dealing with the objections people have against the implementation. It should plan decision points to finalize some open issues at each stage and verifying that all the users are content with whatever they need to do.

Just the technical tasks are too complex to plan without the aid of project management tools. The various dependencies between technical tasks need to be clearly specified and placed within the time frame. Adding the "soft" tasks to the project planning only adds to the need to specify on paper the dependencies, the amount of resources needed, and the description of what needs to be done.

Now enters the TOC technique for managing a single project. ERP implementation is a single project that is extremely important to finish as early as possible. It also uses a lot of managerial and professional internal resources.

The Critical Chain methodology for managing single projects can yield a much more secure implementation. The ERP implementation process includes the definition of the system, which is a critical managerial topic that has been discussed above. The execution itself needs proper management direction above the technical–professional level. The leader of the ERP project should NOT be a software engineer. A business executive should lead the move to find common language between the management issues and the precise professional world of software.

Being focused on the management objectives of such a huge project is part of the TOC basic concepts. One of the common failures of ERP implementations is to be drawn into the technical details and lose the sight of the overall target. It may be the case where the objectives of the implementations were nicely defined in the first stage, and during the implementation much of it was lost. The capability of identifying what detail is crucial for achieving the target is a skill that can be learned.

After the ERP package is functioning and stable, the real challenge begins — using ERP as a trigger to improve the business. With the right mindset, even a lousy implementation process of a mediocre ERP package can be used to generate spectacular results by learning how to use the RIGHT information for making the RIGHT business decisions. Education and constantly striving to better understand the role of information in the prosperity of the business does not stop when the ERP software goes live. The availability of a lot of data does not necessarily provide good information. Just think of playing squash in a room full of mirrors.

Summary

TOC is a pragmatic management philosophy. It is not a well-defined algorithm. Based on the TOC philosophy some critical algorithms have been developed. Drum-Buffer-Rope methodology for planning the shop floor is a TOC technique. While the planning ala TOC considers the amount of uncertainty, it still recognizes the need for a proper control system to be able to fix the hazards of uncertainty. Hence, on top of the planning, TOC has developed a control mechanism called Buffer Management. The task of Buffer Management is to set up the right priorities, identify the exceptions, and warn about threats to the planning. Buffer Management is also an integral part of the project management in the TOC way. Here again we find a planning algorithm coupled with a control algorithm to create a realistic planning and execution system in spite of all the uncertainty around.

Throughput Accounting (TA), or rather Constraint Accounting, is more than a technique for a certain environment. This methodology is an integral part of the TOC conceptual world. It is focused on the *goal* of the organization and how it should be measured. Throughput Accounting offers a different view from traditional management accounting or the activity-based costing (ABC) on how to make decisions about products, services, outsourcing, and investments. Many of the ABC exponents admit openly that TA offers a good decision support for the short term. Experts claim that the TA can be expanded to long-term decisions.

The more generic thinking of TOC can and should lead ERP implementation to be much leaner than otherwise thought. A lean ERP that still encompasses the activities within the organization has the potential of becoming a very effective package.

3 Sales and Operations Planning

The challenge many companies face is that demand exceeds their production capacity or several products compete within the facility for limited resources. If resources were unlimited, then budgets and schedules would not be required. Budgets and schedules are required to ensure that these limited resources are spent in the best interest of the company in order to reach its vision, mission, and goals. Eli Goldratt, in his well-known work, *The Goal*, noted that for most companies the goal is to make money now and in the future. The products scheduled through a manufacturing company should ensure the highest possible level of profitability. This is the basis for the recent introduction of advanced planning and scheduling (APS) tools. These automated computer tools provide the computational power to analyze many possible alternatives before a final schedule is determined. However, before the computer tools can be used effectively, a well-defined sales and operations planning process must be established. Otherwise, the attempt will be made to automate a process that is not well understood. When technology is used before the process is well understood, the results are very disappointing and very expensive.

Why Sales and Operations Planning?

Inherent in the departmental design of most companies is a disconnect in the planning process. Sales and marketing do their analysis of market needs and forecast customer demands. At the same time manufacturing is scheduling what needs to be built that optimizes the use of its resources. Distribution is optimizing its storage locations to provide ready access to those items that experience the highest levels of demand. The finance department is attempting to project sources and uses of cash and determine if the enterprise will have sufficient assets to reach its goals. In addition, an analysis of product costs and overall profit and loss for the enterprise is examined. In the development department, the engineers and scientists are working on the next generation of product to bring to the market. They want to design a better product to provide financial success for the company. In addition, they are probably trying to push the design and technology envelope to stay ahead of the competition. Each of the functional areas has its own goals that it is attempting to optimize. What is the integrating mechanism that brings together these differently focused areas? To be successful, these diverse groups should be aligned on the same objectives and strategies to meet the company's goal. The integrating mechanism that provides that alignment is Sales and Operations Planning.

Dick Ling, the father of Sales and Operations Planning, defines this practice as "the integrated business planning process that provides management the ability to strategically direct its businesses to achieve competitive advantage on a continuous basis by integrating customer focused marketing plans for new and existing products with the management of the supply chain." Sales and Operations Planning provides the linkages between the annual review of the strategic plans as detailed by the specific business plans into the operational detail that is reviewed and adjusted on a monthly basis. Performance measurements encourage alignment on the desired business objectives. This closed-loop process provides feedback on the overall performance of the company in the face of changing markets and competitive factors. One thing is for certain, the only thing that is constant is change. As time moves on, the rate of change appears to be increasing at an increasing rate. Having an effective process that eliminates nonvalue-added activity from the development and execution of the Sales and Operations Plan could provide a significant competitive advantage for the enterprise.

In Figure 3.1, the elements of Sales and Operations Planning begin and end with the customer. The overall strategy and detailed business plans provide the overarching framework while data and information technology provide the foundational support for the senior management business review. The important thing to note in this model is that Sales and Operations Planning provides an integrated alignment of product planning, demand planning, supply planning, and financial planning. As changes are made in one area,

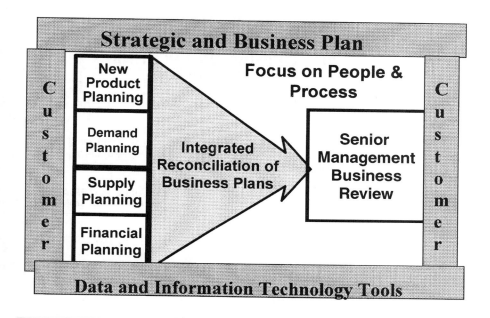

Figure 3.1 Elements of Sales and Operations Planning. (Courtesy of Richard Ling and Andy Coldrick (© 1996). With permission.)

the impacts that are expected in the other areas are identified and highlighted. This reconciliation process provides the opportunity for the senior management to focus on the real issues rather than a large amount of data.

Sales and Operations Planning highlights areas of change and the decisions that need to be made to provide directional leadership. The alternative is to have each functional area attempt to optimize each of its individual pieces. This is the traditional method of managing most businesses. However, experience has shown that this approach will result in suboptimal results for the enterprise. The central box is the focus on people and processes. People come first in this because they are the only ones capable of improving the processes. According to W. Edwards Deming before he died, approximately 94% of the problems within an organization can be directly linked to the process. Only 6% are people problems. However, the authority with the resources to fix these problems is clearly in the hands of management. Sales and Operations Planning provides management with the tools they need to make the appropriate decisions for the enterprise.

In Figure 3.2, the operational areas affected by the Sales and Operations Planning process are noted. This pattern of new products, demand

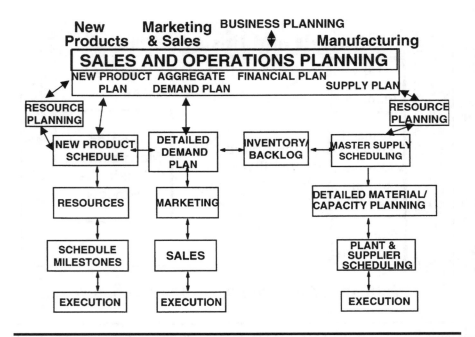

Figure 3.2   Operational impact from S&OP process. (Courtesy of Richard Ling and Andy Coldrick (© 1996). With permission.)

management, supply management, and financial analysis is repeated for each link of the supply chain. To be an effective part of a competitive supply chain, the link containing the internal enterprise must be effective, strong, and capable of responding to its customers' changing needs and wants. Good information is critical to this agile response. What should be especially noted in this diagram are the number of iterative linkages. These two-headed arrows show the flow of information into-and-out, of these different operational areas impacting decisions made in these areas. The integration point for all the gathered information is in the Sales and Operations Planning process.

Figure 3.2 clearly shows how integrated the Sales and Operation Planning process is. As the old joke goes, the good news is that S&OP is integrated and the bad news is that S&OP is integrated. First the good news. Having this integration provides decision-making ability based on accurate facts. In addition, the impact of these decisions can be measured and analyzed. The bad news is that each department can no longer operate as an independent unit without being concerned about the other departments in the company. This may cause some departments to do more work to benefit the company as a whole or to modify their processes so that the information they generate is usable by other departments in the company. To obtain accurate data for use in the Sales and Operations Planning process, it is essential that all departments use the data from the same source. By using the same data source, errors can be noted more quickly and identified for correction. Only by using the same database will all departments be encouraged to be meticulous in their data inputs.

Impact of Change

Most companies will focus their time and effort in planning and managing a variety of different activities. The basic activities for each link of the supply chain include new products, demand, supply, and financial control. Figure 3.3 shows the relative relationship in this planning activity between new products, demand, supply, and financial control.

Transaction systems focus specifically on the supply requirements through the material requirements planning module (MRP) or production planning module (PP). This is because the typical company's largest use of cash is towards the purchase of raw materials. Conversely, financial analysis of company results is the other main catalyst for the selection and implementation of a planning and control system like ERP. The cost justification of ERP is frequently done on the improvement in these two areas.

However, change causes disruption to this planning and control. As noted before, change is constant. Having the ERP system focus on managing these changes provides excellent results for the company. Effectively managing

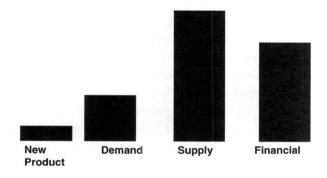

Figure 3.3 Traditional planning system focus.

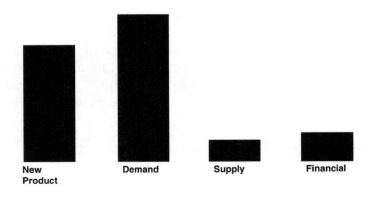

New Product | Demand | Supply | Financial

Figure 3.4   Change introduction.

change is the real purpose for ERP and provides the largest return on investment. When the areas in which most change and unpredictability are identified, the results are often surprising (Figure 3.4).

The area in which most change is introduced is the direct opposite of most ERP systems focus. Traditionally, the use of ERP has been inwardly focused on optimizing the ordering of materials and accounting for results. New products and demand variability introduce more change and, therefore, uncertainty into the company. Since managing change and its impact on the organization is the real reason for a planning system, it would make sense that the areas for focus should be on changing customer demands and new products. One of the largest shifts from MRPII (Manufacturing Resource Planning) to ERP is the incorporation of an outside focus including new product development and customer demand management.

In general, change is triggered by individual events either inside or outside the organization, deviation from established plans, or the replanning process itself. Individual events from inside the organization could include an addition or loss of a customer, a new product introduction, pricing changes to encourage volumes, promotion to encourage market demand, or a financial shortfall that does not allow the company to purchase required materials or other resources. External changes can be the entrance of a new competitor to the market, their pricing and promotion strategies, or supply problems from vendors that do not support the desired production schedule. When these individual events are linked in any series, deviation from established plan is quite likely. This deviation then requires a replanning process that includes customer review, analysis of management information and trends, and performance reviews including reconciling the top down planning comparison to the bottoms up execution data. This results in the strategic decisions that provide direction for the future. Change from any source must be acknowledged and integrated into the overall plan for the enterprise to ensure that the scarce resources are indeed working on what will bring the highest return on investment.

Elements of Sales and Operations Planning

The key elements of Sales and Operations Planning include:

- New product planning
- Demand planning
- Supply planning
- Financial planning

These four elements are integrated and reconciled on a monthly basis to provide detailed business plans for review by senior management. According to Dick Ling and Andy Coldrick in 1998, "all companies have some of the elements of Sales and Operations Planning, but too many have not seen the need to embrace the total Sales and Operations Planning concept." Given that an integrated Sales and Operations Planning process provides real data and information with which to manage the business, and add that an integrated plan will provide better bottom line business results than having each functional area optimizing their individual area, then why have so few companies successfully implemented Sales and Operations Planning? The reason appears to be that incorporating this process into the enterprise is not as easy as purchasing software. Implementing Sales and Operations Planning cannot be successfully accomplished by simply purchasing the latest APS or ERP software and hardware. In fact, a very effective Sales and Operations Planning process can be successfully completed manually or by using a simple spreadsheet to try different scenarios for the best fit. Implementing Sales and Operations Planning requires the active participation of key personnel across the company in a well-defined implementation approach.

Sales and Operation Planning Implementation

Sales and Operations Planning is implemented in three phases:

Phase I. Developing the foundation.
Phase II. Integrating and streamlining.
Phase III. Competitive advantage.

These three phases normally can be expected to take 12 to 18 months to be completed (Figure 3.5).

Phase I

The fundamentals of Sales and Operations Planning include the integration of the functional views of the organization. This process determines product families and planning horizons. It also establishes time fences to ensure that changes can be incorporated at less cost than the value received and manages making the change. Finally, it establishes the policies and procedures to institutionalize Sales and Operations Planning into the enterprise. The integration of the functional views of the enterprise can be a real challenge. From

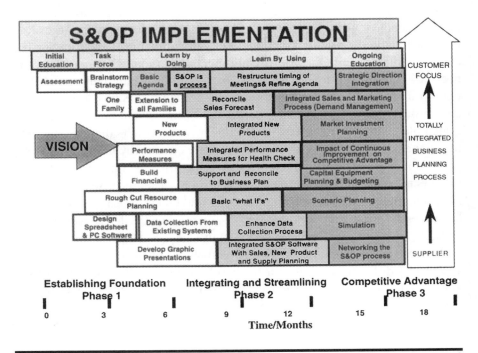

Figure 3.5   Sales and Operations Planning implementation. (Courtesy of Richard Ling and Andy Coldrick (© 1996). With permission.)

the demand planning perspective, the demands are seen in terms of units by part number and revenue. The supply planning function sees this demand as consuming capacity in terms of cash, hours, or other unit of measure required to provide the raw materials and resources needed to make the desired product. The financial planners see the organization strictly in terms of money. New product planners are concerned about scarce resources and timing for competing projects.

Most standard ERP systems do not have an adequate Sales and Operations Planning capability. It's no wonder that developing a Sales and Operations Planning process rarely makes it onto the ERP project implementation schedule. However, even though management cannot purchase software and hardware as the silver bullet for Sales and Operations Planning, the management team has a very important role in successfully establishing this process. Their role includes facilitating continuous improvement in the utilization of the process. This means possessing patience and knowledge that the S&OP process will not be perfect from the beginning. Management should also make decisions for the organization using the information provided by the process and accept Sales and Operations Planning as an ongoing management development process. The ability for the organization to integrate all functional areas into one enterprise-wide plan provides visibility for all managers on how their decisions impact the overall results and not just their own department. This can be clearly seen in the simulation exercise included with this book.

At its very core, the Sales and Operations Planning process is the balance of supply and demand. The variables that must be considered in this balancing act are inventory, material supply constraints, management constraints, lead-time to the customer, actual demand from the customer, new product timing and volume, and the establishment of priorities for customers and products. Too many times the budgets are established based on a projected demand growth while the supply side of the equation lags behind.

Figure 3.6 is the graphic representation of an imbalance between supply and demand. Considering that personnel hires and other overhead expenses are committed based on the budgeted sales, the net result to the organization can be devastating. More people and expenses will be committed than can be supported by the expected level of production. The lead-time required to turn off these expenses can be too long to recover with a positive bottom line. In Figure 3.7, further detail behind the 15% growth can be seen. Part of the growth is expected to come from new product introduction while the balance is expected from increased promotion of current products.

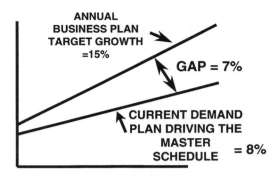

Figure 3.6   An imbalance between sales plan and production plan.

New product launches can have an enormous impact throughout the organization. The target market must first be identified. Promotion to that market must be timed such that demand for the product is experienced at approximately the same time as supply. If the product is sitting in inventory before the demand begins, this is a waste of the scarce cash resource. Conversely, if demand begins before the product is available, customers may be lost. Therefore, it is imperative in a new product launch that the marketing plans, development resources, and new product strategy are in alignment so that the risk is minimized.

Additional issues that must be addressed during the Sales and Operations Planning process for new product include the difficulty in forecasting the

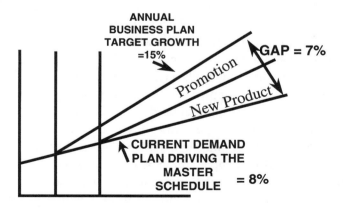

Figure 3.7   Imbalance detailed factors.

acceptance of this product in the market. Given that forecasts are at best an educated guess about the future and by their very definition they are wrong, forecasting new products can look like "Mission Impossible." The three rules for forecasts are

1. Forecasts are always wrong. This is the very nature of forecasts. Forecasts are at best a fuzzy glimpse of the future. Given that the future is subject to many unseen factors, the only thing that can be counted on with certainty is that the forecast will change.
2. Forecasts are more wrong farther in the future. Think about attempting to project where you will be exactly 6 months, 3 hours, and 12 minutes from right now. Impossible, right? Now, where will you be 5 minutes from now? Much more predictable, isn't it? In the same way, forecasts that attempt to predict sales or other events months to years in the future are much less accurate than those predicting sales next week.
3. Forecasts are more wrong in more detail. Given the fact the new products typically have longer lead-times than stock products and forecasts must be made for detailed part number configuration, it is no wonder that the new product introduction is such a challenge.

The impact to current product also must be addressed when new product is introduced. Will this new product replace any current product? If the product does not replace a current product, will the introduction of this product affect other products, either positively or negatively? The company must take into consideration the possibility that the product will sell either significantly more or less than the forecasts. If the product sells significantly more, what is the contingency plan for the manufacturing facility and its suppliers to surge their capacity? An extremely difficult transition is when a product starts to sell well. This is because the supply base typically specializes in either low volume, high-variety products that are built to order when customers requests them or a high volume, low-variety production strategy that builds finished goods to stock. The low-volume producer typically has machinery and facilities that have a wide range of capability but are not efficient in producing large volumes of the same part. These companies tend to compete in the prototype market or small-volume requirements. When the volumes increase such that their prices become uncompetitive, the time has come to switch to a new supplier with high-volume capability. When a product experiences rapid growth, the enterprise can find itself in a very significant transition with a number of suppliers at the same time. All the challenges of a major transition happen at the same time that demand for the product is increasing. Without an adequate plan, success in the form of increased demand could actually kill the product if the transition to new suppliers cannot be done successfully.

Demand Planning

Demand planning is the main driver in the Sales and Operations Planning. Management must determine the objectives, strategies, and expectations of products as they move through their product life cycle. The life cycle begins with introduction and then moves to the growth phase and then to steady state and finally to the decline phase. A diversity of products is needed so that the company does not find itself in a major product-rebuilding situation. Marketing supports this management strategy with market information. This can include the history of the product, external factors that may affect the demand for the product, and overall product plans including the marketing, promotion, and pricing approach. Plans are only as good as their successful execution so the sales area must be in alignment with the overall management and marketing strategy. This includes the possible use of distributors or the establishment of territories. Account plans for target customers are developed which focus on how the product that is available can be brought into alignment with the needs of the customer through the desired market channels. Operationally this plan is further detailed in demand management in Chapter 7.

How people are measured is how they will behave. The use of incentives to encourage the desired behavior from the sales people is essential for overall success of the sales plan. Measurement systems are the most difficult to establish and maintain such that the desired behavior is encouraged. Sometimes what looks like a great idea is, in fact, absolutely the wrong thing to do. For example, if production is held to high efficiency as a measure, distribution is measured on the percentage of orders shipped per schedule, and sales is rewarded for revenue, the result is a dysfunctional company struggling to be competitive in the market. Inventory is high because manufacturing will tend to make large lot sizes of the easy to build products rather than what is really being sold. Distribution will favor small orders and may ship these at the expense of large orders since they take less time to pick. When the percentage is calculated, having all the small orders ship on time will skew the performance results in the desired manner. The company really wants the large orders to ship on time since they are the highest revenue contributors. Sales will focus on selling the high-revenue products regardless of the resulting profitability. In fact, sales often may discount the price in the rush to drive revenue and sell the company right out of business! These measures and their impact can be further explored in the simulator on the CD-ROM that is included with this book.

Unfortunately, these are typical measures used by many companies. Each functional area will focus on maximizing its measure without realizing the overall implication on the profitability of the firm. Other issues that impede the demand planning process include an attitude within the organization that is not conducive to working together for the good of the company. The lack of inventory visibility through the supply chain masks the real demand from the production requirements. Shipping goals cause potential end of month, quarter, or year rushes at significantly increased costs. Systems may not provide adequate visibility and information needed to make timely decisions. The most difficult issue to overcome is the lack of focus on Sales and Operations Planning as a key management process. Demand plans are essential because every business has a lead-time to react. Although the focus has been to reduce response time, there still is a certain amount of time required to order materials, deploy the internal and external capacity, and deliver the desired products to the customer.

Many make-to-order companies believe that they do not need to forecast. A common misconception is that forecasting is only needed for make-to-stock companies. Assuming that the customer is not willing to wait for the company to build a facility, hire personnel, purchase equipment and materials, produce the product, and deliver; every company must include forecasting as part of its essential business process. Forecasts provide the lead-time required to accomplish these activities. The issue becomes what to forecast. This answer is very different for different companies and industry types. Remember the rules of forecasts. Forecasts are never right but they are better than no planning at all. For demand plans to be effective, it requires a significant amount of hard work, timely reviews of actual experience against the forecast, inclusion of customer input, appropriate software support, and, most important, good judgment on how to react. Please note that appropriate software is not the only requirement for effective demand plans, regardless of what the software companies would have you believe. Deciding what to forecast and how the forecast will be used is the first major hurdle. Then the hard work of organizing and analyzing the data to glean meaningful and relevant information can be done. This information is the real key to successful demand planning.

Supply Planning

On the other side of the balance beam from demand planning, supply planning defines the resources and strategies available to meet demand. These supply strategies must align the external suppliers and the internal facilities, labor, and materials to deliver the products that the customer demands. The supply planning process includes planning resources and eliminating undesired constraints. In addition, an overall plan must be developed to meet seasonal demand peaks in such a way that the company ensures the best financial results. The amount of desired flexibility is defined and integrated with the company's market strategy. This buffer resource strategy is further described in Chapter 4. If the company is competing in low volume, high-variety products, their flexibility will focus on multiple use machines capable of producing a wide breadth of products. When the company is competing in high volume, low variety products, the flexibility focus will be on the agile reaction to changes in volume by utilizing machines that have a very focused use. The benefit of the supply planning process is to ensure short, medium, and long-term resource requirements that can be met with available or projected supply. Figures 3.8, 3.9, and 3.10 show different scenarios that a company may need to address.

Figure 3.8 shows a company that has increasing demands on its capacity. A decision must be made to either increase capacity, out source the demands that exceed the available capacity, or reduce the load. When the decisions are made to reduce the load, the most profitable orders and customers should be retained. This is the real power behind the latest business models available in an Advanced Planning Systems (APS). These computer models can provide a schedule that maximizes the desired inputs. This is covered in more depth in Chapter 7.

Figure 3.9 shows a company that experiences spikes in demand. There are two basic ways to address this situation. One method is to increase the inventory to meet the surge in demand. This works very well for a make-to-stock or assemble-to-order company. The forecast is established for the products and then production can build inventory during the slow time to be sold during the surge periods. The difficulty with this strategy is that rarely

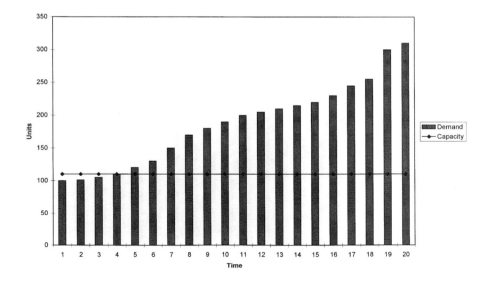

Figure 3.8 Increasing demand.

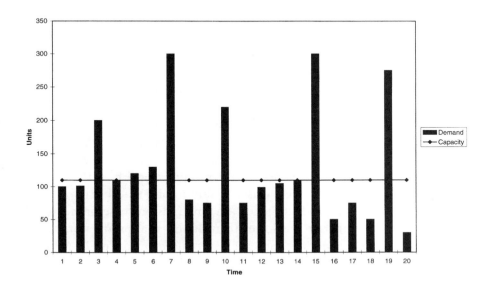

Figure 3.9 Random demand spikes.

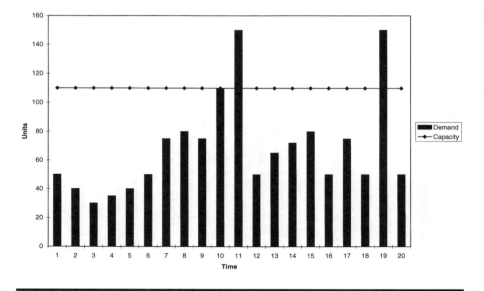

Figure 3.10   Resource underload.

are the same products made over a period of time in a make-to-order company. Another choice is to flex the capacity to meet the surge. The difficulty with this strategy is the degree to which the facility can flex its capacity. Over the short term, 20% upside flexibility in a facility is not unrealistic through planned overtime. However, to ask personnel to work overtime for a long period normally serves to reduce productivity and quality. A third choice is to outsource the amount of production that is required in excess of available internal capacity. This strategy is the most difficult to manage since there is not the same level of direct control over suppliers that is possible internally. In addition, what assurance is there that the supplier will have the capacity at the time when the requirement exists? Assuming also that the supplier cost is higher than internal production cost, the margins on these products will be lower. If the supplier cost is lower than the internal production cost, it does beg the question of why the part is produced inside at all. A fourth choice is to extend the committed lead-time to the customer. Extended lead times provide an increased opportunity for the company to level the load within the facility. If the facility can really make the part in 3 days, but quotes 6 weeks to the customer, there are 5 weeks over which the available work can be spread to meet the customer's due date. The risks of this approach are that the factory may begin to believe that the lead-time to produce the part should be 6 weeks. This would release excess to the shop floor that must be managed and tracked.

Figure 3.10 represents a company that should be aggressively moving any product that is produced outside the facility into the internal production facility. In addition, this enterprise should be actively looking for additional work. Given that the overhead cost is relatively fixed, the company can significantly drive profitability if volumes are increased. The pitfall that many managers fall into is to reduce the direct labor force in this situation in an attempt to reduce costs. This normally begins a downward spiral and poor financial results. The best answer is to aggressively market the company's capability and price products to more fully utilize the available resources. Up to the point where additional resources need to be added, the incremental cost of that utilization is nominal. A close look must be taken at marginal pricing and marginal costs to determine what the real cost is of adding a product to the production schedule. This is one of the advantages of an integrated Sales and Operations Plan. The financial results of sales and operations decisions can be clearly seen and analyzed before decisions are made. This has been simulated in the MICSS simulator included with this book. Without Sales and Operations Planning, it is like running a company blindfolded.

Financial Planning

When all is said and done, what matters most to companies is bottom line results. Even nonprofit companies work towards operational surplus. Non-profit is really a tax status and not a state of mind for these enterprises. Financial planning is where the business plan, the inventory plan, and the revenue, costs, and margins are brought into alignment. Financial planning must be based on current plans for proper financial projections of revenue and inventory. If the Sales and Operations Planning process is followed, there should be no surprises at the end of the year from a financial perspective. Since the final measure of a company's effectiveness is financial, this integration of the Sales and Operations Plan is essential for all departments to improve their understanding of the financial impact to the enterprise from decisions made in their particular areas. Financial planning allows decision making at the appropriate level in the company where demand and supply mismatches can be identified and resolved. The market implications, customer satisfaction, and long-term impacts to the product all must be considered. The integrated financial plan also helps ensure that the new product strategy is being followed and supported through enhanced visibility to the management team. Sales and Operations Planning provides alignment of operational plans with the business plan and the strategic direction of the company.

A demand manager leads the establishment of the Sales and Operations Planning process. Some companies have used the titles of demand coordinator, Sales and Operations Planning manager, and life cycle manager to name a few. This individual should understand the priorities and tradeoffs that are available to meet the needs of all functional areas. This individual is responsible for developing and managing a set of business rules for management approval. The demand manager is also responsible for scenario planning. This process is more than just "what if." Scenario planning analyzes potential demand, supply, new product introduction, and financial scenarios for the business with the purpose of developing and reviewing possible alternatives. Well-defined scenario planning leads to improved understanding and decision making.

Senior Management Business Review

The monthly review by the senior management team should include a review of performance measures such as revenue, cost, customer service, sales plan performance, forecast accuracy, new product launch, and supply performance. From this review, action plans are developed for improvement. In addition, the assumptions behind the plan should be well defined including internal and external assumptions. Any changes in these assumptions should be highlighted during the meeting. After this review, the key issues by customer, market segment, product family, or resource are identified and discussed, including the review of multiple scenarios for the business. Alternative plans are discussed including the opportunities and risks associated with these alternatives. Decisions are made during this meeting to address the alternative opportunities and provide direction for all affected departments. The Sales and Operations Planning processes bring customer demands, business plans, and the enterprise strategic thrust into alignment.

All these wonderful results sound very enticing. The senior management review is not without its difficulty. Some problems that can occur include the perception that the Sales and Operations Planning process is a separate meeting and not the process by which the business is run. A frequent problem is that too much is put on the agenda for the meeting, the meeting runs for hours, and little is really accomplished. The senior management review should be exactly that — a review. Much of the work and analysis should be completed BEFORE the meeting. The converse also can be true, there is too little on the agenda for the meeting and no real discussion occurs during the senior management review. The Sales and Operations Planning process should be an opportunity for different functional areas to be heard and for plans to be made that will be actually implemented. Senior management frequently will not have the patience to let the process evolve to the level where adequate analysis is done and action-focused decisions can be made. Another problem is when the management team will not make a decision. There is a risk of analysis paralysis, where more and more data are requested before a decision is made. The most difficult area in the review process is the establishment of appropriate measures. Performance measures drive behavior so they must be selected carefully to support the strategic plan in an integrated fashion

The Sales and Operations Planning Process

A typical Sales and Operations Planning process is represented in Figure 3.11. Typically new product planning is done during the first week of the month. This is followed by the analysis of demand planning, supply planning, and

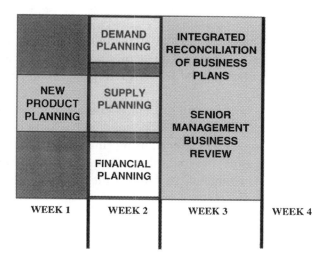

Figure 3.11 Typical monthly timetable.

financial planning. This is because most companies will take the first week of the month to close the financial results from the previous month. This is followed in the next week by the integrated reconciliation of business plans and the senior management business review where the decisions are made and integrated into the master production schedule.

Phase II

Phase II of the Sales and Operations Plan is integrating and streamlining the process into the everyday management of the enterprise. Management learns by doing and learns by using the Sales and Operations Planning process as an integral part of managing the business. During Phase II the company learns that S&OP is a process and, therefore, should be continuously improved. This improvement includes restructuring the timing of the meeting and the refinement of the meeting agenda. The Sales and Operations Planning process focuses on change. The important questions to be considered are

1. What has changed? How has it been measured?
2. Do we agree with the changes?
3. Do we understand the impact of these changes?
4. What decisions need to be made as a result of these changes?

Figure 3.12 shows a typical Sales and Operations Planning spreadsheet where the changes have occurred. This allows the management review to focus on where the impact will be felt in the organization. These changes also can be highlighted in a graphical format as shown in Figure 3.13. The graphical format can provide some additional insights that may not be evident in the grid format.

The important thing to remember during this phase is that S&OP is a process and, therefore, must have a built in continuous improvement process. During the initial critique of the process, the questions that should be asked are

1. Was everyone prepared? This is required to make the most of the time that is spent together and obtain the maximum return on investment.
2. Were the steps on the process appropriate? The Sales and Operations Planning process should fit the business practices and the culture of

Product Family Large Bags

Sales	Past Months -3	-2	-1	1	2	3	4	Future Months 5	6	7	8	9	10	Annual
Last Year		1168	1096	1310	1298	1136	1189	1156	106?	1157	1187	1210	1129	14123
Bus. Plan	1200	1200	1200	1200	1200	1200	1200	120?	1?00	1200	1200	1200	1200	14400
Previous	1211	1197	1225	1225	1225	12?	1225	1?5	?25	1225	1225	1225	1225	14672
Act/Proj.	1211	1197	1298	1275	1275	?50	1250	?50	?250	1250	1250	1250	1250	15045
Backlog				680	350									1030
Diff / Chg	11	-3	98	50	50	25	25	2?	25	25	25	25	25	373
Cum Diff	11	-3	95											

Production	-3	-2	-1	1	2	3	4	5	6	7	8	9	10	Annual
Bus. Plan	1200	1200	1200	1200	1200	1200	?00	?00	1200	1200	1200	1200	1200	14400
Prevoius	1195	1202	1200	1200	1200	1250	?275	?225	1225	1225	1225	1225	1225	14677
Act./Proj.	1195	1202	1197	1200	1200	1350	?350	1350	1250	1250	1250	1250	1250	15099
Diff	-5	2	-3	0	0	100	7?	125	25	25	25	25	25	422
Cum Diff	-5	-3	-6											

Inventory	-3	-2	-1	1	2	3	4	5	6	7	8	9	10	
Bus. Plan	1200	1200	1200	1200	1200	1200	?200	1200	1200	1200	1200	1200	1200	1200
Previous	1190	1195	1170	1145	1120	114?	?195	1195	1195	1195	1195	1195	1195	1195
Act./Proj.	1190	1195	1094	1019	944	104?	1144	1244	1244	1244	1244	1244	1244	1244
Diff	-10	-5	-106	-181	-256	-156	-56	44	44	44	44	44	44	
Cover (wks)	4.14	4.09	3.67	3.46	3.23	3.59	3.94	4.28	4.28	4.28	4.28	4.28	4.28	

Figure 3.12 Sales and Operations Planning spreadsheet example.

the individual enterprise. No two companies will have exactly the same requirements.

3. Did we have the right level of detail? Too much detail and the meeting will get bogged down, too little detail and the right decisions cannot be made.

4. Were the appropriate decisions made? The risk when beginning on the road to Sales and Operations Planning is that too much analysis will be required before the appropriate decisions can be made. Do not fall prey to analysis paralysis!

5. Were we efficient with our time? The speed of business is increasing at an alarming rate. Nobody wants to feel like he has wasted his time. However, when people feel that the time they have spent has made a

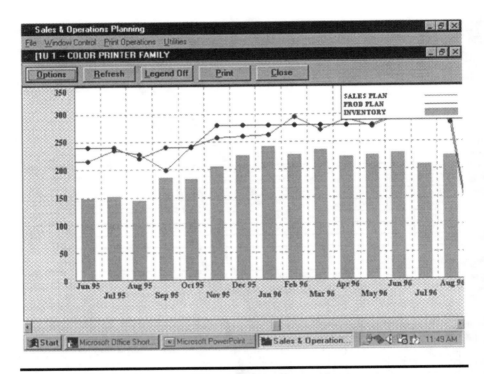

Figure 3.13   Sales and Operations Planning graphical format.

difference, most people are willing to invest in the process because they recognize the potential for long-term return on their investment.

6.   What can we do to improve the process? No process is perfect. Every area has room for improvement. The constraint to improved overall company performance must be identified and addressed through continuous improvement.

Phase III

Phase III is when the company internalizes the Sales and Operations Planning process and utilizes it for competitive advantage. A company that has successfully implemented Sales and Operations Planning is customer driven. This company drives the execution of the business plan by ensuring that plans are integrated and realistic rather than allowing chance to play a large role. A Sales and Operations Planning company embraces change as a competitive strategy and drives internal change through continuous improvement. The underlying advantage is that strategies and tactics have been integrated into one plan that everyone drives towards. Too many times each department attempts to drive in its own direction to the negative impact on the overall enterprise.

Given all these benefits, it begs the question — why don't more companies effectively implement Sales and Operations Planning as part of the ERP implementation? The primary reason more companies do not is that the management team is not educated at the beginning of the ERP implementation on the value of Sales and Operations Planning. Often during an ERP implementation the amount of time, data, and resources required are significantly underestimated. This usually leads to de-scoping the project so that the implementation will finish on schedule and on budget with the reduced scope. Strategies to ensure a successful ERP selection and implementation are detailed further in Section III of this book. Companies are unwilling to publicly admit the increased expense incurred for the disappointing results achieved. However, the high cost of ERP implementations compared to the low return on investment is beginning to show in publications like the *Harvard Business Review* and *The Wall Street Journal.* Even *The New York Times* ran an article entitled, "Software that can make a grown company cry," referring to ERP implementation.

Many companies do not focus on strategy as a key ingredient of the overall business process. Strategic planning is viewed as something done by the corporate staff for the purpose of developing a large document that is left on the shelf to collect dust. Rarely is the strategic plan fully integrated into the business operations planning and implementation. For strategic planning to really be successful, those linkages must exist and be monitored on a regular basis. This brings the process back to the beginning, the role of management in the Sales and Operations Planning process. The management team must provide the leadership to integrate this process into the enterprise, including the insistence on education. Performance measures and discipline can change what someone does. Education changes what someone thinks and believes. Management must also model the desired behavior. "Walking the talk" is louder than any words can be. The Sales and Operations Planning process should be used to make the appropriate business decisions. The appropriate amount of detail should be expected in the reporting process and last but not least, continuous improvement is facilitated and, encouraged by the management team.

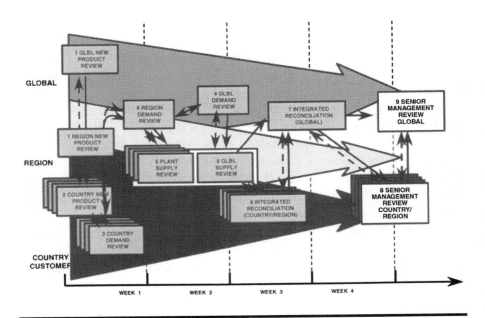

Figure 3.14 Global sales and operations planning process.

Global Sales and Operations Planning

As more companies are competing on a global basis, the Sales and Operations Planning process must also span the globe. Figure 3.14 shows one process example of how S&OP can be implemented on a global basis.

This integrated plan shows how the information from each country or region flows to a final review on an enterprise level by senior management. Having integrated information systems becomes even more important to the effective management of the company as the operating scope of the company gets broader. Failure to integrate the plans from the different regions and geographies will cause the company to operate like an unrelated group of independent enterprises and not gain the results expected from global reach and integration.

Summary

Sales and Operations Planning can benefit the business in a number of different ways. The increased visibility helps achieve the inventory and lead-time objectives by managing supply and demand. When fewer surprises impact the operation, the total delivered cost of the products or services is reduced, thereby yielding higher profits. Customer service is improved through the development of proactive plans rather than waiting until it is too late and reacting when options are few. Overall resource utilization is improved through consistent priorities. All personnel are empowered to make decisions since there is a well-understood direction for the global enterprise. The keystone to a successful Sales and Operations Planning process are people. This is not a software project. The people involved must be educated in the Sales and Operations Planning process, team oriented, actively participate in the process, and possess an attitude of continuous improvement while focused on a common vision. This common vision includes the strategy, goals, products, and services for a company. Developing appropriate measures that reinforce the desired behavior enhances performance and aids in the achievement of the common vision. From companies that have implemented Sales and Operations Planning, the results include management that has been enabled to plan better and thereby improve reliability of information. This results in the ability to manage more effectively with a more effective decision-making process. People understand the business better through these improved strategic and business planning processes. The success factors quoted by the companies that experienced bottom line results were

1. Management was committed right from the start.
2. The affected personnel first obtained an education in Sales and Operations Planning.
3. The vice president of sales and marketing was the champion.
4. A full-time demand manager coordinated the process.
5. Learn by doing rather than planning until perfection.
6. A continuous improvement process was employed.
7. Decisions were made through using the process.

One company executive said, "S&OP has given our management the forum and processes to provide the leadership that is necessary for our business." According to Dick Ling, the worldwide champion of Sales and Operations Planning, "Common sense, improved communications, empowerment, accountability, and PEOPLE are the cornerstones of Sales and Operations Planning and its ultimate success in a corporation." Sales and Operations Planning is the integrator between sales and marketing, manufacturing and distribution, finance, and product development. This integration is a critical success factor in any ERP implementation.

Resources for Sales and Operations Planning

Orchestrating Success, Improve Control of the Business with Sales and Operations Planning, Richard C. Ling, CFPIM and Walter E. Goddard, 1988, APICS # 03111. Available from APICS: http://www.apics.org.

CPFR, The Collaborative Planning, Forecasting, and Replenishment Committee is an industry group made up of several retailers and manufacturers. This group aims to develop a set of business processes that entities in a supply chain can use for collaboration on a number of retailer/manufacturer functions, towards overall efficiency in the supply chain, http://www.cpfr.org.

4 Buffer Resource Strategy

The two most flexible resources in an enterprise are inventory and capacity. Both of these resources can be utilized to buffer customer demand from the manufacturing process. Different types of industries and manufacturing processes require different types of buffers. Inventory is the largest single current asset in most companies today. The investment in inventory must be made very carefully to assure the best profits possible for the enterprise. Even though the inventory has a certain value on the balance sheet, in the event of excess inventory, the true market value is really a small fraction of that value or may actually cost the organization money to unload. Given that customers are demanding higher variety, shorter lead-times, and lower volumes, the modern enterprise must carefully invest its inventory dollars to ensure that they can turn that investment into profit and not loss. Capacity is perishable. The capacity that is not used today is no longer available tomorrow. Both these resources must be wisely spent to realize the best benefit for the enterprise.

Inventory Buffers

Inventory can be successfully used as a strategy to meet the market demand with an acceptable response time. This is similar to a breakwall that is placed in front of a marina to protect the boats. The more violent the waves and weather, the higher the breakwall. The calmer the water, the smaller the breakwall. The company must ask where it desires to meet the market demand: finished goods, work in process inventory, or raw materials.

A make-to-stock company may consider a safety stock of finished goods to buffer the uncertainty of the demand from customers. The level of this buffer is directly dependent on the response time to customer demand and the level of demand variability from the customers. If the company is able to quickly convert raw materials into finished goods, this end item inventory buffer can be relatively small. This is because in the event of any unexpected demands, this agility provides recovery fairly quickly. This requires flexible capacity resources.

A make-to-order company may consider meeting its customer at the level of common component raw materials. This strategy works especially well when the product designers keep the number of raw materials to a minimum. The lead-time and reliability of the supply base also directly affect this inventory investment. The less reliable the supplier's performance, the higher the level of safety stock that will be required. Internal capacity resources should be flexible and the schedule requirements well understood.

To improve response time with a wide variety of goods without investing heavily in finished goods inventory, many companies have moved to an assemble-to-order philosophy. In this strategy, a small variety of semifinished goods are inventoried followed by the final assembly of a wide product variety being accomplished quickly after customer demand by choosing from the list of alternatives.

These different manufacturing strategies also have been referred to as VAT strategies. A "V" plant is one that takes relatively few raw materials to make a wide variety of end items. This type of plant typically practices a make-to-order approach to manufacturing. An "A" plant is the exact opposite and takes a wide variety of raw materials and assembles them into significantly fewer end items. This enterprise is normally a make-to-stock company. The "T" plant holds to a minimum the number of combinations possible until the very last moment. This type of industry is typically an assemble-to-order company. Sometimes references also are made to an "I"-type company. This is a plant that can be considered a make-to-stock/assemble-to-order company. This enterprise is more vertically integrated. Many different raw materials are combined into significantly fewer semifinished goods from which a wide variety of end items can be assembled.

A single correct resource buffer answer for every type of enterprise does not exist. The enterprise must first understand its market response strategy to determine its overall resource buffer strategy. This strategy also must include the product design policies as well as the inventory planning policies.

Decisions made early in the design process can make effective production and inventory management easier or impossible. For example, the desire is to stock inventory at the raw material level in a make-to-order company. The customer does not need to wait for the supplier to order the raw material and then fabricate the parts. If the designers insist on frequently using non-standard materials or sizes for every part that is designed, this investment in inventory will sit on the shelf tying up scarce financial resources while the customer waits for the finished parts. This is a lose–lose proposition even though the designer may have a perfectly logical reason for desiring that particular raw material. The overall implications of these choices must be considered from an enterprise perspective and not just from the functional area perspective.

Inventory reduction and improved capacity utilization are very common expected return on investment items for an ERP implementation. An effective ERP implementation should be expected to reduce inventory and improve capacity utilization in the entire supply chain by providing higher quality planning information more quickly. Capacity should only be used to build those products that will be sold immediately. However, this inventory reduction strategy can be taken too far and leave the enterprise in a position of noncompetitiveness since it cannot ship product when required by the customer. If product cannot be shipped, then revenues are not realized and the enterprise does not make money. You can try this for yourself on the MICSS simulator in this book. The right answer is the Goldilocks Inventory Management approach: not too much inventory, not too little inventory, but just the right inventory at the right time.

Volume/Variety Matrix

To better understand the competitive position of an enterprise, the relationship between the volume produced by the company is compared relative to the variety produced. An interesting diagonal has evolved where most companies are clustered in order to compete effectively. Movements from that competitive diagonal can either be a competitive advantage for the company or disaster. According to Terry Hill in *Manufacturing Strategy*, this can be represented in the following matrix (Figure 4.1). This relationship shows an inverse relationship between variety and volume. In general, as the product volume increases the variety tends to decrease.

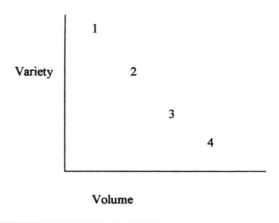

Figure 4.1   Volume–variety matrix.

Project Driven Company: Position 1

Position 1 of the volume/variety matrix is a company that produces a very high variety of products but in very low volume. This can mean that a single product may be developed, planned, and produced once and never produced again. These products or deliverables are typically managed as unique projects. A project-driven company competes in the market based on the wide variety of products that it can produce utilizing the same resources. This type of company rarely uses Materials Requirements Planning (MRP) for determining what needs to be ordered and when. Instead this organization will normally use a project management system to determine the critical path for the activities of the project. The tools of the project management company include PERT (program evaluation review technique) and Gantt charts. These tools can provide the expected finish date once the start date is determined using forward scheduling. The earliest a task in the scheduling network can start is calculated by using forward scheduling. Or, given a desired completion date, the suggested start date can be calculated using backward scheduling. Backward scheduling determines the latest each task can start. In the process of scheduling all the required tasks, some tasks have a difference between early and late start or early and late finish.

When planning material to be available to begin a task, the difference between early and late start is significant. The question quickly arises about when the material should be available: in time for the earliest possible start or hold off investing the capital in inventory until the last possible moment? The project-type company must decide and establish the material policy for ordering needed materials, such as choosing to be available at the early start, late start, or average start date. In most companies of this type, the policy is to have the materials available at the earliest possible start date since a project-driven company's cost is typically driven more from the resources utilized rather than the materials available. These resources are usually the constraint to the company delivering a higher level of output. Having a resource idle because materials are not ready or available can cause a great financial loss, since it cannot be regained once it is lost.

To more effectively manage these scarce resources and improve the overall time and expense required to complete a project, a new scheduling methodology recently has been developed in the project scheduling area called "critical chain scheduling." This scheduling method pulls all the individual slack times from each operation and provides a schedule buffer for significant paths within the overall project. The traditional project scheduling method has slack time broken up at each operation. Project management reality is that since the most critical resources are people and people are driven by deadlines, getting a task completed early is virtually unheard of. The natural tendency is to wait until the last possible finish date to focus on the work and accomplish the tasks since the resources typically have more to do than there is capacity available. Figure 4.2 shows how the individual activity buffers are moved to the end of the project so that real requirement dates for each activity can be identified.

The critical chain method moves the slack time from each task into a resource buffer for a sequence of tasks. This provides more accurate information so that everyone can work to the real deadline but still have some buffer time in the overall project schedule in the event an emergency arises. For more information on this scheduling approach, *Critical Chain,* by Eli Goldratt, is available. An add-in product from Microsoft® Project (ProChain™ Project Scheduling) has been developed to facilitate this scheduling process.

These new tools were developed in response to the overall pressure to reduce lead-times for a project. A competitive strategy for a project-driven company is lead-time. A company that can complete a quality project in less lead-time than the competition can typically demand a premium for this performance. Having inventory available at the earliest expected moment can enhance lead-time response. This is not to say that all materials should be

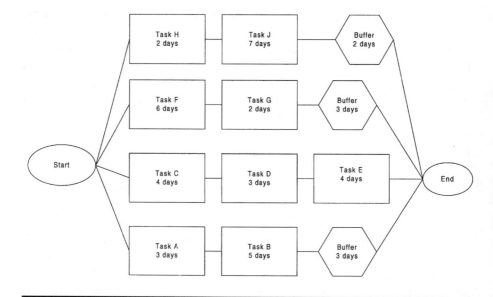

Figure 4.2   Critical chain schedule.

purchased at the beginning of the project. However, the better alternative to guessing when the activities with slack time will really start is to utilize critical chain scheduling. By using these resource schedule buffers, more accurate start dates are calculated with which to determine real material need. The more agile a company is in the execution of a project, the less opportunity there is for cost overruns due to unexpected crises. Or, in the immortal words of Marine Colonel (Ret.) William Scott in the management of a large aviation remanufacturing depot, "The longer the cow is in the pasture, the more grass it can eat!" A direct relationship exists between lead-time and cost. When the business processes are capable and agile, costs dramatically reduce. However, if the quick response time is accomplished by expediting and manual intervention, short lead-times can be financially disastrous. Anyone who has worked on a project that was behind schedule will attest to this fact. Schedule and cost can never be recovered simultaneously. Effective project management requires up-to-date information with which to make quality decisions. Having a closed-loop information system that provides feedback to the plan based on actual performance is essential for success in this environment. Implementation of ERP in this environment has its unique challenges. An implementation success strategy for project-driven companies is discussed in Chapter 18.

Make-to-Stock (A-type company): Position 3 and 4

Make-to-stock companies typically ship to customers on demand. The customers are not willing to wait very long for their needs to be fulfilled. They expect the products they want to be on the shelf, typically in a retail environment. Since manufacturing has to build products in advance of customer demand, the manufacturing schedule is typically driven by a demand forecast. Actual customer demand then consumes this forecast. Ideally, the sales force will sell to the "available-to-promise" (ATP), the uncommitted portion of inventory. ATP assumes that the plan will be executed as designed and provides visibility on how much inventory will be available for customer orders. In Table 4.1, an example of ATP is shown. Available to promise is calculated only in the first time period and whenever there is an expected receipt.

The demand time fence is the expected time within which no additional customer orders are expected. The demand time fence is typically the length of time that customers are expecting to wait for the product they have ordered to be shipped. Within the demand time fence, actual customer demand is used to calculate the projected available balance. Once the planning horizon goes beyond the demand time fence, the projected available balance uses the greater of the forecast or the customer order.

The available to promise line only uses confirmed customer demand. Available to promise is the uncommitted portion of inventory. This is why it is only calculated for the first time period and whenever there is an expected receipt. Another way to think about it is: how long does the inventory need to last given the current customer backlog? Cumulative ATP shows how many pieces are available between receipts that have not already been committed. In some cases, there may be insufficient inventory to cover the demands that are already known in Period 2 to last until the next receipt in Period 4. This is when a process known as backwards ATP is used to reserve inventory to assure that the known customer orders will be covered. In Table 4.1, the real ATP in Period 1 should be 47 pieces. If all 92 pieces are committed to a customer, then the customer's order in Period 3 will be short by 45 pieces. If the order entry personnel use the projected available balance to promise customer orders, customers who have provided the company with sufficient lead-time may be penalized while customers who just called in may get product immediately. Comparing only the two lines (projected available balance and cumulative ATP) in Table 4.1 clearly demonstrates the errors that can be made by using the project available balance.

Table 4.1   Available to Promise

Part A
Demand time fence–3

Beginning on hand–172	1	2	3	4	5	6	7	8	9	10
Forecast	100	90	80	75	80	90	100	100	120	130
Actual customer demand	80	120	75	30	20	10	0	0	0	0
Project available balance	92	122	47	122	42	102	2	52	82	102
Available to promise	92	–45		120						
Cumulative ATP	92	47	47	167	167	167	167	167	167	167
Master production schedule		150		150	167	150		150	150	150

However, remember the three rules of forecasting: forecasts are always wrong, they are worse projecting farther in the future, and worse in more detail. What a terrible situation for this type of company that depends entirely on forecasts to drive its planning for material and capacity. If the forecasts are incorrect, then the planning is incorrect. If the planning is incorrect, then the inventory that is purchased may be exactly the wrong material in exactly the wrong amount. This has a terrible impact on cash flow and can affect overall profitability. The make-to-stock company is the most difficult kind of company to reduce inventory and still provide good customer service without dramatically changing to integrated business planning and supply chain management processes. One proven strategy for reducing inventory is to have a relatively small number of finished goods when compared to a make-to-order or assemble-to-order enterprise. This is the reason why this company is also referred to as an A type. When the bills of material are examined, they look like Figure 4.3.

An A-type company must fight the urge to try to be everything to everybody if their processes are not flexible and agile. The marketing department will try to add small variations to meet the needs of unique market channels. This can wreck havoc in a company if the processes are not capable of easily

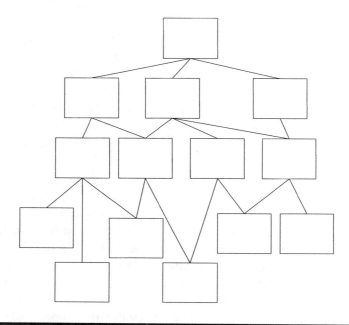

Figure 4.3   A-type company bill of material.

handling these changes. Many make-to-stock companies have successfully deferred the final configuration of products until the customer order is received. The advantage is that the forecast error is significantly reduced since resources to complete finished goods are not committed until an actual order is received. This competitive strategy is covered in the section on assemble-to-order.

This strategy may not be possible for the company if they are delivering products like mayonnaise or canned green beans to a retail market. The customer is not willing to wait for the company to package on their demand. The customer expects to have immediate delivery from the shelf. This is why the make-to-stock company will typically exercise a strategy of carrying a safety stock of finished goods to buffer against the variability of demands from the market. However, understanding what is currently in the entire supply chain pipeline can mean the difference between profits and loss for this enterprise. What may be perceived as consumer variability is nothing more than normal supply chain replenishment cycles. Table 4.2 shows how demand from just a few different retailers through a few distributors can wreck havoc on the manufacturer. This is not because the customer had wide variability in demand but rather the batch ordering of products from the retailer to the distributor and the distributor to the manufacturer has set the manufacturer up for guaranteed failure.

If safety stocks were calculated using the traditional statistical methods, the required safety stock to provide 95% customer service would be 805 units. If this is applied to the planning from Table 4.2, the result can be seen in Table 4.3. The combination of the safety stock and fixed-order quantity yields an amazing average inventory of 1640 units. This is over twice the expected safety stock. When this is considered on an enterprise-wide level, the assets dedicated to this hidden inventory could be significant. As an alternative, if visibility existed of the entire inventory in the supply chain, proactive planning as shown in Table 4.4 could be used to provide a better level of customer service with no safety stock. Supply chain management planning processes to address this situation are more fully described in Chapter 6.

The availability of information for intended demand from distribution centers can result in drastically reduced inventory while providing higher levels of customer service. This is the motivation behind the implementation of supply chain strategies. Having visibility of inventory in the supply chain from the manufacturer to the end consumer should be a priority for the make-to-stock company. This visibility provides the opportunity for the

Table 4.2 Supply Chain Inventory Visibility

	1	2	3	4	5	6	7	8	9	10
Distributor 1										
Beginning on hand–145										
Forecast	100	90	80	75	80	90	100	100	120	130
Project available balance	45	105	25	100	20	80	130	30	60	80
Planned receipt	0	150	0	150	0	150	150	0	150	150
Planned order release	150	0	150	0	150	150	0	150	150	0
Distributor 2										
Beginning on hand–190										
Forecast	90	100	90	80	75	82	125	110	150	50
Project available balance	55	255	165	85	10	228	103	293	143	93
Planned receipt		300				300		300		
Planned order release	300	0	0	0	300	0	300	0	0	0
Distributor 3										
Beginning on hand–272										
Forecast	80	75	80	90	100	125	130	120	50	85
Project available balance	192	117	37	197	97	222	92	222	172	87
Planned receipt				250		250		250		
Planned order release	250	0	250	0	250	0	0	0	0	0
Manufacturer										
Beginning on hand–200										
Total demand	700	0	400	0	700	150	300	150	150	0

Table 4.3   Statistical Safety Stock Impact

Manufacturer
Beginning on hand–200, safety stock–805

	1	2	3	4	5	6	7	8	9	10
Total demand	700	0	400	0	700	150	300	150	150	0
Project available balance	1000	1000	2100	2100	1400	1250	950	2300	2150	2150
Planned receipt	1500		1500					1500		

Table 4.4   Proactive Planning Impact

Manufacturer
Beginning on hand–200, supply chain solution

	1	2	3	4	5	6	7	8	9	10
Total demand	700	0	400	0	700	150	300	150	150	0
Project available balance	0	0	0	0	0	0	0	0	0	0
Planned receipt	500		400		700	150	300	150	150	

manufacturer to be proactive in their planning rather than reactive. Reaction is normally manifested as high levels of inventory.

The next level to consider is that even when the plan looks like everything is in balance, excess inventory can still be in the supply chain. Table 4.3 shows how easily lot sizing can result in excess inventory. Fixed lot sizing is a very common practice in many companies. This excess inventory can hide in the system because no ERP system currently highlights its existence. If the inventory investment in the company seems to be high, try this test:

1. Run a query on the current database to identify the parts for which safety stock has been authorized. Typically safety stock is set in the item master record as a fixed-order quantity.
2. Multiply this authorized safety stock by the cost of the product according to the accounting department.
3. Add these individual numbers to get the total authorized investment in safety stock. If this number does not shock you, then continue to the next step.
4. For those parts with authorized safety stocks, multiply the current on-hand balance times the accounting cost for each part.
5. Add these individual numbers to get the total real investment in safety stock. Compare to the investment in step 3.

When companies run this test, the difference between the authorized and real investments has been as high as a factor of four to six times. The frustration of the senior management team is that after all the money that has been poured into the ERP system implementation, why is this fact so well hidden? Make-to-stock companies typically will order according to some economic lot-sizing rule and buffer with a fixed safety stock. The net result is inventory and lots of it!

Make-to-Order (V-type company): Position 2

A make-to-order company competes in the market by providing a wide variety of products in the shortest lead-time possible. This V-type plant is characterized by a few raw materials with a large number of end items. Figure 4.4 shows a typical bill of material configuration.

In addition to common raw materials, all products in a V-type company tend to go through similar operations. This type of manufacturing facility is

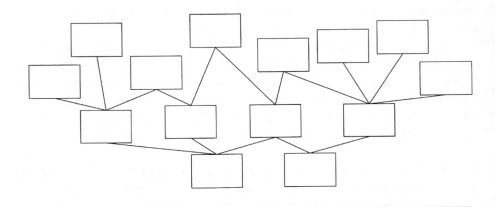

Figure 4.4   V-type bill of material configuration.

generally capital intensive with general-purpose equipment that can accomplish a wide range of processes. An example of this kind of business is a machine shop making sheet metal parts for many customers. The operations used can include punching, forming, deburring, plating, and assembling. Almost an infinite number of finished goods can be produced from these basic operations. To effectively compete in the market, the make-to-order manufacturer tends to focus its marketing on one type of industry, such as aerospace and defense, medical devices, or computer parts, etc. The constraint for growth in this type of company is typically lack of knowledge of the market, including the unique customer demands and potential distribution channels rather than production capability. The cost of adding additional distribution channels is significantly more expensive than adding production capability.

The inventory strategy in this organization is to purchase a safety stock of the commonly used raw materials so that the overall response time to the customer can be reduced. Customers tend to order what they want at the last possible moment. Design changes after the orders are placed are not unusual. Normally, relatively few raw materials are used in the normal course of business. The investment required in safety stock to shorten the response time is not all that significant. Another competitive strategy is to standardize the manufacturing processes to use common sizes of raw materials. Rather than using the size of material that provides the best material utilization, the company may standardize on sizes of raw material that are easily obtainable. Purchasing standard size stock material prevents having to stock safety stock inventory since these standard sizes are normally in stock at the supplier. In addition, these standard size materials are typically less expensive on a square foot basis. However, it is true that more of the material will be wasted than if the best fit material was purchased. The capacity strategy usually focuses on maintaining aggressive cross training with the operators so that they can operate a variety of machines. This enhances the overall flexibility of the enterprise and could lead to a market advantage.

Understanding what the best solution is for the company as a whole must consider the cost of the wasted material, the inventory carrying cost to stock special material, the less expensive stock material, the competitive position for the company with respect to lead-time response, and many other factors that impact the overall cost. This final decision is dependent on many factors and must be considered from an overall competitive position for the enterprise.

Assemble-to-Order (T-type company): Position 3

In the assemble-to-order company, the customer is provided with more product variety than the make-to-stock company if they are willing to wait a small amount of time. The T-type company has a bill of material that looks like Figure 4.5.

Gateway Computer has embraced this competitive strategy with wonderful success. Only the semifinished subassemblies are forecasted, built,

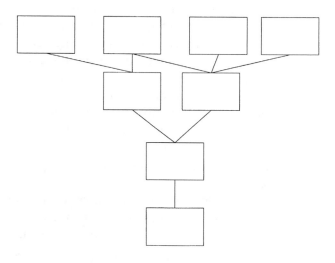

Figure 4.5   T-type company bill of material.

and inventoried. When the customer orders a finished product, these items are assembled on demand to provide a custom product. The ERP system for an assemble-to-order company should contain a linear finite configurator where the order entry personnel can select from a preestablished list of options to build a finished part. Each of the choices promised in a finished product must exist in inventory. This is very different from the dynamic configurator described in Chapter 15. A linear finite configurator usually creates a temporary part number to represent and track the end item. If that exact set of options is ordered again, the demand will be added to the previous order. This provides the enterprise with the visibility of those configurations that are the most popular and, therefore, may warrant a move to a make-to-stock strategy.

A success strategy for setting up this type of configurator is to make the choices that distinguish the product at the very end of the manufacturing process. Having the common parts early in the selection process also helps make the assembly line run more smoothly. In addition to linear configurator capability, capable to promise (CTP) functionality is just starting to develop in ERP systems. Available to promise (ATP) is the process used to commit make-to-stock products. ATP works best on finished goods items that are forecasted and then customer orders are directly received against that forecast. CTP matches the promise capability with how the assemble-to-order company actually plans its products. Material superbills are used for planning. Forecasts in the assemble-to-order company are accomplished at the semifinished good level using percentage product mix as an indicator of relative need. Customer orders are received at the finished goods level. CTP examines the material availability one level down and the available capacity to promise delivery to the customer.

Figure 4.6 shows an example of a superbill that can be used to plan this product. There is little need to know how many Red heat shrink, type C connectors, 12-inch cable with strain relief were shipped. The important issue is to have sufficient wire, connectors, heat shrink, and strain reliefs available. These semifinished goods are placed into inventory pending actual customer orders for the final assembled product.

A very important function for ERP in an assemble-to-order environment is capable to promise. Available to promise is used in a make-to-stock environment where the forecast is for the finished product to provide information on the uncommitted portion of inventory. Customer orders are at the same level that the product is forecasted. Capable to promise would indicate to the order entry person the first available opportunity to ship the customer's

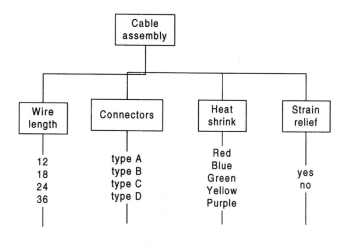

Figure 4.6 Configuration superbill.

order, given the current fabrication plan for each component needed. Capable to promise examines the expected delivery of components based on capacity and material availability to project customer availability.

In an assemble-to-order environment, typically manufactured and purchased parts are common to many assemblies; each assembly is made up of a series of options. For this reason, when promising orders using CTP, it is essential that reservations are made against inventory that has been committed to a customer, otherwise the same scarce subassembly may be promised to two different customers. In addition, capable to promise also may take into account the capacity of the final assembly area when promising an order. Even though all the parts may be available, if there is no capacity with which to assembly them, the product will not be available when expected. The assemble-to-order company is well suited to the expectations of customers for mass customized products on demand. The challenge is having the right building blocks available from which to make the final product. This challenge can be made much easier through the design process as covered in Chapter 8.

Make-to-Stock/Assembly-to-Order: I-type company

Some companies may be a combination of types and encompass a number of positions of the volume/variety matrix. An example of this is the I-type

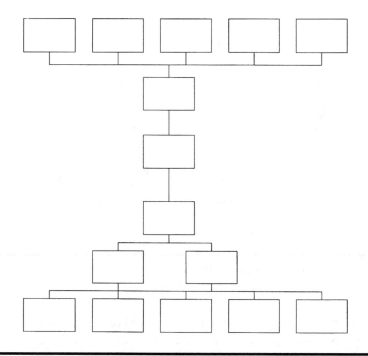

Figure 4.7   I-type bills of material.

company. This company combines a number of different raw materials into significantly fewer semifinished goods and then can explode these choices into many finished products. The bills of material in this company look like Figure 4.7.

An example of this kind of company would be a computer manufacturer that also assembles its own circuit boards and cables. Many individual parts need to be managed and planned to support the assembly of significantly fewer semifinished goods. From these options, a wide variety of final products can be assembled. This company has all the challenges of both the make-to-stock and assemble-to-order companies. This company is driven from forecasts for semifinished goods similar to the assemble-to-order company. The inventory strategy is to have these semifinished goods available based on the overall Sales and Operations Plan by product mix. The I-type company then has to plan and purchase the required raw materials to combine into subassemblies. These needed raw materials are planned using traditional MRP logic. The I-type company has the additional challenge of longer lead-times since they must purchase all the separate components, assemble them into semifinished goods, and then assemble the finished product to customers' orders. The assemble-to-order company has only to worry about the timely response to customers' orders without the complication of ordering all the raw materials. The diversity of manufacturing processes also can be a real challenge in this type of company. An I-type company can include processes as diverse as sheet metal stamping to electronic assembly to painting. This diversity of operations required for fabrication normally requires batch manufacturing which results in on-hand inventory as a buffer between the fabrication and assembly operations since the assembly batches are significantly smaller. The assembly resource capacity is the buffer in this type of enterprise. Having a tight integration of design with fabrication is essential for overall success. Using standard parts in multiple models helps reduce the complexity of the fabrication process and increases the volume of each individual part. The cost per part is usually reduced as the volume increases. The design strategy is a critical success factor for this type of company. This is further covered in Chapter 8 (Product Data Management).

Summary

Inventory and capacity resources are key assets in every company. Just as Goldilocks found when she visited the three bears, a successful company does not want too much inventory or assets will be wasted and the company is restricted in cash flow. Too little inventory and customer demands cannot be met, therefore, reducing overall profits. Just the right amount of inventory in the right place and the company is profitably meeting customer demands and expectations. Too much capacity and money is wasted. Too little capacity and profits may be jeopardize. The right amount of capacity can be a competitive advantage. Knowing what kind of company you manage (V, A, T, I) and what the strategy is for competing on volume and variety is essential for developing an overall resource buffer strategy for success. This strategy is essential for overall enterprise success.

Resources for Buffer Resource Strategy

Critical Chain, Goldratt, Eli, North River Press, Great Barrington, MA, ISBN 0-88427-153-6, 1997, APICS #03203, Spanish version: APICS #03009SP.

ProChain™ Project Scheduling software: Creative Technology Labs, LLC, 37 Grieb Trail, Wallingford, CT 06492, (203) 265-7590, prochain@compuserve.com, http://www.prochain.com.

5 Enterprise Resource Management

An excellent way for an ERP system implementation to fail is to expect the software to be drastically changed to reflect the current business processes. Doing a thorough system selection to ensure the very best possible software fit could save the company millions of dollars in implementation costs. The best advice to a company who expects the new ERP system to look like its old business system is to save its money and stay with the old system. Think about it. Add the cost to purchase the new system plus the cost of modifying it to the cost and frustration of attempting to implement this mess. Then consider that in the end the system will look just like what was there before except the balance sheet will have a big chunk taken out of its asset side. Why bother? It is essential during the selection phase that the key business processes for your company are reflected in the system selected. This selection process is described in Chapter 12.

The good news is that commercial off-the-shelf software has been programmed to reflect identified industry best practices and these best practices can be used as a catalyst for changing the internal business processes. The bad news is that the software is programmed to reflect industry best practices. If every company purchasing the system changes their processes to match the software, then upon which process will the enterprise distinguish itself for competitive advantage? Some recent articles suggest that the competitive position will come from who can least expensively implement the software! This is not an acceptable alternative. There must be room in the implementation for the examination of the current business processes and the recommendation of improved business processes. This must be done in the context of the overall company's strategy. Frequently, the senior management of the company underestimates the number of changes required in the company's processes and the wild enthusiasm at the beginning of the ERP project turns into mass disillusionment. Too many times the next steps are typically to search for the guilty, punish the innocent, and promote the noninvolved. The net result is that the company has invested millions of dollars and has not seen any return on that investment. Like all the tools that have evolved into ERP, the main ERP focus is on planning, but reality is that planning is only one piece of effectively managing the business. Many companies have embarked on major projects to implement ERP systems with very little to show in the way of actual results. The reason many of these companies have failed to realize the full benefits of ERP is because most organizations are not organized correctly to benefit from the new information tools provided by ERP. Many of the companies attempting implementation of enterprise-wide systems have run into difficulty because the organization is not positioned for integration. Departments work to their own sets of objectives. Measurements are functional not global. People are specialists not generalists. Information is spread over many systems and platforms. Systems are often fragmented and there are very few people who have an enterprise-wide view or understanding of the organization.

ERP is only part of the challenge facing most organizations today. It is not good enough to just plan the resources required to run the enterprise. These resources need to be managed as well. Enterprise resource management (ERM) more accurately describes all planning, control, and management functions required to effectively operate the enterprise. Is your company really ready for an integrated enterprise resource management system?

ERM Checklist

This organizational assessment checklist (Table 5.1) provides a simple and practical reference to determine if your company is ready for the competitive business environment of today and its positioning for tomorrow.

To score your own organization on these criteria, review the question and mark your organization's status on a scale of 0 (not at all) to 4 (completely). For an explanation of what is meant by each question, see the following pages.

Table 5.1   ERM Organizational Assessment Checklist

Checklist	Score (0 to 4)
1. Have you transitioned from internally focused performance measurements to customer-focused performance measurement systems?	
2. Have you flattened the organizational hierarchy?	
3. Have you fully educated your personnel in enterprise-wide thinking?	
4. Have you successfully moved to a team-based organization?	
5. Have you reengineered your major business processes and eliminated all waste?	
6. Have you moved from traditional costing methods to value-added costing?	
7. Have you adopted the principles of integrated supply chain management?	
8. Have you implemented completely reliable information networks and communication systems (software, hardware, and human systems)?	
9. Have you changed your evaluation and appraisal systems to recognize both team and individual performance?	
10. Have you become a customer-focused organization?	
11. Have you developed and implemented procedures that ensure standardization of information in all business operations?	
12. Are your business leaders committed to the principle of lifelong learning?	
13. Have you replaced organizational silos with process teams?	
14. Have you adopted a single company compensation program?	
15. Have you benchmarked your organizational performance with "best in class" practices by global leaders?	
16. Can you demonstrate total company-wide process capability performance of 6 Sigma or better?	
17. Have you developed business policies and procedures to ensure complete data integrity?	
18. Have you prepared your people to operate in a paperless environment?	
19. Have you become a truly global organization?	
20. Have you adopted an organizational culture with shared vision, values, and goals?	
21. Have you driven out fear?	
22. Have you developed a truly flexible workforce and process capability?	

Table 5.1   ERM Organizational Assessment Checklist *(Continued)*

Checklist	Score (0 to 4)
23. Have you educated all your business leaders in Integrated Resource Management?	
24. Do you have a formal process for identifying and resolving process constraints?	
25. Have you institutionalized the process of continuous and rapid operational improvement?	

(Score 4 points for full implementation, 2 for partial, 0 for no evidence)

Total Score
90 points or higher: Organization is ready for ERM
70–90 points: Organization is close to ready for ERM
50–70 points: Organization needs significant work
Below 50 points: Organization needs substantial preparation work, do not make the ERP purchase

Source: Courtesy of Keith Launchbury, CFPIM, CIRM and Carol A. Ptak, CFPIM, CIRM, Jonah. © With permission.

Checklist Questions Detail

Have you transitioned from internally focused performance measurements to customer-focused performance measurement systems?

Customers care only about how their needs are serviced. They care little about the supplier's internal efficiencies and utilization. When a company clearly understands the needs of the customer and aligns its business processes to meet those needs, it enjoys a market advantage over the competition. The latest advance in obtaining this data is the use of Customer Relationship Management (CRM) systems. These systems provide analyses of which customers tend to purchase what products. This kind of information is invaluable when deciding how to market new product introductions. Rather than marketing in a shotgun fashion, CRM allows the enterprise to market with laser accuracy. In addition, a CRM system provides insights into the customer's ordering patterns such that the enterprise can begin to anticipate the customer's needs for new products and/or services. The integrated resource model begins and ends with the customer. Without the customer there is really no reason to be in business. The goal of any business, manufacturing, or service is to profitably service the customer. Remember two simple facts: (1) what gets measured will be done and (2) if something cannot be measured then it cannot be improved.

If the performance measures that are used to run the business are customer focused, then the enterprise will be customer focused. If the business measures are internally focused, like efficiency and utilization, then the enterprise will be internally focused. In any case, the managers will focus on what is reported and visible. Competitiveness in today's market requires that the enterprise not only focuses on the needs of its customers but also focuses on the needs of its customer's customer until the final consumer is reached. This is the essence of supply chain management where performance measures are consistent — from the supplier's supplier to the customer's customer. Some customer-focused measures could include:

- **Response lead-time:** This measures the amount of time that a company takes to deliver a product once the demand is received. Customers are increasingly demanding and expecting products that are mass customized to fit their needs delivered in a relatively short lead-time. Decreasing this lead-time also reduces the impact that the market forecast has on the operation. Remember that forecasts with a longer forecast horizon are by their very nature less accurate. Having an agile response capability within the enterprise translates directly into a more accurate market forecast because the time period to forecast is shorter.

- **Product development time:** Customers can provide a wealth of information concerning potential new products. Derivative product ideas easily come from current products as different applications are realized for the current product. Rarely will a customer develop a breakthrough idea like Post-It™ notes, but once this type of product has been developed customers will discover additional uses for it. Listening to this kind of feedback can be very profitable as the company can leverage on what has been already developed. The time to market for these derivative products is another very useful performance measure. The less time it takes, the more market share that should be available.

- **On time to promise:** This measure is a rather traditional measure but still very important. How did the delivery promise to the customer compare to the actual ship date? Having reliable deliveries to customers is a key part of overall customer satisfaction.

- **On time to request:** We may promise the customer a date but in reality this is not the date they requested. On time to request is a comparison of the actual shipping date to what the customer really wanted. This measure can realistically be expected to be more aggressive than on time to promise and some would question its use. On time to request provides very valuable information about the customer's needs and wants, and can provide market-driven target goals for the response lead-time.

Have you flattened the organizational hierarchy?

An organization with many levels of supervision suffers reduced speed of communication and agility. A flattened organization has more direct communication and can respond more quickly to the needs of the customer. The biggest benefit of a successful ERP implementation is that useful information that can be used to make quality decisions is available throughout all levels of the enterprise. No longer are key decisions reserved only for senior management. Given a common vision and good performance measures, decisions can be accurately made at much lower levels in the organization. Flattening the organizational hierarchy means less overhead expense and more rapid communication. A flattened organization has a structural advantage encouraging closer communication between departments since there are fewer levels that must be coordinated. Many levels in the organizational hierarchy lead to nonvalue-added bureaucracy. Reducing the levels of the organization reduces the cost and improves the overall performance, provided adequate information is available.

Have you fully educated your personnel in enterprise-wide thinking?

Only personnel that understand what the organization is attempting to achieve and why can begin to implement customer-focused ideas and processes. Silo-based organizational myopia must be replaced with an enterprise-wide focus. Departments are not in competition with each other but rather must collaborate with an integrated customer focus. This collaboration then extends outside of the enterprise through the entire supply chain. This type of thinking is not taught in schools. In fact, our entire education system is based on silo-focused concepts. Rarely is higher order thinking taught which provides the participant with the tools to understand the impact and implications of actions of one part of the enterprise on other areas. This is the reason why the MICSS simulator was included with this book. This simulator provides an interactive learning opportunity to apply the tools and techniques covered by the text. Integrated resource management is extremely difficult since it causes people to think outside of their box. In addition, having sufficient understanding about the different functional areas to be able to consider implications of strategies and choices requires specific study and curriculum. The functional areas that should be included in this integrated resource management education are

- Marketing and sales
- Field service
- Product design and development
- Production and inventory control
- Procurement
- Distribution
- Industrial facilities management
- Process design and development
- Manufacturing
- Total quality management
- Human resources
- Finance and accounting
- Information systems

This is a wide variety of functional areas but each impact the other within the enterprise. Each should have an understanding of the implication of its choices. An excellent program that is proven to deliver this type of education is the APICS Certified in Integrated Resource Management (CIRM) program. This curriculum was developed by a team of practitioners, consultants, and academicians to ensure that the theory taught is successfully used in practice in a variety of industries.

Have you successfully moved to a team-based organization?

Teams with a clear vision and mission have consistently outperformed individual efforts. The creativity of a high-performing team can successfully move the organization to significantly higher levels of performance. Team skills are not taught in most school curriculums. In fact, our entire education system enforces a model of individual effort and reward. Assigning people to work together does not make them a team, only a work group. Skills needed to ensure an effective team-based organization include facilitation, communication, brainstorming, and problem solving, to name just a few.

Teams normally will evolve through four stages of development, according to Kenneth Blanchard in the *One Minute Manager Builds High-Performing Teams.* These stages are forming, storming, norming, and performing. The forming stage is where the team has just been named and people are trying to determine how they individually fit. This is usually a time of professional aloofness. The storming phase is when the team begins to get to the task at hand. This entails experiencing conflict in roles and responsibilities while the team determines how it will work together. The team can get stuck in this phase and tear the team and the overall organization apart if the leader does not have the necessary skills to move the team to norming. Norming is where the team really determines how it will work together, including roles, responsibilities, and communication. The final stage is performing where the team is able to accomplish more than the individuals separately could. A high-performing team can help ensure a competitive edge for the company. Teams do not just happen. Education and training is required. Above all, leadership is needed to provide the overall guidance and vision of the goal. According to Taiichi Ohno, "Manpower is something that is beyond measurement. Capabilities can be extended indefinitely when everyone begins to think." This is what teams are all about, engaging all facets of everyone's capability in pursuit of a common goal.

Have you reengineered your major business processes and eliminated all waste?

Waste is any nonvalue-added activity upon which the organization expends resources. These critical resources can yield consistently higher profits for the organization when they are focused only on the desired results. A key part of the ERP implementation process is to closely examine the current business processes and how they map to industry best practices. This is not to suggest that processes that have been developed as a strategic competitive edge should be changed just to fit the software. Implementing ERP is an excellent time to re-examine the current business processes to ensure that they really do best fit the organization. Keep in mind the story of the ham in the pan. As the story goes "a little girl was watching her mom make Easter ham. She asked, 'Mommy why do you cut the ham in half before putting it in the pan?' The mother who was harried and trying to get a large holiday dinner together replied that this was the process for making ham and the little girl should just go away. Not to be dissuaded, the little girl then went to see her grandma. 'Grandma, why does Mommy cut the ham in half before putting it in the pan?' Grandma replied, 'Honey, you need to understand that cutting the ham in half is how you make ham! Now go out and play.' (Anyone who has even been around a 10-year-old can appreciate how persistent they can be.) Next, the little girl went to see her greatgrandma. Greatgrandma is happy because she no longer has to worry about putting on the large holiday meals. She pulls the little girl up onto her lap. The little girls asks once again, 'Greatgrandma, why does Mommy cut the ham in half before putting it into the pan?' Greatgrandma responded, 'Well, you see, back when I was a bride the family was so large that we could not fit the whole ham into one pan. We had to cut it in half to allow it to fit.' Three generations later the ham is still being cut in half and the reason why has been lost." When we translate this to manufacturing, this likely means:

1. We have a specification for the allowable variability of the cut from the midpoint.
2. We have automated the process so that robots and lasers are used to cut the ham.
3. We have outsourced this operation to our supplier to provide the extra "value-added" step of cutting the ham.
4. We pay them because we really do not understand why we cut it in the first place.

Upon telling this story to an audience one day, a participant related a question that he asked his new bride once (and only once) why she cooked like she did. Why did she cut both ends off the ham before she put it in the oven? She looked at him like he was crazy and replied that, of course, anyone who knew anything about cooking knew that the ends had to be cut off or the ham would explode! Too many times this is how well we understand our business processes. There is no understanding of why we do the things we do. Nobody in the organization has a clear idea of the impact of a decision on other areas so everyone fears the consequences of a change. The easy way out for companies has been to accept the "industry best practices" that are forced on them during the ERP implementation. Unfortunately, these "industry best practices" may be exactly the wrong answer and may replace some processes that are the competitive advantage for the company. There is no one right answer on how to configure an ERP system. The first step in every ERP implementation is to carefully examine the current business processes and determine which should be changed because they contain nonvalue-added activities and which should not be touched because they provide a competitive advantage. Education in integrated resource management and teamwork is required to be able to know the difference. Blindly accepting processes to implement the system from a consulting group will lead to disaster as the enterprise refuses to internalize these new ill-fitting processes and quickly reverts back to the informal system.

Have you moved from traditional costing methods to value-added costing?

Traditional costing methods spread overhead on direct labor hours. This has caused many organizations to feel that the cost to produce in-house is too high. The result is they purchase at the lowest purchase cost. This encourages large volume overseas procurement while at the same time decreasing in-house production. Overall costs rise from the increased inventory and real profits decline. There is no direct cause and effect between overhead charges and direct labor cost. Value-added costing includes only those direct benefits and costs when considering product line costing. Only those costs that would be eliminated if the product were no longer produced in-house are considered when costing a product. More realistic profit contribution information is available using value-added costing. The theory of constraints has taught us that if the product is not sold to the end customer, we really have not made a profit on it just because we have put it into inventory. Throughput value-added costing provides a more realistic cost assessment based on what is constraining the company's ability to move more product out the door to the customer. Throughput value-added costing is covered in more detail in Chapter 9.

Have you adopted the principles of integrated supply chain management?

The information about the available supply and desired demand must be shared from your supplier's supplier to your customer's customer. These principles of integrated supply chain management provide a seamless integration of supply and demand and provide the ability for the company to deliver products that uniquely meet the needs of the market. Integrated supply chain management can be defined as achieving a sustainable competitive position and maximizing shareholder value by optimizing the relationship of process, information, and physical goods among internal and external trading partners. Supply chain management includes:

- Integrated Supply and Demand Planning
- Order Fulfillment and Customer Service
- Procurement and Strategic Sourcing
- Production Logistics
- Distribution Networks and Warehouse Management
- Transportation and Shipment Management

Real-time information systems are required as an enabler for effective integrated supply chain management. Having accurate information at all links in the supply chain is a necessary condition for good decisions.

Have you implemented completely reliable information networks and communication systems (software, hardware, and human systems)?

The information systems of a company, including software, hardware, and human systems, must be completely reliable for the information to be trusted by everyone using it. Sophisticated computer tools still require the basic building blocks of information to be accurate for the tool to be effective. Data accuracy is so important that Chapter 13 has been dedicated to this subject. As computers and other technologies directly connect more links of the chain, having accurate data feeding into these systems is more critical than ever before. Manual intervention is being replaced by more sophisticated computer systems. However, systems are more than just hardware and software. The humans involved in the process also must be reliable and consistent with the desired processes. Hardware and software are not a replacement for effective management.

Have you changed your evaluation and appraisal systems to recognize both team and individual performance?

This is probably one of the most difficult areas in the checklist. Keep in mind that how people are measured will determine how they will behave. Since personnel are expected to function both as part of a team and also as individuals, measurement systems must be changed to measure and reward the desired team behaviors. This is the area that must be addressed at the most senior levels of the organization. If the behavior is not consistent with the desired direction, check the measurement system. Behavior is likely very consistent with the performance measures. If sales people are rewarded for revenue and not profitability, the likely behavior will be to sell more of the products that have a lower margin because they are likely more price competitive in the field. Measure purchasing on the number of shortages and inventory will go through the roof. When efficiency is used as a measure for manufacturing, the result is usually lot sizes larger than planned so that the factory can show a favorable variance. Unfortunately, this also increases lead-time as these large orders wait behind each other to be processed. Inventory rises and customer service falls — exactly what we do not want! The caution is that "watch what you measure — you will get it!" The other rule of thumb is that we can only improve what we can measure. If the desired state cannot be measured, we will surely not get there. Performance measures are another area where there is not a single right answer for all enterprises. Remember that measures included in annual performance reviews often have only short-term effect. The real measures that people respond to are the day-to-day comments and interactions with their immediate supervisor. The measures should fit the individual overall strategic direction for the enterprise and support process improvement.

Have you become a customer-focused organization?

A key competitive strategy is to focus on the needs, wants, and desires of the customer. How well does your organization understand what your customer really wants? How well is your organization aligned to serve these needs? How do you know what the customer desires? If you asked your employees who is the most important person to the enterprise, would they answer, "the customer?" Becoming a customer-focused organization requires the alignment of performance measurement systems to encourage a focus on the customer. The old saying, "you are what you eat," also applies here. Stop and look at what is in your in-box. You will focus and think about the things that are in your in-box. How many things come across your desk each day that focuses on the customer? If your in-box does not focus on the customer then how do you expect to have a customer-focused enterprise? This question can be asked at every level of the enterprise from the executive office to the shop floor. If the measures and information are not customer-focused then how can you reasonably expect that the organization will be?

Have you developed and implemented procedures that ensure standardization of information in all business operations?

Only when a process is standardized can it be reliably depended upon and improved. This includes all purchasing, production, or distribution processes, together with the delivery of information, products, and services. Creativity is a wonderful thing to an enterprise but not in business information operations. For the enterprise to align itself to achieve its mission, standard information must be available to all areas of the enterprise. This is a driving force behind the benefits of ERP. Having a common database from which to draw information, then making informed decisions based on that information, is a key reason to purchase ERP. The larger the enterprise, the more the enterprise can benefit from having a single database of information and standardized processes. This is not to say that small companies should have multiple databases and processes, but rather the small company has developed informal procedures and an environment of mutual adjustment from which it can be effective. Larger companies have a more difficult time dealing with informal information systems and require a better-defined information standard. During the ERP system implementation, this includes setting standards for part numbers, account numbers, and consolidation techniques since information will need to be shared across the enterprise. Having the same part called by multiple part numbers within the same organization will lead to confusion, increased cost, and reduce the economy of scale and efficiency that the enterprise expected to accomplish. In addition, in the multiple division ERP system implementation, having different part numbers or account numbers precludes the seamless sharing of information and instead the organization is back to manual intercession or expensive interfaces. A large benefit can be realized in an ERP implementation by standardizing information.

Are your business leaders committed to the principle of lifelong learning?

The scary facts are that the half-life of education has been reduced to 3 to 5 years and the rate of change is accelerating. This is to say that half of what you know will no longer be useful or possibly even valid in 3 to 5 years. Consider the growth of the Internet. This single tool has drastically changed the face of business, with small businesses now competing effectively with large businesses. New tools and techniques are being developed on a daily basis, so the need for lifelong learning has never been greater. Lifelong learning is not a luxury but rather a necessity to stay competitive and current. Senior level managers in many organizations were never exposed to how computers can be used as a critical business tool by providing "what if" analysis and consolidating information from multiple divisions. Not too long ago it was considered bad form for an executive to have a computer on their desk. Now, the norm is laptop computers that are getting smaller and more powerful. Without lifelong learning how will the manager know what to do with these new tools? Performance measures have changed in recent years with the introduction of Constraints Management, also known as Theory of Constraints (TOC). This topic is still not covered in most business school curriculum. Traditional measures like efficiency and utilization are being touted as industry norms even though business has moved far ahead of these concepts. Lifelong learning is required to make early identification of industry trends during an enterprise's environmental scanning. Lifelong learning is also required to be able to link and integrate new concepts that are introduced into the market. Effectively running a business is not accomplished by pursuing every latest business fad that comes onto the market but rather by synthesizing and adapting the tools and techniques that make sense for the enterprise based on the desired strategy. Lifelong learning can help prevent the manager from pursuing the latest silver bullet just because everyone else does.

Have you replaced organizational silos with process teams?

Cross-functional teams can begin to understand the sources and uses of information and to work across departmental barriers. Process teams require vision and collaboration rather than competition. These teams must have a common base from which to operate and share a common vision. Effective teams do not just spontaneously appear in an enterprise. Effective teams require a great deal of work and nurturing. A big part of the failure for quality circles in the U.S. in the 1970s and 1980s was because the teams were focused inwardly. A stockroom team would work on stockroom inventory accuracy and quickly discover that production and engineering had a role in maintaining inventory accuracy. Without their participation on the team, getting these two organizations to understand the consequences of their actions, both short and long term is impossible.

An effective team is a collection of people who are able to accomplish more than could be done individually. To be effective, a team must have a clear vision, an inclusive view of the issues surrounding the problem at hand, and the skills that can solve the problem. High-performing teams can accomplish incredible feats for the enterprise. Developing these high performance teams can be a real challenge.

Have you adopted a single company compensation program?

Multiple company compensation programs can cause a great deal of dissatisfaction. Is your compensation program well understood with clear expectation of how increases in pay can be earned? Compensation systems must be perceived to be fair and equitable by all concerned. This includes performance bonuses and salary increases. Just because someone has lasted another year in the organization should not necessarily mean that they are due an increase. This entitlement mentality removes the link between accomplishment and reward. Rewards should be based on achievement of objectives that are in alignment with the overall strategy — not longevity. The organization of the future is quickly looking like a construction team that is used to build a house. A general contractor uses a team of subcontractors from whom they have had good performance in the past. If a subcontractor slips in performance either on quality or timeliness, another subcontractor will be substituted. Company performance measurement systems are beginning to develop to support this approach. Rewards are based on the completion of projects that help the company achieve its goal — whatever that is. Typically the goal is greater profits and market share. To achieve the highest level of effectiveness, the performance measurement and compensation system should be simple, easy to understand, and directly reward the desired behavior.

Have you benchmarked your organizational performance with "best in class" practices by global leaders?

Not only must your company improve on what it has always done, but also it must do better than the competition. Only through benchmarking practices with best in class companies can you begin to understand what is required for your business to move ahead of the competition. This is not to say that you should only have your eye on what your direct competitors are doing. Remember that unless you are the lead dog in the dogsled of competition, the scenery never changes! An organization must look externally to see how well it compares to others in the same industry, as well as compare its processes to best in class. You may not consider your company to be in the catalog business but when benchmarking a customer order entry process, Land's End is the organization that is recognized as best in class. No longer can the enterprise look merely inside the borders of its own country for best in class. Global competition requires that the organization look outside its own company and country boundaries to identify the best in the world. Benchmarking is not just sharing information but rather clearly identifying your own processes first and how you measure them. If you go into benchmarking with the idea of just looking around, you will learn little from the exercise. However, if you clearly understand your own processes and constraints, a benchmarking exercise can yield a dramatic return on investment.

Can you demonstrate total company-wide process capability performance of six sigma or better?

Six sigma quality in all processes virtually guarantees that failures in quality cannot happen. Are your business and production processes that reliable? Motorola is one of the most well known companies in this area. Six sigma is one way to quantify the reliability of your processes. If your company can achieve six sigma performance, the probability of having a defective product or service is less than 3.4 defects per million. When this level of quality is available on a company-wide basis, the need for inspection and double checks is removed and so is the cost of this nonvalue-added activity. Although you may never reach six sigma capability across all processes, setting this as a goal reinforces the consistency of the process as a key focus for the enterprise. If the processes increase in reliability, then the buffers that are required to ensure continuous flow are drastically reduced. This phenomenon is true in the manufacturing area as well as the support function area.

Have you developed business policies and procedures to ensure complete data integrity?

Every sophisticated computer system has the same requirement: accurate input information. When the quantities on hand, bills of material, routings, schedules, and other inputs are accurate, then the outputs are reliable. If any of these requirements are inaccurate the result is that people do not use the system. This issue is addressed in more depth in Chapter 13. The probability of having realistic information output by the system is the product of the level of accuracy of the inputs. If inventory accuracy is 90% (which is considered quite good), bills of materials and routings each have 95% accuracy, and the overall demand schedule is 90% accurate, the probability of having accurate information come from the system is only around 73% (90% × 95% × 95% × 90%). When you consider sending incorrect information automatically to your suppliers one out of four times, it is easy to see why the incorrect materials or quantities will be the result. In an integrated supply chain system, there is not a person double-checking the inputs to assure that everything looks logical. The computer does the calculation and, untouched by human hand, sends the requirement to the supplier. The computer is merely a calculator with a communication function built in. The calculation assumes that the data inputs are accurate since there is no way for the computer to function otherwise. The supplier would have no way to know that the requirement was incorrect. The good news for an integrated supply chain is that requirements are passed very quickly. The bad news is that the requirements are passed very quickly. Only accurate input data will provide accurate requirements for the supplier.

Have you prepared your people to operate in a paperless environment?

The evolution of sophisticated computers should eliminate the need for paper. Are your people and their management ready for such a drastic change in how they do business? Part of an effective ERP implementation is to re-examine the current business processes to determine which add value and which add only cost. Paperwork is a very visible result of a process that is normally nonvalue-added. Adjusting to a paperless environment can be difficult for the operation. In fact, some companies experience more paperwork after an ERP implementation rather than less. For example, the manual process for matching receipts and invoices could be as simple as attaching the packing slip to the invoice and matching it to the purchase order. Once an ERP system is implemented, the process may include printing a receipt traveler to attach to the packing slip, printing a receiving inspection report, matching this to a printout of the purchase order, followed by matching this to the invoice. This whole mess can then be sent to the buyer, materials manager, and accounts payable supervisor to be signed off and matched to a log printed from the system. This "improved process" has only contributed increased cost. Once the automation has been implemented, an effective process could all be done online. The path of least resistance for ERP implementation is to replicate the current manual process. Part of the ROI of an ERP system is the elimination of paperwork and other nonvalue-added activities. Is your organization ready?

Have you become a truly global organization?

Many companies talk about market share in only the U.S. or North America. In today's business world, you must get your products to global markets. Your competition is certainly targeting the traditional marketplace. A large gap exists between a multinational company and a truly global one. A multinational company does business in a number of different countries usually as a series of independent entities. A global organization leverages its global reach to provide a consistent and seamless offering to the customer. Becoming a truly global organization requires an understanding of a variety of cultures, business practices, and customer needs. The employees in the enterprise must think globally for the enterprise to act globally. This means that the performance measures should also encourage global thinking and global considerations. The enterprise will not be global unless direct interaction is enabled between employees and customers globally.

Have you adopted an organizational culture with shared vision, values, and goals?

Shared vision, values, and goals enable an organization to nimbly respond to the needs of the market. When this culture is empowered, the result is an organization that can successfully change to the changing environment. Without shared values, vision, and goals, each department or area will develop its own goals and strategies that best fit it and not necessarily the enterprise. Alignment on the global optimum is impossible. Only when an organization has a clear and articulated vision and goals supported by common values can it possibly achieve a competitive advantage. Part of the vision and goals should include the value proposition for serving customers' needs. According to Treacy and Wiersema in *The Discipline of Market Leaders,* the choices for this value proposition include product leadership, customer intimacy, and operational excellence. They also maintain that these three strategies are not a trade-off but rather choices for focus. A level of competence must be available on all dimensions, but the competitive advantage for the enterprise can be on only one. In any case, the strategy for the organization must be clearly defined, communicated, reviewed, and updated for the enterprise to secure and maintain its competitive advantage.

Have you driven out fear?

This point has been adapted from W. Edwards Deming's 14 points of effective management. Only when company personnel can take risks without fear of failure can the company move to new levels of performance. Fear is a great limiter of creativity. Think of how we learned to walk — by falling down. In the same way, we learn through a process of making mistakes. The best consultants and managers are those who have learned from the errors they have made at previous jobs. You have the opportunity to try different strategies with the simulator without fear of retaliation. You will learn from your failures what the correct answers really are.

What a tragedy for an organization to bear the cost of the learning experience and not enjoy the return on that investment. The reality is that when employees fear making a mistake, they will take the safe and known route. Considering that competitive factors are constantly changing, taking the safe and known route will likely not result in a competitive position. The old saying — "if you continue to do what you have always done, you will continue to get what you always got" — is no longer true. The rules of the game have changed and it is very likely that doing exactly what was done before that led to wonderful success could very likely result in failure given the change of the market demands and expectations.

According to Fran Tarkenton, the famous NFL quarterback, if you ask a truly successful person about their past, you will find that they have had to manage terrible failure. People that have never made an error are afraid that they will and, therefore, they never stretch and never achieve their full potential for success. Failure is liberating in that once experienced, learning occurs and performance can be leveraged to the next higher level. Empowerment truly occurs when people know that they will be supported when they take ownership of the business processes. One company gave its highest award to people who had tried and failed. They called this their "ready–fire–oops" award. The winners had planned carefully and tried an improvement or new idea and it failed. The net result was that this organization found that over

90% of its breakthrough ideas came from these "ready–fire–oops" winners. Once the fear of failure or retaliation is removed, creativity and breakthrough thinking can begin. This type of thinking is essential for an enterprise to truly be successful.

Have you developed a truly flexible workforce and process capability?

Each person in the organization must be truly flexible and focused on constantly improving the process. Are your personnel flexible in meeting changing requirements and information? Have they been encouraged to develop and use multiple skills? If the only tool the workforce knows how to use is a hammer then all problems look like nails. Product life cycles are getting shorter and shorter. Customers are becoming increasingly fickle about their needs, wants, and desires. Processes and products must be capable of changing quickly to meet the needs of the market in a manner that is profitable for the enterprise. A truly flexible workforce is essential in developing and supporting the enterprise as it meets its current and future challenges. A key success strategy to achieve this flexibility in processes and people is described in the next step.

Have you educated all your business leaders in Integrated Resource Management?

Have all the leadership personnel in your company been educated in the details of Integrated Resource Management, including the integration of sales and marketing management, materials management, human resource management, financial management, and production management? No longer is it acceptable to have a monochrome view of the enterprise. The real world has many shades of color. Each functional area should have at least an appreciation of the motivation and challenges of the other areas. Without this appreciation, decisions can be made that do not incorporate the consequences on other areas of the enterprise. This top-level understanding and its implication for enterprise competitiveness is why APICS, The Educational Society for Resource Management, developed the CIRM curriculum. The educational process creates an awareness of the implications, choices, and consequences facing an enterprise when developing products and processes to service demand from the market.

Do you have a formal process for identifying and resolving process constraints?

Process constraints are those things that limit the ability of the company to increase its output. These can be physical constraints or procedural constraints. Are your personnel trained in how to recognize and resolve these constraints? This is a major key to improved profitability. The MICSS simulator that is included with this book allows the user to try out different policy and physical constraints in virtual reality to determine the best fit for the company as evidenced by the healthiest bottom line. Having a formal process for identifying and resolving process and resource constraints allows the enterprise to break those constraints that are limiting its performance. This process continues until the constraint moves outside of the enterprise and becomes a market constraint. When the constraint has been moved to the market, the enterprise then integrates itself through the supply chain to its customer. The next step is to help the customer identify and resolve the customer's process constraint since sufficient capacity exists within the enterprise to deliver an increased amount of throughput. This strategy is known as making an offer the customer cannot refuse. Only when the internal constraints have been identified, managed, and finally broken can the enterprise really begin focusing on the market needs and how to help its customers. Until that time, the solution is to optimize the product mix that the enterprise produces such that the current bottleneck is producing the highest level of profit.

Have you institutionalized the process of continuous and rapid operational improvement?

With the continual changes faced by companies today, internal processes also must be improved in a rapid and continual way. Having this process institutionalized in an organization enhances the overall competitive position of the company. Without it the enterprise will quickly fall behind since the very nature of competition is that your competitors are always getting better. One way to think of this is the old story of the two hikers in the woods. The two hikers came across a bear which began chasing them. One hiker stopped and began changing from hiking boots to running shoes. The other hiker said, "I cannot believe that you think you will outrun the bear just because you are changing your shoes!" The first hiker replies, "I don't need to outrun the bear, the only need to outrun you!" The moral of the story is that, at times, a competitive position is not the enterprise that is way out in front, but rather just one step ahead of the competition. You must keep running. Stand in place too long, resting on your laurels and the bear of competition may eat you. Continuous and rapid operational improvement is the how you stay ahead of the competition.

Summary

This organizational assessment checklist has been developed to aid you in determining if your organization is ready for enterprise resource management. For each of these criteria, score your enterprise on a scale of 0 to 4 (0 is where there is no evidence of the characteristic and 4 is where the enterprise is fully compliant). By critically examining and developing a current score for your enterprise, you can determine the readiness of your organization to be effective in the implementation of enterprise resource management. If your organization scores 90 points or higher, you are well on your way to successfully integrating these sophisticated ERP tools into your business. If your organization scored less than 90 points, this survey will help you pinpoint the areas to target for improvement to position your organization for full utilization of ERP in achieving improved business results.

In many of the characteristics described in this chapter, the first step is adequate education and training. This is not to say that the educational background of the current employees is deficient or lacking. Having a common educational experience that focuses on cross-functional integrated enterprise concepts provides a common framework from which the enterprise can build. The education provides the insight for the affected personnel about the vision of the desired business process and why the company desires to move from where it is today to that vision of the future while providing insights about consequences in other functional areas. Given this "what" and "why," the training and technology provides the tools to accomplish that vision or the "how." Without the appropriate education, the implementation can become the adoption of ill-fitting practices simply because they are inherent to the design of the ERP system.

6 Integrating the Supply Chain to Reap the Rewards

imilar to how a tree grows with the addition of rings, enterprise management systems also have grown with additional functionality (Figure 6.1). More recently these individual enterprise rings have been interlinked through supply chain management. Each of the individual links represent a single enterprise. Supply chain management is when individuals work together collaboratively to focus on the end customer and provide benefit to all the links (Figure 6.2).

In the very beginning products were made by hand only when needed. Then as our society moved from an agragrian base to an industrial base, people began to specialize their talents. A few pieces were made for display to demonstrate the craftsman's ability. Actual products for sale to customers were made only to order. As markets and customer demand changed, an expectation developed for immediately available finished products. Then there was inventory. From inventory came the need for inventory control and then for production planning. In the early days (1950s) these planning tools were called "requirements generation" or BOM processors. The tools continued to evolve by adding additional functionality. These concentric rings continue to grow into the modern ERP systems available today. A full evolution and history was detailed in Chapter 1. As the computer has become increasingly powerful, so have management tools that utilize the computer.

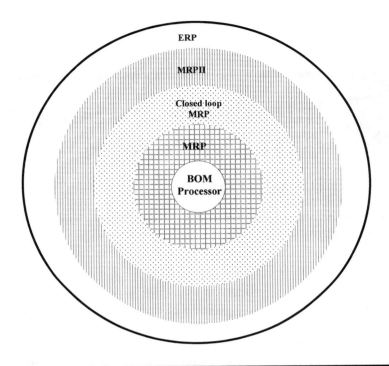

Figure 6.1   ERP growth rings.

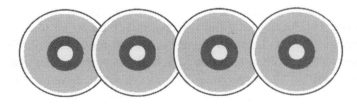

Figure 6.2   The supply chain.

SCOR Model

Until recently the main focus of these tools has been internal to the enterprise. In the mid-1990s, the focus began to move externally from the enterprise to the supply base and customer needs. The term "supply chain management" was coined to capture these linkages from the customer's customer to the supplier's supplier. APICS defines supply chain management as the "planning, organizing, and controlling of supply chain actitivites." In 1996, the Supply Chain Council (SCC) was organized by Pittiglio, Rabin, Todd, and McGrath (PRTM) and Advanced Manufacturing Research (AMR). This effort was supported initially by 69 volunteer member companies. The focus for the group was to develop a process reference model that would describe supply chain management. According to the SCC, "Process reference models integrate the well-known concepts of business process reengineering, benchmarking, and process measurement into a cross-functional framework." This framework contains:

- Standard descriptions of management processes
- A framework of relationships among the standard processes
- Standard metrics to measure process performance
- Management practices that produce best in class performance
- Standard alignment to software features and functionality.

The SCOR (Supply Chain Operations Reference) model was developed and endorsed by the SCC. Figure 6.3 shows the SCOR model.

The SCOR model includes:

- All customer interactions, from order entry through the paid invoice
- All physical material transactions, from the supplier's supplier to the customer's customer, including equipment, supplies, spare parts, bulk product, software, etc.
- All market interactions, from the understanding of aggregate demand to the fulfillment of each order

The SCOR model specifically does not include:

- Sales adminstration processes
- Technology development processes
- Product and process design and development processes
- Post-delivery customer support operations including technical support processes

The four distinct processes for the SCOR model are source, make, deliver, and plan (Figure 6.4). These processes are defined in increasing levels of details beginning with a description of the overall process. The processes are

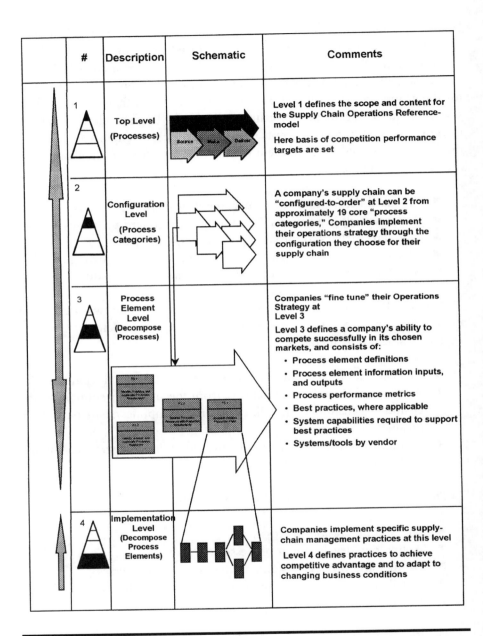

Figure 6.3   SCOR Model. (From the Supply Chain Council, Inc. With permission.)

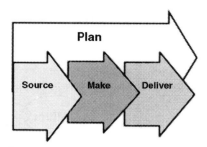

Figure 6.4   The supply chain core processes. (From the Supply Chain Council, Inc. With permission.)

further divided into the process elements, tasks, and activities. The supply chain configuration is driven by:

- "Deliver" channels, inventory deployment, and products
- "Make" production sites and methods
- "Source" locations and products
- "Plan" levels of aggregation and information sources

The real results from supply chain management come from the integration of processes throughout the entire supply chain from the supplier's supplier to the customer's customer (Figure 6.5).

Supply Chain Competitiveness

Most of this book is focused *within* the enterprise in order to "get the internal house in order." However, any chain is only as strong as its weakest link. The big return on ERP investment and the future revenue and profit growth come from integrating the enterprise to its entire supply chain. No longer will a company compete solely on its own merits. An enterprise will compete in the market based on the overall strength of its supply chain. Supply chains will compete with each other for market share and profits. While product is moving forward from the supplier to the customer, information needs to move backward to provide adequate time for planning and replanning. Technology will continue to develop that will enhance and speed these information linkages. The term "supply chain" is really quite descriptive for the concept. The supply chain is the interrelationship of a series of links from

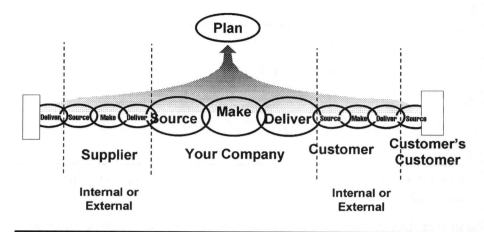

Figure 6.5   Integration of processes throughout the entire supply chain. (From the Supply Chain Council, Inc. With permission.)

individual companies focused on serving and providing value for the end consumer.

Some companies have decided that they wish to implement only a supply chain software system and not implement the supporting ERP management processes. This is like building a house on quick sand. Without adequate control of the internal processes, an integrated supply chain is truly only as strong as its weakest link. The integration of the supply chain is an area where the speed and accessibility of technology will make a large impact. This technology can include EDI, E-commerce, Internet, or a variety of other possibilities including some that have not been developed yet. However, without the accurate data feeding this technology and robust business processes supporting the strategy, the risk is that the same bad information will be the result — now only more quickly. The Sales and Operations Planning process can be used to provide the management oversight and focus needed for effective supply chain management (Figure 6.6).

Plossl's Seven Supply Chain Points

George Plossl, one of the people credited with the popularization of MRP, continues to be a thought leader in the supply chain arena. His frequent presentations on the subject challenge us to remember that Henry Ford was able to produce the Model T car at the River Rouge Plant from the mining

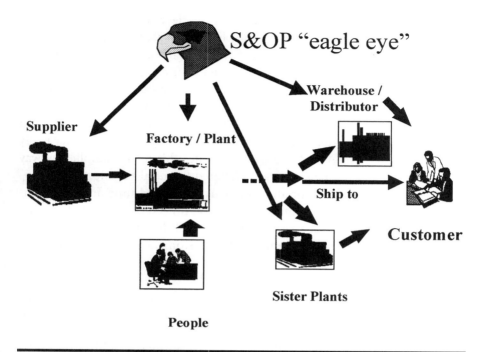

Figure 6.6   Sales and Operation Planning role in supply chain management. (Courtesy of Richard C. Ling and Andy Coldrick. © With permission.)

of the ore to the finished product rolling off the end of the assembly line in a mere 83 hours. This remarkable accomplishment was done without the benefit of sophisticated computer systems including ERP, Advanced Planning and Scheduling, or Supply Chain Management Systems. Too frequently managers reach for technology to solve problems rather than leveraging technology as part of the effective management toolbox. Rarely does a company fail due to technological failure. Companies fail because the management processes are ineffective to compete in the market. Even as computers become more and more sophisticated this fact still remains. Mr. Plossl's seven supply chain points are

1. **Satisfy the customer's real needs not wants.** Communication of real need can be a challenge. Any purchasing agent will usually pad their real need by a few days or weeks depending on the reliability of the supplier. The worse the performance of the supplier, the larger the

time pad. This process moves from the deceiver to the deluder. The supplier knowing that the dates have been padded commits to the customer's wants. The supplier knows full well that the customer's need is really very different. They get confirmation of this when the shipment is late and nobody from the customer's organization calls to expedite the delivery. This only confirms the customer's practice of padding the delivery dates. This unusual dance is continued until whenever we are in trouble we do it right. When the customer really has a desperate need and communicates this to the supplier by way of frequent phone calls and/or offered financial premiums, the supplier can magically produce the parts in record time and fulfill this need. The larger the bonus for being on time, or the penalty for being late, the more probable the shipment will be on time. For effective supply chain management, the real customers' needs must be satisfied, not their wants.

2. **Understand how the real world works.** With all the advertising and marketing about the latest and greatest information system, one constant remains. All benefits increase in direct proportion to the speed of flow of material and information. The more quickly information moves, the more value it has. Information that is old has very little value. Just ask the newspaper printer. The same fact is true for supply chain management. Manufacturers need to know what the retailer has sold as soon as possible after the sale. Sales information that percolates through a complex distribution system taking weeks or months to reach the manufacturer has little value. When demand is synchronized with supply, everyone wins. The customer gets the product they want. The retailer sells the products they stock. The distributor sells the product they have. The manufacturer uses capacity for products that can be sold. Using capacity to build products that cannot be sold, add no value (or revenue) for the entire supply chain. Products that can be made and shipped close to actual demand are more likely to be what the customer wants. Remember that forecasts are less accurate farther into the future. Being able to execute quickly can remove the need to forecast.

   Another real-world fact is that material will expand to fill the space provided. The four walls of the company are what really control inventory. The Japanese have the advantage that space in their country is exceptionally expensive. This provides motivation to reduce inventory and develop pull systems like Kanban to provide only what is needed when it is needed. In North America, space is relatively inexpensive. This is demonstrated by the inventory held in North American companies and the installation of Automated Storage and Retrieval Systems (AS/RS). These high-density storage systems are required simply because there is just too much inventory! Installing one of these systems is an excellent way to add to the excess assets already tied up in the form of inventory. When a company moves to a larger building because the current building is too small to handle operations, within 10 years this new building also will be too small. Many documented cases exist about how embracing JIT principles have led to space savings. The real truth is that unless this space was leased or could be sold, the savings is really a mirage unless increased throughput can be realized from this space savings.

3. **Have a complete integrated system.** A complete system includes both planning and execution management. This is the point where ERP can be so effective as a tool. The fact remains, plans will change but to fail to plan is planning to fail. The planning side of the integrated system uses soft data. Changes and variability are expected events. The more quickly an enterprise can react, the less cost is incurred by the operation. However, implementation requires hard data. This is where the resources of the enterprise are committed and changes are very expensive.

    When designing and implementing a system, remember that system effectiveness is inversely proportional to the complexity. This is why the simple pull signals of JIT work so well. A 2-week class in concepts followed by a hands-on workshop to learn the keystrokes is not required. The pull signal can be explained simply. When the signal comes or the block is empty, build the next one. If there is no signal or the block is full — stop. What could be simpler? One problem with all the advancements of technology is that we can develop the intergalactic solution using the most advanced technology possible and we do. Unfortunately in the process we lose sight of the goal. How do we improve the competitiveness of the company now and into the future? Technology continues to advance so companies continue to purchase and implement it. Competitors also purchase it for fear that they will fall behind. But, does the bottom line improve? We find ourselves swamped with data and starved for information. The

No. 1 success strategy for installing any piece of technology is to have a clear vision on how this will improve the real profit for the enterprise now or in the future.

4. **Accurate data.** Watching the development of middleware systems that automatically links demand from customers and forecasts from sales personnel directly into the ERP system with no review is terrifying. We can now drive all of this bad information into the system — only faster. The computer is a box of electronic components that possess no intelligence or judgement at all. Why is it that we expect brilliance to come from a machine that is really nothing more than a very big calculator with lots of storage? If you take the same bad input data that you have always had and put it into a new and improved supply chain system, what makes you think that you will get a different answer? If the outputs of the system are wrong, check the inputs! The system itself will rarely make a computational error. Without accurate input data, the best hardware and software will be nothing more than a big money pit and provide no return on investment. The management oversight of the Sales and Operations Planning process is required to ensure feasibility of the business solution not just a mathematically feasible solution.

5. **Manage cycle time.** Cycle time is the amount of time that elapses between material entering and exiting a production facility. Given the stress to get orders to customers on time, it is easy to get into the vicious order release cycle. Since orders are late, the desire is to release orders earlier. The belief is that if the orders are released earlier, then there is more time to complete the work and the order should ship on time. The reality is that when more orders are released, there is more work to be managed and longer queues at each operation. The systems become more complex and the resources needed to manage the inventory increase. Orders spend more time waiting to be run. This directly results in more late orders and greater increases in expediting. If all orders could be completed in 1 day, there would be no need for expediting. Consider all that can be completed in 1 day is 1 day's worth of work. Why is there more work on the shop floor than can be completed in 1 day? Do not release orders to the floor unless ALL material and capacity is available to run it. This drastically shortens the cycle time. A company in upstate New York reduced the lead-time on a complex medical instrument from 6 weeks to less than 1

week from following this one simple rule. On-time orders increased and so did revenue and profits.

6. **Eliminate nonvalue-added activity.** Nonvalue-added activity is anything that the customer does not want. Too many ERP and supply chain implementations begin with the best intentions only to succumb to the desire to modify the system to reflect current business process. This is not to say that every implementation should embrace "industry best practices" if these processes do not help the enterprise achieve its goals. This is a tactic that many consulting companies have sold to their customers to keep implementation costs down rather than driving higher return on investment. Eliminating nonvalue-added activity means that one shouldn't automate bad processes.

   One aerospace company found itself developing a complex modification of its ERP software to support what it called the "EAMR" process (early advanced material releases). This allowed the engineers to send requirements to purchasing to get long lead-time parts on order while the design was being finalized. When the process was documented through a flow chart, it was determined that the engineers were spending more time developing and managing EAMRs than they were developing the parts themselves. When this practice was stopped, the lead-time to release drawings dropped and the purchasing department could order from released drawings rather than from blue lines. This saved millions of dollars in obsolete inventory. As the patient said "Doctor, doctor, it hurts if I do this." The Doctor replied, "Then, don't do that!" The same is true for nonvalue-added activity — don't do that!

7. **Fully qualified people.** Many companies will invest in the very best systems, hardware, and software. Managers spent a great deal of time researching and interviewing integration and consulting suppliers. Extreme care is taken before committing to the final purchase. Everything is set and the people who are expected to operate the system are saying, "Huh?" Just as you would not go to a doctor who has not had the proper education and training, turning supply chain management systems over to untrained, inexperienced personnel can be just as devastating. Ask these questions when hiring qualified people:
   - **What business are they themselves in?** Just as there is an external supply chain, so is there an internal supply chain. Two bricklayers working on a cathedral were asked, "What are you doing?" One

responded, "I am laying bricks." The other replied, "I am building a temple for God." Which attitude would you prefer in your business? Does every level of the organization understand the vision, mission, and goals for the enterprise, and understand how they contribute to it? If they don't — they won't.

- **Where does their work fit into the total business?** It is too easy to only focus on the task at hand. Historically, management has reinforced this through a hierarchical organizational structure. This organizational form was necessary at the time to enhance communication. Information was passed from one person to their direct reports for dissemination in a sequential fashion to their direct reports until everyone was notified. Now in the information age, these levels are not required. Communication can occur with many people all at the same time. Each person in the enterprise requires a more integrated view to understand how the decisions that he makes impact the whole organization.

- **Who are your customers? What do your customers need? What are their problems?** Customers can be either internal or external. Understanding the needs, wants, and desires of internal customers is important. The problems facing each functional area must be considered as part of the overall strategy. Effective communications of problems or constraints to higher performance are necessary for the organization to achieve its goals.

- **Who are your suppliers? What are their problems?** With all the focus on customers, suppliers can get lost. Understanding what information the supplier needs or other problems that they face is essential for the organization to be successful. Always remember that the output is only as good as the input or "you can't make a silk purse out of a sow's ear." Effectively communicating and working with suppliers can provide excellent insights for internal processes that need to be improved. Each person should clearly understand from whom or where he receives materials or information.

- **What are their tools (systems, data, machinery)? How well do they use them?** Does the person understand the tools he needs to do his job? Does he require additional training to use them effectively? If a journey-level master is required, putting an apprentice-level person on the job will likely lead to disappointing results. Does the person keep his skills updated in his particular field? Recent studies have shown that the knowledge half-life is approximately 3 to 5 years. That is, in 3 to 5 years, half of what you know is no longer valuable. Just as tools in the production area must be maintained, so must the knowledge tools of individual people.

- **Who is on their team?** How does the person define her team? Does she consider her team only within her department or across the enterprise? Demand for agility is increasing. This agility can only be achieved through dynamic cross-functional teams. Does the person have the team skills needed to contribute effectively in this environment?

- **Who are not yet fully qualified?** After asking the previous six questions, it may become evident that some people are not fully qualified. A decision then has to be made to develop these skills or replace these people. Is there a development plan to bring the people who are not fully qualified up to the needed level?

Strategic Sourcing and Procurement

During the 1940s and 1950s, the largest component of the cost of goods sold was labor. This led to the whole Taylor labor movement and the focus on labor productivity. The labor focus gave rise to our cost accounting methods where overhead is typically spread based on the production labor hours. For almost 50 years management has focused on the shop floor and how efficiencies can be improved. North American managers continue to search for inexpensive offshore labor. Asian and European managers have begun to develop strategic sourcing agreements that move production closer to the market. One only needs to look as far as the automotive and consumer electronic industries to discover a large number of foreign-owned plants in North America. In the 1990s, the cost landscape changed drastically. For most companies labor is an increasingly small part of costs. On average the cost of material for an enterprise comprises about 60 to 80% of total cost. Not surprisingly, the focus has shifted to managing these costs and the market for ERP and supply chain management tools is expected to continue to grow well into the next decade.

This shift has also caused a drastic change for procurement. The role of purchasing has shifted from simply placing orders to providing strategic management of the company's assets and profitability. For example, consider a company with a $100 million revenue and a 30% gross margin. Their cost of goods sold would be $70 million. Given the conservative number above, the material cost can be expected to be $42 million. If a small percentage improvement could be realized through effective supply chain management, say 10%, the cost of materials would decline to $37.8 million ($4.2 million savings). Assuming that the other costs would stay the same, this would increase the profit for the company to $34.2 million. This is a 14% increase in profit. Assuming that all costs are variable, the other way to drive this increased profit would be to increase overall revenue by 14% or decrease other costs by $4.2 million. The most likely place that a manager looks to is production labor. In this example, nonmaterial costs are only $28 million. The average percentage labor is approximately 10 to 15% of the cost of goods sold. Taking the conservative number of 15%, this means that the organization has $10.5 million in labor cost. Reducing this by $4.2 million would be a 40% improvement. Which is really more likely, a 10% improvement in material cost or a 40% improvement in labor cost?

Supplier Partnership Characteristics

The typical view of the supplier is a black box. Order goes in and, *voila*, parts come out. Rarely does reality work like this. As the company moves to effective supply chain management, supplier partnerships are formed to provide a win–win relationship between customer and supplier. Supplier partnerships are characterized by:

- **Longer contracts.** No longer are parts purchased as commodities or with annual contracts. Having contracts in excess of 3 years is not uncommon.
- **More exclusivity in agreements.** The company's total requirement for one part is purchased from a single supplier. This eliminates the variability introduced from multiple suppliers. This also provides the opportunity for the supplier to better understand the customer's business and possibly suggest new products. One company received 60% of its new product ideas from suppliers. This innovation from the supply base had direct bottom line benefits for both supplier and customer.
- **Fewer (but better) suppliers.** A reduction of 60 to 80% of the supply base is not uncommon as a company moves to supplier partnerships. The best suppliers will be kept while the poor performing ones will be eliminated. This reduces the sheer number of suppliers that must be coordinated, and reduces overall supplier management overhead cost.

- **Higher volume between buyer and supplier.** Since many of these relationships are exclusive, the volume typically increases. This increased volume also should decrease product cost.
- **Lower prices.** Since the suppliers do not have to incur additional selling expense to maintain the partnership customer, they can afford to focus on improving manufacturing processes. This should reduce their costs and improve profits simultaneously. A common partnership requirement is a mutual cost control effort. By working together the supplier and customer should be able to improve quality and reduce costs.
- **Quality at the (supplier) source.** Few parts will improve quality on the trip to the customer. A metal part that needs to age after a heat treat operation or cranberry sauce that has not solidified yet are the only two examples that come to mind. Since quality does not improve in transit, quality should be assured before it leaves the supplier. Redoing tests on arrival at the customer site that were just done at the supplier's plant adds no value to the supply chain. Supplier partnerships move to certificates of compliance rather than inbound testing. Demonstrated high-quality performance is a requirement for any effective supplier partnership.

  Documentation also may be required as part of the supplier partnership. If the customer is under FAA, FDA, or other regulatory control, a key part of the quality standard between supplier and customer is having the ability for product and process traceability and other quality documentation.

- **Supplier centered design.** When a part is designed that the supplier can build easily, the part is more likely to be built well. Why spend your engineer's time designing a part that will be built by a supplier? Who is really the expert on the supplier's processes? The supplier, of course! By working with the supplier in a concurrent design process, quality and cost are improved.
- **Frequent delivery of small lots.** Rather than shipping large lots infrequently, small lots are shipped more frequently. The shipment of large lots usually comes from pricing policies. As the sales batch size increases, the price decreases. The customer orders more than he needs simply to get the discount. In reality, the customer does not want more than what he can use daily. Large lots are usually more than 1-day production for the supplier as well. The production batch

does not have to equal the sales batch. Having a long-term relationship allows the supplier to synchronize their production with their customer's needs and both companies win.

■ **Less burdensome order conveyance.** The same paperwork level cannot exist when the lot sizes decline and the frequency of shipment increases. This setup cost is a driving force behind product lot size. The order conveyance process can be simplified through the utilization of technology like EDI or E-commerce.

EDI is a point-to-point solution where a single trading partner is identified and a protocol developed to transmit data. Standard formats, such as X12 or EDIFACT, have helped in the utilization of this technology, but the solution is still customized to each specific trading partner involved. A value-added network (VAN) must be utilized to complete the transaction. The advantage of EDI is that it provides a complete, integrated package to support transactions. However, these transactions usually occur on a batch basis. A complete security package is provided as part of EDI. This network can be optimized for those trading partners with frequent information exchanges.

E-commerce is an Internet enabled process where trading partners can build their own fields using Java applets and then transmit them for a fraction of the cost of traditional EDI. The advantage for E-commerce is that it is less expensive and easier to implement than EDI. However, E-commerce can quickly become expensive and complex when many different partners are involved. E-commerce can support near real-time transactions and can handle a wider range of transaction types. It can also reach everyone that has access to the Internet, which makes E-commerce the logical choice for handling occasional orders. Concerns still exist, however, about the overall security of the Internet. So, which tool should you use? The same answer is true for this question as for so many others while implementing ERP and supply chain — it depends!

■ **Delivery to point of consumption.** As supply chain management becomes more sophisticated and the two companies become more tightly linked, receiving inventory at the receiving dock, putting it into a stockroom only to pull it against an order to be moved to the shop floor, takes too much time and costs too much money. The supplier can be expected to deliver in containers that can move directly to point of use on the shop floor.

- **Mutual openness.** If there is distrust between the two partners, then a true supplier partnership will not exist. Access to each other's factory floor and information systems is essential in making this partnership process successful. Efficient information systems are a catalyst to this openness. Well-trained employees also are required to make this a success. A recurring theme throughout this book is the need for well-trained personnel committed to the organization's success. This is no different for supplier partnerships. A big key to successful supplier partnerships is mutual trust and openness. We have to advance trust before we earn it.

Successful strategic sourcing is dependent on a number of different factors. These include:

1. **Financial stability.** A successful partnership will not last long if one of the partners goes out of business.
2. **Management commitment to excellence.** Any organization reflects the behavior of its leadership. When management is committed to excellence through words and actions, it is very likely the organization will be committed to excellence, too.
3. **Design and technology strength.** Since the customer will be increasingly relying on the supplier for product design, the supplier must possess the design and technology strength to provide a competitive advantage for both organizations.
4. **Quality capabilities.** The supplier's processes must be capable of producing the level of quality that is needed by the customer. Inspecting incoming product does not provide adequate quality assurance. Quality must be built into the processes.
5. **Cost leadership.** One major concern that managers have about long-term relationships with suppliers is being overcharged for material cost. This is why a strategic success factor for supplier partnership must be a demonstrated cost leadership by the supplier.
6. **Service and flexibility.** The question is not *if* things will go wrong, but rather *when* will things go wrong. With lead-times getting shorter and customers becoming more demanding, the ability to provide excellent service becomes an order winner. Jack Welch at General Electric considers his company a service company that happens to make things. Customers are demanding. The flexibility and agility of the supply chain provides a competitive advantage to all of the links.

7. **Manufacturing skills.** Too many times in all the excitement about other things, the basic concern about the supplier's ability to manufacture the needed part is overlooked. Has the supplier kept up with the times by incorporating new equipment and processes?

8. **JIT development.** Having the ability to deliver "just in time" does not mean stocking parts at an offsite warehouse and then shipping just in time. True JIT is when the manufacturer is synchronized with the customer. Inventory, no matter who legally owns it, costs money for the whole supply chain. Inventory should be placed in carefully considered buffers to guard against variability and ensure optimal throughput.

9. **Employee participation.** Once again the idea of people as the most important asset comes to light. W. Edwards Deming said that 94% of the problems associated with a business are process problems. Only 6% are people problems. People solve 100% of the process problems.

Supplier Partnership Cautions

With all the benefits described on supplier partnerships and strategic sourcing, some concerns and cautions also must be considered:

1. **Be careful not to overload one supplier.** We have a tendency to overload suppliers much like we overload employees. A good supplier will be given more and more work until the point arises where they are no longer performing well. The supplier is then replaced with another supplier and the cycle begins again. Rarely is it found that a supplier will turn away business. The supplier may be concerned that if they decline offered business, they may lose other current business as well. The customer may have to exercise restraint when loading a supplier. The customer should clearly understand the supplier's capacity.

2. **Ensure a philosophic fit.** An organization that is committed to agile delivery of mass customized product will not fit well with a supplier that is committed to long runs of uniform product. The commitment to quality and continuous improvement should also be shared between the two partners. The two organizations should be philosophically aligned before they become strategically aligned.

3. **Complete contingency planning.** Life happens. Some people believe that Murphy was an optimist. Having a strategic sourcing agreement

does not mean that the buyers should neglect their duty for planning contingency. This could be to have another plant producing complementary products at the same time. If one supplier goes down, the other can then pick up the production. As the organization moves to single supplier sourcing, having complete contingency planning becomes even more important.

Strategic Sourcing Summary

Different levels of approval are common. A supplier may begin with a customer simply as an approved supplier. This approval status allows the buyer to purchase from this supplier but this also engages a higher level of control on the purchase and incoming product. The ERP system can be used to trigger these controls, including receiving inspection or manual approval of invoices. Once the criteria for acceptable performance have been documented, the supplier may move to certified status. At this level the ERP system can be triggered to automatically move parts into inventory upon receipt. Invoice exceptions are managed rather than routinely approving all invoices in a labor-intensive review process. The next step is to achieve preferred status. This status gives the supplier preferential treatment when work is allocated. This may also mean longer-term contracts and better payment terms. Movement between the levels is based on performance to well-communicated criteria. These criteria should be well documented and communicated to the supply base.

In an effective supply chain relationship, the partnership should provide a win–win situation for both partners. Strategic alignment should be evident between the two enterprises. This relationship can enhance competitiveness as these two companies begin to leverage each other's capabilities to meet the needs of the end consumer. By reducing nonvalue-added activities, profitability is enhanced throughout the supply chain relationship. As W.E. Deming cautioned in one of his 14 points for effective management, "Do not award business based on price alone."

Distribution Networks

On the other side of the supply chain link are the distribution networks. A single level of distribution centers may be able to provide adequate service to the customer. In more complex distribution, a network hierarchy of centers

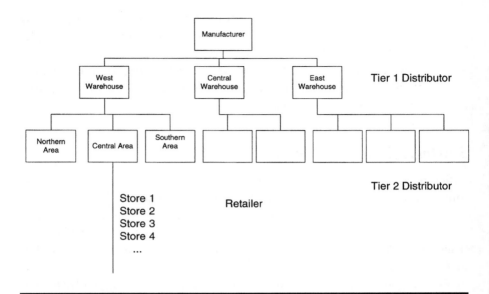

Figure 6.7   Hierarchical distribution network.

could be utilized. An example of this is the auto parts stores. The retail outlet is the final distributor to the customer. Higher sales volume parts are stored directly at the retail outlet. The regional distribution center holds the parts that are expected to have some sales or may be more unpredictable in demand. These parts are available to the retail outlet in 24 hours. To further backup the regional warehouse, a national warehouse may consolidate requirements and provide unique parts that experience unpredictable demand. This distribution network may look like Figure 6.7.

Distribution Requirements Planning

Supply chain management is critical in ensuring that the appropriate inventory is in the right place at the right time. A process known as distribution requirements planning (Table 6.1) is used to determine the need to replenish inventory at branch warehouses. This logic is very similar to MRP logic.

The demand at the retail location for this part has been forecast. Actual customer orders can be compared to the forecast to provide an updated forecast. Abnormal demand should be filtered and ignored. This process is further covered in Chapter 7 (Operations Planning). Based on the expected consumption at Retailer #1, there are two expected orders, one in Period 1 and one in Period

Table 6.1 Distribution Requirements Planning

	1	2	3	4	5	6	7	8
Retailer #1								
Forecast	100	100	150	150	150	200	200	250
Scheduled receipts	500							
Projected on hand	400	300	150	500	350	150	450	200
Planned order receipts				500			500	
Planned order releases	500			500				
Retailer #2								
Forecast	200	200	400	400	500	500	400	400
Scheduled receipts		600						
Projected on hand	350	750	350	1150	650	150	950	550
Planned order receipts				1200			1200	
Planned order releases		1200			1200			
Regional Distributor								
Requirement	500	1200		500	1200			
Scheduled receipts	2000							
Projected on hand	1500	300	300	600	600	600	600	600
Planned order receipts				2000				
Planned order releases	2000							
Manufacturer								
Requirement	2000							

4. These orders have been offset by three periods to allow for the expected transportation time from the warehouse to the retail store. Similarly, Retailer #2 can expect to place orders in Period 2 and Period 5, given their expected demand. Even though the demand at the retailer occurs in every period, due to the inventory at the site and the ordering lot size, the demand at the distribution site is only recognized in half the project periods. This is called "lumpy demand" and is absolutely normal. This condition is further exacerbated as the demand flows down to the manufacturer. Only one large order is expected back at the manufacturing plant. Imagine what this process may look like with thousands of retail locations and hundreds of distributors. Quickly the need for a formalized integrated planning tool is realized.

It is impossible to forecast the demand at the manufacturer. Attempting to develop forecasting methods to project this demand will fail miserably. This is rather like using a hammer to drive a screw into the wall — you may be lucky enough initially, but it sure won't last. Using a more expensive and sophisticated hammer will not yield better results. However, demand can be calculated very accurately by knowing the inventory at each of the other supply chain links and the expected consumption rate at the retail level. This accurate visibility is the motivation behind integrated supply chain management systems across multiple enterprises. Modern technology including open databases and effective networks can share this supply and demand data easily.

Once the overall replenishment plan has been developed utilizing distribution resource planning (DRP) through supply chain linkages, DRPII can be used to plan the key resources contained throughout the distribution system, include warehouse space, workforce, money, trucks, freight cars, etc. This is very similar to the capacity planning validation that is done at the master schedule and MRP planning levels. Chapter 7 covers this planning level in more detail. If there is a resource within the enterprise that constrains the total amount of throughput, an advanced planning and scheduling (APS) system may be considered. APS systems can optimize the schedule to manufacturing based on a number of priorities set by management. Usually this optimization is used to ensure that the most profitable product is built and shipped with the highest level of priority.

Performance Measurements

The Supply Chain Council has done a great job in providing Level 1 metrics in the SCOR model by which to measure the performance of the overall supply chain. These measures are

1. **Delivery performance.** What percentage of orders is shipped according to schedule?
2. **Fill rate by line item.** Orders may contain multiple line items. The fill rate by line item is a good measure of customer service. A customer would prefer to get all the items they order at the time they ordered them.
3. **Order fulfillment lead-time.** The customer does not wish to wait once their order has been placed. Reducing lead-time can provide competitive advantage for the enterprise.
4. **Perfect order fulfillment.** This measures how many orders were filled and shipped on time.
5. **Supply chain response time.** This measure captures how long it will take for the effect to be felt in the supply chain given a change.
6. **Upside production flexibility.** This measure assesses the response time required by the manufacturing facility to surge capacity to meet increased demand.
7. **Supply chain management cost.** Effective supply chain management should provide better returns for a lower cost. A lower percentage is improved performance.
8. **Warranty cost as % of revenue.** These costs directly impact the bottom line in two ways. One is the warranty expense itself. The other is the loss of customer goodwill and satisfaction. This can impact follow-on business from that customer.
9. **Value-added per employee.** Improving the overall financial performance of the enterprise is dependent on improving the value-added per employee. Nonvalue-added activities are a waste and should be eliminated from the process.
10. **Inventory days of supply.** This measure quantifies how long the enterprise could continue to run if all source of supply were cut off. In an agile supply chain this number is expected to be very small.
11. **Cash-to-cash cycle time.** Inventory is a large consumer of the cash asset. When the accounts payable and accounts receivable times are considered, the amount of time it takes for an enterprise to liquidate its investment in inventory and turn that investment back to cash can be significant. A company may be profitable but an unacceptable cash flow can still put the business out of business.
12. **Asset turns.** This measure is more inclusive that the cash-to-cash cycle time. Asset turn is very similar to inventory turn. How many times can the same assets be used to generate revenue and profit. The

Level 1 Metrics	Major Opportunity	Disadvantage	Average or Median	Advantage	Best-in-class	Value from Improvement
Delivery Performance			69%		93%	+ $20-30M
Fill rate by line item			88%		97%	Increase in
Order fulfillment lead time			225 days		135 days	revenue
Perfect order fulfillment			65.7%		92.4%	
Supply chain response time			225 days		72 days	Increased customer
Upside Production Flexibility			22 days		9 days	satisfaction
Supply Chain Mngmt. Cost			14.4%		8.6%	-$2.5M cost reduction
Warranty Cost as % of Revenue			2.4%		1.2%	-$4.2M cost reduction
Value added per employee			$139K		$275K	NA
Inventory Days of Supply			84 days		55 days	-$27M cost reduction
Cash to cash Cycle time			99.4 days		35.6 days	-$6.2M cost reduction
Asset turns			1.7 turns		4.7 turns	NA

Figure 6.8 Supply chain scorecard. (From the Supply Chain Council, Inc. With permission.)

stakeholders expect the assets to be well utilized and will invest in a company who can effectively turn their assets.

In 1998, the Supply Chain Council summarized these measures on a supply chain scorecard (Figure 6.8). The numbers that have been filled in will change for each industry median and best in class. Also the value from improvement will be unique to the enterprise making the assessment. The important thing to know is where your company is with respect to the competition. The current status of this example company is marked with the desired goal identified. For this particular company, the value from the improvements has been quantified in the last column.

Summary

Most of this book is internally focused within the enterprise in order to "get the internal house in order." However, the big return on investment and the future revenue and profit growth come from integrating the enterprise to its supply chain. According to Jan Hammond from Harvard University, School of Business, "In every implementation ... of these types of partnerships and coordinating practices within the supply chain, sales have gone way up and markdowns have gone way down." While product is moving forward from the supplier to the customer, information is needed backwards to provide adequate time for planning and replanning. The term "supply chain" is really quite descriptive for the concept. The integration of the supply chain is an area where the speed and accessibility of technology will make the biggest impact. This technology can include EDI, E-commerce, Internet, or a variety of other possibilities. However, without the accurate data feeding this technology and robust business processes supporting the strategy, the risk is that the same bad information will be the result — now only more quickly. The experts are claiming that in the future it will no longer be single companies competing against each other. The individual company must position itself into a competitive supply chain and the different supply chains will compete against each other. Others would say the future is here today. Are you ready?

References and Resources for Supply Chain Management

Supply Chain Council, Inc., 303 Freeport Road, Pittsburgh, PA 15215, www.supply-chain.org.

Achieving Supply Chain Excellence Through Technology (ASCET), a forum on the next generation of supply chain strategy, www.ascet.com.

Advanced Planning and Scheduling magazine focuses exclusively on the theory, use, implementation, benefits, and challenges of the use of Advanced Planning and Scheduling systems, http://www.apsmagazine.com.

The Featherbone Principle, A Declaration of Interdependence, Charles E. "Gus" Whalen, Jr., Rand McNally Book Services, Nashville, TN, 1996.

Advanced Supply Chain Management: How to Build a Sustained Competitive Advantage, Charles C. Poirier, Publishers Group West, 1999.

Business Logistics Management: Planning, Organizing, and Controlling the Supply Chain, Ronald H. Ballou, 1998, APICS #03372.

Customer-Centered Supply Chain Management: A Link-By-Link Guide, Fred A. Kuglin, Amacom, 1998.

The Executive's Guide to Supply Management and Strategies: Building Supply Chain Thinking into All Business Processes, David A. Riggs and Sharon L. Robbins, Amacom, 1998.

From Mind to Market: Reinventing the Retail Supply Chain, Roger D. Blackwell, Harperbusiness, 1997.

Introduction to Supply Chain Management, Robert B. Handfield and Ernest Z. Nichols, 1998, APICS #03698.

Logistical Management: The Integrated Supply Chain Process, (McGraw-Hill Series in Marketing), Donald J. Bowersox and David J. Closs, 1996, APICS # 03622.

Strategic Alliances: Managing the Supply Chain, Tim Underhill, Pennwell Publishers, 1996.

Supercharging Supply Chains, Gene R. Tyndall et al., John Wiley & Sons, New York, 1998.

Supply Chain Management: The Basics and Beyond (St. Lucie Press, Boca Raton, FL, APICS Series on Resource Management), William C. Copacino, 1997.

Supply Chain Optimization: Building the Strongest Total Business Network, Charles C. Poirier and Stephen E. Reiter, 1996, APICS #03466.

Applying the Theory of Constraints to Supply Chain Management, John Covington, in press.

Note: Book titles with APICS # identifiers can be ordered through www.apics.org or by calling 800-444-2742 or 703-354-8851.

OPERATIONS MANAGEMENT

7 Operations Planning (Material and Capacity Requirements)

Operations planning is the detailed calculation of the material and capacity required to execute the Sales and Operations Plan. Material requirements planning (MRP) pulls together all the requirements for an individual part from the variety of demand sources and calculates a recommended replenishment plan that meets all the requirements. In addition, MRP also provides information by exception when the demands and the expected supply are out of alignment. This information allows the planner to react specifically to those areas requiring attention rather than requiring a routine detailed examination of every part.

Detailed capacity requirements planning (CRP) provides the visibility of demand for each of the workcenters. This forward visibility allows the operations manager to more accurately plan the overall strategy for the addition or reduction of capacity. This proactive approach to capacity management allows the company to make decisions and plans at a time where many options are possible rather than during a time of crisis. The overall costs and benefits of alternative plans can be evaluated and discussed to determine the best solution. If the capacity cannot be changed to accommodate the priority plan, a change in the priority plan may be required. This in turn prevents material from being purchased unnecessarily and reduces the assets dedicated to unusable inventory. Integrating detailed material and capacity requirements planning is a key implementation success strategy as it can help in the overall proactive identification and resolution of bottlenecks and identify suspected data errors.

Demand Management

Demand management is the function of recognizing all demands for products and services in order to support the customers in the marketplace. This demand management process also includes doing what is required to help make the demand happen and prioritizing demand when supply is lacking. Demand management facilitates the planning and utilization of resources for profitable business results. Overall demand management maintains an intense focus on the customer. Demand management can be broken into two levels of control: demand planning and demand control and execution. Demand planning includes forecasting, customer linkage, new product planning, and inventory and capacity strategy. Demand control and execution includes customer order fulfillment, forecast consumption, abnormal demand management, and safety stock or buffer management.

Demand planning is directly dependent on the quality of the demand information. The process must be defined so that the best demand information is available. This process includes a forecast review including accountability. To facilitate this process many companies are establishing the position of demand manager or demand coordinator in order to facilitate and coordinate the development of the demand plans for the business. There should be a formal management demand review of the monthly updated demand plan/forecast as part of the Sales and Operations Planning process. This was covered in Chapter 3.

Forecast

Usually the demand planning process begins with a forecast. Businesses do not work well without a reasonable forecast. The forecast does not need to be 100% accurate. However, a forecast is necessary in order to drive the business. Good usable forecasts result from hard work, timely review, and update by the appropriate people using customer input, judgment, and software support. The answer to good forecasts is not a more expensive forecasting system. The strategic vision and business plan should be supported by the forecast. The forecast also helps provide a target for sales. This, in turn, through the material and capacity planning process, defines the required resources (equipment, people, materials, and services). This integrated plan provides visibility that is required to reach consensus on the support needed to service the customer. The forecast is a driver of the business planning process.

Demand patterns can vary dramatically and it is very important they are well understood. To better understand these patterns they must be analyzed and measured for our ability to understand how to deal with them. This understanding also provides an idea on the accuracy of our forecasts. A basic principle of forecasting is that a forecast is only as good as the assumptions behind it. Sharing the assumptions behind a forecast leads to a shared understanding of the business. When forecasts are wrong it is very likely due to the assumptions that were behind them.

Balance Supply and Demand

Demand management attempts to balance supply and demand. Demand can come from forecasts, customer orders, distribution, spare parts, safety stock, interdivisional requirements, and new products. Supply can come from material in inventory or expected on factory orders, capacity (labor or machine), and directly from suppliers. When demand exceeds supply there must be an effective demand prioritization process in effect until the supply can be increased.

For the generic enterprise. the order entry and promising process is shown in Figure 7.1. In reality the order entry and promising process must address the following three questions:

1. What is the best business practice for the company?
2. Who needs to be involved?
3. What mechanics are required?

Proper forecast consumption mechanics can be crucial to having demand stability. The first attempt at forecast consumption logic is a simple blending approach. If the monthly forecast is 1000 units, the spread would simply be done as 250 units per week or 50 units per day. Although this process is very simple, it does not work very well. Assume 3 days pass and no customer orders are received. What should the forecast be for day 4? The options that exist are to drop the forecast by the unconsumed units or carry the

Figure 7.1   The order entry and promising process. (From Richard C. Ling, Inc. © With permission.)

unconsumed forecast into the next time period. Another alternative is to spread the unconsumed forecast evenly across the balance of the month.

If forecasts are done in monthly time increments, then it probably makes sense to consume the forecast with incoming customer orders over that same time frame. Any forecast left over at the end of the month will be deleted until something tells you to do it differently. In any event all incoming customer orders should be screened for normal/abnormal demand characteristics. Practically speaking, this is not possible for every customer order. However, it must be done on an exception basis to allow correct forecast consumption. Identifying abnormal customer demand for the individual customer order may include considering the demand source — either customer or channel. If all of a sudden, demand for an industrial product is experienced from the retail channel, this demand should set a flag for review. The quantity on the order may also trigger the need for review. This could be the size of the order itself or the percentage of an item's forecast that is consumed by one order. Triggers also can be set for cumulative demand variances. Abnormal demand types include:

- One time demands — this order will never be seen again and should not be included in future forecasts.

- Ordering pattern change for timing — this could be due to a budget cycle being reset. This would impact future forecasts if the new budget cycle were expected to remain.
- Time to change the forecast — abnormal demand may point out where the forecasting process is in error.
- Wrong seasonal timing pattern — this may sometimes be caused by an alternate use being developed for a product such as a waterski board now being used as a snow board.
- Spiked demand — this could be absolutely normal if the demand is dependent on inventory in the supply chain. In this case forecasting is not the right answer. A better result would be obtained using distribution requirements planning. (See Chapter 6 and 10 for more details on this tool.)

In order to maintain maximum user control, there needs to be the ability to code each abnormal demand with a flag so that the planning system will not consume the forecast. In addition, future forecasts should not include this quantity as part of the mathematical computation. Each company needs to have a policy that states there will be a process and mechanism that helps to identify and deal with abnormal demands. Accountability needs to be established in order entry, customer service, and the demand management functions. Many companies must deal with multiple demand streams for the same item. This item may be sold as an end item and is promised through the use of available to promise (ATP). The same item may also be used as part of another assembly and is controlled by MRP. These demand types must be included in the overall company policy.

Safety Stock

Safety stock is a request for inventory to buffer demand or supply variation to better serve the customer. Safety stock is directly related to demand management and the overall buffer resource strategy (covered in Chapter 4). The other buffer strategy is to have safety capacity or surge capacity in order to support abnormal demands. The better term for safety stock is strategic inventory or buffer inventory. A question that is commonly asked is, "How much safety stock should you have?" This level is usually statistically calculated to maintain a specific service level. This is covered in more detail later in this chapter and in Chapter 10. Safety stock also can be visually determined by reviewing demand variation. New products are supported with subjective safety stock estimates. In a supplier partnership, the amount of safety stock may be directly negotiated as part of the procurement contract.

No matter how the safety stock is determined, the important thing to remember is that the system will treat it like a demand rather than a supply. Therefore, safety stock needs to be managed and consumed just like a forecast. If the safety stock is never used, then it is not really needed. The ERP system should provide visibility when the safety stock has been used to fill customer demand. Customer order allocations should also allow the use of the quantity that has been identified as safety stock. If safety stock is being used, it must eventually be replenished. This replenishment should occur with a lead-time that makes sense in your environment. Unfortunately, most ERP material planning functions treat safety stock as a requirement in the current time period. This causes a past due expedited order to be created to simply replenish safety stock that was doing exactly what was intended. It is difficult for the planner to distinguish these expedite messages from the messages that directly impact a customer.

When demand increases rapidly and resources are having a difficult time keeping pace, this is a good time to reduce safety stocks and possibly even prioritize customers. Conversely, as soon as it is apparent that the demand that was anticipated is not going to happen, the forecast and safety stock should be reduced so material and capacity resources can be freed up to handle real demand. This is not an easy process to accomplish, but this is extremely helpful to the internal manufacturing resources and the overall customer service. Manufacturing can then work on the things that are really demanded by the customer rather than replenishing unneeded safety stocks.

Material Requirements Planning

Given a realistic master production schedule, the MRP system provides the answer to the questions of "how much" and "when" for all the items required to support that schedule. The way inventory was planned before the advent of MRP was to wait until a reorder point was reached, order the parts, and hope that the parts got there before needed. Unfortunately, the reorder point system works best for demand that is relatively continuous and stable. This type of demand is found in companies that produce parts that are high in volume and low in variety. When this order point strategy is exercised with very short lead-times and relatively low inventories, this is known as Kanban,

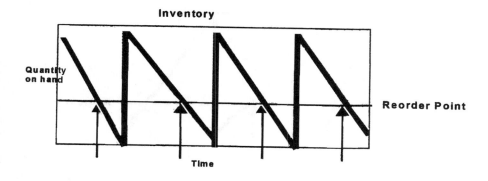

Figure 7.2   Order point inventory pattern.

or automatic replenishment from suppliers, internal or external. The supplier can quickly respond to the need from the customer because the customer is demanding the same thing at relatively the same rate over the same period of time. This type of replenishment is also known as demand pull or demand flow. The other place that an order point system or Kanban system works relatively well is for independent demand items — the items with demand coming from the external customer. Independent demand tends to be relatively continuous and steady over a period of time. The overall demand for the end item is relatively level with some variability. When this occurs, inventory falls in a steady predictable manner, as expected. Assuming that the reorder point method for inventory replenishment is used, an order would be placed as the inventory drops to the predefined level. This predefined level is the quantity of inventory that should cover the expected demand during the lead-time. These reorder points are marked with arrows in Figure 7.2.

This type of inventory pattern is considered a traditional sawtooth pattern. Inventory declines in an orderly fashion until the order point is reached lead-time away from the need. The replenishment arrives just as the inventory reaches zero. Or at least that is how the theory says that it should happen. The average inventory using this theory is the order quantity divided by two. Typically, the order quantity is fixed by part number and reflects an economic quantity to produce or purchase. The reality of the situation is that the demand pattern tends to look more like Figure 7.3.

In this figure the demand has some variability and the inventory runs out either too early for the shipment to arrive and the company experiences backorders or the demand falls after the order has been placed and there is

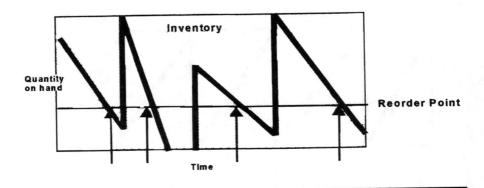

Figure 7.3 Order point inventory with variability.

excess inventory. These problems are exacerbated by long replenishment lead-times. Shorter lead-times allow direct replenishment to occur while mini-mizing the chances of running out or having excess inventory. This is the basis for supply chain systems where the supplier is directly tied to the inventory and consumption of the customer. Direct replenishment works well where the reactive lead-times are short and the product mix stays stable. As soon as product variety comes into the picture, the need for detailed material requirements planning (MRP) returns once again. Suppliers must have some knowledge of requirements by quantity, configuration, and esti-mated timing sufficiently in advance so that they can start their processes in time to deliver the requirements. The exact timing of the replenishment can be through direct linkages to the supplier but the planning information has to be provided sufficiently in advance of the requirement. Imagine if you were a supplier who has been selling blue parts to your customer on a direct replenishment contract. Your customer sends you a fax or EDI-type Kanban to signal the exact timing of your shipments. Today you get a Kanban and the customer now informs you that they would like to have a striped part. Your processes are incapable of producing a striped part! You have never produced a striped part! Your customer knew about their requirement for a striped part as soon as their customer ordered it, but since you are delivering in a direct replenishment pull system, you did not get the visibility until today. Now what do you do? This is a formula for disaster and is the reason why MRP still has an integral role in supply chain direct replenishment systems. Good planning makes for good execution. This fact is still the same no matter what technology develops.

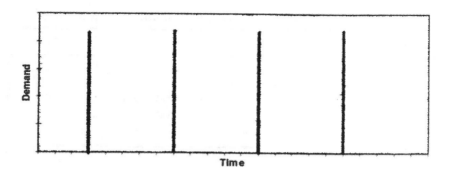

Figure 7.4   Dependent demand pattern.

The other area where MRP fits extremely well is for dependent demand, demand that arises from the need to build the end item. This type of demand, by definition, is lumpy and discontinuous. This phenomenon also was seen as part of the inventory strategy discussed in Chapter 4. The seeming variability in demand surprises many people until they look at it more closely. Once again lead-time and batch sizing makes a significant impact here. Demand for component parts does not exist until an order is released for the end item. At that time, there is a requirement for the parent's lot size quantity times the quantity for each item from the bill of material. If the product being built is a lamp, there is no demand for yoke subassemblies until an order is released to build additional finished lamps. If the order is for 500 lamps, there is an instant demand for 500 yokes all at once, assembly lead-time away from the finished lamp requirement. Even though the independent demand for lamps can be very level, say 25 per day, there is no demand for yokes until the order is released to manufacture completed lamps. The finished goods inventory has lamps with yokes built in. No additional yokes are required until a manufacturing order is begun. When the manufacturing orders for lamps are released, the result is simultaneous demand for all the components (bill of material quantity times the order quantity) to be available when the order is due to start. Figure 7.4 examines the effect on the demand for yokes.

Tables 7.1 and 7.2 and Figure 7.5 show how these spikes in demand can be determined with sufficient advance notice so that little or no safety stock is required. In Table 7.1, the customer forecast is rather level with a small

Table 7.1 Independent to Dependant Demand Planning Grid

Item ID: Lamp	1	2	3	4	5	6	7	8
Customer forecast	200	300	400	400	300	200	500	350
Scheduled receipts		500						
Projected lamps on hand	100	300	400	500	200	500	500	150
Planned order receipts			500	500		500	500	
Planned order releases		500	500		500	500		

Note: Lot size = 500, Low Lvl = 0, OH = 300, LT = 1, Alloc = 0, SS = 100.

Table 7.2 Dependent Demand Explosion

Item ID: Yoke	1	2	3	4	5	6	7	8
Yoke gross requirements		500	500		500	500		
Scheduled receipts								
Projected yokes on hand	1000	500	0	0	0	0	0	0
Planned order receipts					500	500		
Planned order releases		500	500					

Note: Lot size = LFL, Low Lvl = 2, OH = 1000, LT = 3, Alloc = 0, SS = 0.

amount of variability. Based on the lot size and the lead-time, the orders to assembly are expected to be released in Periods 2, 3, 5, and 6. There is no demand for assembly in Periods 1, 4, 7, or 8.

In Table 7.2, the need for lamps to be assembled starting in periods 2, 3, 5, and 6 is translated directly into gross requirements for the yokes in the same periods. Based on the inventory strategy for yokes of only ordering what is needed when it is needed, this translates to two orders of 500 parts, one in Period 2, and one in Period 3. In Figure 7.5, the net result of demand and inventory is shown in one chart.

This pattern of demand bears little to no resemblance to the sawtooth pattern shown in Figure 7.2. However, by using MRP the orders can be proactively planned, providing sufficient lead-time to the yoke supplier of what to expect in quantity and timing.

The other alternative, given the assembly lot size strategy in this example, would be to use the order point method. The demand arrives all at once, quickly depleting the available supply. This unexpected demand often causes expensive expediting as the supplying department or purchasing attempts to

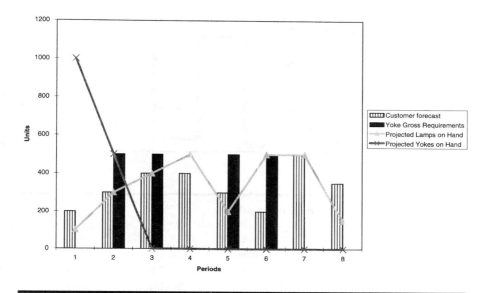

Figure 7.5 Independent vs. dependent demand and inventory.

replenish the inventory. No visibility of declining inventory exists like in the material planning system. Unlike the predictable sawtooth shape of the independent demand graph, the graph of the demand for component items looks like unpredictable discontinuous spikes. This is because all parts are required at the beginning of the process to start the order. Even though sales for the end item may be smooth and relatively continuous, demand for component inventory is affected by the parent's manufacturing lot size as shown in Tables 7.1 and 7.2 and Figure 7.5. The larger the lot size, the lumpier the demand is for component inventory. Figure 7.6 demonstrates the general resulting inventory for yokes given this spiky discontinuous demand.

Using reorder point to manage this type of inventory results in high levels of stockouts. The typical reaction is to react with safety stock resulting in a higher level of inventory overall. The inventory level drops all at once, triggering an order that is already too late. This is affectionately referred to as the OSWO (Oh Shoot We're Out) theory of inventory management. On the other hand, simple logic states that when the parts are not required they should not be sitting in inventory. This use of company cash and other critical resources is wasted on inactive inventory. This is where the analysis suggested in Chapter 4 could uncover this type of incorrect planning tool usage.

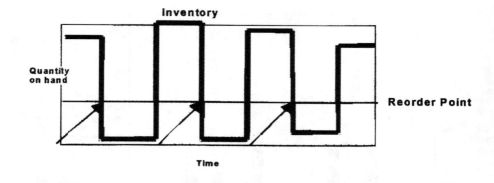

Figure 7.6 Component inventory pattern.

One way to minimize the lumpiness of demand is to reduce the lot size and lead-time of production and/or procurement. This is the secret behind Kanban or pull system replenishment systems. The lot sizes are so small and the replenishments occur so frequently, the lumpiness of dependent demand is not noticed. The reality looks like Figure 7.7

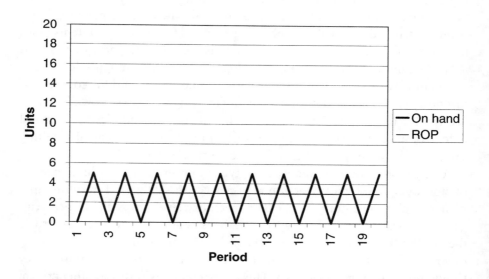

Figure 7.7 Pull system inventory pattern.

The inventory quickly rises and falls given the steady demand. The Kanban quantity is very small and the response time is small. This allows rapid replenishment and very low overall inventory levels. However, for traditional production, the lot size selected must allow efficient utilization of all the company's resources. Even though the inventory would be at a minimum if parts were ordered and built into finished goods daily, few companies have sufficient uniform demand volume to support this strategy of repetitive manufacturing. Another way is to order only what is needed, when it is needed. This is the basis and motivation for the development of MRP systems. Many people would have you believe that MRP is an old tool that is no longer necessary; there can be nothing farther from the truth. MRP is an essential tool in the toolbox of a complete ERP system.

MRP plans all the items that have to be completed or purchased to support the master production schedule. The forward visibility allows the release of orders on time. This allows the planner to take on a proactive role in managing inventory. No longer is the inventory replenishment process reactive, waiting until a shortage occurs. Instead, requirements are projected, thus replenishments can be planned and managed as shown in Table 7.1 and Figure 7.5. The on-hand inventory for yolks can fall to zero with the confidence that any new requirement will be identified with sufficient lead-time to be able to secure the part. Rather than buffering demand with expensive inventory, using MRP can be thought of as buffering demand with adequate planning. The planning is considerably less expensive than the inventory. As computer systems have evolved and become more powerful, different types of scheduling algorithms have become available.

Backward Scheduling

The standard default scheduling process is backward scheduling. The master schedule date is taken as the end point and then all components are offset backward through time by their respective lead-times to determine the required completion and start dates for each. This type of logic is used in everyday life. When determining when to get up in the morning, the thought process may be to work backward from when you want to be at work. Assuming that you are scheduled to start at 7:30 a.m. with a 30-minute drive, you would leave your home at 7 a.m. Assume for a moment that traffic in your city is reliable on a day-to-day basis. Given that you like to eat a hearty breakfast and read the paper. That whole process takes another 30 minutes, you know you should be ready by 6:30 a.m. If it takes 1 hour to get up and get ready for work, you set your alarm for 5:30 a.m. This kind of planning is done in many different daily activities. When you make an appointment to meet someone for lunch at noon, you know that you cannot *leave* work at noon and expect to be at the meeting point on time.

We do not have to physically go on the trip to be able to plan lead-times to schedule when we need to start. Activities that we do most frequently, like the trip to work, will provide the most accurate planning while things that we do infrequently require a larger margin of error to be planned. The same process exists in planning for the manufacturing company. Suppliers who deliver reliably over a period of time can be scheduled to a smaller margin of error than those with whom we do business infrequently. Backward scheduling is best used when the demand is known in advance of the expected lead-time. That is, if demand is known 6 weeks in advance and the assembly lead-time is only 2 weeks, backward scheduling is the best option. This scheduling method provides the least amount of inventory by starting orders at the last possible moment.

Forward Scheduling

At times, scheduling forward rather than backward better meets the needs of the company. Just as if you get up late, say at 7 a.m., in your mind you quickly schedule the things you must do to get to work. Given the same times as used in the backward scheduling example, the projected arrival time at work is 9 a.m. Unfortunately, you have a big meeting with the boss at 8 a.m. and walking in with your coat still on is not a very good idea and could be a CLM (career-limiting move). Some activities must be deleted or changed to accomplish the expedited schedule. You may forego reading the newspaper and eat a smaller breakfast. Using this same technique, companies making high variety and low volume parts will typically plan the quickest completion of a part using forward scheduling. This is because the customer usually wants the part as soon as possible rather than at a defined future date. If the resulting date is not acceptable, the sequence and duration of events, both value-added and queue, is reviewed and adjusted until either there is no additional time that can be taken out or the desired date has been reached.

In the example used of getting to work, sometimes things are done that seem to expedite the process but in the long run defeat the purpose. Getting to work sooner by speeding may seem like a good idea at the time until the local friendly law enforcement officer intercedes or you lose control of the car by attempting to multitask by doing other things while driving. The time it takes to get a ticket offsets dramatically any perceived timesavings accomplished through speeding. Similarly, attempting to speed selected items through the plant by expediting results in similar negative repercussions. The attempt may make sense at the time and sometimes you actually get away with it. When done as a routine practice, in the long run, you will always get caught and the effort is not work the price.

MRP System Requirements

Master Production Schedule

A master production schedule is required to drive the material requirements planning system. This master schedule contains items that are fully defined in bill of material terms. The master schedule is a statement of what is planned to be completed by defining quantities and timing for each parent item. The bills of material define the components for each parent. The two items together are critical to calculating the parts' requirements. The master schedule answers the questions of how much and when for the finished item. The bill of material answers the question of what. MRP uses these two inputs to calculate how much and when given the current inventory position.

Inventory Records

Every inventory item that will be stocked must be identified uniquely and have an inventory record available. Inventory records include information about:

- **On hand.** How many are currently in inventory, available for use.
- **On order.** How many parts have already been ordered from the supplier (either internal or external) and when are they due to arrive.
- **Lead-time.** How long is the replenishment expected to take from the time of order. A common error is to not include the amount of time it takes to place the item on order. Some companies requiring three quotations and awarding the purchase to the lowest bidder can use up significant lead-time in this process. The amount of time required to receive and inspect the parts also must be included. If only the supplier's lead-time is used, the parts will be always late.

- **Planning data.** These factors define the order sizes and timing. This includes lot-sizing rules available in most ERP systems like lot for lot, economic order quantities, order minimums/maximums/multiples, and period of supply.

Unique Item Identification

MRP plans by unique items. Having multiple identification numbers for a part because there are multiple suppliers will not allow MRP to add the requirements for this part together. MRP can suggest the best order quantity possible. In the same way, having the same part at different divisions of the enterprise with different part numbers makes consolidation of an overall enterprise quantity to a supplier a manual process or one requiring a great deal of customized programming. Defining the identification system can evoke many opinions and emotions. The best systems have concise part numbers containing all numeric digits (i.e., nonsignificant codes). The most common error is to encode descriptive information into the part number (i.e., significant codes). The belief is that this will help the shop floor find things and make the system easier to use. The opposite often is true. For example, 127277725 could be a significant code for a guide for a lamp. The first two digits (12) denote the manufacturer. The next three digits are a color key. The last four digits are the model for which this part is usually purchased. Unless all the translations for the codes are known, this just looks like a very long part number. The chance that the entire part number will be used on a daily basis is minimal. The people using the numbers always find some way to shorten them to a usable length, usually less than six digits.

The only people the significant part number assists are the people who designed it. The encoding of information requires a translation key and soon the code is forgotten, leaving long part numbers in use with no benefit. Having short numeric part identifiers allows the users to remember and use the correct identifier for the correct part. The real function of the part number is to uniquely identify the part, period. Additional functionality of the software allows the other information to be attributed to the part which is a simpler fashion through the use of a relational database.

Studies have shown that the chance of repeating the entry of a number with more than 7 digits falls to zero quickly. There seems to be no significant difference between 6 and 7 digits presumably because of the phone number recall ability for most people. In most businesses, the need for a part number in excess of 5 digits is rare. Five numeric digits allow the company to have 99,999 part numbers. Even if the 5-digit number starts with 10,000, the possibility still exists for 90,000 part numbers. This is sufficient to support a company up to a rather significant size. The advantages of nonsignificant part numbers are that they are easier to enter and recall. Accuracy of the inventory is usually better with a shorter number. The company also is poised to support future growth. If all 5 digits are used up, a 6th can be easily added.

The main disadvantage of significant part numbers is that they are longer and the company can easily run out of numbers depending on the coding scheme. Introductions of unexpected new products can throw the entire system into chaos. Usually the floor personnel begin using only a short subset of the number to identify the part or, worse, they rename it to something that makes sense for them. This quickly results in confusion, incorrect part use, and errors in inventory data. Don't be fooled into thinking that bar codes will eliminate this problem. Someone still has to look at and pick those parts with the long number. Part numbers are used for many things in addition to data entry. They are the basis of the language for the entire enterprise system.

In either case, the inventory records define all the characteristics of the parts. If the company wishes to stock a part and/or collect information about a part, a unique number is used. The best rule of thumb is that if there is a change in fit, form, or function, a new part number is required. If a blindfolded person cannot use any part in the bin, a new part number is needed.

Obtaining Quality Output

With only these three requirements — a master production schedule stated in bill of materials terms, unique part numbers, and inventory data — any MRP system will run. Notice that nothing has been mentioned yet about the quality and accuracy of the inputs. Many people like to blame "the system" when the information they receive as output is wrong. In reality, the inputs are normally the problem. Since users expect high-quality results from their system, high-quality inputs are required. Following are the key inputs to obtaining high-quality output.

Accurate File Data

File data must be accurate. This includes on-hand balances, bills of materials, part numbers, planning data, schedules, and everything else that is input into the system. Detailed information on how to achieve accuracy is detailed in Chapter 13. Accuracy in the master schedule means that the schedule is realistic and doable. The master schedule should be a stretch, but not impossible. Since MRP starts the calculation with how many are on hand, inventory record accuracy is essential. Bills of material drive the entire calculation process to determine requirement quantities. The parent–component relationships must be an accurate reflection of the part and quantity used, or shortages or excess inventory will result. Inaccuracy of input data is the most common reason for failure of ERP system implementations.

Realistic Lead-Times

MRP treats lead-times as fixed. Due to expediting and priority changes, lead-times can change based on the time of year or month. The end of the month in most manufacturing companies results in shorter than expected manufacturing lead-times as parts are expedited to completion to achieve monthly revenue goals. Close estimates are good enough for a successful system. Lead-time is one area where a conservative estimate will result in excellent part availability. As the MRP process becomes more fine-tuned with the efforts of continuous improvement and inventory declines, more accurate lead-times are required to prevent inventory from arriving too early or too late.

Timely Inventory Transactions

Every inventory item is transacted into and out of stock as required. At each level of the bill of material, work orders must be opened, component parts issued, and finished goods received. This is not to say that completed subassemblies must physically move into and out of a stockroom. Some of the most accurate stockrooms are in the middle of the shop floor on open shelves. Accuracy does not come from chain link fences and padlocks. Accuracy comes from discipline (with a capital "D") concerning the inventory consumption transactions. This discipline cannot be stressed enough. If the on-hand balance is incorrect, poor schedules and priorities are a guaranteed result from the MRP run.

Order Independence

In MRP schedules all components are available for the start date of the manufacturing order. Orders should not have to wait for parts or people when planning has been done effectively and implementation is well disciplined. For maximum production efficiency, all the parts must be available when the order is begun. An excellent discipline is that no work order should be released if part supplies are short. When shortages are allowed onto the shop floor, the downward spiral is hard to stop. Tracking these partial orders consumes a significant amount of resources. The expected result is high work in process and late orders as extensive labor and cash resources are spent attempting to relieve the shortages. Just finding the order after it has been set aside because of a shortage can be a challenge. The resource is better spent building quality product and delivering it to the customer.

MRP Output

The result of the MRP explosion is a schedule of order actions and messages by exception. The MRP process matches the part requirements with incoming parts or available on-hand quantities. MRP outputs notify the planner of problems and actions. The planner takes action on these messages to bring the production and inventory plan back into balance. Planner messages are provided to release orders to buy or make, cancel orders, or reschedule orders based on the current conditions. Changes are easily incorporated through this plan by this exception process. The key point is that the underlying cause for the imbalance must be addressed and resolved. Just deleting planner messages does not make them go away. The same messages will be back the next time MRP is run. If you do not like the output, challenge the inputs. The problem (and solution) will be found there. This is the real power of an ERP system. The system provides information by exception rather than wading through an enormous pile of information. The complementary process to material requirements planning is capacity requirements planning. When these two tools are used in synergy, the process is known as closed loop MRP.

Capacity Requirements Planning

Even if materials are well planned and available, they cannot be converted to finished goods without adequate capacity. Additional planning is required to determine the availability and need of these critical resources. To aid in the capacity planning process, a tool known as capacity requirements planning (CRP) was developed. Recently the need for capacity planning has received additional attention through the development of Advanced Planning and

Scheduling (APS) systems. Capacity requirements planning is defined in the 9th edition APICS dictionary as:

> The function of establishing, measuring, and adjusting limits or levels of capacity. The term "capacity requirements planning" (CRP) in this context refers to the process of determining in detail the amount of labor and machine resources required to accomplish the tasks of production. Open shop orders and planned orders in the MRP system are input to CRP. These orders are translated through the use of part routings and time standards into hours of work by workcenter by time period. Even though rough-cut capacity planning may indicate that sufficient capacity exists to execute the master production schedule, CRP may show that capacity is insufficient during specific time periods.

Capacity requirements planning follows exactly the same logic as materials requirements planning and plans the amount of critical resources needed to carry out the master production schedule. These resources can be labor hours, machine hours, cash, or any other constraint to the process. APS systems attempt to provide an optimized schedule based on the constraints in the process and the required customer demand. Capacity requirements planning answers the question of how much resource is required and when is it required. APS systems provide a schedule that maximizes the desired results in the business, typically profit. Asking the question of "what must be added to increase output" can identify critical resources. Becoming locked into thinking about capacity in terms of workers or machine time is easy. The first step in planning detailed capacity is to define the resource bottleneck. This is usually easy to spot. The pile of work in process in front of the resource bottleneck is a sure giveaway. If the process is not completed at this resource, upstream and downstream operation scheduling really does not matter. The APS system focuses on these resources. CRP can monitor this bottleneck and other near-bottlenecks closely and provide information about the load projected into the future. Since CRP can track many resources simultaneously, this process will prevent planning capacity for resources that do not affect output and possibly missing resources that are critical to increased output.

Levels of Capacity Planning

Capacity planning should occur at many levels. During the production planning process, a check is made against available long lead resources like facilities, large capital equipment, and total headcount to ensure that the production plan is reasonable. This was covered in more detail in Chapter 4 as part of the inventory and capacity strategy. When this plan is further broken down into the master production schedule, another validation of capacity is done to ensure that the master production schedule is achievable. These capacity requirements are in finer detail and include shorter horizon items like major department capacity and overall shift requirements. Further detail of the capacity planning process is done after material requirements planning to ensure that individual resources are not overloaded and to provide near-term visibility of future needs for critical resources. This detailed capacity planning process is called *capacity requirements planning*. The different levels of capacity planning are not directly linked. The linkage between the capacity plans is through the priority plans.

However, in the process industry, the capacity plans are more closely linked in the process flow scheduling process. This is further covered in Chapter 16. In priority planning, the production plan drives the master schedule (MPS) and the master schedule in turn drives the detailed material plan. The production plan is a total of the more detailed master production schedule. MRP is directly linked back to the MPS. In capacity planning, the resources planned are calculated from each level of the priority plan, not from the higher-level resource plan. The capacity plan validates each level of priority planning. Validating the priority plan with a capacity check closes the planning loop and increases the chances for success in achieving the overall business plan.

Using Capacity Planning

Recall from the MRP discussion that all materials are calculated to be available at the start of the lead-time for the replenishment order. MRP takes the estimated lead-time from the item master file and schedules all material to be available at the time of order release. However, capacity is consumed at different times in different places as the order moves through the shop. Similar to the discussion in the material planning section, capacity can be scheduled backward from the desired completion date or forward from an identified start date.

In Figure 7.8a, the process of backward scheduling is demonstrated. With this logic, the order would be scheduled to start at the beginning of day 3. Provided the lead-time in the item master is 9 days or longer, the materials will be scheduled in advance of the expected order start.

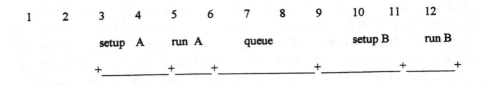

Figure 7.8a Backward schedule.

If the lead-time is less than 9 days (say, 5 days), the order would be scheduled to start before the materials would be scheduled to be available.

Figure 7.8b shows how this schedule changes if forward scheduling is used. Given this forward schedule, the order should be completed at the beginning of day 11. The utilization of resource is very different than the backward scheduled order. Resource A would be needed in days 1 to 4 for the forward scheduled order and would be needed in days 3 to 6 for the backward scheduled order. Resource B is needed between day 7 and 11 for the forward scheduled order and day 9 through 12 for the backward scheduled order. Just the choice of scheduling a single order can result in a very different load profile. This is exactly why sophisticated APS tools were developed to provide the best-fit schedule to optimize the schedule, given the desired strategy.

The expected total cumulative lead-time in this detailed capacity planning has little chance of equaling the estimated lead-time from the item master. The cumulative lead-time is the total of the setup time, run time, and move and queue times. Since the run time is variable based on the size of the lot, the total cumulative lead-time changes as the lot size changes. Materials are planned based on the fixed lead-time in the item master. Capacity is planned based on the desired order scheduling rule to determine how much capacity is needed, at what location, and when.

The capacity plan translates into detailed schedules by day for the shop floor, called *dispatch lists*. Dispatch lists are used by the shop floor to deter-

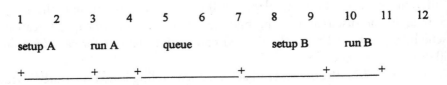

Figure 7.8b Forward schedule.

mine what to work on next and what can be expected in the future. In the examples used previously, work area A would have had the order on their dispatch list starting day 3 for the backward scheduled scenario and day 1 for the forward scheduled order. The completion date on the dispatch list is day 6 for the backward scheduled order and day 4 for the forward scheduled order. Other orders would be scheduled in a similar fashion to provide complete visibility of load for the work area. More important than communicating what to work on next is the forward visibility of future demand for critical resources. This allows an opportunity to be proactive in solving imbalances. Just like planning material, capacity use does not have to be forecast. CRP allows the future capacity plan to be calculated, giving a more accurate and more reliable plan. The real value is knowing that a problem is going to arise *before* it becomes a crisis. A plan can then be formulated to resolve the problem before it goes to the shop floor.

Requirements for CRP

MRP has some very simple system requirements and, similarly, so does CRP. Below are the CRP requirements.

Units of capacity

This is similar to the unit of measure for the item master. The most commonly used unit of measure for planning capacity is hours. This can be machine hours or people hours. Another unit of capacity that is commonly used to validate the master schedule and production plan is square feet. This capacity measure also can be used on a more detailed level to calculate storage area or pallet positions required. If space is a critical constraint, close planning of this resource may be required. The capacity unit of measure answers the question of what do we need to add to increase output. This constraint is the focus for the APS system optimization.

If the ERP system does not provide a specific function for planning tooling requirements, tooling needed for the production process can be planned as part of the capacity plan by treating it as another work center. The unit of measure usually is hours. Another method for planning tooling is to treat it like a component item on the bill of material with a certain amount of hours "in stock" that are consumed as the tool is used. This process allows the calibration, overhaul, or replacement of a tool to be planned into the future based on actual, scheduled utilization. Once again the integration of MRP and CRP allow the accurate calculation of these events rather than having to forecast them (and be wrong).

Routings

Routings are the sequential steps that the raw materials and other parts must follow to be completed. Other commonly used names for routings are bill of operations, instruction sheet, manufacturing data sheet, operation chart, operation list, operation sheet, route sheet, and routing sheet. The most difficult step in developing routings is to make the choice between a routing step and bill of material level. If the semifinished state will be stocked or sold, or if detailed data collection is desired, a level in the bill of material is required. This means that the order must be closed and received in inventory at this level. This part is then issued on the next higher assembly. The requirement for this transaction does not mean that the part must move to a storeroom. A transaction must take place completing one work order before issuing the part onto another order. These transactions can take place without the part moving to a stockroom. If the semifinished state is temporary and the part is moved directly to the next operation within a short period of time, a routing step is all that is required. As companies reduce lead-time and decrease the levels in the bills of materials, steps in the routing are added. The parts do not go into and out of inventory, instead they stay on the shop floor until totally completed and are ready to go to the customer.

Implementing cellular manufacturing simplifies the routings by eliminating all the intermediate steps and routes the part into the cell as a single workcenter rather than a series of individual operations. A cell is a collection of dissimilar machines that perform all the functions required to complete the part. To change from the traditional bill of material structure to these "flattened" bills, phantom parts are used. Phantom parts (make on assembly or MOA) have no lead-time and are expected to have no inventory. Usually the designation is made in the item master that this part is considered a phantom. Using phantoms simplifies the flattening of deep bills of material because the bill does not need to be restructured. The flattened bill is achieved by simply changing the item master to reflect the phantom status. The bill of material continues to match the drawing tree.

Special care must be taken when developing routings to determine the most commonly used sequence and work areas to complete the parts. Many

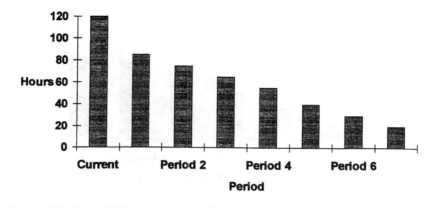

Figure 7.9   Released orders only.

modern systems allow the input of alternate routings but realistically keeping one set of routings accurate is a big enough task for most companies. No CRP system is intelligent enough to reroute a part through the alternate routing. That is the job of the skilled planner. Even the most sophisticated APS system uses the primary routing. The amount of data entry and maintenance required to accurately maintain alternative routings is rarely worth the effort. Honestly, it is rare to find many companies with accurate primary routings much less alternate routings. The defined routing in the computer should be the most likely sequence of where the work will be accomplished and how long each operation is expected to take.

Schedule

The schedule of orders used as the input to CRP is a direct output of the MRP process. Released and planned orders can be used to provide future visibility of capacity needs. If only released orders are used, the load pattern falls off quickly and gives a false picture of the future need for resources (Figure 7.9).

If the actual capacity for this area was 60 hours, the manager could come to the incorrect conclusion that a production window opens up to complete the past due work beginning in Period 5. Using all orders, released and planned, allows the analyst or supervisor to have a more complete picture of the need for capacity. Only considering released orders can cause incorrect conclusions to be drawn about the need for capacity in the future. A realistic

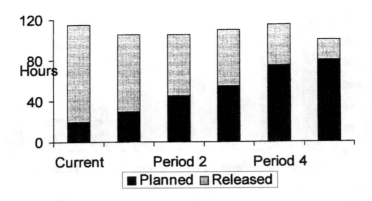

Figure 7.10   Planned and released orders

picture of capacity demands into the future is given when both types of orders are considered (Figure 7.10).

Looking at the total picture, if the capacity of the area is demonstrated to be 60 hours, the realization is obvious that this area is in a significant overload position. There is no conceivable way to complete the work expected in the area. In addition, having planned work still in the current period does beg the question "why?" Normally, the work in the current period should be released and already in work. For this work area there are only two choices. Either capacity must be increased or load must be decreased. The other option is a combination of the first two choices, increasing some capacity and decreasing some load. Ignoring this situation will not make it go away. The guarantee is that it will only get worse.

Shop Calendar

The shop calendar defines what days the shop will work. The shop calendar is also known as the manufacturing calendar or M-day calendar. The benefit of having a shop calendar is that only realistic shop days will be used in the calculation of schedules. If there is a holiday inside the lead-time, an extra calendar day is required to complete the order. A shop calendar gives a more accurate picture of expected completion dates since the nonworking days are removed from the picture. A core requirement to implement capacity requirements planning is the definition of the shop calendar. This is usually done in the administrative function of the system. Different shop calendars are usually available for different sites in a multiple site ERP implementation.

Capacity Management Measures

Available Capacity

Available capacity is the level of resources on hand to fill the demand. Unlike inventory, available capacity cannot be carried from one period to the next. Once the day is gone, the amount of capacity available for the day is gone as well. Understanding this phenomenon is very difficult for some managers. The production schedule should contain no past due work orders because there is no past due capacity. Using past due dates in an attempt to drive priority is the first step on the road back to using the old informal system. A key measure of the effectiveness of the master schedule is how much past due capacity is planned. Determining available time is accomplished by identifying the number of shifts the resource will be available each day and how much that resource can be utilized.

Utilization Factor

The utilization factor is usually expressed as a percentage between 0 and 100%. This is the percentage of time the resource is expected to run compared to the total time it is available. For example, if an NC machine is available two 8-hour shifts per day, but the machine does not run unattended, the utilization of the machine would be reduced by the time for breaks and lunches, assuming a total of 2 hours each day. The utilization factor of the NC machine would then be:

14 planned use/16 total available = 77.5% utilization factor

Planning to utilize any resource 100% of its available time is a certain plan for failure. Every resource requires a certain amount of time for repair, maintenance, and rest. Scheduled preventive maintenance is not included in the utilization number. This activity is planned just like any other work order to use the resource. If the monthly preventive maintenance takes 8 hours (all at one time), it makes little sense to schedule reduced utilization of 15 minutes per day. The better solution is to schedule an order that takes 8 hours of capacity from the machine in one block. In a make-to-order company, utilization is sometimes placed at conservatively low levels to provide a bank of safety capacity. This can be used to react to less than full lead-time orders. These orders tend to have a higher price (higher profit) associated with them and being able to react successfully to them can be a competitive strategy for the company. If the capacity is not used for these last minute orders, usually enough backlog exists on the shop floor to consume the available capacity. The "utilization factor" is used for planning future capacity requirements and is different from the "utilization" calculation many people use to express what percent of the payroll time was actually spent in productive activities. If an organization has utilization as a key performance measure, the result is usually high levels of inventory and low preventive maintenance since employees are being encouraged to just keep machinery running.

Efficiency

Efficiency is one of the most abused measures in manufacturing. Many companies use efficiency as a measure for people and their performance. In reality, efficiency is the measure of how well the standard times were established for each routing step. Efficiency is expressed as a percentage. If the actual time required to complete a routing step is less than the estimate, the efficiency is greater than 100%. If the actual time required to complete a routing step is more than the estimate, the efficiency is less than 100%.

The more humans are involved in a process, the greater the variability of the efficiency. People vary one to another on how quickly they can complete a job. People vary day to day on how quickly they can complete a job. Adding to this normal variability, learning curves come into play for tasks that are repeated. This is the fallacy behind attempting to use the APS system in this type of environment. The data inputs are inherently inaccurate due to this varying performance. Given this wide variability, the suggested schedule can have a wide error factor. People performing a repetitive task get quicker as they perform more repetitions. As the process becomes more automated, the efficiency is less variable and more accurate routing times can be established. This is the best area for APS tools.

Efficiency factors are like a coarse tuning knob for routings. Rather than changing the amount of hours in each routing step, application of an efficiency factor to the workcenter accomplishes a mass change very quickly. A key point to consider is that efficiency is not a performance measure of people. Efficiency is only a measure of the accuracy of the hour's estimate made in the routing. Many different factors can make a difference in the performance of the work area.

Rated Capacity

Rated capacity is calculated by multiplying the planned daily capacity at the workcenter by the utilization factor by the efficiency factor. For example, one machine working one shift equals 7 hours available. If that machine has a utilization factor of 75% and efficiency of 70%, the rated capacity is 5.44 hours (7 × .75 × .7). This result is an estimate of the capacity for the workcenter for each day.

Since rated capacity is a calculated number, there is an illusion of accuracy because of the appearance of numbers to the right of the decimal point. This is also the case in the APS system. The answer may look incredibly precise and, given the input data, it is a mathematically correct answer. However, when using the information from a capacity planning system including a very sophisticated APS system, consideration must be given to the underlying data supporting the information. An easy trap to fall into is that available capacity can be predicted accurately because a formula is used to calculate the number. One of the most exciting and frustrating parts of managing a plant is determining what the available capacity will be for the current day. People do not show up reliably for work. After reporting to work, people can leave suddenly. Day-to-day variations can be noticed in a worker's output. This illusion of accuracy and the inability to determine routing times exactly creates an unstable base upon which to use APS scheduling.

Scheduling Options

Once an estimate has been made of available capacity, orders can be scheduled into position for completion in a variety of ways. Backward and forward scheduling are the two most popular methods. Backward scheduling starts from the desired finish date to calculate the start date. Forward scheduling starts from today to determine the earliest possible finish date. In either case, the resulting demand must be compared against the available capacity. Two methods are commonly used.

Infinite Loading

The biggest criticism lately of MRP systems is that they are capacity insensitive. The netting and scheduling logic will schedule an order for completion regardless of the availability of capacity. One of the assumption of MRP is that all input data are accurate and up to date. This includes the Master

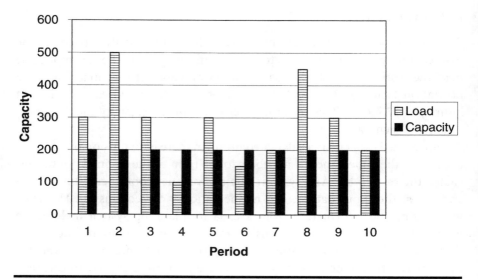

Figure 7.11 Load vs. capacity.

Production Schedule (MPS). For the MPS to be realistic and accurate, the expected load must be compared to planned capacity. The planner is required to level load the shop and typically watches critical workcenters for overload. Fewer routing steps and lower work in process make this job easier and more straightforward. This potential overload situation due to an unrealistic MPS has existed since MRP systems were originally developed. The main job of the planner was to resolve the resource conflicts and smooth the shop loading. Virtually every job shop has a bottleneck operation that can be easily identified by the pile of work waiting to be run. When this bottleneck is properly managed, the flow through the balance of the plant is usually very smooth. Figure 7.11 is an example of an overloaded workcenter. The priority plan must be changed to better balance the capacity and the load.

The drastic fluctuations between overload and underload is an unworkable condition for any facility. An effective planner will find a way to better balance the load and capacity. Capacity requirements planning provides the information visibility for the planner to accomplish the job.

Input/Output Control

Input/Output control is a straightforward way to handle the bottleneck situation. Orders are released only for the quantity of work that has been completed through the bottleneck. Process improvement is focused on this bottleneck to reduce the amount of time required. Buffering this workcenter with some backlog of work ensures that it will not run out of work and, therefore, adversely impact the entire output of the plant. A sufficient buffer is needed to guard against running out of work, but not so much that additional lead-time is created. This buffer is planned by defining queue for a workcenter. This queue time is scheduled into the sequential process for the job and becomes part of the standard flow. The workcenter can then expect to have that amount of planned queue waiting for processing. The actual amount of queue will depend on the reliability of the processes and the feasibility of the schedule.

Finite Loading

The answer to the traditional capacity insensitivity of MRP and CRP is finite loading. Even more sophisticated than finite loading is finite scheduling, as used in APS systems. The simpler finite loading method will never exceed the available capacity of a workcenter during scheduling. If the capacity is already allocated, the system will move the order forward or backward, depending on the scheduling rule, to find an available spot. Since computers are very good at calculating numbers, computing and scheduling according to this rule is computationally easy. However, real life sometimes gets in the way with less than precise estimates of the routing times, utilization factors, and efficiency factors. When the three are multiplied together and then used to compute exactly the load for the plant, the schedule can be precisely built on some very shaky ground. Understanding the underlying accuracy of the data and assumptions made during the development of the routings will enhance the utilization of this valuable tool of finite loading. In reality, the best application for finite loading and finite scheduling is a machine-constrained situation where the routing times are determined with a high level of precision. This type of industry will schedule the capacity first and then feed this information back to the material plan rather than the other way around. This approach to scheduling has been received with expectations of great results and resolutions of problems.

Intuitively, finite scheduling should provide a better answer than infinite loading. Now, let's talk about the real world. Only when the setup, run times, and available capacity are extremely accurate and reliable does the process work well. A big problem faced by the typical high variety manufacturer is the variability in times for set up, run, and available capacity. Learning curve can also play a part, as people become more experienced in producing the product. Just knowing who will show up for work the next day can be a big challenge. One person can make a big difference in the output of a small plant. If a single individual does not show up for work or if a slow or fast person is assigned to a particular job, the capacity can be different. Installing a finite loading or scheduling system does not solve these root core problems. Spending a significant amount of money installing a finite scheduling system or APS system is a poor investment for a plant with unreliable routing times and resource availability. These critical resources can be better spent reducing the variability of the production process. This will enhance the overall throughput of the plant far better than the purchase and implementation of a high-priced finite loading program. Once again the answer is not in automation but understanding and resolving the root cause of the problem.

Capacity Feedback and Control

After capacity has been planned, feedback to the plan is required to close the loop. Demonstrated capacity is the proven capacity calculated from actual performance data. This can vary from the planned capacity based on a number of factors like product mix, process problems, employee training, and other unexpected problems. Adjustments to the efficiency factors are done through examination of the past-demonstrated capacity. If the actual output is consistently less than the expected output, the efficiency factor needs to be adjusted downward. Conversely, if the actual output is consistently more than the expected output, the efficiency should be adjusted upward. Remember that efficiency is only a guide to the accuracy of the routing hours estimate, not a performance measure. A manufacturing execution system (MES) provides excellent feedback and can close the loop directly into the planning system including the APS system. Please remember that attempting to use efficiency as a performance measure causes undesirable behavior where hours are charged to incorrect jobs and other tampering is done to the system to make the measure look good. Combining manufacturing lots to avoid a setup will make the efficiency numbers look good, but the resulting inventory is expensive. The focus on capacity management should be on the capacity process not on the people involved. Processes can be controlled, not people.

Capacity control is essential for any production shop. If too many orders are sent to the shop floor, lead-time increases as parts sit in queue waiting to be run. Promises to customers are broken as lead-times become unpredictable. Orders are released even earlier in hopes of making the desired completion date. Expediting is done to ensure certain orders ship on time, pushing other orders out of the way and into an ever-worsening schedule position. Overall planned lead-times increase and even more work orders are released earlier. More work orders are on the shop floor further muddying the picture and deteriorating lead-times. The overall utilization of the formal system begins to break down and the informal system resumes control. To cover shortages, substantial dollars are invested in safety stocks of raw materials before they are really needed, adversely impacting cash flow. What a bleak picture! Using a few simple tools, this negative picture can be turned positive.

Input/Output Control

Input/output control can be used to keep the amount of work in process on the shop floor constant. When the shop floor backlog is constant, lead-times are relatively constant and commitments to customers are easier to make. The input/output control process only releases as much work to the shop as is completed during that time period. The focus of this input/output control should be on the main bottleneck of the plant. The input/output tool prevents the stratification of work in progress into active, inactive, and sludge. Active work orders are the orders where all the components are available and the manufacturing process can be completed. These orders tend to get worked on first and have the shortest lead-times through the shop. The inactive orders are those that need some assistance to be completed either due to a parts shortage or a process problem. These orders are only worked upon when the active order base is depleted or someone comes looking for them. These orders have longer than expected lead-times. Sludge orders are those orders that no one wants to touch and everyone wishes would go away. Unfortunately, ignoring them does not make them go away. Due to capacity constraints, these orders are not considered unless they are really needed and are usually significantly past due. Top levels of management are required to break these orders loose from their resting place. Lead-times for these orders can be many times the expected lead-times. For these orders to move, the underlying process or material problem must be addressed and resolved. If the answers were easy, the orders would have never deteriorated into this state. The amount of resource required to free these orders may exceed the value of the order. Allowing a high level of work in process on the shop floor encourages these orders to be ignored and the problem to escalate.

Attempting to do input/output control at every workcenter is not advisable. Once again the reality of the bottleneck arises. This work area should be closely monitored for output and load. Using a simple Pareto analysis, only 20% of the workcenters should be closely monitored using input/output control. The same is true when focusing on inputs for finite schedule or advanced planning and scheduling. Practical experience has shown that the number is really closer to 10%. A small number of workcenters make a big difference in overall schedule performance.

Another tool in capacity control is analyzing future needs for capacity and scheduling orders to smooth future lumpy demands. Customers rarely will order so that the load on the plant is level. Skilled master schedulers can revise the master production schedule so that the customer demands are met and the capacity is more evenly balanced. Finite scheduling is not a guarantee of level loads. The master scheduler must integrate all the parts into an effective production schedule. This is exactly the reason why an integrated enterprise system is required.

Summary

Material planning, capacity planning, closed loop management, and control are essential to the overall success of the company. Closing the priority-planning loop with effective capacity planning yields a powerful reality check. Capacity planning is accomplished by selecting and managing the constraint to increased production. When the bottlenecks to increased production are identified and managed, overall throughput in the plant increases. Every resource does not need to be planned and scheduled, only those impacting the throughput of the operation. Typically the implementation of a formal planning system will have the capacity planning activity come online some time after the material planning activity has been stabilized. Too many times, the implementation never gets around to bringing this valuable tool into use. To only plan materials without the consideration of capacity can also lead to failure. Not having the capacity to turn materials into desired finished goods wastes critical resources including cash. The requirements for effective capacity planning are not complex or difficult. Similar to MRP, the most difficult part is the data input accuracy. The benefits of closed loop capacity planning far outweigh the investment. Capacity planning validates the overall priority plan and can ensure long-term utilization of the formal planning system by providing essential visibility of future problems even without an expensive APS system. When this begins to happen, the organization moves from reactive fire fighting to proactive, process-focused fire prevention.

8 Product Design and Development

Effective product design and development is required to support the strategy of quick response to the market. The concurrent design process dramatically reduces the overall time to market. Concurrent engineering uses various computer tools to aid in the design process. The development and use of these computer tools has evolved quickly during the past few years. No longer is it necessary to build prototype parts to test for fit and interference. Building physical prototypes is extremely demanding on both time and expense. Complex assemblies can be put together directly on the computer through the use of computer-aided design (CAD) without ever building a physical part. The use of an effective PDM (product data management) system facilitates the design release, distributes the design data to multiple manufacturing sites, and manages changes to the design in a closed loop fashion. PDM provides the vault infrastructure that controls the design cycle and manages change. Effective utilization of this production engine can save an organization 15 to 20% in product cost. The innovation engine is powered by a virtual product data management system (VPDM) through the collection of what the organization considers best in designs, and provides insight into best practices in design. This innovation engine explores design alternatives and defines innovative options and alternatives including developing products targeted at individual customers. This can be integrated directly into customer relationship management (CRM) via the ERP system. VPDM can result in several orders of magnitude improvement to the product design process. When PDM, VPDM, and ERP are used in an integrated fashion, the Gartner Group refers to this as PDMII.

169

Product Data Management (PDM)

The product data management system not only tracks the configuration of the part and the bill of material, but also tracks the revisions and history of the as-designed and as-built conditions. By utilizing an integrated CAD and PDM system, the quality of the design is improved and the response time to the market is significantly improved. After all the virtual tests, a direct link to manufacturing (CAM) is also possible. Until recently the missing link has been to automatically update the ERP system planning data. This is now possible in a seamless connection due to the openness of the database tools and the sophistication of middleware used to perform the linkages. This integration into the planning system is essential so that the right part with the right configuration can be ordered at the right time.

The other side of product data management is the definition of what goes into the parent part. Where a machine shop may use relatively few materials to manufacture a part, an assembler may take hundreds if not thousands of parts to make an end item. An engineer, when ordering for a company building sophisticated satellites or ships, may use thousands of parts to complete the final unit. The as-designed and as-built configuration must be concisely documented in this type of business since part of the total deliverable is the product catalog to provide critical service information. Keeping track of all these pieces, assemblies, and quantities can be very confusing. A product data management system integrated with the bills of materials provides the planning system with a clear definition of the product and the materials required.

Expected Benefits of PDM

The enterprise is faced with many challenges both internal and external. The benefits of PDM can be broken into four categories:

1. Market share.
2. Customer satisfaction.
3. Profit margins.
4. Returns to stakeholders.

Market Share

The use of an integrated design system should increase market share since the enterprise can be expected to improve the introduction rate of new products and lower costs. PDM significantly reduces the time it takes to bring new products to market by reducing the amount of nonvalue-added time in the product release process. This increased frequency of introduction can help gain a competitive advantage. If the competition is releasing products at a slower rate, there is significant potential to grab market share. This faster and lower cost introduction of new products can also allow the enterprise to introduce products that meet the needs of new market segments or smaller niches that could not otherwise be accessed in a profitable way. In addition, the selling price of these products can potentially be lower since the cost of the design is lower, thus lowering the break-even point for the product launch.

Customer Satisfaction

PDM provides the enterprise with the ability to increasingly fit their product introductions to the market needs. With the ease of design the company can try innovative products that leverage what has been learned in prior designs. Feedback from customers can more easily be incorporated and introduced to the market. Since the design, fabrication, and services systems are integrated under a fully implemented ERP system, the components that exhibit early or frequent failure can be identified and the design can be modified to improve overall service levels. The PDM system supports the low-cost introduction of additional features as the market demands them because the design does not have to start from scratch.

Profit Margin

As discussed in the customer section, the use of PDM and CAD can significantly decrease the cost of developing a product. The number of derivatives that are possible from the same base design increase. A derivative is a product that is very similar to another product that has already been introduced. Typically a derivative product would share production processes. An excellent example is the Kodak disposable camera. Kodak introduced this camera as a standard product, a panoramic product, and a weekender product sealed in a plastic case. The basic design of the product is the same, only small changes were made and very different products are available for the market at a very low incremental cost. PDM facilitates the reuse of previous designs and knowledge because this information is easy to access and use. Where possible, previously proven material and parts are incorporated into new products coming to market. The benefit of this approach is that the volume for these parts goes up and, therefore, the cost goes down.

In addition, when proven parts are used the number of parts that could cause a risk in the project should decline because the startup production problems have already been resolved. Another side benefit of this approach is that the warranty cost should be reduced as the number of different stocked parts is reduced. The strategy of developing a product with all new parts may be exciting and attractive to the design engineers but it sets into motion a series of very expensive consequences. The complexity in managing the overall development processes increases because any one of the new parts could cause the overall project to be delayed. All of these new parts must have an item master added to the ERP system. This addition can introduce errors to the system. The parts then must be added to the bill of material — another potential source of errors. If this is a durable product, replacement parts must be held in inventory to fulfill the field service and internal service demand. As the product variety increases this level of inventory investment can quickly become substantial. When the PDM system is used to reduce the number of new parts used in a design, the warranty cost is reduced. The parts have been proven and the cost to provide service parts is significantly reduced.

Return to Stakeholders

The ability to bring new products to market quickly and profitably has a direct impact on the corporate image. The corporation is viewed in the market as being innovative and fresh in its product design. This competitive advantage usually provides improved market share and increased investment, in addition to improved returns to stakeholders. When this strategy is continued over time, the return to stakeholders can continue to improve as well. This steady growth and profit curve is well received by the financial markets and other investors.

The improvement in product design drives benefits across all elements of the extended enterprise. One measurable objective for new product introduction improvement is lead-time reduction. Without substantial improvement in the underlying processes, the reality is that even though the lead-time may be reduced the amount of resource required for completing the design did not change. This is shown as the transition from the resource line labeled 1 to line 2 as shown in Figure 8.1. The drawn out process shown in line 1 has been simply shoved into a smaller timeframe. The amount of resource required has not changed.

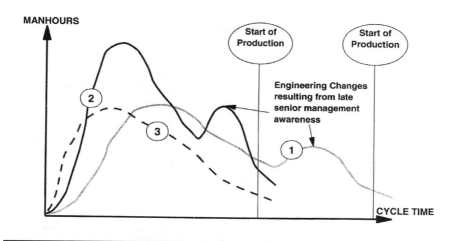

Figure 8.1 Design resource requirements.

The next step in the improvement process results in an overall reduction in the amount of resources required to complete the design. This is shown in Figure 8.1 as the transition from line 2 to line 3. Line 3 shows a reduced resource level through the improved design processes, such as change management using a PDM system. Management's awareness of potential problems occurs very late in the traditional product design cycle. Typically this is too late to really impact the overall cost of the product. Costs are committed because of decisions made early in the cycle, although the actual costs are incurred much later. Dramatic savings can be made when problems and issues can be identified earlier in the product design cycle.

Effective Product Design

Virtual Product Data Management (VPDM)

The VPDM process is really the process of learning from prior projects and designs. VPDM provides the resources to explore design alternatives and define innovative options for release in the next product. VPDM manages the linkages from the early design phase to the final release plan including required tool paths. This integrated process allows the development of the manufacturing information currently with the product design before final design release. This is very different from the iterative steps of drawing release

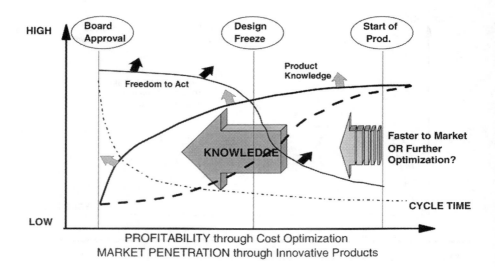

Figure 8.2   VPDM impact on design.

followed by a series of manufacturing engineering changes in traditional product design. The early availability of product and process knowledge offers the option to further optimize the design or push the design to market to capture critical market share. The design engineer can see how product will be built and can quickly determine the tools that may be affected if a design change is made. Figure 8.2 shows the traditional relationship between the freedom to act compared to the knowledge of the design vs. the integrated relationship that can exist under a VPDM process.

The typical relationship is shown with the dashed line and the dotted line. The dotted line falls quickly representing a rapid loss of freedom to act. Unfortunately the knowledge about the product does not rise at the same rate as shown by the dashed line. The high freedom to act is very short lived and drops quickly as the product design solidifies early in the overall product development cycle. A significant number of cost decisions and product decisions are committed early in the design project and although the product will not be available for quite some time, there is little freedom to change the product or the timing of the introduction to the market. As knowledge is introduced into the design process through the use of VPDM, the freedom to act stays very high as shown as the dark solid line with the dark arrows almost all the way to the design freeze. At the same time product knowledge increases at an increasing rate. The dark line with the gray arrows notes this in Figure 8.2. Throughout the entire design phase the freedom to act is very high and the product knowledge is high as well. This combination is because VPDM provides visibility of the design in context. The information is presented to different functional areas in the way or context that makes most sense to them. This could be the electrical systems for the electrical engineers or just the structural layout for the structural engineers. No longer do these engineers need to work from a two-dimensional drawing and translate to their view of the system. The VPDM technology allows the engineer to take a virtual tour of the product. The engineer can look at one part of the overall product and determine if there is any interference. This dynamic tour can also include calculating stresses or pressures at points that are identified during the tour. This ability to create a three-dimensional product in virtual reality eliminates the need for engineering changes and passes off the best design to the PDM system. The PDM system then manages the preparation of the manufacturing bill of material from the engineering bill of material.

By using VPDM, a conscious decision can be made to release the product to market to gain market share or continue to optimize the product in the design phase to reduce product costs. The overall design lead-time is dramatically reduced in addition to the total product cost. The number of designs that can be economically developed and evaluated increases. Figure 8.3 shows how many more product options can be developed concurrently against the project and business requirements. This process allows many decisions to stay fluid until the very last moment when the best options can be locked into the design and taken into production. The benefit of this approach is getting the best configuration at the last moment to meet market needs. The marginal cost to consider additional designs and products is significantly reduced so many more options can be economically considered. This fills the design funnel with additional concepts that would not be possible using traditional methods. Consideration of multiple product options early in the cycle can prevent costly engineering changes after product introduction.

The enterprise implication of this structured approach to design and development allows the extended enterprise to work together in a more seamless way. Concurrent engineering is the process by which different functional areas can work together to design and develop a product that meets the needs of the customer. VPDM is the technology that provides the information support that facilitates that process.

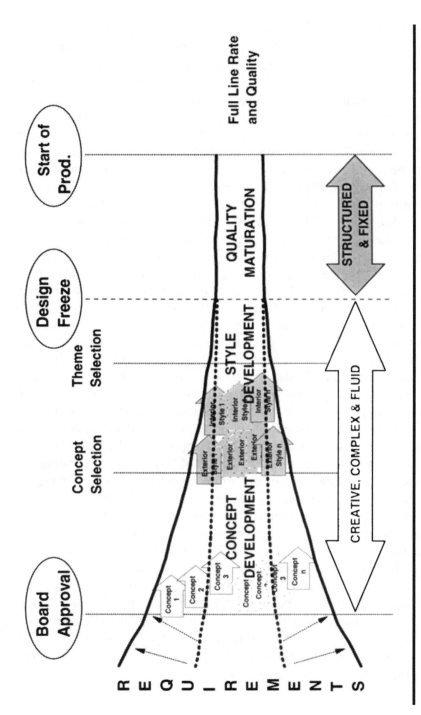

Figure 8.3 VPDM design funnel.

Concurrent Engineering

Figure 8.4 shows the various stakeholders impacted by the design process. A close relationship exists in this model between marketing, design, production, service, sales, and suppliers. These different functional areas interact concurrently in a series of tasks that must be accomplished to complete the product design. This concurrent engineering process also is known as participative design and engineering. The intent of this process is to enhance the design with inputs from all key stakeholders. Decisions made by one functional area directly impact the consequences felt in a different area. As designs are completed increasingly at a variety of sites, this information must be integrated to develop a virtual prototype to validate the final design. The PDM and VPDM technology tools are a significant aid in this communications process. A physical prototype may only be required in the final stages of the design process or may not be needed at all based on the quality of the design process and the confidence in this process. Unlike all previous airplanes, the Boeing's, 777 model never had a full physical prototype built before moving into manufacturing. This resulted in significant time and cost saving for Boeing. The robustness of the design data also allowed them to obtain FAA overwater approval in record time.

Key new product introduction practices are interrelated and have different benefits to quality, time, and cost, but all rely on integration of the factors

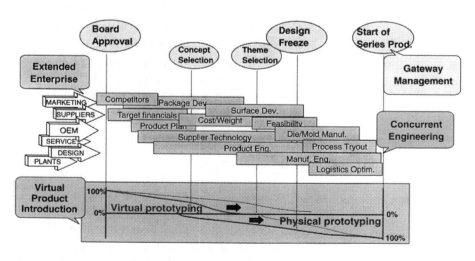

Figure 8.4   Various stakeholders impacted by the design process.

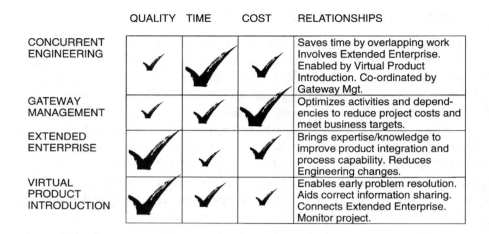

	QUALITY	TIME	COST	RELATIONSHIPS
CONCURRENT ENGINEERING	✓	✓	✓	Saves time by overlapping work Involves Extended Enterprise. Enabled by Virtual Product Introduction. Co-ordinated by Gateway Mgt.
GATEWAY MANAGEMENT	✓	✓	✓	Optimizes activities and dependencies to reduce project costs and meet business targets.
EXTENDED ENTERPRISE	✓	✓	✓	Brings expertise/knowledge to improve product integration and process capability. Reduces Engineering changes.
VIRTUAL PRODUCT INTRODUCTION	✓	✓	✓	Enables early problem resolution. Aids correct information sharing. Connects Extended Enterprise. Monitor project.

Figure 8.5   Interrelationships of product design. (From IBM Consulting Group. With permission.)

of the enterprise, design process, and technology. These relationships are described in Figure 8.5.

Concurrent engineering has its most impact in the area of "time to market" of a new product, but also has benefits on cost and quality. Cost is most impacted by gateway management. This management process assesses the readiness of the product for launch into the market to ensure that the best design is available to meet the needs of the customer. Utilizing a VPDM tool provides extended time where the freedom to act is cost competitive. Quality is most beneficially impacted by the integration of the extended enterprise and the capability of a virtual product introduction through the use of CAM and VPDM. When these four factors are achieved simultaneously, the benefit is felt directly as an improved bottom line.

PDM II = PDM + VPDM + ERP

These engineering best practices have a wide range of interrelated objectives. Concurrent engineering requires the knowledge that is gained during previous product designs be shared across design teams. Issues that may affect the design, including the adoption of ideas and sharing the real intent of the design, must be identified and resolved early in the development process. By drawing on the skills that are available across the extended enterprise, the use of external competencies and skills is possible. With the integration of the ERP system, visibility of materials information and other critical data are possible. When the tools of PDM are combined with VPDM and integrated with ERP, this has been termed PDMII by the Gartner Group.

The use of a formalized PDMII system also helps in collecting and protecting the enterprise's most valuable asset — its intellectual assets. The virtual product introduction allows the product to be built without really being built physically. The PDM and CAD process allow a variety of required parts to be viewed on a computer screen in three dimensions to assure fit with other parts and checked for any interference between parts. An automotive designer reportedly discovered during computer simulation that the oil filter could not be removed from the engine without lifting the engine off its mounts. This electronic discovery allowed a quick redesign of a fender well to provide clearance. This eliminated a potentially costly rework of tooling after the interference was discovered in a completed car. This virtual fit allows the design engineer to visualize multiple configurations and models. Once this virtual design process is completed the gateway management process provides the decision support and impact analysis of the design decisions. This helps in the overall project management and can significantly reduce the risk in the project. Essential throughout in this whole process is one of easy sharing and reuse of information. When creating new products, there is a need to easily present information to the teams and in the form relevant to the specific role, task, or activity to be carried out in context. This is diagrammed in Figure 8.6. Each of the functional areas integrates through a product creation pipeline to provide a single finished design in a cost-effective manner typically in a fraction of the time required for a serial process. To enable the development teams to work in the correct context, data have to be organized, structured, and accessed according to the specific needs of the extended teams and managed along the product creation pipeline. From all of the data available on the product, the **correct data** has to be selected and presented in the **right place** at the **right time** specific to the task to be carried out. It, therefore, must be (or have)

1. **Configured.** Capable of being integrated into the product design.
2. **Maturity Managed.** Ensuring that only those parts with a proven design are incorporated into future designs.
3. **Secure.** These data represent the intellectual assets of the company and therefore must be treated with a high level of security.

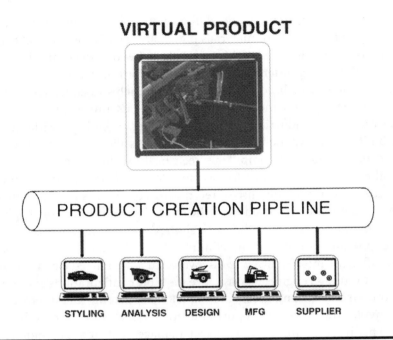

Figure 8.6   Roles impacted by design.

4. **Dependencies Maintained**. If one item is changed in a design, many times there is an impact to other parts in the design. This could be the requirement for tinted glass if there is an air conditioning system installed. Another example could be the need for a particular kind of fastener if a certain kind of wire is used. The linkages back to the tool approach can identify any expensive tooling changes.

5. **Communications Support**. Having information has no benefit if it is not where it is needed when it is needed. Communication support is critical to supporting the concurrent design process.

6. **Traceable**. The source of the information is vital in making good design decisions; not only where the information came from, but also where the information has been used can be tracked in the system. Traceability provides information about other products that may be affected if a change is made to one part.

7. **Activities Managed**. The product design process is directly linked into project management. Completion of parts of the product design is tracked in the overall project schedule.

8. **Extended Enterprise Support.** The extended enterprise includes the suppliers and customers. The data that are developed must be easily shared so it can be used at an appropriate place at the appropriate time.

Gateway Design Management

An effective design management process must include gateway management. The PDM system can track status levels that can represent steps in the design process. These steps can be directly linked to the overall project plan. The status level can also identify substeps. A sophisticated plan may also include transition steps that can be conditional or only take effect on another event happening. Part design maturity is equivalent to an attribute value in this database tracking status levels. The different possible maturity levels are defined in the overall profile for the part. The final level of maturity is the design "freeze." The maturity and status levels are managed separately. The integrated PDM system enables interested parties to be automatically notified as soon as a change occurs. As the status of an object (parts/models/actions) change, PDM has the ability to automatically inform any user (or manager) who subscribes to that object (Figure 8.7).

There is no longer a need to search for information — relevant information is presented to the user automatically. This notification can be inside the company or across the Internet to reach the extended enterprise. Supported by a VPDM system, this notification can also provide an automatic three-dimensional view of the proposed change.

Configuration Management

Configuration management tracks the revisions made to the parts and to the drawings. Part of the ISO9000 requirement is to ensure that the parts were manufactured and assembled according to the desired design. There are a few choices in how to handle this process. The first choice is to change part numbers when there is a change in the fit, form, or function of the part. Some ERP systems provide the functionality of keeping the base part number the same and simply changing the revision of the part in a controlled field. This system would plan part number 140849 revision A independently from part number 140849 revision B. Having the revision code as an integral part of the unique item identification assumes that the parts are not backward

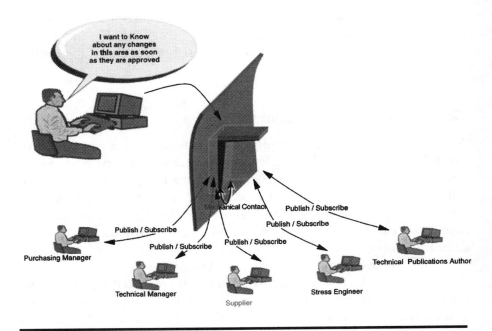

Figure 8.7   Automatic design change communications.

compatible and that a revision A part is not acceptable in the place of a revision B and vice versa.

Buyer beware on this ERP functionality! Ensure that you understand how the system you are considering actually handles this planning process. Many ERP systems will demonstrate that they indeed have revision codes as part of the database only for the users to find out later that it is a text-only field and does not control any functionality. Requirements for revision A and revision B are lumped together. The parts are considered interchangeable in the bin. In addition, getting back to the old configuration at some future point in time may be impossible since nothing is associated directly in the database from this revision code. Some companies have worked around this issue by putting the revision code as the last character in the item identifier or part number. The upside is that the parts are treated as separate and unique parts and the traceability of components is very clean. A customer could order an old configuration of a part with full traceability of requirements and these parts would be separate and distinct in inventory. The downside of this approach is that any customer order for this part must include the correct revision code for that customer's specific requirements. The revision code makes the part number unique and the ERP material planning functionality is very literal in how it calculates. The difference between a 145295A and a 145295B is the same as between a 145295A and a 105827! The system sees the parts as separate and distinct. The other disadvantage is that the part number becomes more difficult to use with the alphanumeric combination.

Another approach to configuration control is to totally change the part number to the next one in a nonsignificant sequence once a change has been made in fit, form, or function. This still provides the traceability without introducing the confusion of an alphabetic character. Some businesses do not require the strict traceability of revision code. The various revisions of a part could be mixed in inventory without any adverse impact on the final product. The important thing to remember is that when a system is selected, this is a critical selection criterion since the different ERP systems handle this process very differently. If a system is required with very strict configuration management, then the buyer should also look for an integrated ECN/ECO (engineering change notice/engineering change order) module in the software tool. Systems exists where the overall part revision cannot be maintained manually but rather an ECN must be started, approved into an ECO, and applied to the part. This is transactionally very expensive. A similar process can also exist for tracking drawing numbers. Drawing numbers can be controlled very similar to part numbers with full ECO/ECN control including revision update and linkages to part numbers. This is the ultimate control for a part in addition to the ultimate in cost. Be sure to purchase and implement the system that is really needed. Simpler, less costly answers may serve the enterprise satisfactorily. This is another reason why the strategy must be fully developed before the tools are selected and implemented.

Implementation

The implementation of PDMII is more than just purchasing technology. An effective PDMII implementation is the unique combination of people, processes, and products including technology that fits the needs of the enterprise. The issues that must be addressed with people to implement PDMII are very similar to those that must be addressed to implement ERP (more detail is provided in Chapter 14). At the very least, the issues that must be address include:

- Teamwork
- An enterprise culture that embraces concurrent participative design
- Sufficient skills for the people who must use the tools
- Education to provide the understanding of what is to be achieved and why
- Effective communication to share this information throughout the extended enterprise

The processes should closely align the vision and goals with the organization's objectives and detailed plans. Customization may be required as the needs, wants, and desires of the customers change over time. Products and technologies include the use of CAD (computer-aided design), CAM (computer-aided manufacturing), CAE (computer-aided engineering), PDM (product data management), VPDM (virtual product data management) tools. The final configured virtual product saves significant time and money. These data must be shared within the enterprise and throughout the extended enterprise so reliable networked computers are needed as part of a complete solution. This is typically achieved through the use of an integration partner to help in the selection and implementation of this technology.

A natural evolution is normal as the enterprise moves from the traditional design process to the fully integrated PDM II. The VPDM is seamlessly integrated with the project management (PM) system to provide real-time and in-depth status of a design. When this is enabled through a secure Internet delivery method, the customer can take a "virtual walkthrough" of the completed product. Many questions can be answered and status can be obtained in an up-to-the-minute manner. However, this agile integrated design process does not come about by itself nor can it be purchased off the shelf. An effective synthesis of knowledge, motivation, and tools is required for this system to be effective. A successful implementation strategy is shown in Figure 8.8.

The tools support the overall strategy of the enterprise. The integration of technology, documentation, and user knowledge is necessary for this strategy to be effective and provide bottom-line results. Any one of these areas alone is insufficient to provide these results. Customization of these tools should be kept to a minimum. Customization can be very expensive to accomplish initially. The cost and aggravation only continues as new releases of the software are completed. Customization should be limited to special reports and queries and not affect code within the application. A help desk needs to be provided so that user's questions can be answered quickly and

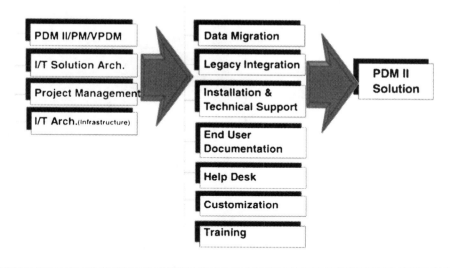

Figure 8.8 A successful implementation strategy.

easily. This is another benefit of not modifying the software; the help desk support can be subcontracted only if no modifications have been made.

Summary

There are many business challenges being faced by industry today. Improvement in new product introduction is critical to address these business challenges. New product introduction was also discussed in Chapter 3 (Sales and Operations Planning) as a major disruptive factor facing the enterprise. To enable design in context, the core requirement is the VPDM which provides an environment to promote product and process innovation and optimization. When this is fully integrated with ERP and PDM tools to provide the real-time access to knowledge and best design practices within the enterprise, the company can realize a significant impact on the bottom-line.

9 Manufacturing Execution System (MES)

Once the plan has been detailed from the business plan through the Sales and Operations Plan and finally through the Material and Capacity plans, the implementation phase can begin. Visibility of actual activity as compared to planned activity is essential in maintaining control of the production operation. This has been named many different things through the years, including production activity control, shop floor control, and, more recently, manufacturing execution systems (MES). The MES system provides a quick and up-to-the-minute view of activities occurring on the shop floor. Recent developments in MES systems have included detailed finite schedulers and optimizers that can quickly replan based on the real-time activity on the floor to provide a realistic schedule to the production personnel.

Finite Schedulers

There are three different basic types of finite schedulers that are typically used as part of the MES system: event-based, job-based, and resource-based.

Event-Based

The event-based finite scheduler only schedules what is immediately visible to it in the best possible sequence. The event-based scheduler is the next technological development representing what the floor supervisor has done for years. Only work that is immediately available is scheduled into the available resources. If the work is not available then no resources are committed. The criticism against this scheduling process is the perception that resources will not be reserved for high-priority jobs. The manual process for event-based scheduling has typically driven up work in process inventory so that something is always available for the resource to work upon. The downside of this manual practice is that this inventory hides the overall effectiveness of the process and drastically increases lead-time. The shop supervisor can only effectively see what is available for work at their individual workcenter and cannot predict the consequences their decisions may have on other workcenters. The MES event-based scheduler provides this true simulation capability and provides a best fit for all jobs based on what is available. In practice event-based systems have been shown to perform better by applying advanced modeling techniques to improve capacity utilization and ensure resource availability for high-priority jobs at the time they are needed. By having sufficient material for processing when the resource is available for work discourages building unnecessary "just in case" work in process.

A major objective of the event-based method is not to waste capacity if demand for the resource exists. The event-based scheduler applies to both critical and noncritical resources and attempts to provide a schedule that best fits the enterprise as a whole using the scheduling objective to eliminate gaps of unused capacity only when there is existing demand for the resource. Of course, if there is no demand for the resource, this resource will be scheduled to stay idle. The event-based scheduler will not increase work in process just to keep a resource busy. The improved scheduling process is designed to reduce overall work in process by the use of more effective schedules.

Job-Based

The job-based scheduler will process the highest priority job first. The priorities can be determined by a variety of methods including first in, first out (FIFO), last in, first out (LIFO), earliest order due date, earliest operation due date, earliest start date, shortest run time, customer priority or manual code. FIFO is a simple process for scheduling that uses the standard queuing process found naturally in most lines. The first job to get to the workcenter would be worked on first. This scheduling process works well if the job arrives in the correct sequence to fit the needs of the customer. However, as variety increases and the process for manufacturing requires more resources to be scheduled in a high variety of possibilities, the likelihood of this happening gets very small. Using FIFO will rarely give an acceptable schedule in the true job shop. As bad a solution as FIFO is, LIFO is even worse. The good news for this approach is that the next job is very easy to find since it was the last one to get here. LIFO is rarely ever used to schedule work in a production environment. LIFO results in FISH inventory — first in still here.

The next approach of earliest order due date begins to introduce the reality of when the order is due to the customer. The earliest due date priority does help in getting attention to the orders that are due first. The downside risk is when the jobs do not require all the same processing time. An order that still has 80 hours and 7 operations to go could be prioritized behind an order that has only 2 hours and 1 operation to go simply because the due date for the second order is first. The reality is that the order with more processing time may need to be started immediately to allow the overall order to be completed on time. This is where using the earliest operation due date as a sequencing tool will usually provide a better answer in a high variety job shop. The operation due dates are calculated either by backward or forward scheduling. In a backward scheduling process, each operation start date is calculated by taking the required completion date and subtracting the number of days of work to calculate a start date. This start date is then further backed up by the desired amount of queue at each operation. This backward scheduling process continues until all operations have been scheduled and a start date for the order is calculated. See the section in Chapter 7 for a detailed description of forward and backward scheduling.

The forward scheduling process starts with today's date and then adds the operation and interoperation times to calculate the expected finish date. The job-based scheduler will then block schedule the resources required for the job depending on the routing for the specific job. In either case, the operation due date incorporates the overall time required for each detailed operation to be completed such that using the operation completion date would provide a more accurate schedule then just focusing on the overall work order due date. An excellent step in getting a shop floor on schedule is to strive to start all orders on the calculated start date. The logic is that if the orders are started on time, then there should be a higher percentage that should finish on time. Using the start date as a priority tool in the job-based scheduling tool provides excellent visibility of what should be started first. This takes into account processing time and overall schedule needs.

Prioritizing shortest run time is a common process for shop supervisors. This is used when the key performance measure is the percentage of orders completed on schedule through a workcenter. If one order requires only 2 hours of work and another needs 20 hours of work, 10 orders could be completed in the same time as only one. If a shop supervisor needed to increase his on time performance, an easy way to do it would be to run all the orders with short processing times. Remember, watch what you measure, you will likely get it! On the other hand, if on-time performance is measured by the number of hours on schedule, then the supervisor will likely place a priority on the longer running orders. There is less time required for setup when one long order is run as opposed to many smaller orders.

Another common way to set priority is by the impact or importance of the customer. Not all customers are created equal. A single customer may account for 40 to 60% of the overall revenue. Another analysis may yield which customers are the most profitable and, therefore, should enjoy priority on the shop floor. Some may say that all customers should be treated alike. The reality is that different customers provide varying amounts of benefit to the bottom line. Why should the customers who are unprofitable get the same treatment as the profitable ones? This process is used in airline frequent flier programs. The more miles a person flies on an airline is directly related to how profitable that customer is for the airlines. The occasional vacation traveler only contributes a small amount of profit to the airline's bottom line. The vacation traveler tends to be more cost conscious and more than likely will select an airline on price. However the business traveler flying over 100,000 miles per year contributes significantly more to the overall profit-ability. They tend to stay with a favored airline due to improved treatment provided the airfare is reasonable. They receive special treatment as their reward. This same process can also be used to schedule work in the shop.

The last prioritization rule is when the priorities are set manually. After all the choices that can be made to set priorities, sometimes discretion is still required for special circumstances. This could be used to manually prioritize a new customer or a new product through the production facility.

No matter which prioritization rule is chosen, the job-based scheduler provides a detailed schedule so that the highest priority jobs are run first. This optimization is done with the impact on each resource examined and a sched-ule is developed with the best overall fit according to the priority rules used.

Resource-Based

The resource-based scheduler is based on the theory of constraints and will schedule the desired sequence to maximize the profit for the firm. This is the logic in the MICSS simulation software that is included with this book. The theory of constraints (TOC) operates from the premise that the enterprise desires to make more money now and in the future. The performance of the weakest link (constraint) limits the degree to which the organization can accomplish its purpose (goal). The integration of TOC into ERP was more fully described in Chapter 2. The resource-based scheduling process sequences product such that the highest profit available is calculated for the firm. The classic theory of constraints problem is referred to as the PQ problem. Assume that the company has limited capacity and that there is no other impact on sales if a customer does not receive the entire product they ordered. The other assumptions are

- There are only two products: P and Q
- There is a well-trained and productive work force
- The quality defect rate is zero
- Selling prices are fixed
- Weekly market demand is fixed
- Labor content is known
- Raw material cost is fixed

In the simulator included with this book, these assumptions and more can be modified and managed. To keep this example simple, a graphic representation of the problem is shown in Figure 9.1.

The finite scheduler would first compare the total requirement to the available capacity. The first pass would determine the bottleneck. In the PQ problem in Figure 9.1, each resource has 2400 minutes available.

For each P	For 100 P
25 minutes of resource A is needed	2500 minutes
30 minutes of resource B is needed	3000 minutes
15 minutes of resource C is needed	1500 minutes
10 minutes of resource D is needed	1000 minutes
$65 material cost	

For each Q	For 50 Q
25 minutes of resource A is needed	1250
30 minutes of resource B is needed	1500
15 minutes of resource C is needed	750
5 minutes of resource D is needed	250
$65 material cost	

Total resource needed to produce total required demand

A	3750 minutes
B	4500 minutes
C	2250 minutes
D	1250 minutes

This put two of the resources above available capacity of 2400 minutes. Both A and B have insufficient capacity. The next question to be asked is what is, "the buffer capacity strategy for the firm?" This was covered in Chapter 4. If the amount of capacity cannot be increased in the short term and the company must produce all the products itself, then the bottleneck or constraint that must be scheduled to is Resource B. There is a 2100-minute overload heading for that resource. To allow all that work onto the shop floor will increase confusion and lead-time incurring cost for materials. When you

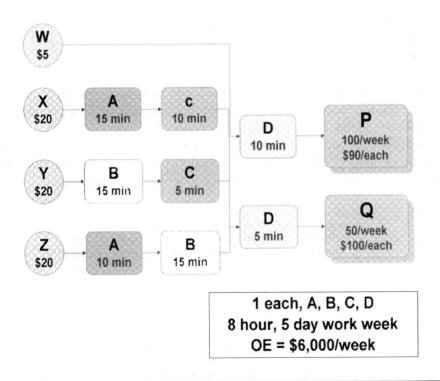

Figure 9.1 P/Q problem.

consider that much of this work will end up sitting for a long time before being worked on, you must question the logic of actually releasing the work to the shop. The cost and cash flow impact of the materials must also be considered. This is why the resource-based finite scheduler is used. Since Q has a higher contribution margin when the throughput value is calculated, it would make sense to build all requirements for Q and consume 1500 minutes of Resource B capacity. The remaining 900 minutes can then be used to build 30 units of P. This plan maximizes the profitability for the firm.

The available capacity for resources A, C, and D can then be utilized to increase production for other products to improve the overall financial results. Until the point that one of these resources becomes the new bottleneck, this incremental capacity can be almost considered as having no cost. This unique examination of cost as it pertains to capacity is the power of theory of constraints as it causes schedules to optimize profitability for the enterprise rather than trying to maximize other less meaningful measures.

Event-Driven Shop Floor Integration

Finite scheduling is just one shop floor management technique that has been developed due to increasing computing power. Although MES has developed quickly as technology has become more powerful, the real functionality of MES goes well beyond the detailed scheduling and optimization advertised by many software companies. The APICS definition provides a better insight into the completeness of these critical tools:

> A factory floor information and communication system includes several functional capabilities, such as resource allocation and status, operation/detailed scheduling, dispatching production units, document control, data collection and acquisition, labor management, quality management, process management, maintenance management, product tracking and genealogy, and performance analysis. It can provide feedback from the factory floor on a real-time basis. It interfaces with and complements accounting-oriented, resource planning systems.

The real power of a MES system is to closely synchronize the shop floor with the demands of the customer while addressing the issues that arise during manufacturing. This is the basis of supply chain. When manufacturing only spends its capacity on what the customer really wants, all links of the chain benefit. This allows the manufacturer to turn productivity into profits rather than into inventory as has been done in the past.

The steps that an implementation will typically experience according to Sami Cassis are

- Accurate plant modeling
- Clear graphical display of results
- Execution management
- "What if" analysis
- Report generation

Notice that once again the first item on the list for a successful implementation begins with the word "accurate." Having accurate bills of materials, routing, and inventory records is essential to be able to move onto advanced techniques like MES and synchronization. Once MES is utilized as a tool, it is also possible to track and integrate tooling and fixture requirements as part of the control system. Without accurate input data, the information provided by the system will be faulty and the decisions made with that information would be incorrect.

Once the data have been entered in the system, the information that can be output can become overwhelming. This is why a graphical display of results is needed. Just like the saying, "a picture is worth a thousand words," a graph can communicate volumes about what is going on in the plant that tables of numbers cannot possibly communicate. This provides the ability to manage the execution of the plan such that only exceptions are identified and managed. The "what if" analysis provides the ability to understand the consequences of decisions before they are put into place at the plant level. Finally, report generation provides hard copy feedback on how effective the plan was compared to the results achieved. This provides the ability to replan where necessary based on what is learned through this closed-loop process. When the input data are accurate and an integrated closed-loop MES process is used to synchronize the plant with demand, the results are quoted to be

- Drastic reduction in cycle time 20 to 89%
- Increased productivity and throughput often as much as 50% or more without additional costs or resources
- 10 to 70% decrease in backlogs and 35 to 90% reduction in WIP
- Significantly improved on-time delivery rate — 90 to 99.9% due date*

---

* Sami Cassis, APICS: The Performance Advantage, June 1997.

Factory Floor Information and Communication

The very first few words in the APICS definition for MES are: "A factory floor information and communication system." For this information and communication system to be accessible on the shop floor, direct connection to the ERP system must be made from the actual work being accomplished. The collection of that data can be through bar coding, direct input from process controllers, integration of discrete counters, or a variety of other methods. The problem has been how to seamlessly integrate these bar code scanners or programmable logic controllers directly to the ERP system. As ERP continues to evolve, systems are becoming easier to link to or more open, but still there must be a connector. This is called middleware. Middleware product includes MQ Series™ and ERP Bridge™. ERP systems are software like JD Edwards, Baan, Oracle, Peoplesoft, QAD, and SAP. This software runs on hardware like Sun, IBM, or HP. Linking software and hardware to these other data collection devices requires middleware. Early in the ERP development process, the ERP software companies saw the benefit of having a standard process for these linkages.

The Open Application Group (OAG) was formed to provide linkage between ERP systems and these desirable subsystems. The OAG is a consortium of some of the world's major ERP vendors including SAP, Oracle, Peoplesoft, QAD, and other technology companies including IBM and Teklogix. The OAG objectives include enabling heterogeneous ERP systems or selected modules to share information and minimize the efforts of performance upgrades. This group realized the benefit for the customer and for the software company to have this kind of connectivity. The OAG process has been for members to define comprehensive business scenarios and the business data, both inputs and outputs required for them to work. The defined BOD (business object document) can then aid in the exchange of information between vendors because it contains all the information required to perform a transaction. The business object document (BOD) is a communication mechanism that requires that each vendor develop middleware to create, exchange, and decompose a BOD transaction. Middleware also supports actual transport of the BOD. Middleware products have become increasingly hardware platform and ERP software independent. This aids in the connectibility of the enterprise system to scanners, bar codes, and other external data collection devices.

Document Control

Document control is a key part of any quality strategy. Documentation of the desired as-designed configuration is essential to building a product that is accurate and meets the design requirements, especially in the companies that build relatively low volumes of individual parts but in very high variety. This is a common requirement in the aerospace industry. Document control includes maintaining traceability of access to the latest version of the drawing.

A key ISO9000 procedure deals with the process of knowing that the latest drawing release is being used for the fabrication and assembly process. An effective engineering change order process must include recognition of document control. However, document control includes significantly more than just drawing documents. Electronic items such as bills of material, item master records, CAD drawings, NC and CNC programs, and routings are also included in document control. Each of these items directly impacts how the product is built and must be controlled to assure the quality of the end item. In medical device, pharmaceutical, aerospace, and defense companies, there also must be control of the work order document as well because this document contains the traceability information required to meet FDA (Food and Drug Administration) or FAA (Federal Aeronautics Administration) requirements. This document contains the materials traceability as well as the operator traceability. The operator must be qualified through a training process to perform the required tasks. This traceability document is usually called the device master record. It is a key document in the overall quality process to assure control of the product and the processes.

The ERP system integrated with the MES functionality are essential tools in the control of these critical documents. The drawing number is normally captured in the item master record. This is usually a text only field. This means that the record captures the information but does not control the planning by this field. This can be a very big issue for a company where revision B is significantly different from revision C. The choices and strategies for managing revision codes was covered in more detail in Chapter 8. One way to assure that only the latest and most up-to-date drawings are being used is to disseminate these drawings and other documents only electronically. The positive side is that the process can assure that only the latest release of the document is being used since there are no authorized paper copies. The downside is that the amount of computing hardware required to provide acceptable response time may be significant. If the information technology infrastructure is insufficient to provide acceptable response time, it is likely that the users will print out the information that they need so they do not have to wait. Waiting for a computer to process is a nonvalue-added activity. This defeats the purpose of distributing this information electronically since there could likely be many different versions of the document on the shop floor, in vendor plants, and innumerable other places.

As the Internet becomes more powerful and access time decreases, multidivisional companies are beginning to use secure web sites supported by PDM (product data management) and VPDM (virtual product data management) systems for the distribution of drawings and other company documents. This provides not only a more convenient way to disseminate this information within the company, but also a way to share this information with authorized suppliers. The use of the Internet is expected to grow as a method to distribute documents and drawings. The main consideration here is if the people use the electronic system. User acceptance is highly dependent on if the site is easy to access and navigate with acceptable response time. Any effective document control system must be easy to use and provide the required information quickly while still controlling the versions.

Data Collection and Acquisition

Data collection and acquisition is the mainstay of any MES or shop floor control system. In the low-volume, high-variety production company, a product may only be produced once for a specific customer order and never again. The desire is to compare the actual cost against the expected cost to determine profitability. This is where labor and materials that are consumed against an order are tracked to that customer order number. Some ERP systems allow materials to be purchased directly to the order without passing through inventory to better support this manufacturing environment. Otherwise, each material that is purchased must have a unique part number and be transacted from inventory to that particular job to be able to track costs accurately. This detailed labor and material tracking is essential for the job shop so that these costs can be compared against the sales price charged on the order to determine the profitability of the order. Data collected may also include component lot numbers and/or serial numbers used on the parent order to allow complete traceability of materials to the end item. This is a key requirement in the aerospace, chemicals, electronics, pharmaceuticals, and semiconductor industries.

Manufacturing shops with higher volumes and lower product variety tend to do process costing rather than job costing. The detailed labor and material data collection provides a validation of the bill of material and routing that is used to plan the part. This validation then closes the loop with the planning systems to ensure that the best possible data are being used to plan capacity and material on an ongoing basis. Statistical process control data also may be charted from the process. Once again the value of the information is directly related to the accuracy of the inputs. If the inputs are poor in quality or lacking in completeness, then the information derived from even the most sophisticated system will be suspect. Having automated data input devices so that the required data collection is a natural by-product of the production process is one way to improve the overall quality of information from the system. The same rule applies to this use of technology as it did to document control. The automated system must be consistently available, easy to use, and have acceptable response time, otherwise the system will not be well used and work-arounds will be developed to obtain the information needed. If there is not a perceived need by the people who supply the data, it is unlikely they will supply complete, accurate data. In the area of product data management, since the data that are collected are typically analyzed and used by an entirely different department, having systems that are easy to use, available, and quick to respond will go a long way in providing usable information.

Labor Management

The traditional use of MES or shop floor systems has been to establish measures for individuals and work groups including efficiency and utilization. This practice is still found in some manufacturing organizations today. Using efficiency and utilization across all operations as a key measure will result in excess inventory as each area attempts to increase its overall output regardless of what is really needed. Areas that are downstream of the bottleneck will quickly become frustrated, as insufficient material is available for them to improve against these measures. Since the overall productivity of the shop is constrained by the bottleneck, the focus of the efficiency and utilization of a resource should be focused only on the bottleneck. Improvements made elsewhere in the manufacturing operation are really a mirage. Only when the capacity of the bottleneck can be increased will the throughput of the operation increase. This is why the integrative measures of throughput, inventory, operating expense, and lead-time are suggested to focus the enterprise on the real goal — making money now and in the future.

Another use of detailed labor management is to feed back information to the advanced planning and scheduling system and the finite scheduler so that the optimal realistic schedule can be produced to guide the plant operations.

If insufficient capacity exists to manage all resources in a cost-effective manner, the main focus can be turned to just the bottleneck and the suspected bottlenecks that may arise if the initial bottleneck is broken. Having accurate data to feed the finite scheduling system will provide better schedules for shop floor execution.

Quality and Process Management

Collection of quality assurance data as part of the manufacturing process provides critical information for overall process improvement. The information on scrap, yield, and defects can be collected as part of the normal shop floor operations and then analyzed later to provide insights on what the core problems may be. Items that can be easily tracked include:

1. The vendors related to the defective incoming parts.
2. The lot numbers that may be suspect.
3. The machines that were used to build the parts.
4. The operator that made the parts.
5. The time of day or shift when the parts were manufactured.

Obtaining this information without an integrated MES system can be very costly and time consuming. As systems become more integrated, getting real-time process data to automatically update the ERP system becomes more feasible. This can include automating statistical process control chart production as the operation is running. It can also include reporting the number of pieces made as a direct result of the machine cycles completed. Computer numerically controlled (CNC) machines can be linked directly to the ERP system to provide closed-loop feedback to the plan. No longer do the islands of automation have to stand isolated; the middleware available for ERP can integrate these multiple systems into a single database. The value of this single database is improved information with which to make decisions.

Maintenance Management

Scheduled preventive maintenance is essential for ensuring maximum machine availability and highest quality parts. Integrating the maintenance management function into the ERP system provides a proactive view of the availability of resources and projected loss of capacity due to maintenance.

Having this proactive view of when machines are scheduled for maintenance allows the planners or the automatic finite scheduling systems to develop a feasible schedule taking this downtime into account. Many companies will run equipment until a breakdown occurs. Murphy's law of manufacturing states that this will always happen at the worst possible time usually when the resource is needed the most. A simple way to begin to incorporate maintenance management into the ERP management system is to put the use of the tools and/or machines on the bill of materials. This way each time a part is made this resource is consumed. When the resource is put into service, the number of expected cycles or processing time is put into inventory. Each work order that uses the identified resource consumes that inventory and the traditional MRP will provide proactive visibility of maintenance requirements based on current production schedules. This way the capacity plan can be determined which allows the refurbishment and/or replacement of the tooling. An example is below.

Bill of Material
Product A
    Material X   3 each per A
    Material Y   7 each per A
    Tool ABC   0.5 hours per A

    Cutter ZDW   1 cycle per A

Tool ABC is brand new and is expected to last for 500 production hours
Cutter ZDW must be resharpened every 1000 cycles

Once we have the schedule for Product A order release, we can calculate cutter use, tool sharpening schedules, and tool replacement timing.

Maintenance Support	1	2	3	4	5	6	7	8	9	10
Product A schedule	200	200	300	200	175	200	200	300	400	200
Tool ABC demand	100	100	150	100	87.5	100	100	150	200	100
Remaining Tool ABC life	400	300	150	50	462.5	362.5	262.5	112.5	412.5	312.5
Planned Tool ABC replacement					500				500	

Maintenance Support	1	2	3	4	5	6	7	8	9	10
Cutter ZDW demand	200	200	300	200	175	200	200	300	400	200
Remaining Cutter ZDW life	800	600	300	100	925	725	525	225	825	625
Planned Cutter ZDW sharpening					1000				1000	

In this simple example above, the tool replacement and the cutter sharpening are scheduled in the same time period. However, as the tools are linked to more common parent items and the cutters are used on more items, this situation can change drastically. The table below is a simple example of how these two resources can quickly become unsynchronized in their maintenance requirements.

Maintenance Support	1	2	3	4	5	6	7	8	9	10
Tool ABC demand	100	100	300	100	87.5	450	100	375	500	100
Remaining Tool ABC life	400	300	0	400	312.5	362.5	262.5	387.5	387.5	287.5
Planned Tool ABC replacement				500		500		500	500	
Cutter ZDW demand	400	400	800	400	375	1100	400	950	1200	400
Remaining Cutter ZDW life	600	200	400	0	625	525	125	175	−25	575
Planned Cutter ZDW sharpening			1000		1000	1000		1000	1000	1000

In this planning diagram there are three instances where the cutter requires sharpening before the ABC tool needs replacement. Also in Period 9 the cutter is not expected to be able to finish all the parts before it needs sharpening. Once the planner has visibility such as this of the requirements and planned replacements of tools and fixtures, the best business decisions can be made based on data and fact. Possibly one of the orders in Period 9 can be reduced in quantity so that the cutter does not have to be sharpened until Period 10. Also, the planner also would have some past actual data from the MES system on how exact the life of the tool sharpening really is. It may be possible to run the tool for an extra 25 cycles without a major concern. This is one of the reasons why having an integrated MES system can provide such a competitive advantage.

Product Tracking and Genealogy

Many industries require product tracking and genealogy. Consumer products, pharmaceuticals, aerospace, defense, and medical devices are just a few examples. Product tracking and genealogy is required whenever there is a desire or requirement to answer the following questions:

1. From what source did the materials come that were used in this product?
2. When were these materials received?
3. Where were the materials used that were received from that particular supplier?
4. To whom were the finished good materials shipped?
5. If a lot is found defective, where else was it used?
6. Who received these lots?

A significant number of transactions are required to provide this level of traceability. The expected process is to have a work order issued for each part or parts lot to which materials are issued and labor is reported. The issue transaction includes not only how many parts were used but also what lot number or serial number was used. Once the traceability process is started this process must be continued up through the remaining levels in the bill of material to the end item. This detailed issuing process fits the low-volume, high-variety production of aerospace and defense very well.

However, in the medical device and pharmaceuticals businesses, the products are usually high volume and low in variety. This type of manufacturing process would normally use a backflushing process for material and labor. Backflushing is when the materials are deducted after the product is completed based on the bill of material multiplied by the lot size. Unfortunately, backflushing is not possible in a traceability environment. This is because there is no possible way for the ERP system to know which lot number or serial number was actually used. The standard process of issuing to work orders is normally used for transacting these orders. However, the timing of these transactions can occur after the product is completed so that the benefits of backflushing can be realized while still capturing the traceability data.

This is just one way that ERP systems can be creatively applied to meet the needs of the business and produce a bottom-line benefit. More examples of detailed ERP application by industry is outlined in Chapters 15 to 19.

Performance Analysis

Performance analysis is the final facet of MES. The main purpose of the MES system is to provide the data from which the analysis can be completed to provide feedback on the performance of the enterprise. Before performance analysis can be effective, the goals and strategic direction of the enterprise must be determined. A 1994 benchmark survey of critical success factors in materials management published by APICS included six key measures. These were inventory accuracy, kit accuracy, on-time supplier delivery, percentage accepted by incoming inspection, bill of material accuracy, and inventory turns. These critical measures still retain importance today in even the most sophisticated ERP systems. The accuracy measures are covered in more depth in Chapter 13. More recently the focus has shifted to theory of constraints (TOC) measures. These measures focus on improving the overall profitability of the enterprise over time. The key TOC measures include throughput, inventory, and operating expense. Throughput is the rate at which the system generates money through sales. This can be calculated as sales minus totally variable expense $(s - tve)$. Totally variable expenses are those expenses that if you didn't have the sale, you wouldn't have incurred the expense. Inventory is all of the money the system spends on things it intends to turn into throughput, including raw materials, work in process, finished goods, all at the price paid to the vendor. Inventory also includes buildings, equipment, other assets, and know-how. Operating expense is all of the money the system spends in order to turn inventory into throughput. Operating expense includes salaries, wages, benefits, utilities, insurance, lease, interest, taxes, etc. Operating expense is not just another term for "fixed costs." These building blocks then can be used for financial analysis including:

Net Profit (NP)	$= T - OE$
Return on Investment (ROI)	$= NP/I$
Productivity	$= T/OE$
Inventory Turns	$= T/I$
Throughput per Constraint Unit (T/Cu)	= Throughput generated per unit of time

More detail about TOC in an ERP environment was provided in Chapter 2. Whatever measure is used, the MES system provides the detailed data to feed the analysis and judgements required to manage the enterprise.

Summary

MES control begins once the plan has been detailed from the business plan through the Sales and Operations Plan and finally through the material and capacity plans. MES provides visibility of actual activity as compared to planned activity and is essential in maintaining control of the production operation. An effective MES system provides a quick and up-to-the-minute view of activities occurring on the shop floor. Recent developments in MES systems have included detailed finite schedulers and optimizers that can quickly replan based on the real-time activity on the floor to provide a realistic schedule to the production personnel. The other functions of the MES system include resource allocation and status, operation/detailed scheduling, dispatching production units, document control, data collection and acquisition, labor management, quality management, process management, maintenance management, product tracking and genealogy, and performance analysis. The real key for MES is to measure what needs to improve and provide quick response and feedback on the progress and performance. You can think of MES as the speedometer and odometer of a car. Unless you know where you are going, the data may be nice but it is not very meaningful. In the same way, MES can provide a significant amount of data, but usable information comes from the context and analysis of that data.

MES Resources and References

MESA, MES Association — MESA was formed in the Fall of 1992 by manufacturing execution system (MES) software vendors. MESA is a not-for-profit trade association providing a legal forum for competitors to work together to expand awareness and use of manufacturing technology, particularly MES and all the related products and services required by the modern manufacturing enterprise. http://www.mesa.org

10 Distribution

Distribution is a key part of the integrated supply chain. The distribution activities are associated with the movement of material, usually finished products or service parts, from the manufacturer to the customer. These activities encompass the functions of transportation, warehousing, inventory control, material handling, order administration, site and location analysis, industrial packaging, data processing, and the communication network necessary for effective management. During the 1997 World Symposium in Sun City, South Africa, Hal Mather's keynote address focused on the fact that for the first time the cost of logistics now exceeds the cost of labor for most companies. Distribution is being reevaluated as the cost to move material is changing and information flows become more global.

Managing distribution effectively through the enterprise system can mean the difference between an agile supply chain that is responsive to the customer or piles of excess inventory in the wrong place at the wrong time. Truly integrated ERP systems have tightly integrated distribution function rather than just a loose interface.

Warehousing

Synonymous with distribution for many people is warehousing. In fact, warehousing is only one facet of distribution. Warehousing is limited to the activities related to receiving, storing, and shipping materials to and from production or distribution locations. These activities are directly supported by the ERP management system. The ERP system collects all the information about material movements and storage locations. These transactions provide the information required to promise customer orders and track inventory investment. Warehousing, therefore, is transaction intensive due to the use

205

of multiple locations and possibly multiple warehouses. The detail of site location and rack location is needed to provide correct material allocation and an efficient pick route when filling customer orders. In a company that requires lot or serial number traceability, the warehousing function becomes even more transaction intensive. This environment is an excellent fit for utilizing bar code technology. Bar coding reduces the time required to complete a transaction and improves the overall accuracy of the information. The bar code equipment reads the information that has been encoded by the chosen bar code format. This is transacted directly into the computer system with little or no human intervention.

The layout of a warehouse contributes greatly to its overall effectiveness and efficiency. Material movement distance should be minimized. Driving inventory around a warehouse is in fact a nonvalue-added activity. By developing an efficient warehouse layout, this kind of activity can be kept to a minimum. It is preferable to accept receipts at a different location from where shipments are made. Having these two functions separated prevents cross tracking inventory and minimizes confusion. A clear flow can be established where product arrives, is stored, then picked, and shipped. Figure 10.1 shows a warehouse with an effective flow through design. If this is not possible then discipline must be established in the warehouse to ensure that incoming shipments are put away in the desired location before the outbound shipments are staged.

Fixed Location Storage

Three methods exist for storing distribution inventory. The first is to store the parts in a fixed location. This location is allocated to the part regardless of the level of inventory that is on hand. Fixed location can provide easier memorization and recall of part location. This strategy is used in many companies where location tracking is not done. Distribution personnel remember where parts have been located. When this process is used these companies will typically store inventory sequenced by part number. This is also known as stocking in rotation. Storing inventory in sequence by part number may appear to the uninitiated to make sense since the inventory is in a predictable order and, therefore, should be easy to find. Additional transactions are not needed to track the unique locations. The reality is that this requires the highest level of maintenance and control. Rarely do consecutive numbers have the same shelf space or storage requirements. Having

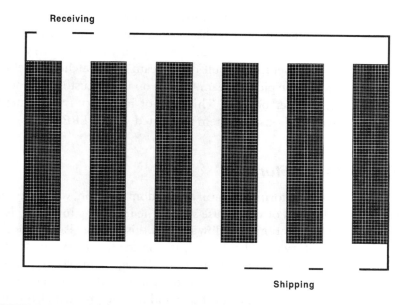

Receiving

Shipping

Figure 10.1   Warehouse with effective flow through design.

fixed locations results in wasted space in the warehouse since allocated shelf locations are held open waiting for inventory to arrive. The space on the shelf must be able to accommodate the total receipt quantity for the part. This means that for most of the time, available space is not being well used since the reserved space will be larger than the inventory in it. If the received quantity is larger than expected, then the stockroom is forced to either reposition the entire inventory to accommodate that quantity in the correct sequence or, more commonly, the excess inventory will be placed in an overflow position. If the company does not transact inventory locations, finding this inventory in overflow can be a real challenge. Manual systems are developed in an attempt to track this inventory and the location. Rarely do they work very well.

Another option for fixed location supports a warehouse that tends to have low product variability. If the warehouse tends to ship the same product mix over a period of time, then fixed locations can be used effectively. An optimization program can be run on the products that are shipped. Those items that are shipped frequently are stored closest to the shipping area. Those items that are used less frequently are stored farther away. This strategy is used to minimize the pick time required to assemble an order. To aid in the picking process, the pick locations are only those locations that can be accessed without using a forklift. This speeds the picking process dramatically. Overflow inventory is stored in random locations on higher racks. When the pick location runs low on inventory, a pull-down team is dispatched to relocate the needed inventory. The picking team focuses on filling customer orders in the most efficient manner possible. This type of inventory management is part of an effective warehousing system integrated within ERP.

Random Location Storage

The second method for storing inventory is random location, which provides the maximum utilization of warehouse space. The incoming inventory is put away in any available location. The downside of this strategy is that the exact location of the inventory must be documented in the formal system through transactions. A more sophisticated warehouse management system may suggest the best location based on the expected future orders for the product based on forecast or backlog. The past demand for the product also may be used to determine a suggested location. The assumption is made that future consumption should look like the past. In the random location strategy, the same part number could potentially be stored in multiple locations in the same warehouse. The order picking logic then provides visibility of these different picking locations and based on the picking rules can suggest a picking order.

This strategy assumes that stocking locations are uniquely identified. Identifying specific locations assists in finding the exact location of the part. An easy method for coding locations is the descending significance relationship. Unlike part number identification where significant numbering creates complexity, having significant identifiers for inventory locations simplifies the inventory management process. If multiple storerooms are used, the first digit could be the location of the storeroom. This could also be indicative of the warehouse location as well. Alphabetic characters work well and for most companies will give ample uniqueness with one digit. This also prevents the confusion of part number and inventory locations. Part identification should be only numeric and utilize no alphabetic characters or other miscellaneous characters. The next set of characters is the rack on which the parts are stored. Usually two digits are sufficient. The next digit is the shelf, starting at the bottom with zero or one. Numbering is started at the bottom shelf to allow growth in the upwards vertical direction. Additional specifics can be built in with the location on the shelf. For example a part stored in P2634 is stored in distribution center P, on rack 26, on the third shelf in the fourth position. A part in R1401 is in stockroom R, on rack 14, on the bottom shelf in the first position. With very short identifiers, over 200,000 locations can be uniquely identified. Parts are easier to find because the system is very consistent, predictable, and simple. This system provides maximum utilization of space but does require transaction control supported by an ERP system to effectively manage distribution inventory.

Zone Management Storage

The third method for storing inventory is a combination of fixed and random. This is known as zone management. Zone management is used to manage inventory with different storage requirements. All components sharing a storage characteristic are stored in the same zone. Within the zone a random location or fixed location strategy can be followed. For example, all electronic components can be stored in a rack that is specially designed with static discharge functionality. Centralizing these components in the same area minimizes the duplication of this equipment to properly manage this inventory. Small parts can be stored in a location that has a weigh scale close by. This minimizes the amount of travel time required to count parts to fill an order. Parts that require special temperature or humidity can then be centralized into one location. Components requiring special equipment like a crane or forklift are stored in a different zone. The zone management method requires some inventory location tracking. If a random location strategy is utilized within the zone, then the requirement for location tracking is the same as the random location strategy.

Three Strategies for Picking Inventory

"Out and Back" Picking

There also are three strategies for picking inventory. The first is an "out and back" pattern. The out and back pattern is when the storekeeper moves through the stockroom to collect items for a single order or customer. The advantage of this approach is that one order is fully picked at a time until completion. The storekeeper who picked the order is directly accountable. The arrival of orders into the shipping area is fairly steady throughout the day. The disadvantage of this approach is that a storekeeper may retrace his steps many times in single day. Although the arrangement of inventory can help minimize the travel distance, the amount of time spent picking orders can be quite significant.

Route Collection Picking System

The second strategy is a route collection system. The route collection system sends the storekeeper through the entire warehouse collecting parts for a group of orders. This approach minimizes the travel distance for the storekeeper. The downside of this approach is that orders arrive in large quantity at the shipping location. Working through this queue can take significant time and the shipments may be delayed. Also, there is a potential for confusion of parts between orders that are picked at the same time.

Zone Picking System

The third choice is to utilize a zone system. The zone system approach consolidates the picking in one zone for a group of orders. The parts from each zone are then sent to the shipping department. Specific customer orders are then separated in the shipping area. The advantage of this approach is that an individual storekeeper can become an expert in a particular zone. The amount of travel required for each storekeeper is also minimized. The disadvantage is that secondary processing is required in the shipping department and potential errors may result. Understanding the advantages and disadvantages of each approach is important before deciding which is the best for your particular enterprise. The warehouse management system functionality within an ERP system can provide a recommended shortest pick route for any of the three strategies.

Lot Tracking

In addition to inventory location, the warehouse may also need to track lot number, serial numbers, or expiration dates. This product traceability is required in many industries in the event that a product recall is required. This product lineage is continued from the manufacturing process all the way through to the customer who receives the product. This additional information also may be used to develop a recommended pick sequence. The two most common pick sequencing strategies are FIFO (first in, first out) and FEFO (first expiration, first out). LIFO (last in, first out) is a costing alternative but is not suggested for inventory management. This results in FISH inventory management (first in still here). FIFO is when the first parts that are received are the first parts to be shipped out the door. FEFO is when the system looks at the expiration date and suggests the pick sequence based on the first product to expire. This is used for an enterprise that may receive products with expiration dates that are out of sequence with the receipt date.

Transportation

The final operation of warehousing is transportation. Transportation is the function of planning, scheduling, and controlling activities related to mode, vendor, and movement of inventories into and out of an enterprise. The choices facing the enterprise can include the trade-off of lot sizes for transportation costs. Large inventory quantities can be moved for low costs by using ocean containers and railroad cars. The lead-time for delivery is also very long. The low cost is offset by the high inventory carrying costs resulting from these large batch sizes and long travel times. Smaller batch sizes that minimize the inventory carrying cost cannot be carried by these low cost shipping modes. The selection of a transportation supplier is a key decision. Choosing a supply partner based on geographic location can provide a cost advantage for the enterprise. Logistics is more than just trucking. Working with the best partner as part of a fully integrated supply chain can provide a competitive advantage. The linkage to the supply chain was explored in Chapter 6.

Site and Location Analysis

Selecting the site for the distribution center is a key decision for the enterprise. This is a decision that is not routine or made every day. However, it is a decision that needs to be regularly reviewed as the customer base, product mix, transportation cost, and tax advantages change. As the rate of global competition changes increase, the distribution decision should be reviewed at least every 2 years. Understanding the impact of all these costs and potential benefits on the enterprise is important when selecting the best site for distribution. The transportation method is a quantitative approach that can help solve multiple facility location problems. This method utilizes computer-modeling tools to provide an effective allocation of work between enterprise locations. The distance material has to travel is minimized by using this analysis. The transportation method does not solve for all facets of the multiple facility location problems, but is acceptable for reviewing allocation of work between facilities.

A heuristics solution utilizes guidelines or rules of thumb to help simplify the site and location analysis. The advantage of a heuristics solution is that past experience can be incorporated into the decision with easy to understand guidelines. This can include proximity to a highway network or a preferred geographic location. However, even though heuristics will provide a feasible solution, the guidelines may not provide the most optimal solution. Heuristics can provide an acceptable solution for a relatively small distribution network at a reasonable price.

Optimization requires more sophistication in modeling the enterprise and typically utilizes a computer. This computer program can be as simple as a spreadsheet or as complex as a full simulation model. An effective optimization program can minimize the various costs and maximize the benefits for the enterprise. If distribution represents a large portion of the company's business, developing these sophisticated computer models is probably a worthwhile investment. The initial cost of development can be significant. However, the incremental cost to change the individual parameter values is relatively low. Unless this is a core competency for the enterprise, this is an excellent area to engage outside resources. A company that does simulation for their core business likely has templates that can be adapted to your company at a fraction of the cost to develop them from scratch. Computer optimization also provides the resources needed to run several "what if" scenarios to evaluate options that could potentially benefit the business.

Inventory Control

Inventory control in the distribution enterprise is different from a manufacturing enterprise. In manufacturing a high level of accuracy is possible when ordering materials because the component materials are directly related to the master schedule for the parent items. If manufacturing is scheduled to build 200 chairs, the calculation to determine requirements for legs (800), seats (200), and backs (200) is relatively simple. This requirement is compared to the projected available inventory and the need to order can be correctly determined. This high level of accuracy in calculating requirements means that little safety stock is required to ensure availability of parts when needed. Inventory control for the distribution company can be anything but predictable. Demand on the distribution center usually comes directly from the customer. When customer demand is analyzed over time, it is relatively continuous. Different forecasting methods are used to analyze past demand and project future demand. Safety stock is used to guard against variability in demand. Regional consolidation warehouses experience very lumpy demand as the end item distribution center restocks its inventory in batches. This multilevel distribution network is an excellent situation in which to use DRP (distribution requirements planning).

Forecasting

In distribution the lead-time to procure and receive a product exceeds the time that the customer is willing to wait. This is the reason why the distribution center exists. Therefore, demand must be forecast so that inventory can be available when the customer places their order. The three basic rules of forecasting are

1. The forecast is always wrong.
2. The forecast is less accurate farther in the future.
3. The forecast is less accurate in finer detail.

However, forecasts should pay dividends in excess of their cost to develop. A forecast that is 20% wrong is still 80% right. Not forecasting will always provide an answer that is 100% wrong. In distribution another alternative to forecasting is to use an order point system. The order point system is simple to set up and use. When the inventory falls below the established order point, an order is placed to replenish. This works well if the demand for a product stays relatively stable over time, experiences no seasonality, and is stable for configuration. If any of these requirements are violated, the order point system does not work very well. In addition, order point will not provide proactive planning for distribution management.

Forecasting can take two major forms, qualitative and quantitative. Qualitative forecasting is often a gut feel opinion of what sales will be. By default, every company has used this method of forecasting. The qualitative method is most commonly used because there is a general lack of understanding about how to do quantitative forecasting. Quantitative forecasting uses past sales numbers to calculate a reasonable estimate for future demand. A phobia about doing numerical calculations can inhibit the use of quantitative forecasting for some people. Reasonably priced forecasting systems are being incorporated into integrated ERP systems. This reduces the fear factor and allows the forecast to be prepared using the data that are collected by the system as a product of normal operations.

For companies without this functionality in their ERP software, some simple but commonly used quantitative tools for forecasting independent demands are described below.

Simple Moving Average

This is the simplest, most commonly used method of quantitative forecasting. Simple moving average can be completed with very basic tools. The last few periods of actual demand data are added then averaged. The result is used as the future forecast. The advantage of this method is that it is easy to understand and compute. The disadvantage is that it is rarely the best solution. The best use of simple moving average is for relatively stable data. The number of periods that are chosen to average will determine the responsiveness of the forecast. Including more periods means the forecast will respond more slowly to the changes in the data. Fewer periods mean that the forecast will respond more quickly to data changes.

Example
Most recent sales: 120, 125, 135
Forecast for next period: $(120 + 125 + 135)/3 = 126.6$ or 127
However, the sales for next month were really 140.
Forecast for next period: $(125 + 135 + 140)/3 = 133.3$ or 134.
(The forecast was rounded up even though arithmetic rules would state that the number should be 133. When any remainder is left, the number is always rounded up. Since partial parts are not an option, the best choice is to always increase the forecast by one unit.)

Another disadvantage is that this only provides a forecast one period into the future. To project farther into the future increases the risk of error. The downside of this method of forecasting severely limits its application, but simple moving average is commonly used because it is simple to understand and calculate.

Weighted Moving Average

This method is an improvement on the simple moving average. Weighted moving average takes advantage of the fact that, usually, the most recent past is a better predictor of the future than the remote past. The weights are at the discretion of the forecaster. The amount of weight given to the most recent past is one way that management can influence the overall inventory and responsiveness strategy. The more weight put on the recent past, the more reactive the organization will be to changes in the market. The less weight put on the recent past provides a more stable schedule for manufacturing. No matter which strategy is chosen the total of all the weights must equal 1. Most commonly used weights are 0.7 and 0.3 or 0.5, 0.3, and 0.2. The important thing to remember is that the heaviest weight goes to the most recent history and that all weights must add up to 1.0.

Using the same data that the simple moving average used in the previous example, changing the forecasting method and this results in a very different answer.

Example
Three period weighted moving average
Forecast for next month (using the first 3 months of data and weights of 0.2, 0.3, and 0.5) would be $(0.2)(120) + (0.3)(125) + (0.5)(135) = 129$.
Assume that the actual demand for the previously forecasted month was 140. Forecast for next month would be $(0.2)(125) + (0.3)(135) + (0.5)(140) = 135.5$ or 136.

The weighted average is more responsive to changing demand than the simple moving average. The forecast picked up the change in the demand and increased the forecast accordingly. The amount of weight put on the most recent past is a management decision. More weight put on the most recent history causes the forecast to react even more strongly. If the weights used are changed, the answer also changes.

Example
Two period weighted moving average
Forecast for the same two periods would be $(0.3)(125) + (0.7)(135) = 132$.
Compare this to the three-period simple moving average answer (127) or the three-period weighted moving average (129). The fewer the number of periods that are used, the more responsive the forecast.

The next period experiences the same phenomenon when the forecast is calculated at $(0.3)(135) + (0.7)(140) = 138.5$ or 139.

Given just a few data points and two simple forecasting techniques, three very different answers have been calculated. Which one is right? The answer is that they all are. The best tool for the job is one that fits the data patterns best.

Trend Analysis

Sometimes there is a strong pattern to the data. One of the strongest patterns is trend. Trend analysis acknowledges that the sales of an item can sometimes be predicted by the passage of time. The ever-increasing sales over time is the best-fit application of this forecast technique. Simply looking at the graph or calculating a trend line using past demand data can do the calculation of the forecast. Another method is to use a spreadsheet to find the line of best fit. When trend is suspected, the best way to confirm the impression is to graph the data. Remember the old saying, "a picture is worth a thousand words." This is true in forecasting. A good first step when manually developing forecasts is to graph the data. Insights can be gained from just looking at the data displayed graphically.

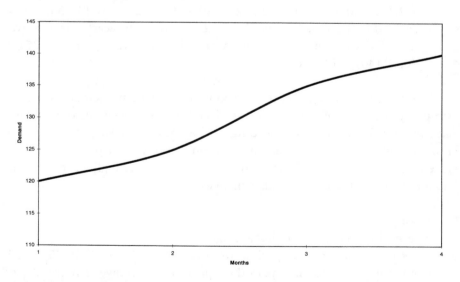

Figure 10.2   Trend demand pattern.

Just by inspecting the graph in Figure 10.2, the next logical forecast for Month 5 would be greater than 140. Examining the graph, the forecast could be set around 145 with some confidence. Another way to calculate the trend is to take the end point and the beginning point and calculate the average trend.

Example
Trend calculation
Trend = (End point − beginning)/number of periods
Trend = (140 − 120)/3 = 6.67
Forecast = End point + trend
Forecast = 140 + 6.67 = 147

Using a spreadsheet, the best-fit line gave the result of 147.5 or 148. The difference between the naïve method (145), the average trend method (147), and the more precisely calculated method using a spreadsheet (148) is minimal in this case. Given a different set of data, the results of these three methods of calculating trend may not be as close. The best initial tool to use with any method is the graph. Looking at a graphical representation of the data can reveal many insights that are not evident in the data table.

Seasonality

Some product demand is seasonal. Examples of seasonal business are manufacturers of snowmobiles, snow skis, camping equipment, water skis, and lawnmowers. Items are built all year but are used mainly during one period of the year. This pattern of consumption tends to recur on an annual basis. Seasonality forecasting tools, also known as indexing, are used for seasonal products with higher accuracy than any of the tools described so far. Indexing calculates the recognizable pattern in the data and uses it for forecasting future data. The pattern can be calculated rather precisely. Only the average change in baseline from year to year must be forecast.

Product Sales

Quarter	Year 1	Year 2
1	50	60
2	75	90
3	62	75
4	45	52

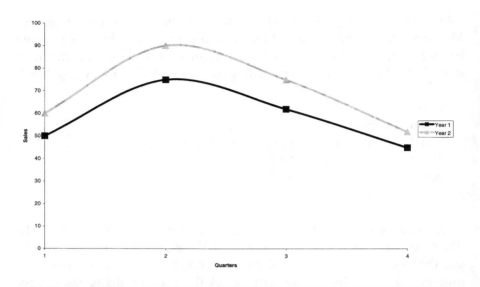

Figure 10.3 Seasonality demand pattern.

Assume that the above table contains the previous 2 years of sales data. Once again the data are graphed and the seasonality of the demand is very apparent. There is an increase in sales during the second quarter and sales decline during the final quarter of the year. In addition, the product has increased in sales between Year 1 and Year 2. Not only does the product appear to experience seasonality, a trend is also evident. The forecast must take into account both phenomena. To calculate the forecast, first the seasonality is determined (Figure 10.3).

Step 1: To calculate the seasonality, the 2 years are totaled. This is displayed in the column labeled Step 1. The simple average is then calculated for this total. The number "127.25" is not indicative of any sales projection but is a necessary step in the computation.

Step 2: The next step is to take the average of the totals (127.25) and divide it into the total for each quarter. This results in the numbers displayed in the column marked Step 2. The first entry is $110/127.25 = 0.86$. The display has been rounded to two decimal points for clarity. These index weights should add to the total number of periods used for indexing, or in this example — four. The meaning of these numbers is that in the first quarter, typically only 86% of average sales is experienced. The second quarter is greater than average with an index of 1.30. This means that in the second quarter the firm can expect to sell 130% of average. If the demand pattern were level each quarter, the indexes would all equal one. Since the data are seasonal, these weights are essential in the forecasting process. If only a simple average were used, sales would look very bad in the first quarter, great in the second and third quarters, and very bad again in the fourth quarter. Actions could be taken that are unnecessary to correct an expected and repeatable fluctuation in demand.

Step 3: The next step is to forecast the average sales per quarter for the next year. Since the first year's average is 58 per quarter and the next year's average is 69.25 per quarter, a trend of 11 units per quarter is used. This results in an average forecast of 80 per quarter (69 + 11). But, since the data are obviously seasonal, this forecast must be reseasonalized into the appropriate quarters. This projection is multiplied by the seasonality factors calculated in Step 2. The forecast for next year is displayed in the column marked Step 3.

Product Sales			Step 1	Step 2	Step 3
Quarter	Year 1	Year 2	Total	Index	Forecast
1	50	60	110	0.86	69
2	75	90	165	1.30	104
3	62	75	137	1.08	86
4	45	52	97	0.76	61
Average	58	69.25	127.25	4.00	80

The advantage of using a seasonalized forecast is that unusual trends can be identified sooner. For example, if sales during the first quarter are 80, the forecaster will suspect that possibly sales may be higher than expected for the year since only 69 were expected to be sold. On the other hand, if the sales for the first quarter are 68, this is accepted as a normal fluctuation and is not cause for concern. The sales in the first quarter are expected to be less than the average. Seasonality allows the calculation of patterns for demand and removes this expected pattern from interfering with the real forecast issues.

Selecting a Method

Using a combination of these simple methods can result in rather sophisticated forecasting models capable of high levels of responsiveness and accuracy. Selecting which tool to use can look confusing. Actually using different possible methods on demand data that are already known makes the selection much easier. A forecaster might take actual data from 2 years ago and test several methods to forecast last year's sales. The forecaster would then compare the forecast to last year's actual sales. The method that most accurately forecast the known actual sales would be selected for future forecasting.

For a distribution operation of more substantial size, software packages are available that automatically do these calculations and best fit the forecasting method to the data. These forecasting packages can be costly but should be justified based on improved inventory management. If higher forecast accuracy is needed than can be developed with the simple tools described here, the software investment is perhaps worthwhile.

Since forecasts are at best an estimate of the future, measuring and managing the amount and type of error is important to manage effectively. Some tools used to measure forecast accuracy are error, bias, and standard error.

Error

This is the simplest of the accuracy measures. Error is calculated by subtracting the forecast from the actual number (actual – forecast). When all the error numbers are added together (cumulative error) and the pluses and minuses are allowed to cancel each other out, a rough measure of accuracy can be obtained. This error measure is individually calculated for each forecasted part.

Actual Sales Compared to Forecast

Quarter	Actual	Forecast	Error
1	69	72	−3
2	104	101	3
3	86	82	4
4	61	59	2
Cumulative error			6

The closer the error number is to zero the better the forecast. If the total error is positive, the conclusion is that the forecast has been consistently too low. If the total error is negative, the forecast has been consistently too high. In this example, the forecast has been cumulatively too low. Adjustments can be made based on the size and direction of the total error. One weakness of cumulative error is that it depends on where the starting point is identified. Bias can be better used to measure overall performance.

Bias

Bias addresses the question of the cumulative starting point by averaging the error over the number of periods for the forecast. Bias is calculated by adding all the errors and dividing by the number of errors that were added. Positive and negative numbers still are allowed to cancel each other.

Bias Calculation — Actual Sales Compared to Forecast

Quarter	Actual	Forecast	Error
1	69	72	-3
2	104	101	3
3	86	82	4
4	61	59	2
Cumulative error			6
Bias			6/4 = 1.5

Just like error, if the bias is positive, the forecast has been too low, on average. If the bias is negative, the forecast has been too high, on average. In this example, the forecast has been too low on average. The closer the bias is to zero means that the forecast, on average, is more precise. The problem with average bias is that when each period is examined, the amount of error could be huge but the errors could average out in the end. A seasonal demand pattern could have a very small error or bias over the course of the year, but be way off in any single month or quarter. From a real world approach for effective distribution, forecast accuracy is required for each replenishment period, not just over a long average period. This variability of demand is the reason behind safety stock inventory in distribution. An improved way to assess the real accuracy of the forecast is to use the standard error.

Standard Error (Standard Deviation)

The disadvantage of the error and bias is that the positive and negative errors can cancel each other out. The error and bias can both be zero and the forecast can swing wildly. The usefulness of this highly variable forecast is questionable. The effect on customer service and inventory levels is devastating. Either there is insufficient inventory to service demand or excess inventory on hand. When the forecast is less than demand, the customer could be asked to wait. The customer may not be willing to wait and will take the business to another distributor that can supply the item when requested. This effect can severely impact a distributor. In distribution, items are forecast individually and the customer expects a rapid order fulfillment time — the worst of both worlds.

Standard error does not allow the pluses and minuses to cancel out each other. The benefit of the standard error is that the dispersion of the forecast is calculated. Standard error assesses the overall variability of the forecast error. Variability is the gremlin of any distribution process. When a process is extremely reliable and predictable, no inventory or excess capacity is needed. When a process is widely variable, safety stock or capacity is used to buffer against unexpected events. Forecasts are estimates of the unknown. The more reliable these estimates are, the less safety inventory and capacity are required to provide excellent customer service. Even though the forecast may jump around due to expected events like seasonality and promotions, if these changes can be identified correctly, safety stock is still not required. Managing abnormal demand was covered in detail in Chapter 7.

Calculating Standard Error

Step 1: The standard error is calculated by first squaring all the errors (multiply the error by itself).

Step 2: Add the squared errors together.

Step 3: The next step divides the cumulative error by the number of data points minus one and then the square root is taken to find the standard error.

Sales Standard Error Calculations				Step 1
Month	Forecast (F)	Actual (A)	Error (A-F)	Error squared
1	100	97	−3	9
2	100	110	10	100
3	100	102	2	4
4	100	105	5	25
5	100	115	15	225
6	100	103	3	9
7	100	124	24	576
8	100	130	30	900
9	100	100	0	0
10	100	103	3	9
11	100	120	20	400
12	100	122	22	484
Step 2: Total				2741
Step 3: Standard Error				15.79

At first glance this process looks confusing and difficult. The truth is that if many standard errors have to be calculated manually, it is. Fortunately, even the most rudimentary spreadsheet software can calculate the standard error for a column of numbers in one simple formula. The real usefulness for this tool is in its application. Remember, the smaller the standard error, the better the forecast.

Safety Stock

The information captured in the standard error affects many areas of customer service and forecasting. Once the standard error is known, this number can be used to calculate the safety stock required to maintain a desired level of customer service.

Traditionally, companies use qualitative judgment or heuristic rules to determine safety stocks. Favorite rules are to keep a 1-month extra supply or a fixed quantity always in stock. The fixed quantity is also usually established by a heuristic rule. Rarely does this method give the desired service level. Using the standard error method, the safety stock provides a more realistic coverage of the true demand variation. First a customer service level is be chosen. Then the safety stock required delivering that level of expected customer service could be calculated. This is a far better method than throwing a dart at the board or just picking a number.

An example of setting safety stock based on standard error and desired customer service level is given here. The process described above: multiplying the standard error by the appropriate safety factor developed the following safety stock levels. These safety factors can be found in any statistics book in a Z-value table. A few commonly used factors are provided.

Desired Customer Service Level	Safety Factor
90%	1.28
95%	1.65
98%	2.05
99%	2.33
99.999999%	4.00

In the example used, the safety stocks required for each desired level of customer service are listed below using the standard error calculated earlier.

Desired Customer Service Level	Safety Stock Required
90%	20
95%	26
98%	32
99%	37
99.99%	63

Ask any manager what level of customer service is required and, of course, the answer is 100%. Intuitively there is an acknowledgment that provided there are no other changes made to the process, inventory must be increased to improve the customer service level. Understanding the relationship between the desired customer service level and the safety factor required provides data and fact for the decision rather than intuition. A comparison can be made of the cost of carrying 37 parts in safety stock to provide 99% customer service compared to 20 parts and only provide 90% service level. Depending on the cost of the part involved, this could mean a notable cash investment in inventory. The inventory strategy can then be determined for the part that provides the best overall return on investment. Try this for yourself in the MICSS Simulator included with this text.

The overall forecasting process capability can be measured by the standard error over time. Even though the forecast is never expected to be perfectly accurate, the reduction in standard error will show how the forecast has improved. This is shown in Figure 10.4.

This forecast in Figure 10.4 shows a steadily improving forecasting process. Since the standard error is moving closer to zero, the amount of safety stock required to deliver the same level of customer service also should be declining. Any improvement in the level of forecasting accuracy reduces the level of safety stock required and maintains overall customer service. A forecasting system integrated with the ERP system can provide this kind of analysis.

Recent development in the ERP system functionality also provides the ability to define dynamic quantities of safety stock. If the product experiences seasonal demand, then the effective management practice would be to increase safety stock going into the season. This would be followed by decreasing safety stock after the rush season. This dynamic safety stock also can be linked directly into the standard error to provide an automatic management function. This feature is not widely found across all ERP systems so if this is a key requirement for the enterprise, having a thorough demonstration before purchase is recommended.

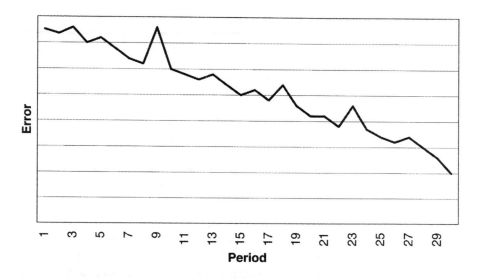

Figure 10.4   Standard error reduction.

Distribution Requirements Planning (DRP)

Distribution requirements planning (DRP) is a parallel process to material requirements planning (MRP). Material requirements planning determines the quantity of component items that are needed to make or assemble a finished good. DRP is an automated management process for the activities and techniques of maintaining the desired levels of finished goods items. DRP provides the proactive visibility of requirements based on the forecast and safety stock. Table 10.1 shows a simple example of how DRP would work.

In this planning grid, an expected receipt can be seen in Period 2. This order has already been released since the quantity appears in the scheduled receipts row. Additional receipts are expected in Periods 3, 4, 6, and 7. These orders must still be released in Periods 2, 3, 5, and 6. This visibility of order release and receipts provides the enterprise the capability of maximizing load configurations for transportation utilizing a DRPII or distribution resource planning process. In addition, the forward expected order releases are an essential link in an integrated supply chain. This was discussed in Chapter 6.

When DRP is used within the enterprise to proactively plan replenishment orders, these expected orders also could be used to provide reliable promises

Table 10.1   DRP Planning for Tables

	Periods							
	1	2	3	4	5	6	7	8
Customer forecast	200	300	400	400	300	200	500	350
Scheduled receipts		500						
Projected tables on hand	100	300	400	500	200	500	500	150
Planned order receipts			500	500		500	500	
Planned order releases		500	500		500	500		

Note: Lot size = 500, Low Lvl = 0, OH = 300, LT = 1, Alloc = 0, SS = 100.

to customers on available shipments through the use of available to promise (ATP). ATP is the uncommitted portion of inventory and is frequently used in distribution. ATP is calculated only in the first time period and whenever there is an expected receipt. Another way to think about ATP is how long does the inventory need to last given the current customer backlog and the expected receipts.

Cumulative ATP shows how many pieces are available between receipts that have not been already committed. In some cases, there may be insufficient inventory to cover the demands that are already known in later periods. If the entire inventory from the previous receipts is used up then a customer who provided greater than expected visibility of their order may not get what they ordered when they wanted the product. To ensure that this inventory is available, a process known as backward ATP is used to reserve that inventory to assure that the known customer orders will be covered. If the order entry personnel use the projected available balance rather than ATP to promise customer orders, customers who have provided the company with sufficient lead-time may be penalized while customers who just called in may get product immediately. The ATP quantity should be used to promise orders to distribution customers. Refer to Chapter 6 for more detail on ATP.

As supply chain systems have become more powerful and sophisticated, the ATP concept has been expanded to include AATP — allocated available to promise. Even though a customer's order may not be actually placed in the ERP system, the product is allocated to that preferred customer and is not available for general consumption. An example of AATP is shown in Table 10.2.

When the preferred customer places an order, the allocation is reduced by the quantity that customer's actual order. If the quantity exceeds the level

Table 10.2 Allocated Available to Promise (AATP)

Part A
Demand time fence–3

Beginning on hand–172	1	2	3	4	5	6	7	8	9	10
Forecast	100	90	80	75	80	90	100	100	120	130
Actual customer demand	80	120	75	30	20	10	0	0	0	0
Project available balance	92	122	47	122	42	102	2	52	82	102
Allocated for customer		30	20		20					
Available to promise	92	–45		120						
Cumulative ATP	92	47	47	167	167	167	167	167	167	167
Allocated ATP	92	17	17	117	117	97	97	97		97
Master production schedule		150		150		150		150	150	150

that has been reserved, the overall available to promise is then reduced. This kind of functionality is normally only found in supply chain integration systems and not as part of a traditional ERP system.

Material Handling

A large part of the overall distribution cost is material handling. Material handling covers the process of moving, packaging, and storing a product. Automation has been used very effectively to help make this movement more efficient. Automated guided vehicles (AGVs) can drive on installed tracks or lines on the floors to automatically bring pick orders to the shipping department for packaging and shipping.

Higher density product stacking is available through the use of automated storage and retrieval systems (AS/RS). These units can store relatively large amounts of inventory in smaller spaces by best utilizing all the cubic space available. The operator stands in one location and the machine will bring the parts to them. This minimizes the movement for the operator. The good news is that these units can store a great deal of inventory. The bad news is that these units can store a great deal of inventory. Requiring automation to access inventory because there is so much around does not utilize the assets of the enterprise to the best return possible. Remember, the goal of distribution is to have the right part in the right place at the right time to quickly be able to deliver customer orders. The goal is not to squirrel away as much inventory as possible and move it as efficiently as possible just in case an order arrives.

No matter what storage methodology is chosen, one of the frequently overlooked subjects is that of industrial packaging. The packaging for the part should adequately protect the part from damage during routine handling. This could include static discharge bags for electronic components or specially treated wrapping paper for storing iron ingots so they do not rust. Inventory is commonly the largest component of a company's current asset base. Selecting the appropriate industrial packaging helps protect that asset.

Order Administration

Order administration in the warehousing function can be handled in a variety of ways depending on the technology that is utilized. High tech warehouses may have RF mobile scanners that interactively walk the storekeeper through the picking function. As parts are wanded by the bar code equipment, the ERP system is completing the issue transaction in the background. This transaction can include lot number, serial number, and/or location number. Once the order is completed, a packing slip will be printed in shipping. Some ERP systems even have the functionality to automatically calculate the weight and best shipping method for the order. It can even prepare a bill of lading automatically.

Other companies may manually print picking paperwork for the storekeeper to pick parts. As each part is removed from inventory, the pick slip is marked with the exact serial number, lot number, and location. These data are then manually entered into the ERP system later. No matter which process is chosen, the key to effective warehouse management is the discipline of transactions completed on time.

An integrated ERP system can also effectively handle returns. Since the customer order database is directly linked to the inventory database, when a return comes back the system can provide information very easily about when the product was first shipped. If manufacturing is also integrated into the same ERP system, the full product traceability would also be available — complete to raw materials used — provided all the transactions were done. The price that was charged to the customer on the original shipment can be quickly identified. This allows for a quick replacement of the defective part or a credit for the value of the product if the customer prefers. These transactions can normally be completed with relatively few keystrokes. The accounting automatically is updated and booked as the parts move through the system. This integration provides quick feedback to operations on products returned, reasons for returns, and possibly customers that may be taking undue advantage of the company's return policy.

Summary

Distribution is where product production meets the outside market. Distribution includes activities such as transportation, warehousing, inventory control, material handling, order administration, site and location analysis, industrial packaging, data processing, and the communication network necessary for effective management. Effective distribution management has quickly become reliant on the use of appropriate technology including ERP management systems, warehouse management systems, bar coding, AGV, and AS/RS. Having a single integrated enterprise database at the core of distribution management provides accurate reliable information with which to promise customer deliveries. ERP also aids in the effective management of the inventory asset. This is a key success factor for maintaining an acceptable cash flow. There are many choices and strategies available in the distribution manager's toolbox. Tools selected must fit the overall desired strategy for the enterprise. When done effectively, distribution can be a key link in a competitive integrated supply chain.

Distribution References and Resources

Distribution Resource Planning: The Gateway to True Quick Response and Continuous Replenishment, Andre J. Martin, 1993, APICS # 03104.
The Distribution Management Handbook, James A. Tompkins and Dale A. Harmelink (Eds.), 1994, APICS #03283.
Distribution Planning and Control, David Frederick Ross, CFPIM, 1996, APICS # 03442.

ERP SELECTION AND IMPLEMENTATION

11 ERP System Requirements

The requirements for an effective ERP system implementation are relatively few. Even the most complicated ERP implementation has at its core the same basic requirements. These basic requirements are the building blocks of every ERP software package no matter what platform or operating system. Many companies during their implementation will get carried away with the technology that is available to them and will overlook the importance of having these very simple building blocks in control and the resulting implementation crumbles. After a career of watching and participation in ERP implementation, it has been noted that having good control of these requirements moves a company quickly through the implementation process. Instead of fighting the basics, the enterprise can focus on the successful application of the software to their specific company and situation so that bottom line results can be achieved. No matter how simple these requirements look, each one is critical to overall success. The basic requirements are

- Unique item identification including part number, lead-time, order sizing rules, stocking policies, and safety stock
- Demand input including quantities, timing, and risk
- Dependent materials required to make the part that will be shipped
- Supply including quantities and timing

Unique Item Identification

The item identifier defines the basic language of the enterprise. The item identifier is commonly referred to as a part number, product number, stock code, stockkeeping unit, or stock number. The key to success is that each item must be uniquely identified so that there is no confusion in the communication of requirements and supply. The development of part numbering systems can be a point of significant discussion in the implementation process. There are many ideas and inputs into when and how a part number should be used. There is a cost for the addition of a part number because it must then be identified, tracked, and managed. This discussion typically breaks into two groups; the "lumpers" and the "splitters." The lumpers will try to avoid adding a part number at any cost. If two items closely resemble each other, the lumpers will attempt to use one part number. The splitters will attempt to put a unique part number on everything. The following example is taken to an extreme, but this is an example of how a company handled castings. A casting is metal that has been formed into a desired shape. Typically the casting will have some machining done to allow the attachments of other pieces to complete an assembly. This casting could also be painted or heat-treated before shipment to the customer. The lumper school of thought would put one part number on the casting no matter its state: raw, machined, heat treated, assembled, or painted. In their mind, it is still a casting. The splitter is just the opposite; they would demand to have a unique part number at each stage of the process: raw, machined, heat treated, assembled, and painted. Now, who is right? This is where an understanding of the operation and business approach is required because the real answer is that "it depends."

The well-known theory for part numbers is that if an item is unique for fit, form, or function, the item must have unique item identification. Theory is great but what is the real-world application? The real-world application is that if the part will be stocked, stored, or if there is a desire to manage costs at that level, then a new part number is needed. If a particular stage occurs only in transition as the part is made, then a unique part number is not needed. Our simple casting could have many different answers. Only one item identifier would be needed in an operation that takes molten metal, forms the casting, immediately moves it to machining, then heat-treats, paints, and the first time the casting moves to inventory is when it is completed. A common scenario is where the casting is made and then stored until needed for machining because the lot size that makes sense in the casting operation is larger than the machining lot size. Also, more than one machined configuration may be able to be made from one casted part. If this were the case, then it would be best to have a part number for the raw casting and one for the machined casting. Similarly, once the casting is machined and heat-treated, the same part may be painted different colors. If this is the case, it may make sense to have a number for the completed casting without paint and a different one for the painted casting, especially if the lot sizes for machining and heat treating are different than the lot sizing for painting. However, if the normal practice was to machine only what is needed for painting, then a single part number would be an excellent choice. So, what is the right answer for the number of part numbers needed? It depends!

The needs and uses of the part number must be clearly understood from all perspectives in the enterprise to make the right decision. No two companies are the same, so do not expect that the utilization of part numbers to be the same. The level of detail must be sufficient to effectively manage the business but not be a burden whose cost is higher than the value received when considered from an enterprise perspective. To change the level of detail of part numbers is cost prohibitive once the ERP implementation is well down the road. Many companies fall into this trap and consume an incredible amount of resources making changes instead of taking the time to do it right the first time.

The flip side of the part numbering coin is whether the identifier should be significant or nonsignificant, all numeric or alphanumeric. This discussion is typically quite emotional with individual past successes and beliefs being championed. This is another area where there is a theory supported by industry best practices affected by a big dose of "it depends." Once upon a time, back in the early days of material planning, before the invention of the computer (yes, there are still people living today who remember that time — it was really not all that long ago!), having significant part numbers was the only way people could track parts. By just glancing at the number, you could tell if it was a resistor or capacitor, red or blue, machined or raw. Many people still believe in this system because they feel it is easier to manage and control the parts. For those people with the decoding sequence in their mind, this may be true. The downside of this type of system is that part numbers are typically long alphanumeric things that are so difficult to remember or use for conversation, so therefore virtually no one uses them in their entirety. A study done a few years ago noted that the probability of entering a long part number correctly was almost impossible. The results in accuracy were directly related to the number of digits. Figure 11.1 below is a graphical representation of that study.

The study showed that the maximum number of digits that could be effectively used was about seven. This is not totally coincidental with the fact that many phone numbers are also seven digits. Once seven digits have been

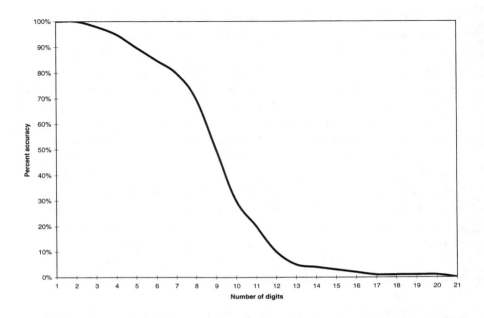

Figure 11.1   Input accuracy vs. part number digits.

passed in length, the probability of entering a part number successfully drops dramatically. If your company has long part numbers, try this test. Go out to the stockroom and ask one of the storekeepers for a part number. The answer will most likely be six digits or less. In addition, if a number greater than four digits is used, then an accepted pattern break in the number also will be used. For example, if the answer is 136609, the verbalization will likely be one thirty six, six oh nine. If you do not believe the importance of this break, attempt asking for a part as a thirteen sixty-six oh nine and watch the looks that you get! Even though you may have asked for the correct number, the message was not received.

Ever wonder why a non-native speaker of your language is so difficult to understand? Likely the words were correct but the accent on the right syllable was not. In the same way we remember phone numbers, social security numbers, or zip codes, we will naturally break things down into smaller pieces to make them easier to remember. This is true even in our basic communication of words where we accent certain syllables. A proven psychological fact is that the human brain is only capable of holding five to seven bits of data at any time with accurate recall. Think about the new employees. They must learn complex part numbering translation codes and deal with part numbers so long that no one uses them anyway, and the probability of accurately entering them into a computer is the equivalent of *Mission Impossible!* This makes one wonder why these complex numbering schemes were ever used? The answer is that there was no other alternative.

At the time, this was the only way that information about the part could be tracked. Since the invention of the computer and especially relational databases, the part number has moved from needing to be all the information required to a simple, unique identifier against which different characteristics can be related. As technology has changed, industry best practices have changed as well. The current industry best practice is to have short (6 digits or less), all numeric identifiers. This provides the company 999,999 possible part numbers and is a sufficient pool for most enterprises. Very few reasons still exist today to have significance in the part number.

This does not mean that there should be no significance anywhere in the part identifier. The best area for significance in the modern ERP system is in the description field. Virtually all the ERP systems available will allow the description to be searched directly for a given string of text. One strategy for the transition from the old paradigm of long, significant part numbers to the short, all numeric identifier is to put the old part number as the first item in the description. That way, all the people who are accustomed to that system still have the information that they expect and the person having to do the transactions does not have to deal with that many digits for transaction entry. Since the computer software program will allow the search of the description field to find a particular string of characters, the part can be found in a number of different ways.

To further ease the process of reporting and analysis, all ERP systems allow codes to be defined and entered against a part so that ad hoc reports can be quickly run. This type of coding allows someone to quickly pull a report only for resistors or capacitors, finished goods or raw material, castings or sheet metal, or even a combination of two categories such as finished goods castings. Extreme care must be taken when defining these codes such that the desired reports will be easily available. The best way to determine what codes should be used is to examine what reports are typically run or questions that are typically asked. This allows the database to be defined in a number of different ways. Figure 11.2 is one way to look at segmenting a database.

The illustrated segmentation of this database would allow reports of electronic raw materials or sheet metal work in process or total work in

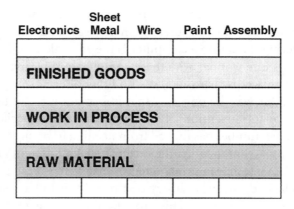

Figure 11.2 Segmenting a database with commodity code classifications.

process to be run. Any database can be cut into a number of different pieces and then the intersection of those pieces can be quickly defined. The diagram shows a very simplistic two-dimensional relationship. Imagine the answers that would be available at your fingertips if this segmentation was set up correctly for your needs. This is at the very heart of the relational database.

A relational database is "a software program that allows users to obtain information drawn from two or more databases that are made up of two-dimensional arrays of data."[1] Very in-depth analysis requiring relationship reporting is easily accomplished using these two-dimensional arrays. The relationship database is a standard backbone for any modern ERP system. The advent of the relational database has removed the reason for the significance in the part numbering systems. As a result, current industry best practice is nonsignificant part numbers because more information is available on the part without the hassle of the long significant numbers.

To be able to adequately manage these parts, planning data about each unique part number is required. This includes lead-time, order sizing rules, stocking policies, and safety stock.

Lead-Time

Lead-time as associated with the item number is the expected time between the recognition of need and receipt of supply. This can be broken into a number of different lead-times such as ordering time, processing time, vendor time, inspection time, stocking time, and transportation time. Depending on the functionality of the ERP system, these individual components may be broken out separately or only one field may be available where a sum of the parts would be entered. Typically the ordering time, inspection time, and stocking time are fixed for the organization and do not vary by part. The processing time for make parts and the vendor time for purchase parts typically varies by part number, as does the transportation time. Having a conservative estimate of the lead-time is essential for the ERP system to do its planning. At the core of the ERP system is the calculation that examines what is needed, what is currently available, or coming in to determine what is needed and when. The answer of the question "when" is the real secret to success of ERP through the reduction of inventory and improvement of response time.

Order Sizing

Order sizing rules suggest the quantity to be ordered. Rarely do the quantity of materials ordered exactly equal the requirements. The business needs and goals must be considered when choosing the most appropriate lot-sizing rule. The most common order sizing rules are

1. Lot for lot, also known as discrete ordering.
2. Fixed lot sizing, including economic order quantity (EOQ), minimum, multiple, and maximum.
3. Dynamic lot sizing, including period of supply and period order quantity (POQ).

Lot for Lot (LFL or Discrete)

This order quantity is the simplest of the lot sizing rules. This lot quantity orders only what is needed, no more, no less. The lot size rule is most appropriate for make-to-order work where the company is very adverse to inventory buildup and the probability of selling exactly the same thing again is very low. Even though it is the simplest to understand, this method creates the most orders. Each requirement for a component material is matched with a corresponding order. The benefit of this method is that inventory is minimized. Table 11.1 shows the result of lot for lot planning for Part 142708. The planned order releases exactly equal the real needs offset by the planned lead-time. The resulting inventory after all this planning is truly just in time!

Table 11.1 Lot for Lot Planning

Part number: 142708	1	2	3	4	5	6	7	8
Demand	200	400	200	600	100	300	300	100
Scheduled receipts	200	400						
Projected on hand	0	0	0	0	0	0	0	0
Planned order receipts			200	600	100	300	300	100
Planned order releases	200	600	100	300	300	100		

Note: Lot size = LFL, Low Lvl = 0, OH = 0, LT = 2, Alloc = 0, SS = 0.

Economic Order Quantity (EOQ)

EOQ recognizes the tradeoff between the cost of carrying inventory and the cost to process the order and set up a machine. The same logic is applied to purchase orders comparing the cost of carrying inventory with the cost of placing the purchase orders. Many would have you believe that this is an old lot-sizing tool and has no place in the current ERP systems. This could not be further from the truth. Remember that how we are measured and rewarded is how we behave. From a financial perspective, as more inventory is carried, the cost of carrying that inventory goes up proportionately. The financial people are usually rewarded when inventory is reduced. On the other hand, because manufacturing is rewarded on low product cost, they favor long runs to spread the cost of the setup. This method leads to higher inventories. Each group attempts to optimize their own area and a conflict begins. The economic order quantity, although very old, is still used to determine the order of magnitude of the optimal order size and understand why the inventory is there.

Without understanding why the current practice is in place, the risk to damaging the operation by just changing things is very high. It is true that many people have been carried away with the EOQ formula and attempt to apply it inappropriately. EOQ still has a fit in the business process that experiences long setup times and comparatively shorter run times. The pressure to reduce those setup times can be quantified through the resulting reduction of inventory by using EOQ. Also, there must be a reality injected into the EOQ calculation. The business must need all the parts calculated by the EOQ. If the company has only make-to-order demand and the EOQ calculates a lot quantity higher than the demand, those extra parts should not be made just for the sake of EOQ. EOQ is an approximation of the order quantity. The calculation gives the appearance of precision, but the resulting order quantity is really just a guideline.

$$\text{The EOQ formula is} = \sqrt{2US/IC}$$

U = Annual expected usage in units
S = Setup cost in local currency
I = Inventory carrying cost expressed as an annual percentage
C = The cost of the item in local currency

The resulting order quantity will be in units.

U: The annual expected usage in units can either be the historic consumption of the past year or it can be the forecasted usage based on the master schedule or other source of demand for the upcoming year.

S: The setup cost in local currency includes all the costs associated with changing from one production run to another. Setup time can be considered as the time from the last good part of the previous run to the first good part of the next run. All costs associated with that time and procedure should be included in the setup costs. Usually these times are estimated in terms of hours of production and are costed by applying a standard labor rate for the area and adding overhead burden. For purchased parts these costs include the entire order preparation cost for the purchasing department to process one PO. The costs are increased for each purchase order as it moves through the receipt process, receiving inspection, storage, and invoice payment. The traditional approach is to add all these overhead costs and divide by the number of purchase orders issued during that time period. The caution is that some purchase orders take significantly more time than others. For the purposes of calculating the economic order quantity, the average is sufficient. This factor begins to explain why supply chain management with automatic communication with customer's customers and supplier's suppliers is so essential. As the communication becomes easier and less expensive, the EOQ drops and the result is that the amount of inventory required will fall.

I: The inventory carrying cost is one of the most difficult costs to determine. The most frequent way this cost is determined is to ask the head of the Finance Department. This person usually has some strong feelings concerning the value of the money currently tied up in inventory. A rough estimation can be made by adding the cost of borrowing money to the cost of running the warehouse including all the people, computer systems, and floor space. Other factors to be included in the cost of carrying inventory are the risk of obsolescence, damage, theft, or spoilage. The largest part of the inventory carrying cost is the opportunity cost of that money. Opportunity cost is what the yield could be if the money were not tied up in inventory. This can be significant in an entrepreneurial business that has the potential to grow quickly. After all those quantitative factors are considered, the norm for inventory carrying costs is in the range of 40 to 70% per year.

C: The cost of the item used in the EOQ formula is usually the fully loaded cost including overhead used to value the inventory for bookkeeping purposes. These costs include material, labor, overhead, and outside production services. If the part being considered comes from an offshore supplier, the import costs should also be included as part of the costs.

With all this wonderful mathematical precision, there are some underlying assumptions to the EOQ formula. The first is that inventory is consumed at a regular and continuous rate. This assumption supports the belief that the average inventory is half the order quantity. Realistically, inventory is consumed in most companies in a lumpy, noncontinuous way. The difficulty in managing this demand pattern is the reason MRP was developed in the first place. The precision that results from using the EOQ formula is really quite an illusion. Drastic changes can be made in each of the components with little difference in the optimal order quantity. The real application of the EOQ is to determine the order of magnitude of the optimal order quantity, not the exact quantity; for example, should you order 100 or 1000, not 100 or 110.

EOQ Sensitivity

Annual Usage	Setup Cost	Inventory Carrying Cost	Cost of the Item	Quantity (EOQ)	Percent Change	
					EOQ	Usage
1000	$1000	40%	$250	141		
2500	$1000	40%	$250	224	58%	150%
5000	$1000	40%	$250	316	124%	400%

| | | | | | Percent Change | |
Annual Usage	Setup Cost	Inventory Carrying Cost	Cost of the Item	Quantity (EOQ)	EOQ	Carrying Cost
2500	$1000	30%	$250	258		
2500	$1000	40%	$250	224	–13%	33%
2500	$1000	60%	$250	183	–18%	50%

This table clearly shows how the economic order quantity changes significantly less than the selected input. The annual usage increased by 150% and the EOQ increased only 58%. When the carrying cost for inventory was doubled, the EOQ only decreased 18%. This shows that best estimates can be used for each of the inputs without adversely affecting the accuracy of the output. Order quantities can be adjusted around the EOQ without suffering a significant cost penalty.

The real message is that since the main driving force behind lot size is setup cost, the focus for process improvement should be on reducing the setup cost. Once the setup cost is reduced, smaller lot sizes can be run. Smaller lot sizes result in lower inventories. Lower inventories typically yield higher profit and better responsiveness to the market.

Order Minimum/Multiple/Maximum

When purchasing parts, sometimes there is an "order minimum" set by the supplier. Rather than having MRP plan frequent orders that are less than this minimum quantity and then manually adjust the results, this planning rule plans the order quantity to be at least the known minimum. If the needed order quantity is greater than the minimum, the quantity planned will match the requirement if no other lot-sizing rule is defined.

"Order multiple" takes advantage of natural order quantities due to production batch size like a full oven load for heat treat or a multiple cavity die. Suppliers may deliver parts in cases that are subsequently stored as "each" by the customer. This could be cases of fasteners, gloves, or adhesives. Orders to the supplier must be in case quantities or multiples of the "each" that will eventually be stored. If the quantity required is less than a multiple of the specified amount, the order quantity planned will be automatically increased to the next higher multiple. Many ERP systems will automatically convert the "as purchased" unit of measure to the "as stocked" unit of measure; for example, one case of 144 to 144 each.

"Order maximum" may be used because of a limitation of space or restriction on the amount of the product than can be transported or stored. A common usage for order maximum is chemical compounds that are restricted in quantity for safety reasons.

Period of Supply

The most useful of the order sizing tools is the period of supply. This allows the planner to determine how many times each year an order should be placed and the lot size adjusts dynamically to demands. If the period of supply is set to five, the order quantity will be calculated starting at the ordering point and all requirements five periods into the future are grouped into the planned order quantity. If the periods were days, this would mean that the item would be ordered once per week. The advantage to this approach is that at the end of the each week, the end of the inventory is also reached. Like lot for lot, no leftover inventory remains in stock unless safety stock has been defined for the part. If safety stock has been defined, the inventory level will fall to that safety stock quantity at the end of the each defined period. This is not true of any of the other described lot size methods except lot for lot, which would plan to bring inventory to zero each day.

One way to choose how often the part should be ordered and, therefore, how many should be ordered at a time is to use the economic order quantity as a starting point. For example, if the economic order quantity for a part with annual sales of 10,000 parts is 500 parts, this means that the planner is expected to order 10,000/500 or 20 times per year. Given there are 240 average workdays per year, the period of supply would be 12 days. This process is also known as period order quantity or POQ. Each time the need for ordering arises, the planning system would look out the next 12 days and group all

Table 11.2   Period of Supply = 3

Item ID: 142708	1	2	3	4	5	6	7	8
Master schedule	200	400	200	600	100	300	300	100
Scheduled receipts		300						
Projected on hand	100	900	700	100	700	400	100	100
Planned order receipts		900			700			100
Planned order releases	900			700			100	

Note: Lot size = POS(3), Low Lvl = 0, OH = 300, LT = 1, Alloc = 0, SS = 100.

the requirements for that part into one planned order. Now, the same Part 142708 used in the example before will be planned with a different order sizing rule. The planned orders are different in quantity and timing than the previous examples.

The answer to how much to order can vary widely based on the characteristics of the parts and the goals of the organizations. Understanding each of these order-sizing tools is essential to managing the part such that the goals of the overall enterprise are met.

Demand

Demand is "a need for a particular product or component. The demand could come from any number of sources including customer order, forecast, an interplant requirement, or a request from a branch warehouse for a service part or for manufacturing another product."[1] Managing demand was covered in Chapters 3 and 7.

The demand must be defined by unique part number to enable the ERP system to perform the necessary calculations and ensure that sufficient supply is timed to match the required demand. Technological advancements provide the opportunity for suppliers to know almost real time what is being sold and what the expected reorder amount and timing will be. This is the goal of the integrated supply chain; to have real time accurate information from the customer's customer to the supplier's supplier in a seamless reliable information process such that only what is being sold is built. The Sales and Operation Planning process oversees the impact of that demand on the whole supply chain. At each link of this integrated supply chain this demand drives the overall planning process as the computer calculates what must be made and purchased to satisfy that demand based on current inventory or expected receipts.

Dependent Materials

For each part that is manufactured, a list of materials to make that part is needed. This list is known as the bill of material. Bills of material are a list of all the items required to make another part. The end item is called the parent item and the items that are required to make the parent item are called components. The quantity on the bill of material for each component is sufficient to make one of the parent parts. The toolbox for defining bills of materials provides many choices and options to represent the configuration of the products. Just like construction, having the right tools make the whole job easier and quicker. Choosing the right tool for the bill of material job enhances overall utilization, accuracy, and improves the results of the MRP system.

Usually the number of chief engineers that a company has had can be determined by looking at the number of different ways bills of materials have been structured. The topic of bill of material structuring usually evokes strong feelings from everyone in the organization who uses these tools very similar to the item number discussion. Since bills of materials are used for costing, scheduling, product definition, work orders, and many other functions, almost everyone in the organization has an opinion. Properly structured bills of materials make the job easy while improper structures can create nightmares, extra work, and errors.

We normally think in term of bills of materials without realizing it. We cook from recipes that are bills of materials for food. Recipes are doubled or halved by adjusting each item on the ingredient list by the same factor. This is the same as changing a lot size for a manufactured product. We assemble our tools and supplies for our hobbies — another bill of material. This bill of materials logic allows us to think of groups of parts as belonging to other parts or assemblies. All items on the bill of material are needed to complete the parent item.

Bills of material are used by virtually everyone in the organization. Frequently, different areas will develop and maintain their own bills of material. The inconsistency in this approach is that each area believes that their bill of material is the one that is correct. The reality is that often none of the bills accurately reflects all the materials and resources used. People who would not dream of having multiple policies and procedures for each functional area support having multiple bills of material in the company. The bill of material is a company document just like the company policies and procedures. Everyone in the company should use only one bill of material. Each functional group may use them for different purposes, but one definition is required. There may be different views available but these views come from one source document. The bill of material is like a language definition. We all use it for different purposes, but one common standard is needed for effective communication. That is what ERP is at its core purpose, an integrated communications system.

Supply

The simplest definition for supply is "the quantity of goods available for use. This includes the actual or planned replenishment of a product or component. The replenishment quantities are created in response to a demand for the product or component or in anticipation of such a demand."[1] Supply is the inverse of demand. To be competitive, any enterprise must be able to match these two better and faster than their competition. The core function of the ERP system is matching the timing and quantity of available supply and required demand. The hardest part of the integrated supply chain is not the technology required to pass information from customer to supplier to supplier. It is the assurance that the information about demand and supply is correct. Accuracy must be found in all the input of the ERP system or the old adage of computing will be true. "Garbage in — garbage out!" Data about current inventories and expected purchase order and work order receipts, including dates and quantities, all must be correct for the planning process to be effective. Chapter 13 has been dedicated to this subject.

Summary

The requirements of an ERP system are really few: unique item identification, demand, dependant materials, and supply. These four items are the four basic elements of ERP just as oxygen, fuel, and a source of ignition are the basic elements of fire. If one is missing, then ERP is not possible. To have an effective integrated system that yields a positive return on investment, each of these items must be very accurate. Without that accuracy, the users of the system will second guess the output of the system and develop manual processes instead of using the desired integrated planning and control process. This becomes even more challenging when the individual ERP systems are connected into an integrated supply chain. If there is any inaccuracy in the output, no human intervention is possible and the entire supply chain is adversely affected. As is normal, nothing that is worth having is ever easy. Obtaining accuracy in these four input elements is a substantial part of the work of the ERP implementation.

References

1. APICS — The Educational Society for Resource Management, APICS Dictionary, 9th ed., Alexandria, VA, 1998.

12 Selecting the Right ERP System

ost enterprises can expect to change its computer information system either to a new system or with a major upgrade at least every 5 to 7 years. With rapidly developing technology and the advent of new features and functions, it is essential that the company makes the best choice possible in a new system. This includes the hardware platform, database tool, and the overall philosophy of the ERP system. Some ERP systems are well designed for the entrepreneurial business with decentralized controls while others offer an excellent fit for corporate standardized business processes. Given that there are hundreds of ERP systems available globally, how can a company be sure that they got the one that is the best fit? Does it really matter which software is purchased? Why not just purchase the same system that everyone else seems to have? There must be a reason why particular software has most of the market, right? The volume of questions needing to be answered to successfully select the best system for the enterprise can seem overwhelming. Don't we all think our company is unique? While many aspects of all businesses are similar, each business does have its uniqueness. To fit a system well, we must answer all those questions from the point of view of our individual company.

Type of Business

The first step of any successful system selection is to decide what kind of business you are and what kind of business would you like to be. Are you a

249

make-to-order company producing high variety and low volume, competing in the market on lead-time response? Conversely, are you a make-to-stock company with all the difficulties of forecasting demand because your internal production times exceed the time the customer is willing to wait for your product? Are you a process industry producing a commodity product competing on price and need to optimize your capacity utilization?

How strong is the desire to purchase a single integrated system to run the enterprise? One option is to select a single integrated system with the best fit for most areas of the company. Business practices that do not fit the software will be changed or the software will be modified to fit the business processes. Another alternative is to select a combination of "best of breed" solutions where the separate subsystems are interfaced rather than integrated. The advantage is the functionality of the individual software may more closely fit the enterprise, but the downside risk is that the seamless integration of these products may not be possible as each software vendor releases new versions. Which is the best strategy to select? The right answer is, "It depends!" There is not one right answer for all companies.

Understanding and asking the right questions during the selection of a system can not only help select the software that best fits your company, but also can build support and commitment within your company for the final selection and implementation. Selecting the right system the wrong way can be as damaging to the enterprise as selecting the wrong system. If there is not a commitment by the people affected by the implementation of the ERP system to making the system work, the results will likely be disappointing. Selection and implementation of an integrated system is a significant project for any organization. It is unrealistic to expect that any off-the-shelf software product will meet 100% of the company's requirements. Even selecting a best of breed approach will not cover 100% of the company's requirements. However, finding at least 90% of the identified requirements should be possible.

During the selection process, the most important thing to remember is that this system selection and implementation should improve the overall performance of the company. The system is a tool to improve the overall company bottom-line business results. The process should not be just an information technology project. If the project is only meant to replace a previous computer system without identifying the core business processes that should be improved with results to the bottom line, then what is the justification of the project? Utilization of technology just because everyone else seems to be doing it is NOT the goal!

It is realistic to expect that the selection and implementation of an integrated system should produce improved bottom-line results. If it doesn't, then why would any company want to begin on this journey? The ERP project should be considered and evaluated under the same criteria as any other project requiring a major investment. The costs of alternatives including upgrading the current solution are compared to the purchase and implementation of a new solution. Another alternative to consider is not changing anything. What would be the expected return on investment and the competitive position of the company if the status quo were maintained? Many companies use the selection and implementation of a new ERP system as a catalyst for global business process reengineering. If this is really the company's objective rather than just installing a new computer system, then sufficient education and training on the new business model is a critical success factor. "To truly change what people do, you must change what people think." This age-old advice is as good today as it was when it was first said many years ago. Without the appropriate education and training, changing what people think is impossible.

Selection Strategy

Two distinct methods can be used for system selection. One is to implement the overall business strategy by focusing on information technology infrastructure. The other method is to determine features and functions that are required to run a business. Larger companies can benefit more from the centralization of data because there is a substantial cost associated with data duplication and data synchronization. The difficulty of coordinating data and information across the enterprise when the enterprise is large, complex, and possibly multinational makes the identification of an information technology strategy critical to the overall company's success. Smaller companies do not have these same problems simply because their size does not generate the same complexities as large companies. Similar to how a large building structure requires a larger base than a small structure, a large company has a more complex infrastructure than a small company. Small companies can successfully rely on more informal communication and less complex data systems. The real benefit of an ERP system implementation for small and medium companies is how the business can be managed more easily because of the functionality of the software. In addition, a company of any size can expect the benefit of integrating the demands from suppliers and customers automatically. A small company should expect to focus more on the feature-function analysis while the large company should expect to spend its time on overall information technology strategy.

Information Technology Infrastructure Selection Strategy

An overall corporate strategy for information technology should consider:

1. **Control.** What is the level of desired control from the corporate level on the individual business units?
2. **Structure.** How extensive is the organizational structure on a global basis and how tightly integrated should these resources be?
3. **Database.** What is the desired structure for the enterprise database and how accessible should the data be to the individual users?
4. **Customization.** How willing is the company to customize the software that has been purchased to fully meet the needs of the users? Will the company expect to complete these modifications with internal resources or is the software supplier expected to provide these modifications as part of the implementation?
5. **Best practices.** Is the company willing to embrace "industry best practices" in its implementation? How integrated does the company desire to have these best practices in the software?

Control

There are as many possible different organizational structures as there are companies in the world, plus a few more. There is not one right answer for the best way to structure an organization. In the same way, there is not one best way to manage a business. The managers of a business must decide the overall company culture and levels of management control. Some of the choices that must be made include the level of detail that the corporate entity would like to have on specific transactions. Some corporations desire to have detailed transactions available to answer questions even from the highest level of consolidation. This level of data storage is required to provide the "drill down" capability that many enterprises desire. Drill down capability allows the summary data to be displayed in finer and finer levels of detail until the transaction that began the process is displayed including identification of the person who made the transaction. Some financial controllers desire only aggregated information on the corporate basis and do not expect to be able to drill-down to the transaction level online. In the event of an audit, the ability to get the data is still possible but online accessibility is not expected. If detailed transaction visibility is required and the software purchased does not support this approach, then the enterprise will be quite unhappy with the software no matter what its other qualities. In the same way, if only the aggregated data is required and a detailed transaction system is purchased, the company will chafe against the transaction load.

Another part of corporate control is the ownership of the data. The data can be maintained at each separate operational site or the system can be run from a centralized database at a corporate location. The advantage of multiple databases is that the software can be customized and configured to meet the specific needs of the individual divisions. The disadvantage is that if there is not a corporate standard for the data, then sharing the data across the divisions is more difficult. Most multiple division companies expect to enjoy some economy of scale and the ability to share data is a key success factor. In addition, having the data on a central repository can reduce the overall information technology expense since these resources (including hardware, software, and information technology people) can be centralized in one area. Having T1 lines, ISDN lines, or other dedicated network connections between the divisions can provide response time equal to or better than having a computer at each location. Of course, a disadvantage of having a centralized database is that in the event of a disaster, all divisions are affected simultaneously rather than just the disaster site.

Procedure development and deployment are another consideration of control. The desire of some companies is to posses and follow well-defined policies and procedures that are consistent across the entire global enterprise. The ERP software can facilitate this directive type of procedures as an integral part of the process. Conversely, other organizations desire to have each division or business unit develop the best policies and procedures that fit their unique strategies and goals. Imagine the difficulties in an organization if a software is selected that has incorporated into it strict adherence to policy and procedures and the desired corporate strategy is to allow agile development and change of accepted business practices. This is why the organization must first decide what kind of organization it is and how it desires to do business. Having a mismatch at this level would be very difficult to overcome during the implementation and could set the scene for extensive (and expensive) modifications to the software. The better alternative is to select software that fits the overall operational intent of the organization.

Structure

A closely linked decision point to the desired control is the organizational structure. An organization with global reach faces an entirely different set of issues and concerns than an organization that operates solely within one country. Does the organization desire a tight or loose integration within the enterprise or does each division operate as a stand-alone entity? The simple question of when a transaction was entered becomes more difficult in a global enterprise with a centralized database since many times zones are spanned by the operation. The impact of language and currency must also be addressed within the system including how difficult it is to display data in a language that is understood by the user. The typical approach is to have a cross-reference table in the system where the different language translations are held. In some software, these translations are already accomplished, in others the tables are available and the translations are considered the responsibility of the user. When the challenge of double byte display like what is required for Japanese and Chinese characters is considered, this challenge can look daunting. In addition, the process of revaluing payables and receivables as the exchange rates for currency change must be considered if the organization intends to consolidate their financials on a frequent basis. If the consolidation only occurs on an infrequent basis, then a batch process of update would be acceptable. The legal and financial reporting needs for the countries and geographic areas in which business is engaged could also be a critical decision point in the system selection. This provides the business with the data it requires for value-add tax, business and occupations tax, income tax, and import and export quotas. Local laws and specific data requirements must be considered when selecting the ERP software.

These financial reporting needs may include different sets of books: tax, financial, and managerial. The format for tax accounting is well controlled by the taxing authority. Controlled product movement reports and all the other demands placed by government and financial authorities must be available. Financial accounting is normally consistent with GAAP (generally accepted accounting principles). The managerial accounting can be as different as the organization itself. The strategy for treating indirect cost must be determined. Are these a period expense or directly related to products? Some systems support ABC (activity based costing). Others are beginning to incorporate TVA (throughput value add) cost accounting based on the theory of constraints. TOC measures were detailed in Chapter 9.

Database

The standard in modern ERP systems is a relational database. This means that the system possesses a multitude of tables that are linked to provide quick access to the information while at the same time allowing one entry to be used throughout the system. How the master control settings are determined is an entirely different story. Some software have a parameter driven methodology for defining master settings and others accomplish the same end by using multiple tables to store these data. The parameter-driven systems tend to be more difficult to change once they have been configured while the multiple tables allow the master settings to be changed more easily. However, the parameters can be set more quickly in the parameter option than in the multiple table option providing a lower initial implementation cost. If the business is in a rapid state of change and expects to change drastically in the next 5 to 7 years, this database approach can be a significant cost savings in the long run and should be considered in the system selection.

The selection approach for an integrated system or a best of breed approach will impact the accessibility of the data. Typically, if a best of breed approach is followed then the data must be downloaded and uploaded or synchronized in batch processes among the interfaced applications. If the system is expected to be available 24 hours per day, 7 days a week, there may not be time to have the system unavailable to perform a large batch operation to synchronize data. Large expensive multiplexed systems may allow this through mirroring hardware. However, this is out of the financial reach of most companies. If this is the case, then a fully integrated system with real-time connectivity is required. Operationally speaking, a large difference exists between a system that is interfaced and one that is integrated. An interfaced system tends to be more batch oriented and does not provide real-time information. An integrated system is a real-time information system.

Customization

No software can be expected to fit a company 100%. Having at least a 90% fit should be a reasonable expectation. However, the company must still develop a strategy for customization of the software. How willing is the company to customize the software that has been purchased to fully meet the needs of the users? Most users will attempt to make the new system look exactly like the old one because the old one is familiar, not necessarily better.

A process must be established to determine this type of request from a real request for needed functionality. Once the determination has been made to customize the software, will the company expect to complete these modifications with internal resources or is the software supplier expected to provide these modifications as part of the implementation? If outside resources are used, the expectation is that the customization should be well documented and accomplished in a resonable time. If inside resources are used, customization may take longer since the IT staff is not as familiar with the software as an outside expert. Frequently these changes are not well documented and can be difficult to maintain in the future. Customization can have a large impact on the overall cost of the project and should be considered carefully.

Best Practices

A very common practice in implementation is the integration of business best practices coincident to the ERP implementation. The ERP implementation is used as a catalyst for overall process improvement. The inclusion of industry best practices in the ERP software provides guidance to the company in their implementation process to identify those practices that need to be changed. The downside of this approach is that the company has developed unique competitive advantages over the years and to abandon these to embrace industry best practices may actually result in a disadvantage in the marketplace. The logic could be followed that if everyone embraces the industry best practices during the implementation of ERP then competitive advantage would be how quickly the ERP implementation could be accomplished. The ERP implementation cost is significantly reduced if the company will change its practices to fit the software. However, this may be exactly opposite of the desired competitive strategy for the business. This is an area where extreme caution must be taken when selecting a software package. Some packages tightly integrate these industry best practices into the software and to deviate from these preprogrammed processes is an expensive and time-consuming implementation.

Since it is unrealistic to expect that the software will fit the organization 100%, some modifications should be expected to the software. The goal of every company in implementing a newly purchased system is to "go vanilla." This means to implement the product as-is out of the box. While this is a laudable goal, it is rarely achieved. However, a good rule of thumb is that no modifications should be made to the source code for at least 6 months to 1 year after implementation. A list of desired modifications should be kept during this period. Typically, after the 6-month period the list is really only a few critical items that really required modifications. Early in the implementation users frequently request many changes to make the new system look like the old one. After 6 months most of the early change requests have become unnecessary. A successful implementation should only require modification to output reports rather than to the core source code. Modifying the source code makes accepting future upgrades difficult if not impossible and drastically increases the cost of the implementation.

A key issue identified during virtually every system selection is to have an easy to use report writer that can be learned quickly by the average user, not requiring a programmer, to provide on demand ad hoc reports. When this type of report writer is available, most programming changes are no longer required. Some software packages make customization easy through the use of configuration switches or preconfigured templates during the implementation process. As discussed in the database section, changing these switches after the initial implementation can be very expensive depending of the package chosen.

The largest part of the implementation cost is often not the software or the hardware but rather the implementation consulting support. Usually implementation services cost compared to the software cost is a 1:1 ratio. The range can be from 1:2 all the way to 2:1 depending on the software and the readiness of the company. Many companies believe that they are too busy to participate in the implementation and bring in a large number of consultants to complete the implementation for them. Other companies believe that they do not have the expertise to implement such sophisticated systems and turn to consultants to complete the implementation. In either case, if the implementation is relegated to the consultants, then there typically is a dependence on those consultants for the foreseeable future. Provided that sufficient financial resources exist in the company to support what is typically several times more expensive than the internal resource per hour, this option is totally acceptable. An alternate approach is to develop the internal resources to complete the implementation with a minimum number of outside people involved. This usually means that the implementation will take longer initially, but the results are better understood by the users and the return on investment is typically significantly higher. There is a large learning curve for the project team, including education on the concepts of integrated resource management, training on the software tool itself, and then the political challenges of changing current business practices. Further detail on the organizational readiness for ERM can be found in the checklist in Chapter 5. There can be a challenge in retaining these people during and after a successfully implementation due to their increased market value. Chapter 14 details the approach options for successful implementations. This strategy should be discussed at the early stages of system selection so that the appropriate resources are available.

Feature/Function Selection Strategy

Another approach for system selection is through the identification of the features and functions that a software package is expected to have. This list could include detailed items grouped under heading such as

1. Forecasting
2. Master production scheduling
3. Planning
4. Inventory
5. Bills of material
6. Routings
7. Material requirements planning
8. Purchasing and receiving
9. Capacity requirements planning
10. Shop floor control
11. Product costing
12. Order entry and sales management
13. Distribution requirements planning
14. Accounts payable
15. Accounts receivable
16. Payroll
17. Personnel
18. Fixed assets
19. General ledger
20. Service dispatch
21. Computer integrated manufacturing
22. Telemarketing and catalog management
23. User interfaces
24. Information system strategy and general environmental questions

Database Enabled

The above list was taken with permission directly from Expert Buying Systems Choose Smart™ package. Expert Buying Systems is a system selection company that accomplishes the feature/function definition through a detailed questionnaire. The company's answers are compared to a database of answers from the potential ERP software suppliers. This process utilizes a PC-based tool with over 2000 feature/function points that its research has determined to be the best differentiators of available ERP software packages. The Expert Buying Systems approach is an on-site requirement definition workshop facilitated by an experienced consultant. The advantage is that there is a person to whom questions can be asked to assist the selection team to understand, evaluate, select, and prioritize the set of features and functions. This trained facilitator ensures that there is a common understanding of each of the questions and can explain the intent of each question. The Choose Smart service includes a screening of the key selected issues by a research team to ensure the best possible fit. The value promised by this organization includes saving time, cost savings, reduced confusion, high-quality package software short-list, consensus, support, and project momentum. When sending a specification document from this type of service, the software company is quite likely to respond since the software has already been shown to be a reasonably close fit.

Other choices to determine feature/function needs for ERP software include a do-it-yourself approach with resources such as the *CTS Guide to PC-Based Software for the Manufacturing Industry* or through the *Buyer's Guide* available from APICS. These resources provide a matrix of features and function against which you can compare your needs to determine the best match.

Determining needs can be a real challenge in any approach. Every functional group that is directly impacted by the system or the system's output should be involved in the development of the needs identification. These needs can be identified in a number of ways.

Brainstorming Session

In the brainstorming session all the wants and needs are identified through a technique called "nominal group." Each person is asked to bring a list of the key requirements for the system. Each person in turn adds one of their ideas to the master list until all the lists have been exhausted. Usually during this process, the addition of items not originally thought of would be made as each functional area listens to the concerns of other areas. After all the ideas have been consolidated, the list is prioritized into features that must be included in the software for the business to run, items that would be great to have, and items that are nice to have. This list forms the basis for the request for proposal (RFP) that is sent to prospective software suppliers.

During the demonstration of the software by the supplier, the issues that are critical to the business should be demonstrated and well understood. The downside of this approach is that a few very vocal people with strong opinions can skew the results to their desires. Also, the rapid addition of features and functions to modern ERP systems provide capability that could be unimagined by the selected users. Unless a person has had an experience with a system with those functions, they would not know to ask for it in a system selection. This zero-based requirements definition is likely the most expensive when the amount of time and effort is considered. The results from this approach are also the least helpful. Given the speed with which business is changing and competitive edges are secured and lost, it is a wonder why a company would follow this approach, but still many do.

Solution Providers

Some of the solutions provider companies provide a service of developing the requirements document for the business so that appropriate fit solutions can be recommended. The cost of this work is usually very reasonable. The downside is that the solutions recommended would most likely be one that the solution provider carries. If the highest concern for the system selection is to ensure objectivity, do not use the same company to specify a system and to install it. An independent source can be used to determine specifications and recommend possible solutions. This is the advantage of the Expert Buying Systems approach. This company does not support any implementation consultants nor takes any money or financial resources from the ERP software companies themselves.

Good advice is to plan to use a different resource to select a system than you plan to use in the implementation to assure independence and objectivity. The time for an integrated approach is during the system implementation where it is very desirable to have the same organization sell the software, hardware, consulting, and integration services. This strategy provides a single point of contact and no excuses or finger pointing if something goes wrong.

Consulting Services

Many consultants are happy to develop and write system specifications. Similar to solutions providers, beware of using the same consultant to specify and support the implementation of the system. The recommendation made will most probably be one of the systems they represent.

Selecting Software

Once the specifications have been written, the really hard part starts. These wants and needs are documented and sent to prospective software suppliers. A request for proposal is made. If the process used for selecting the short list has already examined the features and functions of the potential software and only those companies who fit best are included, do not send this full feature list back to the supplier. You already know the answers. The RFP should be less than five pages. Many companies believe that the quality of an RFP is measured by the weight of the document. This is not true. Normally the response rate from the prospective software supplier is directly dependent on the research done during the specification development. If requests for proposals are sent only to software companies that are known to fit the overall needs, the response rate will be quite high. Typically these RFPs are characterized as being very short and to the point. Unique questions are asked that are not in the standard grid. Asking if their system provides an item master is a sure sign of a company that has not done its homework and the response rate will be very low. This type of RFP is typical of the nominal group technique for requirements. If the request for proposal is sent out in a shotgun fashion to any known MRP solution provider, the response rate can be only about 10 to 20%. Likely the software companies that would fit the organization well will not respond because it would take too much time. From the software company's perspective, they will spend time where they believe they are likely to close a sale. Given the level of effort required to develop the specification document, putting some time and effort into researching potential suppliers is time well spent. Not doing this does a great disservice to your company and to the software company. Using consulting services or solution providers can facilitate this process. This is a process that your company likely will do only every 5 to 7 years. Using an outside resource that does system selection as a specialty is money well spent. These organizations are proven to provide a high quality result in shorter time at lower cost.

The number of proposals reviewed should be no more than five. After the responses are received, each response is critically reviewed. As part of the proposal preparation, weighting of critical elements should be developed such that the proposals can be quantitatively compared. Figure 12.1 shows a potential comparison. The rating for each attribute is in the left side of each column and the product of the weight times the rating is in the right side.

This method of quantitatively rating subjective criteria is just one way to compare the proposals at hand. The selection team should determine the

Attribute	Feature/function		Cost		Support		Years in business		Database design		Total
Weight	9		7		8		3		5		
Vendor A	4	36	1	7	2	16	3	9	3	15	83
Vendor B	3	27	3	21	3	24	2	6	2	10	88
Vendor C	2	18	2	14	4	32	1	3	4	20	87
Vendor D	1	9	4	28	1	8	4	12	1	5	62

Figure 12.1   Company ERP choices.

weightings before the results come in. Otherwise, the team may be tempted to skew the process towards a fancy proposal rather than meeting the needs of the company. Doing this before the proposals are received allows some time for the team to establish what is really important to the company and how will this investment in technology help the company achieve its goals. At this point, the proposals can be narrowed down to the top three.

In Figure 12.1, the companies who would be invited for a demonstration would be Vendors A, B, and C. After the top three are selected, each of these companies is asked to provide a demonstration of its system. Beware of the canned presentation with a script. The sales personnel will attempt to sell you on the sizzle and graphics of the system rather than real functionality. Clearly communicate to the prospective supplier the unique needs of your business and ask for a demonstration of those items identified in the proposal as "must have." Remember that no commercial software is likely to fit every need and want for your business perfectly. However, it is reasonable to expect at least 90% fit between your business practices and the software. The task at hand is to select the best fit not the perfect fit. If you purchase a software package with a particular paradigm and that paradigm does not match the business practices and paradigms in your company, you are setting yourself up for a significant expense in modifications.

Other considerations when selecting software include how long the company has been in business, how many copies of the software have been sold, and how many were successfully installed. This directly relates to how risk adverse your company is. If you desire to have the latest leading-edge technology, then the software that you will select will not have many copies installed. If your desire is to play it safe with a tried and true package with many installations, you will likely not get the leading-edge technology. ERP software functionality is changing at an amazing rate. The best decision is the one that best fits your needs at the time of the selection. Something better is always on the horizon. A local user's group is a wonderful resource as you begin your implementation. This provides you an opportunity to network with a number of users at different levels of implementation. User's groups are typically found with software that has been in the market for some time.

Be very careful about being a "beta site" for software. Beta sites test the software for bugs and expected new functionality. In return they usually receive the software at a significant discount. Given this is a mission critical system, this might be like taking advantage of a sale on brain surgery. Understand that there will be tradeoffs between the latest and greatest utilization of technology and the number of installed sites. Companies that have been around for a long time tend to have outdated technology and proprietary database structures in their system. The advantage that they have is a large installed customer base and the code is well tested and very robust. However, their beta tests of new functionality will likely be as fraught with difficulty as any newcomer to the market. The new companies on the scene can have the latest bells and whistles but without many people running it, the reliability can be severely lacking since the full functionality of the system may not be used in the market. The best advice, unless your company can successfully withstand the loss of the business planning system for a period of time, do not beta test software in a live database environment. This is where it is better to be second and let someone else be the guinea pig.

The worst thing that can happen is to purchase your software, begin to implement the system, and have the software provider go out of business. Having this contingency covered in the original contract is a good idea. Many software companies sell to small business through value-added resellers. These independent organizations support the product and receive a payment from the company or directly from the customer for this support. The advantage of this approach is that the support for the software is local. The customer does not have to be concerned with time zone differences between their location and the software supplier. The disadvantage is that the value-added reseller may not know the software as well as the programming company or may run into unrelated business difficulties. Again, this is an excellent contingency to cover in the contract. A quality solution provider will back up their value-added reseller chain in the event they go out of business. This is where selecting the right resources for system implementation is so important.

Summary

System selection is a critical milestone in the path of an ERP project. The features, functions, and technological approach must be right for the company. Given that the latest magazine articles show that 75 to 90% of ERP system implementations will not achieve the bottom-line business results that were identified in the project justification, getting started with a good selection is critical. With rapidly changing technology and the advent of new features and functions, it is essential that the company makes the best choice possible when considering a new system. This includes the hardware platform, database tool, and the overall philosophy of the ERP system.

Some ERP systems are well designed for the entrepreneurial business with decentralized controls while others offer an excellent fit for a corporate standardized business process. The first step of any successful system selection is to decide what kind of business you are. How strong is the desire to purchase a single integrated system with the best capability available? Another alternative is to select a best of breed solution where the separate subsystems are interfaced. Asking the right questions during the selection of a system can not only help select the best fit but also can build support and commitment for the final selection. It is unrealistic to expect that any commercial off-the-shelf software product will meet 100% of the company's requirements. However, at least 90% of the identified requirements should be possible.

In addition to determining the overall strategic approach and then features and functions of a desired system, the investment required must be considered. The costs of upgrading the current solution are compared to the purchase and implementation of a new solution. Many companies use the selection and implementation of a new ERP system as a catalyst for global business process reengineering. If this is the company's objective, then the question of including sufficient education and training on the new business model must be asked. A project off to a bad start has a very difficult time overcoming this obstacle and achieving the expected financial success.

System Selection Resources

Expert Buying Systems, 311 South Wacker Drive, Suite 3500, Chicago, IL 60606, 800-832-6434, www.choosesmart.com.

CTS Guide to PC-Based Software for the Manufacturing Industry, 11708 Ibsen Drive, Rockville, MD 20852, 301-468-4800.

APICS, The Educational Society for Resource Management, 5301 Shawnee Road, Alexandria, VA 22312, 800-444-APIC, www.apics.org.

13 Data Record Accuracy

Without exception, every failed implementation has as either a prime or contributing factor, the lack of data record accuracy. If data are inaccurate, then users will not trust the information from the system. When data are not trusted, then data are not maintained since people don't bother. Once the users of the system can no longer trust the data contained within the system, they begin to second-guess the information coming from the formal ERP system. The informal system is always standing by ready to take over. This unfortunately is a very insidious process that can sneak up on the company until the overall data from the ERP system that may have cost millions of dollars to purchase and install is absolutely worthless. The company must be ever vigilant on the accuracy of its data records. The use of an ERP system can have a very high return on investment if this accurate common database is used for developing reports that provide critical business management information. This common database supporting enterprise decisions eliminates the nonvalue-added wasteful discussion of who has the correct data. When the system contains accurate data, the fact is that everyone in the company does. The agility of the enterprise is enhanced as decisions based on valid data can be delegated to lower levels of the organization. The cost of inaccuracy is higher inventory, lower profits, and a significant amount of nonvalue-added work by a large group of people. In the worst case, the overall implementation may fail totally taking with it the overall investment in ERP.

To have an effective ERP implementation, data accuracy is required for inventory records, bills of materials, routings, sales orders, work orders, purchase orders, and execution transactions. An ongoing process of improvement and validation is required to assure this data quality. The enterprise planning system is really a communication system providing distributed information from a centralized database. The quality of the information is directly dependent on the accuracy of the input data.

Inventory Record Accuracy

The three most common methods used to ensure inventory record accuracy are mass balance, annual physical inventory, and cycle counting.

Mass Balance

The first method, mass balance, adds up all the incoming receipts and deducts materials used based on what has been shipped to the customer. The resulting mass balance is that quantity that should be found in inventory. This method is used in cases where the inventory is especially difficult to count like bulk material stored in silos or rail cars. The reality of this approach is that the resulting actual on-hand balance usually bears little resemblance to this balance. Unexpected events occur that use extra inventory and if the operation is of any significant size, tracking multiple items in this manner can be very unwieldy. In the face of having no other system, many companies use this mass balance method to value and validate their inventory.

Physical Inventory

Next, the most commonly used and the second least preferable method is the annual physical inventory. This process closes the entire facility for the duration of the counting and uses everyone in the plant to count unfamiliar parts. The worst inventory adjustment in one company's history was directly attributable to the annual physical inventory. One of the counters was unfamiliar with the parts and proceeded to count some electrostatic discharge sensitive parts (translation: very expensive and damaged easily) by stripping them from their protective sleeves and weigh-counting them. This part's handling process caused many of the parts to be scrapped and thousands of dollars of inventory write-off for the company. Further problems were caused because the assembly department was now short these critical parts and expedited replacements had to be air shipped from the supplier.

To perform an effective physical inventory the following steps are required:.

- Ensure all transactions are completed. This is essential for an accurate count. All receipt and issue transactions must have the same deadline. After all the transactions are completed, freeze all activity with the inventory. Receipts from suppliers and shipments to the customers must have a clean cutoff point so that the perpetual inventory records can be updated. Many companies send messages out to the suppliers and customers communicating the expected dates of the annual physical inventory and that there will be no shipments received or delivered during this inventory time.

- Control counts through inventory tags. Each item that is counted is tagged with a control tag. Part of the tag is left with the item and part is brought back for entry into the computer or validated against the manual records. Leaving a portion of the tag on the item ensures that all items have been counted. Items not expected to be counted are identified with a tag that says "Noninventory item." This rigid approach to identification of counted and uncounted items and a clean cutoff from shipments and receipts attempts to ensure positive control of every item in the plant. After the inventory has been counted and the tags have been entered into the computer or validated against the manual inventory, comparison reports are run.

- Run analysis reports. These reports summarize the total inventory changes in dollars and are usually sorted in descending order by the variances against the perpetual inventory record. This report is usually run by total extended value variance rather than by part count. In some companies, these reports are processed twice, once by value variance and once by count variance.

- Recount significant variance items. If the errors are great, items may need to be recounted. Expect that 80% of the dollar problems will be attributed to 20% of the errors. After recounting the items with significant variances, the accountants then verify the inventory and clear approved sections of the plant to continue return to production. Depending on the size of the plant, this process can be completed in one day or several days. Considering that the people who prove to have the best skills in counting are rewarded by being required to stay until the very end while the people who have difficulty counting get to leave early, it is no wonder that the overriding goal of the day is to simply get done. This results in lack of concern for accuracy and it does make one wonder why this approach is so popular with so many companies.

■ Audit and consider the inventory completed. Now go back to work producing items that the customers want; real work that adds value and profit to the bottom line, not like the annual physical inventory-taking process.

One thing remains constant, the annual periodic physical inventory always takes longer than expected or desired. The result of this antiquated process of annual physical inventory is an unfounded confidence in the accuracy of the inventory records since the perpetual record is updated during this time with these hurried counts. Reality is that approximately the same number of records will be corrected as are made incorrect. Many companies compound this pain by taking physical inventories quarterly or even monthly.

World-class organizations rarely voluntarily disrupt their entire inventory and operation by imposing an annual physical inventory. The commonly held belief that accounting auditors require an annual physical inventory is not true. The process of validating the asset called inventory is required, not an annual physical inventory. Keeping well-organized accurate perpetual inventory records benefits the enterprise more than just eliminating the physical inventory. Without real-time accurate records, having a successful supply chain solution is impossible.

Cycle Counting

Cycle counting is the preferred method of validating the inventory process. This allows small quantities of the inventory to be counted daily or weekly by personnel that know and understand the parts. The real benefit of cycle counting is not the update of the physical inventory records but rather the identification and resolution of the root causes of inventory record inaccuracy. There is less time between the error cause and the error detection. The investment for cycle counting is significantly less than the annual physical inventory. Because a little is done each day, the risk for large inventory losses is greatly reduced. Just eliminating this financial impact and the management shock of the annual write-off can be sufficient to support a cycle counting program. The people counting the parts are familiar with the parts and their required handling. Since cycle counting is part of their everyday duty, the learning curve effect is seen and they become very efficient and quick at accurately performing these counts. More counts can be accurately completed accurately at a lower cost than the annual physical inventory.

Cycle Counting Requirements

Unique part numbers. As in many other parts of the ERP system, each item in inventory must be identifiable through a unique number. This means that if a part is in inventory stocked in a number of different conditions such as unpainted, painted, and plated, each condition of the part must have a unique part number. If a part has the same part number, the fit, form, and function must be identical. A good test is that if a blindfolded person could reach into the bin and use any part drawn, then all the parts in the bin should be one part number. If a sort would have to occur to have a usable part or if someone needs to remember which customer or order can get a specific supplier or color, then a different part number is required. Unique part numbers are required for material requirements planning (MRP) to run, as a rule. Without unique identification, the calculation of what is needed cannot be completed. Unique item identification is not a new requirement to support cycle counting. Unique part identification allows error free communication about parts.

Experienced counters. The people performing the counting should have experience in counting and be able to handle numbers accurately. This means that people responsible for maintaining the inventory should be evaluated for their ability to read and write numbers accurately. Even very intelligent people can be challenged when it comes to handling, correctly recording, and inputting complex part numbers. Each person that is responsible for counting the inventory should be validated in the counting process so that one uniform process is used throughout the company. These experienced counters have the responsibility and accountability for accurate inventory. Careful attention to detail is required in this position.

Control group. A representative group of parts is selected for testing the overall cycle count and inventory process. This group should contain representatives from each product group and dollar category. The control group is used during the early stages of cycle counting to validate the inventory control process and is used from time to time to validate any changes made in the counting process. Establishing a control group is a key factor for success in any cycle counting program. This is usually the overlooked part of the process. The effectiveness of cycle counting is not measured by the number of different parts that are counted, but rather the process improvement that is accomplished through judicious counting processes.

Small amount of time each day for counting. The best time for counting is when all transactions have been posted against the database or manual record. Counting first thing in the morning is the most common practice. The amount of time dedicated to counting and validating those counts should not exceed 30 to 60 minutes. The main thrust of cycle counting is to accomplish a small bit each day and not impact the overall operation. This dedicated small amount of time each day yields major benefits for the operation. The discipline required to dedicate this time each day can become a challenge as the company becomes busier and the time demands of the storekeepers increase. Discipline is necessary to maintain accurate inventories and allocating time to count is only a small part of the total requirement, but it is essential for the process to be successful.

Cycle Counting — A, B, C

Many different approaches are used to accomplish cycle counting. A proven method is to follow these steps:

Count the control group repeatedly. Many companies attempt to pass over this step, but it is the most critical for long-term success. The control group items should be counted daily until 100% inventory accuracy is achieved and maintained for 10 days. Any error in the count is documented. The underlying systems and inventory control processes must be improved before moving on. The process of recounting a control group gives intensive attention to a small group and identifies issues that are likely problems for the balance of the parts in inventory. By identifying and fixing problems for this group, the balance of the inventory should be similarly affected in a positive way. Expanding the count to additional parts before the control group is 100% accurate is an exercise in futility. Unless the underlying process issues can be identified and resolved, the overall inventory record accuracy will not improve.

Identify process issues. Process issues are any event or cause that result in less than 100% inventory accuracy. Common errors are: failure to make timely transactions, transposing a number, or undocumented usage of a part. These process issues are easiest to see during the control group counting because the time difference between error cause and effect is very short. Additional process issues will likely be uncovered after the cycle counting practice has expanded to the remainder of the item records.

Correct process issues. For any process issue resulting in inventory inaccuracy, the root cause must be determined and resolved. This may include updating the inventory control process, training storekeeping and production personnel in the correct procedure, or insisting on discipline in the inventory control process. Just as a bank will not allow anyone to come in and take what they want without a transaction, manufacturing and distribution inventory must be accounted for in a reliable, consistent, and dependable fashion. With the advent of ATMs, no longer is the teller required to document the transaction at the bank. Similarly a storekeeper is not required to document inventory movement; discipline of transactions is required. More companies are moving to having parts stored directly on the production line. This increased availability does not eliminate the need for discipline. Actually, online or point of use inventory stores increases the amount of discipline required. Having access to inventory creates a challenge in having foolproof processes. The developed processes should be easier to complete correctly than to work around.

Expand to other part numbers. Only after the inventory control process has been proven reliable with the control group and the inventory accuracy for this group has remained at 100% for a period of time (5 to 10 days), should the cycle count process be expanded to the rest of the parts. Inventory record accuracy will take an initial jump and then gradually move up from there. The goal of the company is to have 100% inventory accuracy. Any inventory inaccuracy causes distrust of the system output in general, incorrect ordering, and poor decision making.

Continue to resolve process issues. As problems arise, resulting in inaccurate perpetual inventory records, the process issues must continue to be identified and resolved. Don't be too quick to blame an operator for the error when there is usually an underlying process issue. Having simple tools enhances inventory accuracy dramatically. The inventory process must be simple enough so that it is easier to do it correctly than to go around the system. The simple solution is always the hardest to achieve. Also, remember that the less inventory that is in the plant, the easier it is to count.

Selecting Parts to Count

Now that a process has been defined for cycle counting, the control group has maintained 100% accuracy for at least 5 to 10 consecutive days, how do the counts take place and on what cycle? A few different philosophies exist for selecting the cycle. The most common are listed below.

Part value. Once the cycle count process has been established, the highest return on investment is to validate the highest value parts in the inventory. The benefit with this approach is that a significant part of the total value of the inventory can be counted in a very short period of time with confidence that the on-hand balances are being corrected. During the same time that the high-value parts are being counted, the control group is still being counted, although not as frequently. The control group should be validated at least on a weekly basis during the time that the cycle counting process is still in its early stages. Once the high-value parts have been validated, attention should turn to working methodically through the balance of the inventory.

Calendar frequency using ABC classification. The traditional definition for cycle counting is to count parts based on a combination of the calendar and their ABC code. "A" items would be counted the most frequently; for example, once per month. "B" items would be counted less frequently, such as once per quarter. "C" items may cycle once per year. One way to calculate the frequency of counting is to examine how many counts required each day. For example, assume a 2500 part item master and 250 work days/year. We would expect 500 "A" items, 750 "B" items, and 1250 "C" items.

If "A" items are counted monthly that would be 6000 counts per year
If "B" items are counted quarterly that would be 3000 counts per year
If "C" items are counted annually that would be 1250 counts per year
Total counts per year = 10,250
Average counts/day = 41

The daily work load for counts must be realistic when compared to the resources available. Otherwise, the job will not be done. Better to plan ahead and reduce the frequency than give up on the process all together. An experienced counter can normally process approximately 40 counts per 8-hour day so if the above scheme was used, one person would be required full time for the cycle counting activity. Fortunately, there are other ways to select items to count.

Receipt time. Verifying inventory at time of receipt takes advantage of the fact that the inventory should be at its absolute lowest point. Another advantage is the person is at the inventory location already and is handling the exact part. Unfortunately, although this is very easy to count, it can be compared to locking the barn door after the horse ran away. Finding out that there is excess or missing parts upon receipt of an order does not leave much recovery time. This method is best used in addition to other count strategies.

Negative inventory. Many modern computer systems allow the inventory quantity to become a negative number. This does not mean that if a quantity of parts equal to the negative quantity were placed on the shelf, they would immediately disappear into some magical black hole. Having negative inventory means that more parts were issued than the perpetual inventory records had available. Knowing the magnitude of the negative number is very helpful in identifying the underlying root cause. Usually negative inventory is caused by a failure to transact the receipt of an incoming quantity before it is used. Similar to counting when the product is received, this method is best used in conjunction with a regularly scheduled cycle count. In any event, negative inventory counts should be validated on a daily basis. Anytime the inventory record goes negative, this is an indication that the inventory control process is out of control.

Counting by location. A creative and simple way to cycle through the inventory is to count by inventory location. This will uncover parts that have been misplaced and other surprises lurking on the shelves. The process works by obtaining a perpetual inventory listing by inventory location. This assumes that locations are uniquely identified. Identifying specific locations assists in finding the exact location of the part. An easy method for coding locations is descending significance relationship. If multiple storerooms are used, the first digit could be the location of the storeroom. Alphabetic characters work well and give ample uniqueness with one digit. This also prevents the confusion of part number and inventory locations. The next set of characters is the rack on which the parts are stored. Usually two digits are sufficient. The next digit is the shelf, starting at the bottom with zero or one. Numbering is started at the bottom shelf to allow growth in the vertical direction. Additional specifics can be built in with the location on the shelf. For example, a part stored in D2712 is stored in stockroom D, on rack 27, on the first shelf in the second position. With very short identifiers, over 200,000 locations can be uniquely identified. Parts are easier to find because the system is very consistent, predictable, and simple.

This declining significance method supports easy production of a report that lists inventory by expected location. Once this report is produced, the storekeeper takes it to the stockroom and begins to validate the inventory. If the parts are easy to count or there is an obvious error, an actual count is performed. If the parts are difficult to count and there is no obvious error, the part is bypassed. For example, when looking at location C2321, there is a quantity of 7 parts of item 136609. The storekeeper validates that part 136609 is indeed expected in location C2321. Since 7 is an easy number to count, the count is validated or error noted and reported back to the perpetual system. Moving to location C2322, the bin holding part 142708 should contain 8794 parts. When looking at the bin the storekeeper can see that there is a large number of parts. 8794 seems reasonable and counting them would take at least 15 to 20 minutes. Since spending all that time does not add any value, these parts are bypassed. No count is entered for part 142708. This is not included in the hit or miss report. The storekeeper moves to location C2323 where the bin holding part 24536 should have 9703 parts. Upon examination, the bin is holding only about 100 parts. The storekeeper makes an exact count. This part is then subject to problem solving to discover the root cause for the discrepancy.

Using this method storekeepers can verify many more parts than counting every part in every location. Since the purpose of cycle counting is to validate the inventory control process, the ability to collect more data about the accuracy of the inventory and the reason for possible inaccuracy is better than slogging through the tedious count of parts that look to be correct anyway. The downside of this approach is that it takes a judgment call on the part of the storekeeper. Often in cases where inventory is stored in multiple locations, there is a working stock supported by reserve stock. The working stock would be counted during the cycle count while the reserve stock is counted at receipt time, sealed, and labeled with the count and stored. As long as the reserve stock seal is intact the label count is used.

Some managers do not believe in letting the storekeepers see the perpetual inventory counts when doing cycle counting. The reality is that the storekeepers are the most motivated to have accurate inventory and withholding this information will only make their job more difficult. Indeed, many times the first action of the stockkeeper is to go to the inventory system and copy the expected quantity onto the cycle count worksheet — an activity that takes a person several minutes and which could have been performed by the computer in nanoseconds. Using proper measurement systems they will respond with overall process improvements for inventory accuracy rather than spending the time and effort attempting to circumvent the system. Everyone is a winner. Allowing the storekeepers this judgment really puts the control in the correct hands — the process owner who knows most about it and is motivated to improve the process.

Defining Accuracy

Accuracy seems like an easy term to understand. Intuitively either something is right or wrong. However, the APICS definition for accuracy reveals that things are more complicated than first glance might reveal. The APICS definition for accuracy is "the degree of freedom from error or the degree of conformity to a standard. Accuracy is different from precision. For example, four significant digit numbers are less precise than six significant digit numbers; however, a properly computed four significant digit number might be more accurate than an improperly computed six significant digit number."[1]

Inventory accuracy can be thought of in similar terms. Accuracy is similar to tolerance limits of a manufacturing process. If parts are counted by hand, the counts should match exactly with no tolerance. If a scale is used to count the parts, a realistic tolerance is 3 to 5%. Overall inventory record accuracy is calculated by adding all the accurate counts and dividing by the total number of counts performed. This is then expressed as a percentage. Inventory accuracy is not the percentage of parts found compared to the actual inventory. For example, a part is not 85% accurate if only 85% of the parts are found. That part would be 0% accurate. Inventory accuracy reflects the overall summary of "hits" and "misses." A hit is a count that falls within the defined tolerance and a miss is a count that is outside the defined tolerance. Overall inventory record accuracy is calculated by adding all the counts within tolerance and dividing by the total number of counts performed. This is then expressed as a percentage. The overall expectation for inventory accuracy is 100%. If you think that inventory accuracy is expensive, try inventory inaccuracy.

Expected Results of Cycle Counting

Obviously the first expected result of cycle counting is accurate inventory balances. The investment required is minimal and can yield exceptional results that directly benefit the overall operation. One positive benefit is the elimination of the dreaded annual periodic physical inventory. Even if the accounting firm thinks they need an annual physical inventory when it is shown that the annual physical inventory actually reduces inventory accuracy, they will quickly change their minds. Another benefit is that the cycle counting process as described is consistent with the closed loop process improvement approach of the Shewhart "plan, do, check, act" cycle. Inventory accuracy is an easily measurable result for a cross-functional team that benefits the company directly. Imagine if there was never another inventory value write down. Let's face it, those unexpected adjustments to inventory come directly from the bottom line. Obviously the parts went somewhere. We may think we are making money on an order when we really are not due to the inventory that is used.

Bill of Material Record Accuracy

A bill of material lists all the physical items required to make a parent part. If a part is inadvertently left off the bill of material, then the planning system will have no visibility that it is required. If too many parts are on the bill of material then excess inventory will be the result. Validating the bill of material is essential to ensure that the correct parts are purchased in the correct quantities. As systems become more integrated and automatic supply chain linkages are used to pass requirements to suppliers, the cost of any inaccuracy in the bill of material can be overwhelming.

Initial Product Releases

When a new product is released to manufacturing, one of the last checkpoints in the process should be to validate the bill of material. A bill of material is "a listing of all the subassemblies, intermediates, parts, and raw materials that go into a parent assembly showing the quantity of each required to make an assembly. It is used in conjunction with the master production schedule to determine the items for which purchase requisitions and production orders must be released."[1] The bill of material has been developed incrementally throughout the design process and before it is released to manufacturing a final check is required to ensure accuracy. This validation is done against the part's engineering drawing. Using product data management (PDM) can make this process easier. This was covered in Chapter 8. The quantity and specifications of the components required to build the parent part are validated. This process is normally accomplished by the engineering function such as manufacturing engineering.

Ongoing Validation

Rarely does a design stay stagnant. Demands from customers or insights gained during the manufacturing process require that changes be made to

Table 13.1   Sample Bill of Material and Validation

142709 Lamp	As Planned	As Built	Hit/Miss
136509 Bulb	2	3	M
154670 Yoke	1	1	H
134957 Bulb socket	2	2	H
145604 Shades	2	2	H
198473 Base	1	1	H
157604 Wire assembly	1	1	H
938472 Wire (feet)	6	7	M
836485 Plug	1	1	H

the engineering drawings and/or the parts list. The engineering change order (ECO) process must include the update of the ERP system so that the bill of material stays accurate. Part of the ECO sign off should include a validation of the bill of material. In addition, periodically the as-planned bill of material needs to be validated against the as-designed and as-built bill of material. This process can be accomplished by producing a special piece of paperwork to follow the part in the fabrication or assembly process. Each person who comes in contact with the order then validates what is actually used and compares it to the system record. The most important part of this process is to make the required corrections in the ERP system. Frequently the checking process is done only to not reap the benefits because the system is not updated. Table 13.1 shows a sample bill of material and how it has been validated.

The resulting performance measure for accuracy is calculated by counting the number of line items on the bill of material that were found to be accurate divided (hits) by the total number of bill of material lines checked. This quotient is then expressed as a percentage. An example is shown in Table 13.1. There are six lines that match the "as planned" to the "as built" out of eight possible lines. The accuracy of the bill of material would be calculated at 6/8 or 75%.

Routing Accuracy

Just as bill of material record accuracy is required to ensure that the correct parts are ordered in the correct quantity, routing accuracy assures that the right resources are available to complete the fabrication and assembly of the item. The APICS Dictionary defines a routing as "information detailing the method of manufacture of a particular item. It includes the operations to be performed, their sequence, the various work centers involved, and the standards for setup and run. In some companies, the routing also includes information of tooling, operator skill levels, inspection operations, testing requirements, etc."[1] A routing is how the materials from the bill of material are converted into a finished product. Having the correct workstations, times, and resources identified on the routing is a prerequisite for developing an accurate capacity plan, either finite or infinite.

If the company has any plans to implement an Advanced Planning and Scheduling (APS) system, routing accuracy is critical. APS systems recommend the product mix that will result in the highest profits for the enterprise given the available resources compared to the requirements from customer orders. If the routing steps are inaccurate or the times are incorrect, poor decisions may be made on which orders to accept or not, and overall company profitability may be adversely affected. The bill of material provides the materials upon which to work, the routing provides the resources required and their required sequencing to accomplish the transformation. Similar to the bill of material, the routing should be validated for accuracy when the part first completes the design phase and on an ongoing basis. The initial validation of the routing after the design is completed is normally part of the manufacturing engineering sign-off. The ongoing check can be accomplished as part of the bill of material validation, accomplishing two critical tasks in one. As manufacturing progresses, each person coming into contact with the order validates the operation, the machine upon which it is accomplished, and the time required completing the setup and each individual piece.

The times used in the routing should be realistic. Unlike bills of materials, where the number of parts used to make the parent part is fixed and known, the routing hours can vary depending on who is doing the task. The more reliance there is on humans resources completing the tasks rather than machines, the more variability and error there will be in routings. This is a normal phenomenon of human beings. Some people are very quick in accomplishing tasks while others take significantly longer, even using the same process. This resource requirement variability is what makes the implementation of sophisticated APS scheduling tools a real challenge for this type of business. Although the theory of optimization and sophisticated scheduling sounds wonderful and very sophisticated and useful, the reality is that the required data accuracy is not feasible in most labor driven enterprises.

Determining routing accuracy is not as easy as bill of material accuracy. The number of checked routings steps that fall within a given tolerance are counted as accurate and are compared to the number of routing records checked to get the accuracy percentage.

Sales Order Accuracy

Sales order accuracy is an area that is frequently overlooked in an ERP implementation. Having accurate demand drive the planning system is essential for the overall success of the system. Imagine the impact of having incorrect demand driving the whole planning process. Everything downstream from the customer order is inaccurate and unusable. When the automatic supply chain integration is considered, the results could be disastrous. The process used to validate sales order accuracy is a gradual improvement strategy.

Normally the backlog of orders can be very large even in a relatively small company. An easy way to incrementally improve the overall sales order accuracy is to look at the first page of a sales order summary. If there is a difficulty with an order, this is usually found when an order becomes past due. It is not unusual to find companies with orders on their books over a year past due! Although this may seem surprising, the reality is there. If each week the first page of the customer order summary is printed in due date order, validated, and corrected, a large number of problems can be addressed. Since it is impossible to ship an order in the past, when the sales order summary is printed, the very oldest order should not have a date that is past due.

If the sales order has a past due date, the materials required to build the part will have a requirement date that is way in the past and anyone looking at the system will know that the information is in error. This begins the downward spiral of distrust and second guessing. This leads to less use of the system until finally the current informal systems are back running the business. The best way to keep sales orders accurate is to really use the system to manage the business. The more the system is used to manage the business, the more people are dependent on the data and become more watchful of the accuracy of that data. Using the data and information from the ERP system to hold people accountable quickly results in improved accuracy.

Work Order Accuracy

Similar to the sales order accuracy strategy, keeping work orders accurate is an incremental approach. The first of the easy steps for work order accuracy is to only release work orders for those items that will realistically be put immediately into work. Releasing work orders before they are needed provides no value to the operation. In fact, releasing work orders before the material and the capacity are both available to build the parts creates a great deal of confusion and manual systems since there is no clear visibility of priorities. The manufacturing area can easily hide behind the excuse that either the materials or capacity or both are not available to complete the order so, therefore, they cannot be held accountable to the dates on the work order. Quickly the dates on the work orders become meaningless and it is impossible to look at the formal system and make any assessment when a product will really be completed. This puts the "capable to promise" and "available to promise" functions at risk of providing any realistic information.

When work orders are released that have the materials and capacity available, the dispatch lists can show realistic due dates to which manufacturing can be held accountable. The available to promise and capable to promise functions can provide a realistic answer to the customer on when they may be able to expect their products. While this process is evolving to having only the workable orders open, validating the oldest orders on the dispatch list will typically yield excellent results. Holding the shop supervisors accountable to the completion dates on the dispatch list will also help develop accuracy in those dates. To begin the process, similar to the process used to validate sales orders, printing the first page of work orders sorted by due date, validating them, and providing realistic due dates (dates after today's date) provides an immediate return on investment. The validation of work orders must continue on an ongoing basis as part of normal system maintenance to ensure that the very past due order condition does not return.

Master Production Schedule Accuracy

Master production schedule accuracy is not simply the schedule input into the system accurately to reflect the current schedule. Master production schedule accuracy also reflects the feasibility of the schedule as validated through Sales and Operations planning described in Chapter 3. The master schedule should be a realistic statement of what can and will be built. The master schedule accuracy is established by balancing the required load against the available capacity. The measurement of accuracy for the master production schedule according to *The Oliver Wight ABCD Checklist for Operational Excellence,* 4th ed., is

1. Past due, which can be measured as a percentage of current output rate or the percentage of current inprocess aging.
2. Percentage of schedule changes within the near (firm zone) horizon.
3. Performance vs. schedule in finishing/final assembly per customer order.
4. Linearity of output (by department and to finished goods and/or shipping). Linearity of output measures the level of variability that is inherent in the whole output process. This measure is excellent for measuring overall operational effectiveness.

Purchase Order Accuracy

Purchase order accuracy is necessary for the manufacturing planners to know when the raw materials will be available to release the required manufacturing orders. If items are purchased and then distributed to customers, having accurate purchasing information allows the available to promise (ATP) and the capable to promise (CTP) functions to accurately project when a customer may expect an order. The process to validate purchase orders is very similar to the process validating work orders and sales orders. This is an ongoing operation where the problem orders will quickly rise to the top as past due. Examine the first page of a purchase order listing by due date. This page will typically hold the problems that must be resolved. Once this first page is resolved, the overall accuracy of the information will improve dramatically. Continue to work through the report one page at a time until the first purchase order is an order that is valid and due sometime in the future. This process must be ongoing to ensure that all orders remain valid. This may be a surprise to some people, but it is not possible to turn back the hands of time to order or receive parts. Therefore, all purchase orders should have an expected delivery date that is sometime in the future. Realizing that all suppliers are not on time with all deliveries, this means that this process must be under constant review to ensure that valid due dates are being fed into the system initially and that they are being maintained with the passage of time.

Manufacturing Execution System (MES) Accuracy

Manufacturing execution systems are a "factory floor information and communication system with several functional capabilities. It includes functions such as resource allocation and status, operation/detailed scheduling, dispatching production units, document control, data collection and acquisition, labor management, quality management, process management, maintenance management, product tracking and genealogy, and performance analysis."[1] MES collects all the detailed information from the actual execution of the plan to close the planning loop and compare actual against planned. This topic was covered in more detail in Chapter 9.

Knowing where parts are in the manufacturing process, what the expected yield is, and how many operations are still to go is critical in providing customers with status on their order including when the product will ship. The MES system is critical in providing feedback to the APS systems so that the required capacity can be identified for each part. One strategy for ensuring accuracy of MES data is to utilize these data as key performance measures for shop floor personnel. ERP has the functionality to report on-time statistics both for start and completion date, lead-time, and process capability as a normal function from the system. If the output from the system is used to drive and report performance measures, the motivation will be there to keep that data accurate. The typical response when first examining the dispatch list is that the orders listed are not in the work area. If the department is measured by on-time orders out of their department and the dispatch list is used to calculate the on-time statistics, the cleanup of the dispatch list is very quick. The other strategy for ensuring accurate MES data is to have the reporting function as an integral part of the process. When someone has to remember to write something down in a log, errors will naturally occur. A MES process that is linked with the material movement system, process controllers, or machine counters should provide a more accurate result. A truism about all data inputs into the ERP system is that when information is used from the system as performance measures directly related to those inputs, the inputs will be more accurate. If there are many legacy systems or parallel systems that are being used in addition to the ERP system, this is a sure sign that the data inside the ERP system are inaccurate.

Summary

Make the assumption that the market pressure to reduce lead-time will continue into the future and the company that is more agile will have a competitive edge. By ensuring that accurate data is used by the ERP system, the information that is generated by the system is also accurate. When the information from ERP is accurate and timely, all decision-making personnel will use this information to make decisions. These decisions will be able to be made more quickly since the manual correlation and checking of data and information is not required. When an enterprise uses consistent information for decisions, the quality of decisions is improved and everyone in the enterprise should be pulling for the same goal. When everyone in the company is aligned on the same goal, the company is more likely to achieve that goal and overall success. Having a common database of information is one of the key motivators in the purchase of an ERP system. The ability to make quick accurate decisions is directly related to having that common database. In fact, this is what drives a large part of the overall return on investment for ERP. Input data integrity is the first domino that starts the chain reaction in making that goal a reality.

References

1. APICS — The Educational Society for Resource Management, APICS Dictionary, 9th ed., Alexandria, VA, 1998.

14 Implementation: Generalized Industry Application

mplementation of ERP has received a great deal of attention in the press. *The Wall Street Journal* named ERP implementation "the corporate equivalent of a root canal." *The New York Times* called ERP "software that can make a grown company cry." ERP software suppliers make promises of huge savings and increased efficiencies, but the business press continues to report millions of dollars invested with little or no return on investment. Quoted failure rates are in the range of 60 to 90% with failure defined as an implementation that does not achieve the return on investment identified in the project approval phase. It is no wonder that companies of any size approach ERP implementation with hesitation and apprehension. Even with all the negative hype about ERP implementation, the "rules of the road" required for a successful implementation are well understood. Violate a number of these rules and failure is sure to follow. This is no different than running red lights or driving the wrong direction on a highway. You may be able to get away with it for a short period of time but soon your luck will run out. ERP implementation can be straightforward if the following template is followed. This is not proposing to fit the business to some arbitrary software model but rather to take advantage of proven, effective business practices.

Determine Industry Type

The first step of an effective system selection is to determine what type of business the enterprise is or intends to be. How will the ERP tool be used to

285

support and implement the company's overall strategic goals? A very common error is to select the right system for the company and implement the wrong one. Similar to the office product software today, commercially available ERP systems have a wealth of features and functionality that can easily dazzle even the most experienced practitioner. The big ERP suppliers are spending millions of dollars each year to add even more! It is very easy to be entranced by the siren's song of these features and get pulled down the path of attempting to implement every part of the system rather than taking from that toolbox what the company really needs. Setting the overall company goals is clearly the job for senior management and should not be abdicated to lower levels in the organization.

Industry application includes how the company has decided to go to market including how the company will meet the customer demand: stock finished goods, forecast raw material, assemble final products to order, or exercise quick response manufacturing. Is the company a high-variety low-volume producer or a high-volume low-variety producer? To better understand the competitive position of an enterprise, the relationship between the volume produced by the company is compared relative to the variety produced. An interesting diagonal has evolved where most companies are clustered in order to compete effectively. Movements from that competitive diagonal can either be a competitive advantage for the company or disaster. According to Terry Hill in *Manufacturing Strategy*, this can be represented in the following matrix (Figure 14.1).

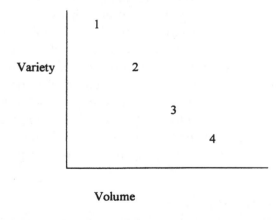

Figure 14.1   Volume/variety matrix.

This relationship shows an inverse relationship between variety and volume. In general, as the product volume increases the variety tends to decrease. This topic was more fully covered in Chapter 4 with respect to inventory and resource strategy. This relationship must be well understood to develop the overall strategy for competitiveness.

The answers to the questions of what kind of enterprise the company is in how it desires to compete in the market, and the volume and variety of products manufactured determine the best strategy for the selection of the individual tools, and the application of those tools for success. Specific strategies for different industry types such as repetitive, project manufacturing (complex manufacturing), remanufacturing, and process industry are covered in Chapters 15 through 18.

The overall ERP implementation process can be broken into three steps: get ready, get set, and go. If a good job is done on the planning and process for an ERP implementation, when the system is ready to be turned on, the implementation should go very smoothly so the expected results will be achieved.

Get Ready

The first step in any project should be to determine what is the objective or expected deliverable from the project. The objective of the system implementation should be a SMART goal; that is specific, measurable, achievable, related, and have a timeline associated with it. The implementation of ERP is a major project for any size organization. The project will go through its very difficult times and having a SMART business goal provides the focus for the team to keep them going during the difficult times. These objectives can be separated into two objective types: strategic and economic. Examples of strategic objectives include integration of processes, customer responsiveness or flexibility, improved information, cost, productivity, and new application infrastructure. Economic benefits include inventory investment, financial management, personnel cost, information technology cost, supplier management and procurement, or order management. Sample metrics can include:

- Reduction of inventory from 27% of revenue to 20% of revenue
- Reduce $15 million out of $350 million inventory
- Reduce procurement time by 25%

- Reduce overall cost of raw material by 5%
- Reduce financial personnel by 10%
- Increase revenue by 25% without increased hiring
- Reduce end of month closing time from 12 days to 4 days

The important thing to remember is that whatever goal or objective is chosen, it should be meaningful to the enterprise as a whole. This provides the motivation for the project during the difficult times. Having the goal of information technology update is insufficient for project motivation. The next step of the "get ready" phase is to determine the approach for the implementation. There are three basic possible approaches for implementation.

Do It Yourself Approach

The first approach is to accomplish the implementation entirely within the enterprise with no outside assistance. The benefit of this approach is that the out of pocket cost will be the lowest. However, if the expertise does not exist within the enterprise to accomplish the wide variety of tasks required in an ERP implementation, the project could take much longer than expected and the returns could be very disappointing. If the enterprise seriously considers this option, all involved personnel must be well acquainted with the underlying concepts of ERP and supply chain management through an intensive educational effort. This approach has been proven very successful in companies with a common understanding of the concepts led by internal personnel with extensive experience in previous ERP implementation. To consider implementing ERP without having anyone inside the firm with previous implementation experience is a sure plan for disaster without outside support.

Hire Outside Resources

Another approach that many larger companies take is to contract for the additional resources required to accomplish the ERP implementation. There are many consulting firms happy to provide this resource at a price that is relatively high per hour compared to the company's current salaries. This can be a source of hard feeling within the project team if the billable rate becomes public knowledge. Add to this the fact that some of these consulting firms hire bright, well-educated, young people directly from college. The benefit of this approach is that their billable rate is significantly below the rate charged for the experienced personnel. The primary downside is that although these fine, young people may have an excellent theoretical background, they could very likely be learning their practical application at your company's expense. In addition to learning the practical application of theory, they also must become familiar with your company and its processes. If insufficient resources exist within the enterprise to accomplish the implementation, this may be your only practical choice. The secondary downside, in addition to the expense, is that your operation will quickly become reliant on these additional people. Before they disengage from your company, there must be a plan on how the knowledge transfer will occur from the consulting team to your team.

The other risk is that the decisions made during the implementation may not take into account some of the finer business process intricacies. The typical large consulting company approach is that they will apply predeveloped templates based on industry best practices. The risk is that these best practices may not be the best fit for your specific company. Without the integral involvement of key personnel from your company, the consultants will not know that. Recently because of the negative press around ERP implementations, the consulting companies are beginning to quote a project at a firm fixed price given a negotiated statement of work. This statement of work should be well understood including the measures for performance and payment.

Mentor Resource Model

The mentor resource model is a cross between the two extremes of doing it all yourself and having a busload of consultants move in with you. This model requires that the overall project team leader is a resource that is internal to your enterprise. Outside resources are used only when needed to support the implementation, provide answers to specific questions, and provide overall strategic support. Usually the rate for these resources is negotiated at the beginning of the implementation but only the amount of resource that is actually used is paid for. This should result in a lower cost than the previous option but the risk is that the most of the budget can be easily consumed very early in the project.

Scope Development

Whatever approach is chosen the overall implementation must include a clear statement of work or scope of the project. This scope should include the modules selected for implementation as well as the business processes that will be in scope and out of scope. Scope creep is a very common phenomenon in ERP implementation. As the implementation team becomes more familiar with the software tool and can see application within the enterprise for other functionality, the project can easily expand to incorporate this new scope. Unfortunately, the budget was not developed with this increased scope and the costs can quickly spiral out of control without an adequate return on investment. This experience is very common and can be difficult to control if there is insufficient scope control at the beginning of the project. The scope determination includes not only which modules of the software that will be implemented, but also the business processes that are in scope for reengineering consideration and automation.

Any ERP system implementation can quickly turn into a major enterprise-remodeling job. Anyone who has ever attempted a home improvement project can identify with this. The project may be a very small project with a well-defined scope such as adding an electrical plug. Once the hole is cut in the wall it is determined that the wiring in that wall is not really the best. Now the whole wall needs to be rewired. Once this is started quickly it moves to rewiring the whole house. The next thing discovered is that the structure behind the walls is unstable and should be replaced. Now the entire wall is torn out for renovation, this continues on and on until it really would have been less expensive to tear the house down and start over than it would be to add one outlet. This is an excellent example of scope creep. Tight scope control must be exercised not only on modules but also on business processes. Once it has been determined which processes are included on the project then an assessment can be completed on which industry best practices fit the desired overall strategic direction of the enterprise. Instituting industry best practices without assessing their fit to the company's strategy will drastically increase the resistance to change as the implementation moves forward.

Budget

ERP implementation is an excellent time to reassess the competitive advantage of the enterprise, present and future. This top-level strategic direction then provides the guiding principles for the implementation. These guiding principles include the measurable expected results and help to determine the budget required. The breakdown of costs for a typical ERP implementation are cited as 20% hardware, 30% software (ERP, database, operating system, middleware), 10% education and training, 30% consulting services, and 10% other. Although the exact percentage may vary widely from company to company, these percentages may aid in preparing an overall budget. The exact budget is determined in detail by the specific approach taken by the company.

Part of the budgeting process is an expected timeline for the investment and the anticipated return. The budget must include the resource models and the overall assumptions made for the project. This should be well documented early in the process so that later in the project these assumptions can be easily identified. The typical timeline is project preparation of 1 to 3 weeks followed by business blueprint preparation of 3 to 6 weeks. This planning phase is followed by detailed application of the software to the company's process including at least two conference room pilot demonstrations. This step takes the bulk of the time and can be accomplished in 1 to 9 months depending on the motivation and resources of the project team. This application phase is followed by the actual "go live" process where the system is utilized to run the chosen business processes.

After the system goes live, the final version of the new business processes must be documented and communicated to all affected personnel. If a consulting company was used to support the implementation, this final phase includes training all personnel in not only how to accomplish the detailed transactions but also how these transactions fit into the overall system.

Get Set

The "get set" phase is where the application of the software to the selected processes is made and the gaps between "as is" and "to be" is identified. According to Karl Kapp, this process can be summarized by the acronym USA. USA means Understand existing processes, Simplify, and Automate. Understanding the existing processes includes using such methods as diagramming the overall system inputs and outputs. Story boarding can be used to examine the cause and effect of different processes. An excellent way to identify waste in the process is to "walk the process." Act like you are an order received by the company. Walk through the process from the very beginning when the customer decides to order through all the paperwork and planning to get the work planned on the shop floor and finally through production to shipping and then to the customer. "Walking the process" quickly exposes nonvalue-added activities and long lead-time queues that can be eliminated to speed up the overall process.

Simplifying the process includes eliminating the waste identified during the first phase. Each affected business process should be examined for its intended purpose. Why is this process being accomplished? How does it move the organization closer to its goal? During the simplification phase, processes can be improved by rearranging, eliminating, or combining methods and processes. Once all the processes have been well understood and improved in a manual process or with the current system then the automation can be effectively applied. Automating processes with nonvalue-added activity only provides the same bad information only quicker.

"Get set" also includes identifying the roles and leadership required for the successful implementation. Leaders are found in many areas of the enterprise. Many times the real leaders are not those with the title but rather those that demonstrate the trait of leadership. These informal leaders must be carefully aligned with the overall system implementation goals. One way to obtain that commitment is through education. Education provides the overall understanding of what the company is attempting to implement and why. Many implementations fail because of confusion on how the system will fit into the normal business or how the normal business must change to accommodate system implementation. This confusion manifests itself in data inaccuracy as the system is not maintained and used. Using the old informal system is perceived to be easier than learning the new tool even though the new system makes the job easier. Overtime data inaccuracy grows and grows. Soon the new system has lost all credibility and things are no better than before as everyone returns to the old informal system. If this happens, most likely the old informal system was never really abandoned.

A real possibility exists that things could be even worse. The management team has lost their credibility with the workforce or at the ultimate worst, the company cannot continue to operate. So how can these dismal possibilities be avoided? The first step on the road to competitiveness is a common understanding of the destination. Every journey is easier when the final destination is well understood and communicated. This common understanding is only possible through education.

Education

Rarely does a small company have the resources for an internal trainer. This means that this crucial education must be secured from outside the organization. One excellent supplier of education for this type of implementation comes through an organization called APICS, The Educational Society for Resource Management (for information, call 800-444-APIC or see the Website — www.apics.org). Since 1957, this organization has standardized the language of manufacturing worldwide. Almost all ERP system software has been programmed consistent with the APICS body of knowledge. Although many consultants provide education directly at the plant site, the experiences shared in the classroom are those from only within the company. An APICS educational opportunity provides an opportunity for people from the company to network with other manufacturing people facing the same issues and problems at different companies. These educational opportunities are available at a fraction of the cost of an on-site consultant. This networking for benefiting the common good was the original motivation behind the founding of APICS in 1957. This networking has moved to the Internet and complimentary list servers are available on the APICS Website (www.apics.org) in a variety of industry focus areas. Why reinvent the wheel when someone else is willing to tell you how to successfully build it?

The need for education cannot be stressed too strongly. Imagine entrusting an accountant with no education the responsibility of preparing financial statements. No sane business owner would make that move. Daily, the same business owners entrust the management of their inventory, the largest portion of current assets, to incompletely trained people. When you consider that the inventory is an asset like cash, educating the workforce to effectively manage this asset does not look like a luxury. As an old sage advisor once said, "If you think education is expensive, try ignorance." Education is required for all employees to help in a successful implementation. Well meaning people can do exactly the wrong thing for the right reasons. Recommended education includes the basics of manufacturing control and a detailed understanding of how MRP systems work. The education program should answer the question "why?" The software training will provide the knowledge to answer "how?"

Roles and Responsibilities

Another area that must be considered in the "get set" phase are the roles and responsibilities for different functional areas in the project. A surefire way for an ERP implementation to fail is to put the MIS or IT department in charge of the project. This is not because they are not wonderful people who are very committed to the enterprise. Unfortunately, having an IT person in charge of an ERP implementation sends a strong message that ERP implementation is an IT system project and, therefore, is only for the computer room. In reality ERP is a business management process and should be expected to have a positive return on investment like any other business project. The most successful projects are led by a business manager with credibility within the company and in-depth knowledge of the company's processes. Essential tools for this manager to have are in-depth project management skills, ability to secure the appropriate resources for the implementation, credibility in the organization, and sufficient power within the organization to make lasting decisions.

Change Management

A great deal of change can be expected during any ERP implementation. To successfully manage change, communication is essential in assuring the climate and atmosphere surrounding the implementation remains constructive and positive. When problems are encountered, they should be communicated early to the affected personnel. If the team attempts to hide problems and issues from the users of the system there will develop an overall mistrust of the entire implementation. In the void of real facts and information, the affected personnel will fill in with their own ideas and rarely do these ideas reflect reality. One way to assure the appropriate climate is to confidentially survey the affected personnel by asking how the change is perceived, if the area is ready and how well the change is supported. When this index is tracked over time, problem areas can be more readily identified and resolved through improved communication or education. If these trouble spots are ignored, then larger problems will surely surface later in the implementation.

Many companies use an ERP implementation newsletter to keep all areas apprised of the pending changes or challenges. Another frequently used communication process is the company bulletin board or company meetings. No matter how it is accomplished, effective communication is essential to ensure the best possible climate and atmosphere for the ERP implementation.

Go

Once all the planning and preparation has been completed, it is time to really begin the implementation process. Normal time for the implementation should be in the range of 4 to 18 months. If the implementation takes longer than 18 months, the motivation of the team will wane and the enterprise will lose its dedication to the successful changes that must be made. The ERP software companies are beginning to leverage intellectual assets leveraged by technology to shorten implementation time and still provide an implementation that fits the enterprise. The benefit of this approach is that the enterprise can leverage the previous experiences, successful and unsuccessful, from other companies in their industry. This technological approach to implementation can dramatically reduce overall implementation time and costs.

Schedule

However, no matter what tools are used, the time the implementation will take is directly related to the current condition of the business. If the company is already using unique item identifiers, bills of materials, and possesses good data accuracy, the implementation can take even less than 3 months. One company had a documented cutover from one ERP system to another in less than 30 days from system purchase to full functionality on the new system. The reality was that this company was already a world-class ERP user and the system move was simply a change in how the transactions were accomplished rather than a change in how the business operated. Since the business currently functioned well within the expected best practices, there were few modifications required in the system so the cost and lead-time were very small. However, if item identifiers, bill of materials, and routings still need to be developed, the time will be closer to 12 to 18 months.

Implementations taking more than 18 months tend to never achieve success. Interest and energy wanes with the lack of accomplishment and the implementation dies. The accuracy of data is a project that can be started well ahead of the software tool arriving on the scene. In fact, by having a team carefully examine all business processes for value added and nonvalue-added activities and improve those processes found lacking, much of the expected return on investment can be achieved early in the process.

Project Resources

When managing an implementation, there are three control knobs, scope, resources, and time. If the scope of the project is reduced, the project will take less time. If the resources are reduced, the time required will be longer. Finding the resources to support the implementation can be the most difficult issue to face. Two successful approaches can be taken. One is to bring in temporary help for the routine duties. These temporaries can be low-wage people to perform the repetitive tasks. The concern is that supervising the temporaries might take more time than they save. Another type of temporary is a college intern. These interns are usually well educated but do not have practical experience. They can be used to augment the team during the implementation and are usually very quick in coming up to speed in the organization. This opportunity provides them work experience and the company the extra resources needed at a reasonable price, a winning combination for both parties involved.

The second way to free resources is to begin doing the existing job differently. Each task that is currently being done must be examined to see if it really adds value to the organization or just adds work. Many people are very busy working hard but are accomplishing little. Many daily tasks are done without their need being challenged because "we have always done things that way." The most important part of the implementation process is the reengineering of current process. There is no time like the present to begin the process.

Part of the reengineering process requires many decisions to be made. The decision process is just one of many processes that must be established early in the project. The implementation team should be from a sufficient level in the organization to be able to make decisions that the organization will implement. The implementation team should expect to experience the normal team evolutionary steps of forming, storming, norming, and performing. These steps mean that the implementation team must first be selected from the appropriate level of the organization. Given the level of personnel involved in the project, conflict is normal and should be expected. Having a well-defined process for incorporating innovation and conflict resolution into the implementation will provide the best results and outcomes.

Project Plan: Major Milestones

Select Project Team

This team should have a common vision of the implementation's goal. These people are responsible for the application of the selected software to their own business environment. The project team should have an extensive understanding of the concept of ERP and a detailed understanding of the specific software tool. These people become the in-house experts that should answer questions as other people begin to use the system. An excellent way to kick off the project implementation is for the project team to attend the software training together. Some ERP companies have begun to provide intensive classes where a team from the same company can come together, learn the system, apply it to their base business process, and begin to understand the gaps that exist between current and desired processes. The people selected for this team are usually not people who can afford to be away from their regular job to support the implementation. The project team is made of those people who are the core of the business. Relieving some of their regular workload is needed to provide the time the implementation will require. It is not possible for these people to continue to perform their regular job in addition to implementing ERP. Skimping on the competency of the project team reflects directly in the implementation results. The ERP implementation should set up future desired business processes for the enterprise to enable future competitiveness. Don't you really want your best people working on your future?

According to Phil Quigley, CFPIM, in a recent article in the *APICS Performance Advantage,* the groups that should be involved in an implementation include:

- **Users from your own organization.** This group should be representative of each functional area of the enterprise. The personnel selected should be able to speak with authority on the business processes in the area and make decisions that will be accepted by their respective areas.
- **Consultants from the ERP provider.** Even the smallest company can benefit from detailed advice from the software company. In a larger implementation, the software consultant is a key member of the team and should be able to provide time and cost saving insights on tool application and utilization.
- **Information systems people contracted through agencies.** The implementation of ERP requires a significant amount of data transfer, linkages to/from legacy systems, and custom reports. Given the time frame for the implementation having outside information systems personnel to accomplish this programming is very common.
- **Your own systems people.** Your own internal personnel are expected to support the implementation and the system after it is complete. Successful maintenance of the system is dependent on understanding the intent of the implementation and any changes that were made. Any modifications should be well documented so that traceability is provided.

Size, Install, and Test Hardware

Before even attempting to use any software be sure that the hardware is reliable and running as expected to support the desired implementation. This includes the operating system, database, and any communications links to legacy systems or supply chain partners. A common error is to load everything, operating system and applications, onto the new computer at the same time. When the combination does not work, it is almost impossible to determine the cause. The hardware and operating system should be installed well in advance of the beginning of the implementation.

A major frustration for the users is when the system has inadequate response time. Installing undersized hardware can cause this. Using a reputable hardware provider and utilizing their services to establish the correct machine power may cost a little more at the beginning but can save significant investment later on. Some hardware companies will even provide performance guarantees that ensure the correct hardware is used. Under the guarantee, if the system does not perform as desired the hardware will be upgraded at no charge until the computing power is sufficient. Buying bargain basement hardware is rarely a real bargain. The enterprise system is a mission critical system for the organization. The entire financial, customer service, and production information are resident on this computer. One company recently spent hundreds of hours and thousands of dollars entering and reentering data only to find a defective (really cheap) network card worth less than $100 was corrupting the data faster than they could enter them. This integrated system implementation is often one of the largest investments made by the company. Attempting to cut corners in hardware can lead to many hours of problems and frustration. Selecting an integration partner you can trust to be there in the long term will yield benefits for the investment made up front.

Attend System Training

In addition to the education required, training is needed to operate the software. This training is typically included directly or indirectly in the purchase price of the software. Training answers the question "how?" Software training will teach the people using the system the keystrokes and transactions required to run the company. This training class is an excellent opportunity to network with other users of the software and use their experiences to benefit your company. The recommended process is to send the implementation team together to this class. Each person on the team tends to filter the class through their functional eyes. By sending them together, the probability of getting a complete picture is much higher. Some ERP companies are now providing the opportunity to utilize the actual hardware and software configuration that will be shipped to the company as part of the class exercises. This option can dramatically speed implementation.

Typically the instructor of the class is not only an expert in the software but also has implemented this software in many companies. Feel free to pick their brain for application suggestions and pitfalls associated with the implementation. Given the reduced cost of laptop computers, taking one to this session allows for the immediate application of the class training to your specific company requirements if it is possible to load a client version on that machine. Your questions can be answered during the class. Attempting to implement software without this type of training is like putting someone with no pilot's training behind the controls of an airplane for the first time and encouraging them to take the airplane for a short flight. They may be very motivated and the trip can be exciting but the results can be deadly. The same situation happens when untrained people are given an ERP system and asked to implement it. The enterprise may crash in the process. Part of the expected support from the software company is the ability to communicate a complete knowledge of the software functionality and limitations, in addition to an understanding of how it should be applied to your industry.

Each software package has different ways of accomplishing the required tasks. Although the concepts underlying the system may be the same, the detailed navigation and transaction approach is very different. Attending specific system training is essential to understanding the system and will shorten the overall implementation time. Usually the software company will provide this training at a reasonable price because having the implementation team well trained in the use of the system reduces the number of technical calls that they will receive and have to answer. Many valuable hints about effectively using the software come out of these classes. Use this class to its maximum potential. A wealth of information is possible from the instructor and fellow participants. Ask how they handled problems that are currently facing your business in previous implementations. If they successfully overcame that problem, they will be very happy to tell how they did it. Class can be a wonderful source for free consulting. Also, usually the participants will freely share how they attempted to solve the problem and failed. Sometimes learning what does not work can be more valuable than learning only what does work.

Complete Conference Room Pilot

A conference room pilot exercises the whole system and tests the users' understanding of the system. The conference room pilot takes the business processes from the beginning, when a customer order is received to the end when the customer order is shipped. This step is unwisely skipped in many cases in the hurry to implement the system. To continue the flight example, this would be like taking a plane up for a solo flight immediately after finishing ground school. The probability of completing this initial flight safely is very small. Without a conference room pilot the new system can go online and suddenly no one knows how to ship a part, relieve inventory, and invoice the customer using this new tool. The conference room pilot provides the opportunity to simulate all the activities of the business in one focused exercise. The other benefit is that each functional area can see how actions taken in their area affects the other areas of the enterprise. A thorough conference room pilot process can reveal wonderful insights opportunities to reengineer.

A draft checklist for the conference room pilot is listed below. The implementation team expected to use the system should be able to:

1. Enter a part, including all item master information.
2. Completely define the bill of materials from inbound purchased materials to finished goods so that it reflects the desired manufacturing process.
3. Enter a customer order.
4. Run the planning cycle and output reports.
5. Analyze reports for needed purchased and make parts.
6. Place a purchase order for a purchase part.
7. Receive a purchased part and enter the invoice.
8. Match the purchase order to the receipt to the invoice and pay the invoice.
9. Open a manufacturing order.
10. Alert manufacturing of the authorization to build. This could be through a work order or a manufacturing dispatch list.
11. Issue material to the manufacturing order.
12. Report progress on the manufacturing order.
13. Look at the status of the manufacturing order.
14. Complete the manufacturing order and receive to inventory.
15. Ship the product to the customer and send an invoice.

16. Receive cash for the invoice.
17. Run basic general ledger reports.

These tasks should be completed without hunting and pecking around the system in confusion. Each person must know very clearly how to do their job using the new system. Remember that the implementation team is the training resource for the rest of the enterprise. If the implementation team does not know how to perform the process adequately, how can they hope to teach someone else? The other choice is to retain a team of outside consultants to train the balance of the users. This option is significantly more expensive.

In either case, only when the system is well understood should the implementation move to the next step. Once the standard business processes that are defined in these initial pilot steps are developed, begin handling the exceptions that happen on a daily basis. Define routine scenarios that happen in reality that cause consternation and problem in today's system. The conference room is a better place to work out these issues than the shop floor after the system goes live. The conference room pilot will save many hours and frustration later because everyone is in the same room where options can be defined and discussed. This is the beginning of developing the policies and procedures for using the system. Document these policies and procedures as they are developed. This will save significant time later and will assure they are completed.

Set Up Security and Permissions

Every system has a method of allowing only authorized people to look at and transact portions of the data. These permissions must be developed early to prevent surprises later in the process. Different systems have a variety of ways to set these security switches. The first step in developing security and permissions is to have open permissions during the training phase. This allows everyone to see all the features and functions of the system. People can explore areas that are not their particular area of responsibility in an environment where they can do no harm. Once the training phase is completed, during the conference room pilot, begin setting the security and permission definitions to assure that everyone has what they need. This begins to simulate the access that will be available in the live system. Having access to only your own specific area of responsibility forces communication between functional areas to practice transactions and test scenarios. Having test data entered by the department that will have final responsibility for it in the production environment eliminates the chances for an unseen surprise when the system goes online. The other option is to leave open access to the system through the conference room pilot phase. This invites a great deal of frustration as one user inadvertently causes problems for another user. The conference room pilot process should test out all production processes including communication and integration points. The risk of waiting until the system is brought online is that there is a high probability that security settings will not be correct. People may be getting in and "playing with" things they should not be handling, adversely affecting financial reporting in the live system. The other possibility is that sufficient permission has not been given to allow the staff to do their job and frustration results. Security and permissions are an important part of the conference pilot process.

Company Specific Pilot

If the conference room pilot has completed the supplied test database from the software company, now is the time to enter a few real parts that are built by the company. Picking a product that is well known and well understood is recommended. This product should not have any major problems or issues associated with it. These parts should be put through the same recommended steps of the conference pilot. Once the system is well understood, then all the issues and problems that normally arise in daily production can be simulated. Some examples of these problems are inventory adjustments, customer changes, engineering changes, credit holds, machines down, people not showing up, and parts shortages. Be creative in testing scenarios that face the company. Run all the steps of the conference room pilot process including the impact on the financial reporting.

Errors in setting up the chart of accounts can be debugged during this process. These errors can be very difficult to track down and even more difficult to fix once the system goes live. Getting the chart of accounts set exactly right is a key deliverable during this stage of the process. Having the entire project team address these difference scenarios and issues brings excellent insight to the overall process. Reengineering the process is best during this time. Implementing the current processes into the new system only to change it shortly after implementation reduces the overall return on investment that is possible.

Identify Beginning Pilot

If possible, it is preferable not to bring the entire company online in one shot in a big bang cutover. The big bang approach does not allow for incremental correction of errors in processes and procedures. No matter how thorough the planning, the actual implementation will always reveal unexpected problems and issues. Better to have these issues and problems show up in a small slice of the business rather than bringing the entire company to its knees. In addition, the resources required to implement the whole company at once are probably not available. A good way to begin the actual use of the system is to identify a part of the business that can be segregated and brought online. This segment of the business should be something that is expected to continue after the implementation is complete, have no major production or technical issues, and reflects a credible test of the overall system. The pilot approach allows for the new policies and procedures to be tested in actual use with a minimum data set that people are familiar with before the entire company is committed.

Some companies attempt to bring up the new system and run the old system in parallel. This approach is even worse than attempting big bang. Parallel systems result in a complete overload on the people and often conclude in a failed implementation when people revert back to the system they are more comfortable with. The resources to keep the current system running are already consuming all the company's capacity. When a second system is added, neither gets the attention or resources needed. As a result, they both flounder and everyone is frustrated. If there is a concern about the new system, running a reasonable pilot data set in parallel while increasing the workload somewhat, allows all users to be fully trained, to gain confidence in the system, and greatly eases the full company conversion. At the time of conversion, the system will not run in parallel. The tried and true approach is to continue to implement slices of the business until the whole business is online.

Cutting the whole company over cold turkey is a gutsy approach best done when several conference room pilots have been completed successfully. This is done successfully in very small companies where the project team is the entire user community. This cold turkey cutover approach also fits a company with a single product line, simple product, or starting from a greenfield opportunity. The potential benefits and risks must be assessed for each option before the best one can be selected for the enterprise.

Entering Fixed Data: The System Building Blocks

Most ERP systems will allow the automatic transfer of any existing item masters, bills of material, customer masters, vendor masters, and employee masters. These data are the basic building blocks of the system and are required before orders can be placed. If this transition process from the legacy system can be completed quickly and accurately, this can be a real time saver. This automatic transition process can however cause many strange problems later in the implementation. Sometimes, since the old data are so bad the decision is made to enter the data manually and ensure the accuracy for each segment of the business brought online. If the amount of data is not overwhelming, keying the data into the new system is usually the best alternative. The system will perform the edits necessary to ensure integrity of the database.

These edits are not performed when directly populating the database with uploads of old data. In an implementation of a significant size rekeying all the fixed data may not be a feasible option. Auditing this building block data for accuracy is a key strategy for success. This is the foundation for the new system. The output is only as good as the inputs. Getting caught in GIGO cycle (garbage in, garbage out) begins at this first critical input stage.

Entering Variable Data

Most systems will not allow the automatic upload of variable data like purchase orders, open work orders, and accounts payable. Opening these orders and moving them through the process affects many areas of the system including financial impact. For best results, these items should be manually input into the database. Transfer onto the new system is an excellent opportunity to clean up these orders and ensure accuracy. The data input of customer orders, purchase orders, and work orders is one of the last steps before the system is turned on live. Bringing over history from the previous system can also prove to be "Mission Impossible" at worst or a very expensive proposition at best. Companies always desire to have all the history from their previous system available on the new system. The reality of the situation is that this is a very costly customized process to accomplish so detailed data history is rarely carried forward to the new system. The financial history is normally entered from the end of month balance sheets and income statements for the purposes of comparing financial results. The other detailed history is typically input to a data warehouse for later access when needed.

Document Policies and Procedures

This last task is the one that unfortunately does not get done effectively. Documenting policies and procedures is not glamorous work. Thankfully, many ERP systems are beginning to provide templates for policies and procedures as part of the base system. These templates can then be modified to fit the unique enterprise. Documenting policies and procedures is an excellent place to use a college intern. Policies and procedures do not have to be the thickness of *War and Peace* to be effective. The best policies and procedures are no more than one page, front and back. The policy statement of what is intended to be accomplished is on the front. The procedural steps to accomplish that objective are detailed in a flowchart format on the back. What could be simpler? This approach is consistent with ISO9000 and will not bury the plant in paperwork. Quality is not measured by the pound but rather by how well these procedures are utilized on a daily basis. Experience has shown that these one-page procedures often get posted on the wall or file cabinet for quick reference by their users. Isn't that how polices and procedures should be used, rather than collecting them in a book to gather dust on a shelf? Figure 14.2 is a sample of this process flow procedure. The steps taken in this procedure fit on one piece of paper in flow chart format. This would be the equivalent of a four- to five-page written procedure. Which do you think will be really used?

Cutover

The whole company is eventually brought onto the new system. The approach of bringing up chunks of the entire company at a time allows for continuous improvement to take place in the utilization of the system during the implementation. After the whole company has been brought online, this is an excellent time to review the performance measures for the system and determine what positive results have already been made. This should be compared to the expected returns from the original justification. Return on investment from the early slices that are implemented should fund the continuation of the project to its full completion. Expected results should include increased customer service, lower inventories, and a reduction in the overall stress level. These benefits allow the business to be more profitable and provide it the ability to grow without additional resources.

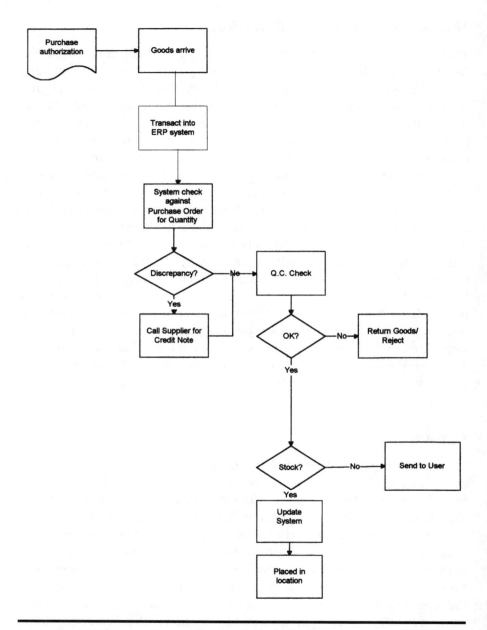

Figure 14.2   Sample of a process flow procedure.

Celebrate

This can be the most important step. The journey has been worthwhile. The whole company has just completed a major project. Celebrating recognizes this accomplishment and clearly demonstrates the importance to the company. This step is frequently forgotten.

Failure Strategies

ERP can be a complex, expensive, difficult to implement paperwork blizzard that drains the resources of the company, or this integrated approach to management can yield significant bottom-line results. Since ERP implementation can be so challenging it is not surprising that the pitfalls preventing a successful implementation are well known:

1. **Lack of education.** This does not mean a lack of degrees and diplomas. People with Ph.D.s and MBAs are well-educated people, but these degrees do not include in-depth understanding of integrated management systems like ERP. If these subjects are covered at all, it is typically part of a single semester treatment of the subject. The use of computers in the educational process has only come into common usage during the past few years. Without an understanding of the integration of this business management system, the implementation will fail. Education means a common understanding of how an integrated system works, what the vision for the implementation is, and why it will make a difference for the company.

2. **Lack of top management vision and active participation.** Too many managers view ERP as a necessary evil that can be purchased and then delegated to lower-level personnel. This lack of active participation will ensure failure of the implementation. Top management must provide the resources and motivation when the difficult times arise in the implementation. Without a clear understanding of the status and details of the implementation this support will not be possible.

3. **Lack of data accuracy.** This issue is such a common pitfall that a whole chapter has been dedicated to the topic (Chapter 13). Data that must be accurate include item masters, on hand balances, bills of material, customer demand, work orders (including completion status), and purchase orders. If any one of these critical data elements are invalid, the information provided from the system will be inaccurate.

4. **Buying vaporware.** Software sales personnel may promise that their software will do anything and any functionality that is not currently present will be in "the next release." *Caveat emptor* on this vaporware — buyer beware! Ensure that performance guarantees are put into the contract so that if the promised functionality does not actually come into reality, significant financial penalties should. Vaporware can be easily detected during the system demonstration if the input screens are not live. Screen shots can be easily assembled to look like the live system. Asking detailed questions about their functionality and requiring actual transactions in a live system goes a long way to prove the functionality is a reality in the current release.

5. **Buying the right system, installing the wrong one.** Too many times a company will spend incredible time and expense documenting how they desire to do business and what features and functions that they want in the new system. Quickly the wild enthusiasm about the new system turns into mass disillusionment when the system that is installed looks exactly like the old one only the company has spent a great deal of money to do it. The other failure strategy is to attempt to install every feature, function, and bell and whistle that is available on the system whether or not it is required. This can take the whole implementation down a rat hole of never-ending expense and resource consumption.

6. **Allowing the consultants to do it for you.** If you are too busy to do the implementation with your own resources, hiring outside people to do it will ensure that the implementation will most likely look like the last implementation they did rather than fitting the specific needs of your business. Abdicating the responsibility of the company's future to outsiders will be met with resistance by the people who have to change processes and procedures without a clear understanding of how it fits their needs. Change management is more difficult and the probability for success is close to zero. Consultants can provide excellent insights and a variety of experiences to the implementation. They have a place in a successful implementation; however, consultants should be a resource to the implementation and not take over the implementation.

7. **Analysis paralysis.** The fear of making a mistake paralyzes the implementation team. The team waits for direct instruction from senior management that will never come. Senior management should not be involved at this level of detail. This is why the implementation

team exists. An unempowered implementation team will fear making a mistake and will continue to analyze a situation and delay action. This paralysis can stop an implementation in its tracks. Determining every problem or challenge before implementation is impossible. When implementing ERP every area of the enterprise is affected. Cross-functional teams identify the potential problems and issues that can be identified. However, other problems may arise and this should not be punished. A team that does not fear retaliation is more capable of solving the problems that will arise.

8. **Being penny wise and pound foolish.** The ERP system implementation is a large investment for any company. Saving cost where possible is one way to improve the return on investment. The company needs to spend adequate money to ensure that sufficient quality is purchased in hardware, software, and consulting services. Making a purchase based solely on cost can result in getting exactly what you paid for.

9. **Not challenging the status quo.** The implementation must begin to ask questions about the current processes and what adds value or only cost. A company that is not continuously improving will be quickly overtaken by the competition.

10. **Expecting the software to do everything and NOW.** The ERP software is not the magic silver bullet for the company. Purchasing the latest word processing software does not make you a world class author. In the same way, just because the leading ERP software has been purchased does not mean the company will be world class. The software is merely a tool that can be used by a talented team to improve the overall company's success. Software is not the whole solution.

11. **Cowboy implementation approach.** Shoot first, ask questions later. In the cowboy implementation approach, no planning is done and the implementation moves off at breakneck speed. Quickly, routine problems that could have been prevented arise and can take the implementation off track into failure. In the hurry to get things done, nothing gets done because there has been no planning. An implementation never plans to fail but frequently fails to plan.

12. **Lack of communication to the affected users.** Having an implementation team work away from the main department isolates the users from the changes that will be needed to make the implementation successful. A key success strategy is communication, communication, and communication. Failure to communicate will cause the rumor mill to fill in the blanks and rarely is this fill constructive or accurate.

13. **Trying to go it alone.** In the attempt to save cost, one strategy is to attempt the implementation without any outside help. Some outside expertise and guidance is required in almost every implementation. Having a knowledgeable outsider on the steering committee to oversee progress and ask the right questions can save far more expense that it costs.

Summary

Selecting and implementing a new manufacturing control system can appear overwhelming. Using a few simple tools, success in the form of bottom line results can be achieved in very short time. The most important tool in the implementation toolbox is education. Attempting to implement what is not well understood is very difficult to impossible. A common vision of the goal and clear expectations of the outcome including benefits to the company expedites the whole process. When ERP systems are carefully examined, 80 to 90% of the system is the same; 10 to 20% is different and makes the system uniquely fit the company. Expect that the selected system will last for 3 to 5 years because changing technology will introduce new tools and increased benefits. The financial benefit of an integrated planning system should be realized within the first 18 months. The largest benefits typically come from reduced inventory, improved cash flow, and improved customer service. These factors combine to allow profitable growth for the company without the addition of overhead resources. This improves the overall profitability and allows for high payoff investments for further growth. Selecting a new system is not a random shot in the dark but like any other new tool, must be carefully selected, understood, and applied to support the future of the company. Avoiding the known pitfalls and following the proven success strategies can result in bottom-line benefits for your company.

15 Repetitive Manufacturing Application

The implementation and application of the ERP system into a high-rate, low-variety repetitive manufacturing company is unique. Unlike the traditional process of a master schedule netting gross to net through to a detailed material plan, the repetitive manufacturer needs to perform rate-based material planning supported by rate-based parts delivery schedules. In some companies this rate-based schedule must be tied to a mixed model sequenced line or may require traceability. The processing of individual work orders either by the practitioner or under the software covers by the computer does not add value for the enterprise. Rather than detailed job order costing the variance of expected vs. actual output rates over time is a key performance measure. Linearity of output provides key insight into the overall effectiveness of the process. Product costing changes to a four-wall period approach rather than performing detailed issue transactions to a work order.

General Repetitive Application

A repetitive manufacturer makes high-volume products in low variety. Most commonly this type of manufacturer competes in the market based on lead-time response and/or price. The manufacturing strategy utilized to meet the market is usually make to stock or assemble to order. The ability to promise delivery to the customer very accurately is very important for the repetitive

manufacturer. Less important is the ability to track costs to a specific production unit. Costs are considered over a period of time rather than for a
particular unit. Bills of material have relatively few levels and routings are
fixed and reliable. This is a very different environment than the traditional
discrete job shop for which MRP was originally developed. The discrete job
shops have a wide variety of potential routings, capacity planning is a major
challenge and costing is accomplished by job. Clearly these two different
environments require different tools. The full functionality of the ERP tools
with repetitive manufacturing capability can really help that type of enterprise be more effective and profitable.

In a repetitive manufacturing operation, the conversion process is accomplished through a very predictable series of sequential operations. Work in
process is relatively low and these sequential operations are highly dependent
on each other. Fitting repetitive manufacturing control into job shop-ori-
ented computer systems is possible. A barrier to this successful fit is the
amount of paperwork and transactions. Since the lot sizes are so small, the
amount of paperwork is quite large since a unique order is still expected for
each production lot that is released in a discrete manufacturing system. If
the same process of paperwork and transactions are used to build repetitive
product as discrete product in a job shop, the production work force is soon
buried under mountain of paper.

$$\text{Economic Order Quantity} = \sqrt{\frac{2\ US}{IC}}$$

where: U = Annual usage
      S = Setup cost
      I = Inventory carrying cost
      C = Cost of the item

Although the EOQ formula is very old and many consider it obsolete, it
helps make the point of why different management processes are needed to
support the repetitive operation. Even though this formula may not be explic-
itly used to calculate the lot size, an effective management process does this
kind of analysis to determine the optimal lot size. A repetitive manufacturer
wants to have very small lot sizes with the eventual goal of producing in lot
sizes of one as close as possible to market demand. This formula can also be
analyzed in reverse to identify the factors that must be changed to allow these
small lot sizes to be achieved in a cost-effective manner.

When the four factors that determine the lot size are considered, the only one that meets these criteria is the setup cost. Changes in lot sizes should have no significant impact on annual usage. The total demand is not dependent on the production lot size. Given that the inventory carrying cost is typically a fixed overhead cost divided by production volume, this factor should also not be affected by a change in lot size. The same is true for the cost of the item. The case could be made that one of the expected benefits of reducing lot size is that quality should improve. This should benefit product cost. However, in the short term, a decision to reduce lot size will not have a major impact on the product cost. Therefore, the only factor that can be adjusted to reduce the cost impact of the decision to produce in smaller lot sizes is the cost of setup. A significant part of the setup cost is the fixed time and expense required to issue work orders, transact parts, close paperwork, and all the other routine expectations that are found in a job shop. This cost is not dependent on the number of parts on each work order but rather is directly related to the number of orders processed. The repetitive manufacturer has no time for all this nonvalue-added activity for each individual part in lot sizes of one. The process must be reengineered to provide the required information without the nonvalue-added cost.

Since product is built in high volume through a repetitive process, there is a not a requirement for a detailed level of progress reporting since this feedback does not add value, only cost. Detailed progress reporting is required in a job shop where the level of work in process varies based on the product mix at that point in time. This detailed progress reporting is a key success strategy to manage the work in process inventory asset in a job shop. However, in a repetitive manufacturer the manufacturing process can be thought of as a river that continuously flows at a relatively stable level. When the flow of inputs is balanced with the flow of outputs, the overall level in the river stays constant. The water level in the river reflects the lead-time through the plant and the inventory in the operation. Since the lead-time for a repetitive manufacturer is so short, the work in process is very low. Critical feedback processes for the repetitive enterprise includes the ability to report rate variances in addition to the expected cost variances.

The repetitive sequential operations are directly related to each other so, if one operation stops, the balance of the line soon stops. Piles of inventory are not allowed to build up between operations. This stable level of work in process simplifies the control and reporting systems. Some ERP software companies have developed true repetitive systems. True repetitive systems have rate-based production scheduling and backflushing capability. The system does not create workorders in the background. When a job shop system attempts to masquerade as a repetitive system, this background creation of workorders is common practice. The creation and processing of work orders in the background can consume a great deal of computer power and processing time. A real risk exists that insufficient computing capacity may have been provided to support the implementation.

Traditional systems can still be used with some minor modifications to answer these specific needs. One method is to plan production in weekly rate-based buckets using the order modifier on the item master called period of supply or days of production. This concept was further explained in Chapter 7. This allows the MRP function to total requirements for the next week and plans an order for release on the first day of the week. The traditional system then does all the background planning and transactions that would have been completed for a job shop. All materials are scheduled to be available at the beginning of each week. For most companies weekly delivery is a major improvement over the current processes. If the enterprise is capable of receiving parts more frequently than once per week per part number, then this system will quickly become difficult to manage. The processing time and computing power required are much larger than expected for the number of transactions entered. True repetitive systems have simplified the internal processing of the system to really reflect the overall repetitive manufacturing process.

Kanban

High volumes and very low variety characterize the repetitive product. The raw materials needed are repetitious in quantity and timing. The end items are still discrete but are produced in a very short cycle time, typically less than 1 day. The management of this type of operation turns to balancing the capacity along the line rather than planning detailed routings. The bills of materials tend to be very flat meaning that they have very few levels. Routings are simple with only one or two steps since the operations are closely coupled with each other. The entire line is either running or not. The option of having some workcenters working while others are idle is not a common option in this environment. Costs for this type of operation are easy to allocate directly to these focused lines.

The "four wall approach" is used to track inventory. Receipts are transacted when the product arrives and deductions are made to the inventory

KAN BAN SI SU TE MU

看板システム

KANBAN System

Figure 15.1 Japanese kanji characters for kanban system. (Courtesy of Toshiyuki Okai, Sanyo North America.)

when the final product leaves. Intermediate tracking does not add value to the process, only cost, so this tracking is not done. The traditional intermediate tracking is no longer required since the materials are in process only a very short period of time.

JIT execution tools are used to bring materials to the line very close to the time of need like kanban. Kanban is a Japanese word that literally means "sign board." According to APICS, a kanban is a "method of 'just in time' production that uses standard containers or lot sizes with a single card attached to each. It is a pull system in which workcenters signal with a card that they wish to withdraw parts from feeding operations or suppliers. This is also known as a move card, production card, or synchronized production." Figure 15.1 shows the actual Japanese kanji characters for kanban system.

A kanban can be a light that signals replenishment, a card that is moved, or an empty container that is sent to the supplier to be filled when the active one is empty or even a fax or e-mail message that authorizes movement of material. The supplier then quickly refills the container and sends it back to the line directly to the point of use. This replenishment can happen many times in a day to bring parts to the production area as needed. Dr. Rachel Zhang from the University of Michigan wrote an article ("Easily Implementable Inventory Control Policies") in the summer of 1996. The article computes the reorder point and kanban quantity. The primary factors for a kanban system are lead-time, item cost, and consumption rate. In addition, user variables include how often are you willing or able to receive the material and what is the desired level of certainty that a particular item will be on the shelf at any given time. Dr. Zhang presents a mathematically complex algorithm for calculating the kanban size. Kanban is really very similar to the order point system that has been in use for many years. The important thing to remember when sizing a kanban is to consider the potential demand and supply variability for the part and the total cost to the enterprise.

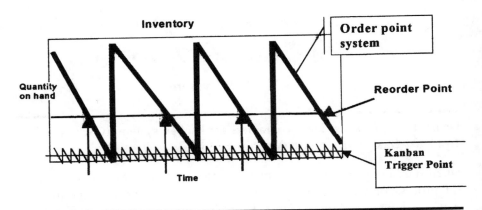

Figure 15.2   Expected inventory pattern using an order point system compared to a kanban system.

The order point system sends out a signal for parts when the inventory has fallen to the level defined as the order point. The expected lead-time to replenish parts should be equal to the inventory of parts left. If the lead-time were 2 weeks, then the order point would be set at approximately 2 weeks worth of parts. The delivery is expected to arrive just as the parts run out. The main difference between kanban and the order point is the time elapsed between signal and replenishment. The order point signal may take days or weeks to replenish. The kanban is typically replenished within minutes or hours. The kanban process works extremely well when the volume and variety stay constant over a period of time. Provided that the future looks like the immediate past, a supplier, either internal or external, experiences stable demand. Figure 15.2 shows the expected inventory pattern using an order point system compared to a kanban system.

This sawtooth inventory pattern works well when the demand for the parts is relatively stable. This stable demand provides a predictable run out for the inventory. The kanban average inventory is significantly less than the order point system average inventory because the replenishment lead-time is also significantly less. The small amount of inventory stored in the kanban also translates to relatively stable demand to the supplier. This is very different than the lumpy demand seen by the supplier of an order point system as shown in Figure 15.3.

Given the very quick replenishment, the demand to the supplier in a kanban environment looks almost straight line and stable. This is very dif-

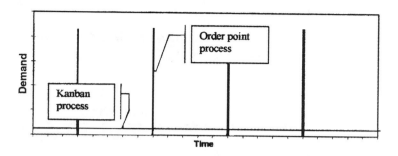

Figure 15.3   Dependent demand pattern.

ferent from the spikes in demand found in an order point process. There is no demand for the parts until the order point is reached and then all of a sudden there is a large requirement. This is followed by a period of no requirement. This pattern is also known as lumpy demand.

The scheduling task for the kanban supplier is relatively easy provided no configuration changes or wide variability in volume occurs. Some people will have you believe that all material should be ordered through this kind of pull or kanban system. Theoretically this may look very good, but the real world is rarely so easy to manage. The risk in using kanban only, without MRP to plan materials, is when a change in configuration is required. Since the kanban is sent to the internal or external supplier only minutes or hours ahead of requirement, the supplier may be unable to respond in time and the whole line can be disrupted or stopped until the supplier is able to provide the needed part. There is insufficient response time for the supplier to react to a requirement that blindsides them. If a supplier has been delivering blue parts at a constant rate and then all of a sudden a kanban shows up with a demand for a striped part, the chances that the striped part will be available are very small without having some forewarning that the demand is coming. This is why a materials requirements planning (MRP) system still has an integral place in a repetitive manufacturing business. MRP can very effectively plan to the day, exactly what is required and when. Practically speaking, most facilities find a daily schedule to be sufficient to support production. Rarely can an enterprise schedule to the hour or exact time. The kanban can then become the execution tool of less than one day's duration with the exact timing of the replenishment when production is ready.

Rate-Based Scheduling

Rate-based scheduling is when a production schedule is directly entered into the system as a date range with volumes. Following could be an example of a rate-based schedule:

Product 135948	Production Per Day
June 10–August 15	12,000
August 16–September 22	15,000
September 23–October 31	20,000
November 1–November 30	30,000
December 1–March 30	20,000
March 31–June 9	10,000

The rate-based schedule also can be entered as rate per shift if that level of control is desired. This higher level of detail is required to plan the staffing for each shift. The increased visibility prevents surprises and allows the shop supervisors to adjust the affected resources to match the desired production rate.

Product 135948	Production Schedule		
	Shift 1	Shift 2	Shift 3
June 10–August 15	6000	3000	3000
August 16–September 22	10,000	3000	2000
September 23–October 31	10,000	5000	5000
November 1–November 30	10,000	10,000	10,000
December 1–March 30	10,000	10,000	0
March 31–June 9	10,000	0	0

This example provides the necessary visibility required identifying when additional shifts are required. Since there is usually a premium paid to the off shifts, the strategy that is usually followed is to maximize production on first shift before adding additional shifts. There are no work orders created to track these requirements. A true repetitive system will have the function to input the expected schedule in a way very similar to the chart above. This makes schedules changes and "what if" analysis much simpler to accomplish.

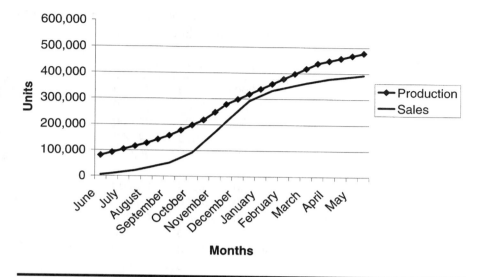

Figure 15.4 Production–Sales–Inventory (PSI) report.

Production Sales Inventory Analysis

In a repetitive manufacturing company the product is usually built to stock. Customers expect their orders to be fulfilled very quickly from a finite number of possible configurations. Forecasting is used to project future demand so production rates can be scheduled. The production rate is compared to the projected sales rate to determine the impact on inventory. If the production rate exceeds the sales rate, then inventory will rise. If the sales exceed the production rate, inventory will fall. Inventory can consume significant cash and physical space in the enterprise. These resources should be planned in advance to assure that sufficient capacity exists to support the overall plan rather than being reactive if cash or space runs short. This production–sales–inventory report or PSI report compares the planned production rate to the sales rate.

In Figure 15.4, the cumulative production rate climbs at a steady slope. This relatively stable production rate is used to fulfill the more variable demands. This strategy is commonly followed when the capacity flexibility is insufficient to track to actual demand. The risk is that expected demand will not be realized and excess or obsolete inventory may result. The table below reflects the raw data that were used to generate the PSI figure. Using the PSI graph is far easier to identify problems or issues than attempting to use the raw data. "A picture is really worth a thousand words."

	Production	Sales	Inventory
June	10,000	5000	75,000
	12,000	5000	82,000
July	12,000	6000	88,000
	12,000	6000	94,000
August	12,000	10,000	96,000
	15,000	10,000	101,000
September	15,000	10,000	106,000
	20,000	20,000	106,000
October	20,000	20,000	106,000
	20,000	40,000	86,000
November	30,000	40,000	76,000
	30,000	40,000	66,000
December	20,000	40,000	46,000
	20,000	40,000	26,000
January	20,000	20,000	26,000
	20,000	20,000	26,000
February	20,000	10,000	36,000
	20,000	10,000	46,000
March	20,000	10,000	56,000
	20,000	8000	68,000
April	10,000	8000	70,000
	10,000	5000	75,000
May	10,000	5000	80,000
	10,000	5000	85,000

In a PSI graph the distance between the production and sales lines represents the amount of expected inventory. In Figure 15.4, it can be noticed that the system started with some inventory on hand. The expected surge in demand during months of December to February is covered by the production rate from previous months. This PSI report shows that all demands are expected to be covered at the desired timing. No customer should expect to wait to have their demands filled. In Figure 15.5, an expected backorder situation can be identified.

Since the sales line crosses the production line, backorders to customers can be expected. There will be insufficient inventory from late December until early April to fulfill expected demand. This is where knowledge of the

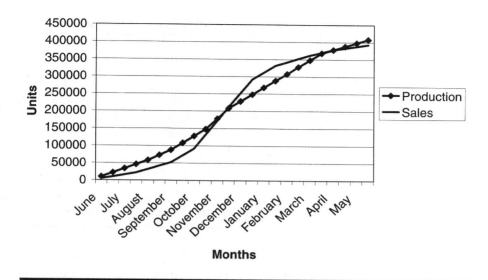

Figure 15.5   PSI showing a backorder stituation.

business is required to determine if this is a feasible plan. Provided that customers are willing to wait for this production output, all customer demands should be filled by May. However, if this is an item that will not tolerate a backorder situation, such as a gift item that is desired during the holiday season, the unfilled sales could potentially be lost sales. Including these sales as part of a revenue forecast would be unwise. The PSI report provides the visibility to this risk and allows the proactive management and alternative identification. This situation can be simulated on the MICSS Simulator included with this book.

The comparison of production and sales also provides the capability to calculate available to promise (ATP), which is the uncommitted portion of inventory and is frequently used in make to stock companies. ATP only includes actual customer orders and planned and expected inventory receipts. The forecast is not used to calculate ATP. This topic was covered more fully in Chapter 4. As supply chain systems have become more powerful and sophisticated this concept has been expanded to include AATP — allocated available to promise. Even though a customer's order may not be placed in the ERP system, the product is allocated to that preferred customer and is not available for general consumption. An example of AATP is shown in Table 15.1.

Table 15.1   Example of Allocated Available for Promise (AATP)

Part A Demand time fence–3 Beginning on hand–172	1	2	3	4	5	6	7	8	9	10
Forecast	100	90	80	75	80	90	100	100	120	130
Actual customer demand	80	120	75	30	20	10	0	0	0	0
Project available balance	92	122	47	122	42	102	2	52	82	102
Allocated for customer			30	20		20				
Available to promise	92	–45		120						
Cumulative ATP	92	47	47	167	167	167	167	167	167	167
Allocated ATP	92	17	17	117	117	97	97	97	97	97
Master production schedule		150		150		150		150	150	150

When the customer orders actually orders the product, the allocation is reduced by the quantity the customer has actually ordered. If the quantity exceeds the level that has been reserved, the overall available to promise is then reduced. This kind of functionality normally is only found in the supply chain integration systems and not as part of a traditional ERP system.

Once the production schedule is developed and approved, the stage is set for putting the plan into motion. Some unique tools are used to control the materials used in the repetitive manufacturing facility.

Backflush

The deduction from inventory records of the component parts used in an assembly or subassembly by exploding the bill of materials by the production count of assemblies produced is called backflushing. In the low-volume, high-variety production process (job shop) a work order is used to collect the costs for material and labor. Since repetitive manufacturing usually determines individual product cost by collecting direct costs over time and dividing them by the number of units completed, the work order transactions specific to an individual part or group of parts are not necessary. In addition, since the bills of materials are stable in a repetitive industry and the product cannot be released to the line without availability of all the parts, the detailed tracking of material to a work order is not needed. This is why the process of backflushing is used to deduct components based on the number of finished goods completed.

If 200 lamps were produced then 200 bulbs, 200 yokes, 200 bases, 200 shades, and 200 electrical cords had to have been used. Only exceptions to the bill of material need to be managed and reported to the system. These exceptions could be parts that are scrapped, rejected, destroyed, substituted, or otherwise are different than the bill of material. Having a good process for capturing and reporting these exceptions is essential to having an effective backflush. **If the bills of material and inventory records are not 100% accurate, do not attempt the backflushing process.** Attempting to implement backflushing with errors in the bills of material or inventory is inviting disaster. Effective inventory control is not possible and the information used by the ordering process will be incorrect. This incorrect information will likely result in shortages to the line which will shut down the whole operation. Backflushing may look very easy and theoretically as a process it really is. With one transaction, the finished good part is received into inventory and all components are relieved. Almost looks like "automagic." However, without good control of exceptional usage or inaccuracy in the bill of material, this magic can become a nightmare.

A more advanced process of backflushing is called pay-point backflushing. Pay-point or count point backflushing is used when the manufacturing process extends for more than 1 day. Documenting material movements with transactions more than 1 day apart makes controlling inventory very difficult. Daily cycle counts must take into account the inventory that is on the line semicompleted and not yet transacted. This problem does not exist in the job shop since all materials are transacted at the time of material issue from stock.

Product 136593 Widget

Bill of Material	Routing Step
142604 Component A	10
142496 Component B	10
148375 Component C	20
193857 Component D	30
103857 Component E	50

For this product, if Routing Step 10 is considered a count point (pay-point), a transaction would be done that would complete that operation and the two parts (142604 and 142496) would be consumed from the line inventory and moved to work in process. The next pay-point may not be until Operation 30. When this transaction is done both Component C & D will be consumed. If the transaction was missed at Operation 10, the system also should consume the materials assigned to Step 10. Component E is not consumed until the very end when the product is transacted as completed and put into inventory. At this time the ERP system will transact all parts that have not already been consumed, relieve work in process of the temporary staging, and receive the part into finished goods. This is all accomplished by a single completion transaction. By using the pay-point backflush method, validation of inventory on the line is a much simpler process since less work in process needs to be considered when reconciling inventory.

A good inventory management process to support backflush is to perform a transaction when moving a bin of parts to the line location and then backflush from the line location. This does create an extra inventory transaction for the bin of parts but the control may be worth it. This provides a clear demarcation between the active inventory on the production line and any inventory that should be in the stockroom. If the inventory in the line location goes negative, it is much easier to detect and resolve the process problem that is causing it rather than allowing the error to continue and impact the main stockroom. Ideally there is no inventory in a main stockroom as a backup for the line. Unfortunately, most companies do not have sufficient reliability in the supply stream performance for this to be true for all parts.

Backflushing in an enterprise that requires lot or serial number traceability can appear like an impossible mission. ERP does not support backflush capability for parts requiring lot or serial number traceability. This is because the lot number of the component parts must be identified when material transactions are done. The answer to this problem has been the process of issuing material to work orders including detailed lot numbers of component parts. However, this does not mean that a facility with lot or serial number traceability is doomed to a life with work orders. Creatively applying the backflush process is still possible. Rather than using the standard backflush feature, the work order issue function is utilized at the end of the manufacturing process. This is known as a post-deduct process. Rather than attempting to predict which lot of parts will go onto a particular end item through the traditional job order release and parts issue function, the information on what lot numbers of parts are really used is collected as the part flows through manufacturing. This is usually tracked through a travelling piece of paper with the part and then transacted at the end of the process. Another option is to utilize bar coding technology to collect that data and automatically deduct the parts from inventory as the parent part is flowing through the process. At the end of the process, a hard copy can be printed for the device master record. This process has all the benefits of backflushing but still provides the required traceability.

In addition, some ERP systems provide the option of backflushing labor as part of the transaction. The backflush transaction creates a general ledger transaction for labor at the same time the material is relieved. Another option could be to consider the labor a period expense and simple divide it by the number of units that are completed.

If backflushing is a critical requirement for the enterprise, be sure that you have this feature demonstrated in the system selection process since not all systems are created equal in this regard. Many ERP systems will provide a place in the bill of material for routing step identification. However, this field is usually for reference only and does not actively link to any functionality. Not all systems provide for period costing and pay-point backflushing may not be possible at all without a great deal of modification.

Period Costing

A steady level of work in process and a reliably short throughput time makes period costing possible. Work in process is directly related to lead-time. When lead-time stays constant then so does the level of work in process. Keeping track of every detailed transaction costs more than the value of the information that is received. Statistical process control charts can be used to track costs over time. Using the same rules as would be used when managing part dimensions, costs can be expected to vary within a certain tolerance. When the trend begins to move out of control or a special occurrence happens to cause a one-time spike in cost, this can be quickly identified. This kind of reporting is now available through the use of data analysis tools on the relational ERP database. Figure 15.6 shows an example of how this cost analysis may look.

As would be expected in a new product development, the costs are more widely variable at the beginning of the analysis. Once the product has become stabilized the reliability of cost is very high over time. One exception can be seen around time period 40 when the cost sharply spikes. This out of control condition can be readily identified and resolved. This would not be possible in a regular costing process where this spike would be averaged in over time and likely could pass by without being noticed. Performing analysis like this requires access to the tables inside the ERP system normally through a custom report writer. This type of report is not typical in ERP standard reports.

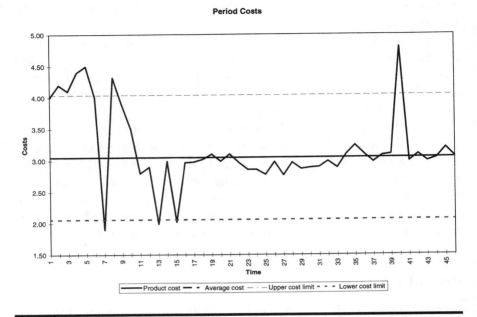

Figure 15.6 Statistical cost analysis.

High-Volume, Mixed-Model Manufacturing

The repetitive approach to ERP implementation can also be leveraged into a mixed model discrete manufacturer where the processes are repetitive. Examples of this type of manufacturer are automobiles, consumer electronics, computers, or airplane overhead bins. Every end item could be absolutely unique but each one utilizes the same process. The variety differences could be color, hole patterns, attached parts, or name plates.

Material and process traceability is also a very common requirement in this type of environment. This means that the end product needs to track the lot number of the materials used and the operator that worked on the units to an end item batch or serial number. High-volume, high-variety repetitive production has one foot in the discrete work order world and the other in the rate-based world. Managing the material and capacity planning can be a real challenge. The same repetitive tools can be used for a final assembly operation where many different configurations of parts are running down the same line. MRP can be linked into the execution on the shop floor to determine the material configuration and the day required. Normally the

SEI ZOU BAN GO KAN RI

製 造 番 号 管 理

SEI BAN

製 番

Figure 15.7   Japanese kanji characters for Seiban. (Courtesy Toshiyuki Okai, Sanyo North America.)

smallest planning time bucket for MRP is a single day. A kanban process can still authorize replenishment to the minute supported by MRP scheduling the configuration of the parts to the day.

Some industries require that the component parts come to the line in a specific sequence and the response time from the supplier is longer than is manageable using a simple kanban. Functionality tying less than daily planning buckets to a serial number is rarely found in ERP. In this environment it is very common that line sequencing of the desired models must also be netted through to the planned purchase order so that the supplier can sequence the incoming materials to the needs of the line. This process is known as Seiban. The literal translation of Seiban comes from three Japanese words that have been shortened into one term. SEIZOU is production, BANGO is number, KAN RI is management. Therefore Seiban can be translated to be management by lot number. The kanji for this term is in Figure 15.7.

This type of line sequencing is commonly found in automotive and truck assembly. Replenishments from suppliers are received many times each day and having the right part on the truck in the right order is essential for the overall productivity of the assembly line. This is one of the areas where all ERP systems are not created equal. *Caveat emptor!*

Configurators

Repetitive manufacturing frequently uses the configurator tool. Configurators are software systems that create, use, and maintain product models that allow complete definition of all possible product options and variations with a minimum of entries. Things to ask about configurators in a repetitive environment are

1. Is the configurator a linear finite model or does it have dynamic capability? Linear finite models are when a limited number of choices can be made. Dynamic model is when measurements and sizes can be added. Dynamic configurators are used for the fabrication of windows, doors, and wire cable lengths. Does your enterprise require a dynamic configurator?
2. Is the configurator an integral part of the ERP system or is it a "bolt on" that must be interfaced?
3. Does the configurator interface or integrate with the front office tools to provide seamless pricing and quoting capability?
4. Is the configurator Web-enabled to allow your customers to configure their own products and determine prices before the order is placed?

The development of configurators is continuing at a rapid pace. In a few short years, this elegantly complex, yet simple functionality is being included as part of the basic ERP system.

Summary

The repetitive operation is the most simple to comprehend, yet can be the most difficult to manage. Any unexpected breakdown can cause the entire plant to shut down. Material is closely synchronized with the production process. Traceability may be required to the end item level. The positive side of repetitive manufacturing is that there are not piles of inventory covering up the problems. Any disruption is quickly identified. A sense of urgency is common in the identification and resolution of the problems encountered in this type of facility.

The capacity planning is more straightforward as the products move down a highly predictable series of machines either on a transfer line or through a manufacturing cell. The routing in a repetitive operation is usually only one step. Lead times through the process are less than 1 day. Processes that take more than one day are supported with tools like pay-point backflushing.

A variety of unique tools are available to the repetitive manufacturer. Kanban, Seiban, configurators, AATP, backflushing, post-deduct, and period costing are all available for use at the appropriate time and place in the process. Understand each of these tools and their applicability and management of the repetitive enterprise can be simplified. As my father taught me, "Use the right tool for the right job and the job is easy. Use the wrong tool and you will fight the job every step of the way." Fighting a job shop ERP system in a repetitive manufacturing shop can be very costly. Buy and implement wisely.

16 Process Industry Application

Process flow industries comprise about half of manufacturers worldwide, with the proportions much higher in Australia and New Zealand. Process industry has always been a challenge for traditional MRP systems. Process industries are typically highly automated plants with a large capital investment. Examples of process industries include food processors, refining, pulp and paper, beverage, primary metals, plastics, and chemical manufacturers. To realize the best return on investment and the lowest product costs, these plants generally run 24 hours a day, 7 days a week. The changeover of the line from one product to another is very expensive since the whole plant is usually down during the changeover. The entire production workforce is idle and the expensive capital assets are not producing revenue, but the equipment cost continues. For this reason, the main focus for any enterprise planning system in process industry is effective capacity management including product sequencing and optimization of orders through the plant. The two main tools are called process flow scheduling (PFS) and advanced planning and scheduling (APS).

Process Industry Overview

Process flow scheduling provides the highest utilization level possible in the plant including sequencing changeovers and scheduling by-product and co-products. Once the capacity is planned, then the priorities are confirmed against the order book or optimized for profitability given the capacity

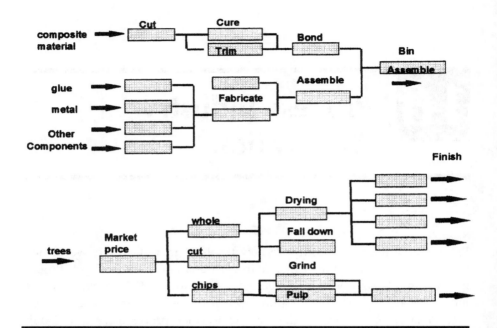

Figure 16.1 (Top) Standard MRP scheduling logic (A plant). (Bottom) The basis of PFS scheduling logic (V plant).

constraint — exactly opposite of the process for discrete manufacturing. Beware of any ERP system that claims to be the best fit for both process and job shop manufacturing. The features and functions that are required are very different. The standard manufacturing business model is to first plan the priorities of the enterprise and then confirm the capacity availability.

Figure 16.1 shows the difference between the bills of material from a traditional MRP plant and the process industry. The traditional MRP scheduling logic is used in the "A" plant, while the process plant is exactly the opposite or a "V" plant. Other differences between A plants and V plants were covered in Chapter 4.

If all process plants were only V-type plants, ERP implementation would be difficult enough to manage all the by-product and co-products. By-products are materials of value that are produced as a residual of the production process. In an injection molding operation the material that is used to hold the part in the die is called a gate. These gates are removed as the part is removed from the injection mold and collected. Customarily this material can then be reground and stocked as regrind. The regrind is blended with the virgin material to make a blend that can be used to mold more parts. The percentage of regrind that can be optimally used by part and by specific component material will change. The ability to use regrind dramatically reduces the cost of manufacturing these parts.

Co-products are those products that are typically manufactured together or sequentially because of product or process similarities. This could include grouping parts of many different sizes and shapes to be cut from one piece of material to optimize the material use. In corrugated plants, different customer orders may be run as co-products to maximize the utilization of the corrugated web. In process plants, such as chemical and refining, operations are the result of very complex "stochiemetric" models. These models use process conditions or are state controlled by raw material quality, temperature, pressure, and flow to determine how production should be scheduled. This provides an additional level of complexity.

The process plant is rarely a single V-style process. It is not unusual to find a blend of manufacturing types inside a process plant. The initial processing of the main product may occur in a continuous flow, but it is very common to find final packaging is done in lots or batches. Food processing is a good example. The product may be produced continuously, but then must be packaged into a finite number of different package sizes. The scheduling interface between the long continuous runs of product must be integrated with the final product configuration so that the product meets all manufacturing requirements, including how long the work in process can be held in bulk before packaging, the forecast market demands are met, and the best profit is achieved. This schedule is further detailed into the individual retail pack. The retail pack then usually has some kind of shipping or case overpack for sale to the distributor. These distribution packs can be simple (one product put in each case) or a complex pack (mix of products or assortment put into one case pack). These distribution packs then must be consolidated onto a pallet for shipping purposes. The pallets are tracked through the system but the visibility to the individual retail pack must be maintained. Having advanced planning and scheduling tools is essential in this environment so that the very best schedule can be developed.

In addition to this type of bulk to pack manufacturing processes, process industries utilize different quality measures. The discrete plant typically inspects parts with a binary result. The part is either good or not good. Good parts are used and bad parts are scrapped or reworked. A process plant can test a batch or a part to determine its potency or grade. The result is not as simple as good or bad. The same production costs may be incurred to produce a batch of product with a low- or high-grade result. The low grade can only be sold for a low price. The high grade demands a premium in the market. The high grade may be affected by storage time. If the product is stored too long, the grade may deteriorate into a lower grade saleable product or may deteriorate into unsaleable product. In refining, during the summer season gasoline is in higher demand and commands a higher price than other products. In the winter, heating oil has the priority. The profitability of the operation is dependent on being able to shift the production schedule between these two seasons, taking into consideration market demand, the quality of the crude being received, the physical contraints of the process equipment, major maintenance, overhaul requirements, and storage capacity for building inventory in the chosen market location(s). Traditional manufacturing only has to worry about where a part was placed in storage so that it can be retrieved. Many process plants can go back to the same location and the product has changed by virtue of sitting on the shelf. This is yet another complication in scheduling the process plant.

The most common return on investment for an ERP implementation in a discrete manufacturing plant is the effective planning of component materials as measured by inventory reduction. Process industry is unique in that it generally uses few raw materials that are purchased in very large bulk quantities like rail cars or ships. These materials are commonly purchased at a commodity price that can fluctuate widely in the market. Detailed material planning by exploding requirement through bills of materials does not provide the same benefit for process industry. The detailed material planning capability of the discrete ERP system must be replaced with PFS. Attempting to implement a traditional ERP system in the traditional job shop manner in a process industry is guaranteed failure.

Adding to the difficulty caused by the conversion process, the inherent characteristics of the process flow business cause challenges for traditional ERP implementation. Process plant businesses are continuously shuffling brands and product line. These businesses are constantly selling and acquiring lines of products to align with the desired strategic plan. The ERP system must be sufficiently flexible to adapt to these changes after the initial implementation. This can be a very different approach than some implementations take where the configuration of the system is locked down and difficult to change once the system has been configured. Providing the ability to quickly reconfigure is essential for the process business overall success.

Another area that is unique to process industry is the inherent nature of supply chain management. Due to the purchase and sale of plants, one week a supplier could be a feeder plant and quickly this plant can be a sister plant owned by the same corporate entity. A process business requires a well-designed business model to understand the impact and consequences of customer and supplier locations so that a holistic solution can be developed that benefits the entire supply chain. Since the operating cost of the plant equipment is relatively fixed, overall profitability must be assured by best utilizing the people operating the plant and providing overhead functions. In some process industries, tolling and exchange contracts with complementary or competitive suppliers also are used to balance supply and demand for multisite operations, which may have a significant geographic distribution.

Process Flow Scheduling

Process industry is characterized by having relatively few raw materials that can explode into a variety of end products, co-products, and by-products. A proven method for scheduling this type of output has been developing over the past 25 years under the guidance of Dr. Sam Taylor and Dr. Steve Bolander. As mentioned previously, this type of scheduling is known as process flow scheduling. This book is not intended to be a complete discussion of this scheduling technique since available technology has been changing its application so radically and is expected to continue for the foreseeable future. This chapter is intended to create an awareness of these tools and their fit in an overall ERP implementation. References have been provided at the end of this chapter for further resources in process industries and process flow scheduling. The close integration of the internal schedules, the reliability of constrained capacity usage, coupled with the impact of outside events have positioned process industry as the leader in APS.

APS engines include the business application of simulation, heuristics (best of business rules), linear programming (LP), and MILP as well as constraint controlled intuitive modeling such as TOC and fuzzy logic. These sophisticated mathematical modeling tools embrace all aspects for the business that can be impacted by a supply chain management implementation. Integrating demand information from the customer's customer to the supplier's supplier is enhanced also by incorporating additional dimensions of the business such as the revenue chain. This allows more comprehensive "what if" scenario planning in evaluating new market potentials, corporate take-over return on investment analysis, price sensitivity analysis, and logistics configuration analysis.

The first process flow scheduling tools were implemented in the late 1980s and focused on the consumer good industry. The calculation models were rather simplistic and attempted to provide the single best answer based on the model input. As computers have become more sophisticated, the models representing the business have become more sophisticated as well. It is now possible to create almost "virtual reality" for the business to evaluate alternate plans. Even the technology that was used to develop the MICSS CD ROM at the back of this book allows the user to make changes in running an enterprise and to realize that the impact on the profit statement was not available at a reasonable cost a few short years ago. This simulator functionality can be easily expanded to simulate the entire enterprise. Similar to running a real business, a single, large model is insufficient to represent all the integrated functions within an enterprise. Effective process flow scheduling systems contain the ability to define multiple models to best describe the business.

The three main approaches for solving the scheduling problem include simulation, heuristics, and optimization. Simulation attempts to represent in a computer the interrelationships of a business. An effective simulator directly relates to the business and allows the iteration of many different decisions to determine the impact on the enterprise. The simulator can be as simple as a spreadsheet that provides "what if" capability for different production schedule. The openness of ERP systems provides the opportunity to download information from the main system into spreadsheets for seamless manipulation in "what if" analysis. The simulator can handle important trade-off's analytically and clearly identify the impact of certain decision. This quantifiable analysis allows decisions to be made on the basis of fact and they make fewer decisions based on intuition. At times, the amount of data becomes overwhelming, causing difficulty in building a mental picture of a particular problem or solution.

The simulator can be used to develop a more sophisticated model to reflect a particular enterprise. These simulators can provide an excellent teaching tool such as the one included in this book or can help in managing a real business by allowing the management to see consequences of decisions before implementation. With the continuing growth of computer processing power and the decline of computer processing cost, simulations are sure to become more widely used in day-to-day operations.

Heuristics are simplifying rules that are used to develop a feasible schedule. These rules are based on intuition or experience instead of by mathematical optimization. These rules may be required because the simulation and optimization may not be able to provide a feasible solution without them. Another use for heuristic rules is to develop an initial solution from which improvements can be made. An example may be that production cannot be increased or decreased more than 10,000 units for each major schedule change. Another rule may be that major schedule changes can only be incorporated once a quarter. Reasons exist for these business rules, but they cannot be quantified sufficiently for incorporation into the simulator. Remember that the computer tools will not take over for good management of the company. Materials, capacity, and other resources have been managed well in the past. The computer tools should not replace effective management but rather should augment it.

Optimization is based on the theory of constraints (TOC). Chapter 2 provided more detail about TOC in the ERP world. For the purposes here, optimization attempts to calculate the best solution given the bottleneck to achieve the desired results. Optimization could include most profits, shortest total lead-time, best customer service for a preferred customer, smallest total changeover time, or making whatever measure that is selected the best that it can be. For optimization to be effective there must be a system defined for which the demand exceeds the possible supply. Optimization then provides the best possible solution to a problem in terms of this specified objective function.

ERP System Requirements

This section lists the typical requirements and a brief explanation for an effective ERP system in a process industry. These requirements are not listed in any specific order of importance.

1. **Supply chain management.** Collaborative forecasting and planning is a real must for the process industry. Having visibility of customer inventory and sell-out data patterns in addition to the traditional sell-in information can provide proactive requirements information. Promotion, sale price, and competitive impact are integral in this supply chain solution. Hard and soft allocation should be allowed in the

system. Soft allocation promises product based on overall volumes. The reality of execution is that the process for filling orders is first come, first served. A preferred customer may find itself without any product. Hard allocation makes an assignment of inventory to a particular customer order. The hard allocation process allows preferred or more profitable customers first availability of the product rather than first come, first served. This hard allocation may also be supported by contract agreements and pricing. Tolling and exchanges also can be used for balancing supply and demand within the supply chain.

2. **Multiple plants, warehouses, and branches.** Most process industries must control inventory at a number of different physical locations including multiple factory and packaging locations, distribution warehouses, and possibly branch retail locations. Some of the process industry products are in liquid form and, therefore, are distributed via public or private pipelines. The control parameters for this mode is different from standard ERP distribution approaches.

3. **Multiple units of measure for each item.** The units of measure can be very complex for a process industry. A piece may be tracked in inventory as an "each," but the part may be sold by the pound. The system must have the capability to recognize the part as both units of measure and convert between these units of measure automatically. The unit of measure conversion should also include tracking retail packs to case packs to pallet packs. These multiple units of measure also require very sophisticated and complex pricing models available to support the business as well. The same product may have different prices dependent on the location it will be shipped. Volume and customer discounts are also normal. The product can change composition during transit, (i.e., liquified natural gas) due to external influences, pressure or temperature, or internal influences such as product mixing in common pipelines or storage tanks. The ERP system must be able to take these variations into account.

4. **Formula management.** Similar to how a cookbook is written, a different formula is required for different production batches in a process plant. Unlike the discrete business, these formulas are different from the bill of material in that if a double batch is required, each component in the formula may not be doubled. Any good cook can relate failed attempts at doubling a recipe. A big issue in process industry is how exactly is a recipe scaled to a desired batch size. These different recipes should be able to be tracked in the ERP system for

different batch sizes. Also lots need to be tracked to meet government regulations for processing particular in food and pharmaceutical operations.

5. **Quality tests and specifications.** Since quality is not a binary function for the process industry, the quality tests and specification should be traceable in the ERP system. This includes the ability to grade material at different levels of quality and then automatically allocate orders based on that grading. Assume grade A is superior to grade B and grade B is superior to grade C. If a customer orders grade C and no grade C inventory is in stock, the system should follow predefined business rules for allocating available B grade material or A grade material to the order. This type of functionality is very unique and normally is handled through a suffix at the end of the part number to denote grade. When grading is done by this method the automatic allocation of this inventory becomes almost impossible without extensive system modification.

6. **Pack bill of materials.** Another unique bill of material function is the pack bill of materials. This defines which items are packed and shipped together to the customer. This can include packing multiple items into a single package for sale such as an assortment of the same product or packing complementary products together for sale as a complete unit. One example would be to pack a television, VCR, and stereo speakers together for shipment as an individual entertainment unit.

7. **Flexible planning solutions.** The planning solution must be able to incorporate and manipulate pack quantities including substitution of items that are not available with items of equal or higher value. Defining these business rules can take an extensive amount of time during the implementation, but can assure that customer demand will be filled most expeditiously. Part of this planning process should also include the recognition of shelf life. If a part will expire on the first of next month, the system should recognize that the lot would not be available for an order that is scheduled to start on the 15th. Any established priorities such as customer or profitable products should also be recognized in the planning process. Multiple variant allocation should also be supported by the planning system. Examples could include product grade, colors, or size.

8. **Lot tracking and product genealogy.** This tracking includes knowing which lots of raw material were used to manufacture the finished goods. The destination for each lot must also be traced in the event a

recall is required. All lots shipped to a certain customer should be easily identifiable as well as all customers who are shipped a certain lot. This traceability is essential for risk management and is required in industries like pharmaceuticals, medical devices, and food processing.

9. **Process costing.** The costing system should be able to allocate costs across multiple parents on the same work order. These parent parts could include co-products, by-products, and grade variants. Fall down in grade targets must also be handled. Fall-downs are usually sold at a significantly reduced price against an almost nominal cost. The variance of the production cost to the product value must be handled within the costing system. Large process plants are required to operate at or near capacity for 24 hours per day with preference being for only planned maintenance outages. The budget for maintenance is typically 20 to 30% of the total operating budget or higher depending on larger process unit turnarounds. This is an area where some ERP systems are venturing or partnering with best of breed solutions. The requirement for robust asset management which considers planned, emergency, preventive, predictive, and turnaround or outage maintenance requirements is a priority. Key areas which must be integrated include material procurement, stores inventory, and maintenance systems.

Summary

Process industry is very different than the traditional job shop. High-volume products made in relatively few varieties characterize this industry. Capacity is a critical constraint in process industry. The first material requirements planning systems were developed for the job shop to manage the complex flow of materials through variable capacity. The priority plan assumes that there is infinite capacity. Capacity planning is used to validate the priority plan in the discrete enterprise. Process industry accomplishes its planning exactly in reverse. Capacity is planned first and then the priority plan is determined. Materials are ordered based on the availability of capacity rather than the other way around. Therefore, it is not surprising that these systems do not fit the process industry well. Unique scheduling tools are used for process industries including process flow scheduling. The ERP system must have some unique functions to allow this integrated system to best fit the process enterprise. Using the right tools for the right job makes the job much easier. Attempting to use the same tools to solve every problem is asking for disaster. Successful ERP implementation in the process industry is the ability to know the difference.

Resources for the Process Manufacturer

APICS Process Industry SIG, www.apics.org, 800-444-2742, 703-354-8851. Resources available that provide educational and technology resources designed to increase productivity, profitability, and competitiveness for process industries through creation, expansion, and dissemination of the planning, scheduling, and logistics knowledge and technologies.

Enterprise simulation, MBE Simulation Ltd, Eli Schragenheim, mbe@mbe-simulations.com.

17 Remanufacturing

Remanufacturing has traditionally been defined as an industrial process in which worn-out products are restored to like-new condition. Today, the concept of remanufacturing is expanding to include elements of repair and overhaul as well. A repaired product normally retains its identity, and only those parts that have failed or are badly worn are replaced or serviced. Overhaul is a specific course of action to ensure that a certain level of performance is restored or a higher level achieved through upgrade. Integrated planning and control systems help coordinate and schedule the difficult job of having the right part in the right place at the right time to support this industry. As difficult as standard manufacturing is, the remanufacturer has a task that is an order of magnitude more difficult. The first step in the remanufacturer's planning process is to take a product that is no longer usable and based on the past replacement or repair history, have the right components available to return the product to usefulness. This requires very sophisticated planning tools. Not only is there a statistical probability attached to which parts may be replaced, there are also many different routings that the part could take to be put in "as-new" condition. To further complicate the issue, the planning of materials and capacities in the remanufacturing environment is highly dependent on the quality and availability of the carcass assets from which the process starts.

Another challenge to the remanufacturer is the simple process of tracking inventory. The product may have the same part number before and after the remanufacturing process. This requires some unique identification of part condition to accurately plan the supply and demand. A standard material planning system usually considers the status codes as information only and will combine the rebuilt and the core product quantities together. The most common solution is to apply a different part number to the different status parts so that they can be kept separate on the planning system.

Another complexity is when the components of a particular asset must be tracked directly back to that particular asset and cannot be used interchangeably for other products with the same item identification code. Add to this complex web of inventory tracking, the desire to track the costs of the parts back to the parent item and one can only begin to imagine how to effectively plan and manage this enterprise. Effective integrated systems can help provide clarity in this web of complexity.

With the advent of environmental responsibility and the ISO14000 standard, it is not surprising to see remanufacturing processes utilized in an increasingly wide variety of industries. This industries include automotive, electronics, defense, communications, education, electrical, healthcare, food, furniture, glass, graphic arts, mining, transportation, retail, metal fabrication, pharmaceutical/chemical, plastics/rubber, lumber/paper, textile, and apparel. As remanufacturing processes and planning become better defined and understood, it is not surprising to find that remanufacturing is good business and good for business. No longer is this operation one that consumes profits from the company, remanufacturing can produce profits for the company.

Remanufacturing Similarities and Differences

Remanufacturing companies have long held the belief that they are very different from the traditional manufacturing enterprise. In April of 1996, in the *APICS Aerospace and Defense SIG News,* George W. Plossl addressed the question of just how different are remanufacturing and manufacturing. His summary was that there are more similarities than differences.

Similarities

1. Both involve suppliers, plants, and customers.
2. Both have two fundamental questions: Are we making enough in total and are we working on the right items now?
3. Both have the same basic logic guides:
   - What will we make?
   - What resources are required?
   - Which are now available and adequate?
   - Which are on the way and should arrive soon?
   - What else must be procured and when?
4. All activities fall into one of two categories: planning and execution.

5. The same system framework is common to all manufacturing, including aerospace and defense and remanufacturing.

Differences

1. Disassembly is required of cores in remanufacturing but not in new product manufacturing.
2. Capacity planning involves less predictable rework, classic capacity requirements planning is not justified, and rough-cut capacity techniques are generally better.
3. Material requirements planning programs must handle decimal fractions and negative lead-times showing when components from disassembly will be available for final assembly.
4. Final reassembly operations are no different than the standard assembly process.

His conclusion was that there are many apparent differences between repair/remanufacturing and manufacturing, but the real differences are few and far outweighed by the similarities. This chapter will concentrate on the differences.

Managing Remanufacturing Material

The starting point for a remanufacturing company is the receipt of the core or carcass. This provides the basic working material for the process to begin. The core or carcass is a nonserviceable item that is intended for remanufacturing or repair. The finished remanufactured part may or may not go back to the same customer. If you have ever purchased brakes, a carburetor, or radiator for a car, there is a core charge that is commonly charged when you purchase the part. This cost is refunded when you bring in the nonfunctioning part that was removed. This rebate is to motivate the consumer of the rebuilt part to return sufficient raw material to be available for the remanufacturer. Even with this financial incentive, a key problem for the remanufacturer is to assure sufficient quantity of high-quality cores that can be cost effectively remanufactured.

Once this part has been received, the first operation in every remanufacturing company is the assessment process or inspection and evaluation of the carcass. A skilled person is required to examine the received part and first determine if the part can be repaired or refurbished economically. Those parts that cannot be economically returned to a usable condition are scrapped at this point. Some carcasses can no longer be economically salvaged. There is a fine balance between utilizing all material that is returned and accomplishing the process in a manner that can be profitable. Some companies will set aside material that cannot be currently reclaimed until a later time when the part's value may increase. This assessment process could be as simple as a visual inspection or it may require disassembly and testing to determine the part's internal condition. Care must be taken in this initial operation not to create a disorganized junkyard where the assessment process is done.

Remanufacturing Bills of Materials

Once the part has been assessed as having economic value for salvage, it is time to begin the remanufacturing process. However, parts and capacity are needed to support that process. This is similar to how a traditional manufacturing company plans to have the appropriate level of material and capacity available through the use of bills of materials and routings. The remanufacturing enterprise develops the disassembly or teardown bill of material followed by a reassembly bill. Figure 17.1 shows a graphical example of what this complete bill of material looks like.

Remanufacturing bills of material have the shape of a diamond. A single part is disassembled, component parts repaired or replaced, and then reassembled to a single parent part. The ability to plan for this type of disassembly process requires a very special bill of material function.

The disassembly bill of material shown here assumes that only traditional ERP functionality is available in the system. Lately some ERP systems have begun to develop and introduce functionality that specifically meets the needs of the remanufacturer.

142095 Clock, Disassembly

142503	Inner works	−1 each
123291	Hands	−2 each
123032	Face	−0.5 each
136958	Clock	1 each

Notice that the bill of materials contains a negative amount for three of the items. This allows standard material planning systems to be used to control a remanufacturing operation. Since MRP was originally designed to

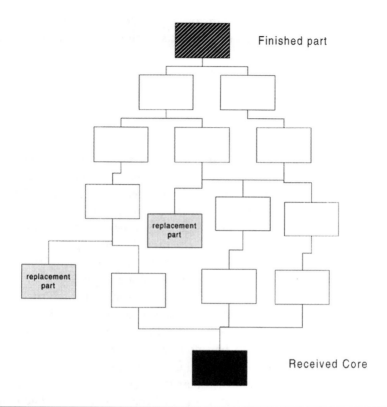

Finished part

replacement part

replacement part

Received Core

Figure 17.1 Remanufacturing bill of material.

support a one-to-one or many-to-one relationship between components and parent parts, attempting to plan multiple parent parts on a single order is not possible. Having a negative amount in the bill of material allows a standard system handle the fact that one item is made into many parents in the initial remanufacturing disassembly phase.

The first step in a standard work order release is to create a work order number and then issue the materials to the order. In this case, the order would be created for the disassembly clock (part number 142095). A partial issue is then done to remove the 136958 clock from inventory. The 136958 clock is the carcass that has been returned for refurbishment. After physically disassembling this clock, the issue transaction can then be done for the inner works, hands, and face. When a negative quantity is issued, the result is that these parts will actually be placed into inventory as usable parts. The parent part is received as normal. The costs also will be credited to the work order correctly. Labor time is charged to the order just like any other manufacturing order. Notice that the expected by-products of this clock assembly include:

142095 Clock, Disassembly — 1 each
142503 Inner works — 1 each
123291 Hands — 2 each
123032 Face — 0.5 each

You cannot physically have one half of a clock face. This fractional amount represents the probability that the face will be usable after assembly. In this case, 50% of the faces will be usable for the reassembled units. The issue transaction is performed at the end of the process with the actual amounts realized from the disassembly process. The parent part for this order, the 142095 clock disassembly, usually represents the largest part of the carcass that is tracked through the process. This could be the frame of the radiator, the main airframe for a plane, or the chassis of a computer.

The disassembly bill of material is used as a guide for the inspector/evaluator in the tear down and evaluation process of an item intended for remanufacturing. Once the process has been performed a number of times, the quantities for the material can be updated. Depending on what comes off the assembly that can be reused, the bill of material is subsequently modified after evaluation to create a bill of repair that represents the required scope of work. A repair bill of material is a bill of material that has been created to define the actual scope of work required to return an item to serviceable condition. This bill results from the actual examination and evaluation of an item intended for repair and is used for master scheduling and MRP explosion purposes.

For the example given previously, the bill of repair could be

242095 Clock, Refurbished

242503	Inner works	1 each
223291	Hands	2 each
123032	Face	1 each
142095	Clock	1 each
239853	Gift box	1 each

Notice that in this repair bill of material there is a new part number for the inner works and the hands, but the part number for the face has stayed the same. This is because the inner works and the hands had to be processed through other processes to make them ready for the reassembly process. This is very difficult to track on a single work order since different parts are going many different ways. One way to handle this problem is to have a minibill of materials to process these parts with the supporting routings. These bills of materials and routings can then be used in the standard fashion to take components and process them into parent parts. The amount of processing to bring the face to usable condition is very small so the same part number is used to track this item. Also this bill of repair also shows a new part — a gift box that is required to complete the product for sale.

Recall that for this particular item, the face had a 50% chance of being replaced or reused. This is called an occurrence factor. Within the repair/remanufacturing environment, some repair operations do not occur 100% of the time. The occurrence factor is associated with how often a repair is required to bring the average part to a serviceable condition and is expressed at the operation level in the router. The planning system must have full visibility of the repair bill of materials including the occurrence factors to effectively plan material and capacity. For the example used here, this bill of material entered in the planning system would be

242095 Clock, refurbished

242503 Inner works	1 each
142503 Inner works	1 each
223291 Hands	2 each
123291 Hands	2 each
123032 Face	0.5 each
223032 Face	0.5 each
142095 Clock disassembly	1 each
142503 Inner works	−1 each
123291 Hands	−2 each
123032 Face	−0.5 each
136958 Clock	1 each
239853 Gift box	1 each

This can quickly become very confusing. A picture is worth a thousand words, so Figure 17.2 is the same bill of material represented in a graphic form.

In this representation of the bill of materials, it is much clearer that the new face (223032) and the gift box (239853) are parts that are purchased from the outside and used in the assembly. The core clock that is returned (136958) is expected to provide the chassis (142095), the hands (123291), the inner works (142503), and the face (123032) required for the reassembly

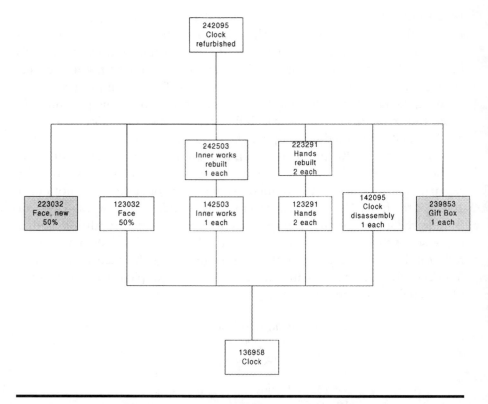

Figure 17.2 Bill of material for 242095 clock, refurbished.

process. However, this disassembly process only yields the face half of the time. The other half of the time a new face (223032) is required to complete the finished product. The inner works and the hands are expected to require additional processing after disassembly before they can be reassembled.

Remanufacturing Routings

Similar to a standard material planning requirement, routings must be prepared that describe the process by which the components are transformed into the parents. In this example, routings would be required for:

242095 Clock, refurbished
242503 Inner works

223291 Hands
142095 Clock disassembly

Notice that no routing is required for the face (123032) because this is a by-product of the disassembly process of the 136958 clock. These routings may have probabilities attached to them similar to the occurrence factors in the bill of material. A standard material planning system requires that the probabilities be reflected in the routing input to the system. A system that has been built specifically for the remanufacturing industry allows the entry of occurrence factors separately. If this is a requirement for your facility, be sure that functionality is demonstrated as part of the system selection process.

The routing below could represent the planning routing for the processing of the hands.

223291 Hands

Step	Description	Workcenter	Hours
10	Cleaning	Plating	2.0
20	Polish	Buffing	3.5
30	Reassembly	Assembly	1.0

Assuming that this routing is accurate, it could still be misleading. This routing could actually be the planning for a product that really is requiring the following process.

223291 Hands

Step	Description	Workcenter	Hours	Occurrence Factor
10	Cleaning	Plating	8.0	25%
20	Polish	Buffing	7.0	50%
30	Reassembly	Assembly	1.0	100%

This routing more accurately shows the factors and times that are used to plan for this product. Another level of complexity is when the parts sometimes can be used and they only need to follow this process a certain percentage of the time. This factor is known as the repair factor. The repair factor is sometimes referred to as the frequency of repair. This defines the percentage of times an average item must be repaired for return to a serviceable condition.

The other option is to use the part as-is or replace it with a new part, such as the face in the example. Planning to have these parts available requires defining the replacement factor. The replacement factor defines the percentage of time an average item will require replacement. In a remanufacturing industry not only do the times and quantities need to be correct, the occurrence, repair, and replacement factors must also be maintained to provide accurate inputs for planning. Even with all these factors and planning, unexpected things can happen and a part will need to be replaced or repaired. This is called unplanned repair. Unplanned repair is repair and replacement that is unknown until remanufacturing tear down and inspection.

Remanufacturing Inventory Management

Not surprisingly inventory management in a remanufacturing company is quite similar to any other manufacturing company. However, it does have its unique twists. When receiving a carcass for repair or remanufacture, the part number on the product is the same number as a good unit. Some systems will have status codes as active field in the database such that it becomes part of a unique identifier and is traceable through the system. For example:

136604 Clock
A code: 145
F code: 53
G code: 97

This record could represent a single part with three different statuses. The A code parts may be the parts that are available for customer orders. F code could be parts that have been evaluated as repairable but are waiting for parts. The G code may be carcasses that have not been examined yet. Each business will have different codes for different inventory states, but the advantage of this system is that the same parent part number is used throughout the process and only the status code changes. However, beware that some systems will have grades or status codes that are informational only and do not become part of a unique identifier. In this case the ERP system would see a total of 295 pieces of 136604 clocks in inventory from the above example with no distinction for usable grade.

Traceability is another requirement to many remanufacturers. Due to product liability and configuration control, the enterprise may wish to link the parts that come off an assembly directly back to the original assembly. As the disassembly parts move through the refurbishment process, the intended destination product may be part of the record. This becomes very difficult to track and is, at best, transaction intensive. The end item to which the part is destined must become a significant part of the item identifier. The impact is that each part in the shop must become uniquely identified. The database required to support this is very complex.

The other risk is that the part that is intended for use on the end item somehow falls behind in its processing due to quality or material problems and a part for a later unit comes to the assembly line. Normal behavior would be to use the available part and document it on the assembly paperwork. This now leaves another unit missing its legitimate part and the process can get out of hand quickly. This process is known as backrobbing. This also occurs when a part is directly taken from another unit that cannot be completed and used on a unit that is close to completion and is missing that part. When backrobbing starts it is terribly complex to track and virtually impossible to do it accurately. The short-term benefit of using the part is far outweighed by the system complexity to track it. The probability of getting the parts traceability to all balance out in the end is close to zero.

Managing the inventory asset in the remanufacturing enterprise is quite similar to other manufacturing companies. Sufficient investment in inventory assets is needed to be able to support the ongoing business. Too much inventory and cash is wasted. Too little inventory and the production operation cannot complete its work. In addition to the inventory strategy choices described in Chapter 4, the remanufacturing enterprise must also consider at what replacement factor should the inventory investment be funded. If a replacement factor is less than 30%, it is very likely that too much cash may be tied up in slow moving inventory. At lower replacement factors the material planning system may require only a fraction of a part based on the scheduled volumes. However, the smallest quantity that any part can be purchased in is one piece. This one piece may never be used and may remain as obsolete inventory. Another strategy for these parts is to wait until the part is required and then order. A part that is currently on site in inventory should be quicker to get than a part from a supplier. Clearly the trade-off is response time. If the part has a sufficiently low replacement factor, this process may still be capable of providing acceptable customer service. As in all decisions, the consequences must be weighed against the possible alternatives and the best overall decision made for the enterprise.

Glossary

APICS Dictionary Terms Related to the Remanufacturing Industry*

Carcass: A nonserviceable item obtained from a customer that is intended for use in remanufacturing.

Disassembly or Teardown Bill of Material: The bill of material (BOM) used as a guide for the inspector/evaluator in the teardown and evaluation process of an item intended for remanufacturing. This bill is subsequently modified after evaluation to create a bill of repair that represents the required scope of work.

MRO: Maintenance, repair and overhaul (an alternative definition for this abbreviation used in the remanufacturing industry).

Occurrence Factor: Within the repair/remanufacturing environment, some repair operations do not occur 100% of the time. The occurrence factor is associated with how often a repair is required to bring the average part to a serviceable condition and is expressed at the operation level in the router.

Remanufactured Parts: Components or assemblies that are refurbished or rebuilt to perform the original function. Syn: refurbished goods, refurbished parts.

Remanufacturing: An industrial process in which worn-out products are restored to like-new condition. In contrast, a repaired product normally retains its identity, and only those parts that have failed or are badly worn are replaced or serviced. In general, the remanufacturing environment is where worn-out products are restored to like-new condition.

Remanufacturing Resource Planning (RMRP): A manufacturing resource planning (MRP II) application in the remanufacturing sector.

Repair Bill of Material: A bill of material that has been created to define the actual scope of work required to return an item to serviceable condition. This bill results from the actual examination and evaluation of an item intended for repair and is used for master scheduling and MRP explosion purposes.

Repair Factor: The repair factor, sometimes referred to as the frequency of repair, defines the percentage of time an average item must be repaired for return to a serviceable condition. This factor is also expressed as a

---

* APICS — The Educational Society for Resource Management, *APICS Dictionary,* Alexandria, VA, 1998. With permission.

percentage applied to the quantity per assembly on the bill of material assembly/component relationship. It is used for forecasting material and required capacity in advance of carcass receipt.

Replacement Factor: The replacement factor defines the percentage of time an average item will require replacement. This factor is expressed as a percentage applied to the quantity per assembly on the bill of material assembly/component relationship. It is used for forecasting material and required capacity in advance of carcass receipt.

Unplanned Repair: Repair and replacement data which is unknown until remanufacturing teardown and inspection.

References and Resources

Remanufacturing Resource Book, 1996, John S. W. Fargher (Ed.), APICS #01179.

Discover a New Level of Performance: *Proc. Aerospace and Defense Remanufacturing Joint Symposium,* 1995, APICS #04217.

Reuse Operations: Community Development Through Redistribution of Used Goods, Michael Lewis et al. (Eds.), Institute of Local Self Reliance, 1995.

1996 APICS Remanufacturing Symposium, *Best in Class Basics,* 1996, APICS #04219.

1994 APICS Remanufacturing Proceedings: *Facing the Challenge,* May 11–13, 1994, Orlando, FL, APICS #04214.

REMAN Seminar Proceedings: *Doing it Better the Second Time,* APICS 1992 Remanufacturing Seminar, September 23–25, 1992, Salt Lake City, UT, APICS #04210.

Remanufacturing Seminar Proceedings: May 24–26, 1993, Oklahoma City, OK, *Real Solutions from Real People,* APICS #04210.

Note: All material marked with an APICS # can be ordered from www.apics.org. The APICS Remanufacturing (REMAN) SIG is a specific industry group designed for individuals working in the areas of remanufacturing, repair, reprocessing, overhaul services, and asset recovery in industries including automotive, electronics, commercial aviation, and defense.

18 Project Manufacturing

A ccording to Ralph Currier Davis in *The Fundamentals of Top Management*, a project is "any undertaking that has definite, final objectives representing specified values to be used in the satisfaction of some need or desire." For a project control manufacturer this final objective is a physical product that meets the requirements of the customer. The project control manufacturer builds products that are very low in volume and extremely high in variety. It is not uncommon to build items that are one of a kind. At the other end of this production spectrum are the process and repetitive manufacturer. The project control manufacturers also have a requirement to track costs to a top-level project. Projects may span multiple years and the cost collection must continue at the very top project level. Managing scope, time, and resources including costs are essential for the enterprise. Integrating the overall project plan with the ERP function can help provide that management control.

Project management adds a great deal of complexity to the ERP system since the basic assumption under the MRP engine is that all materials and activities are scheduled on the critical path. The fundamentals behind project management are that there is one critical path and the slack time on the parallel paths is used to balance capacity. The project manufacturer's dilemma is how should the ERP system plan the materials to support the activities not on the project's critical path. Should they be available at the early start or late start date of the activity? When are resources really required?

The standard logic of a material requirements planning system assumes that if the part is the same for fit, form, and function as designated by the part number, it can be used anywhere that part number needs to go. The project manufacturer may purchase materials specific to a single project that potentially can be used for multiple projects. The desire is to track the actual costs of these materials to the top level project but this is in direct conflict with the standard costing process that is the default of most ERP systems. These complexities of material planning and scheduling and overall costing are some of the project manufacturer's uniqueness. This chapter is not intended as a comprehensive reference in project management but rather highlights the application of ERP to this environment.

Project Life Cycles

Too many project managers believe that the phases of a project are

- Wild enthusiasm
- Mass disillusionment
- Search for the guilty
- Punish the innocent
- Promote the noninvolved

This belief has evolved from the personal experience of many project managers as they have been striving to do a good job managing the project. Effective project management requires effective management skills and techniques supported by appropriate technological tools. Unlike some projects where the overall statement of work can be descoped to bring the project in on schedule and on budget and declare accomplishment, the project manager for a manufacturing company cannot usually descope the final product to be shipped and still declare victory. The product must still meet all the requirements set by the customer.

According to David I. Cleland and William Richard King, the phases of effective project management include:

- Conceptual phase
- Definition phase
- Production phase
- Operational phase
- Divestment phase

Conceptual Phase

The conceptual phase is when the design team is working with the customer to determine the overall requirements for the product and potential deficiencies of the existing processes and products. The initial feasibility of the technical, environmental, and economic reality also is examined during this phase. One example would be the recent development of super fast ERP/SCM systems. Conceptually these systems were conceived many years ago but only recently have become a reality. The reason is that the available technology could not support it. Now that computers have multiple gigabyte memory available, these calculations can be completed directly in the active memory core without incurring the slow down of reading and writing to the hard drives.

In the conceptual phase the project team provides the answers to:

What will the product cost?
When will the product be available?
What will the product do?
How can the product be integrated into the existing systems?

The overall design and production approach is determined during this phase and an initial statement of work is prepared for further detail in the definition phase.

Definition Phase

The definition phase is when the detailed plan is prepared that determines the realistic cost, schedule, and performance requirements. This plan determines the quantity and timing required for human and other critical resources. A good project manager will also identify those areas that are risky or cause for concern. These areas are then further detailed for recovery and contingency plans. This is very different than the traditional ERP environment where the master schedule is entered, supported by a bill of material. In the traditional ERP environment the assumption is that everything will work exactly as planned. Any variability or unexpected events are typically covered with safety stock inventory or available surge capacity. In the project manufacturing industry the likelihood of the same inventory being used again is very small. Capacity must be carefully scheduled to provide optimal cost performance.

In the definition phase a detailed statement of work is developed and broken down to the necessary level for control purposes. An effective statement of work (SOW) should clearly define the objective for the project and how success will be measured. The statement of work should include cost

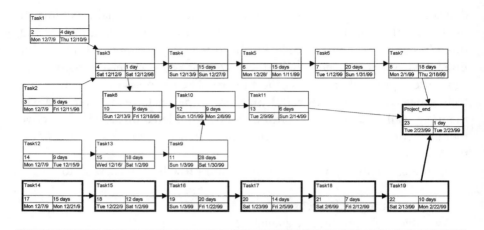

Figure 18.1   PERT chart representation of work breakdown structure.

and schedule targets as well as quality targets and usually becomes the contractual statement of work. Since revenue is directly related to the statement of work, it is very important to have agreement with the customer on the definition of key words. For example, a customer may desire to have a product tested in water. Your intent is to test the product in a local lake. The customer meant water, as in the Pacific Ocean. The cost implication can be significant. Even establishing the documentation format for the product manuals can be important since manuals created using new versions of software are not readable by previous versions. The project manufacturer also may be paid at certain points in the completion of the product so having measurable completion criteria is essential for each significant step in the work breakdown structure.

Once the statement of work has been defined and approved, the work begins on the work breakdown structure. A graphical representation of the work breakdown structure looks like a bill of materials that has been laid on one side. The duration of each task and the relationship of one task to another can be clearly visualized in this structure as shown in Figure 18.1.

This breakdown of activities allows scheduling materials and capacity based on the timing that is required. When this work breakdown structure is phased against a time-line, the timing for each task can be calculated. Project management tools like Microsoft Project or Primavera can be used to manage this work breakdown structure and the impact on schedule and resources. Table 18.1 shows how these tasks can be displayed in a tabular

Table 18.1   Tabular Work Breakdown Structure

Task	Duration	Start	End	Predecessors	Resource
Project Part 1	74d	Mon 12/7/98	Thu 2/18/99		
Task1	4d	Mon 12/7/98	Thu 12/10/98		A-Resource
Task2	5d	Mon 12/7/98	Fri 12/11/98	2	A-Resource
Task3	1d	Sat 12/12/98	Sat 12/12/98	2,3	B-Resource
Task4	15d	Sun 12/13/98	Sun 12/27/98	4	A-Resource
Task5	15d	Mon 12/28/98	Mon 1/11/99	5	C-Resource
Task6	20d	Tue 1/12/99	Sun 1/31/99	6	D-Resource
Task7	25d	Sun 1/11/98	Thu 2/18/99	7	C-Resource
Project Part 2	70d	Mon 12/7/98	Sun 2/14/99		
Task8	6d	Sun 12/13/98	Fri 12/18/98	4	E-Resource
Task9	28d	Sun 1/3/99	Sat 1/30/99	15	E-Resource
Task10	9d	Sun 1/31/99	Mon 2/8/99	10,11	B-Resource
Task11	6d	Tue 2/9/99	Sun 2/14/99	12	C-Resource
Task12	9d	Mon 12/7/98	Tue 12/15/98		C-Resource
Task13	18d	Wed 12/16/98	Sat 1/2/99	14	D-Resource
Project Part 3	78d	Mon 12/7/98	Mon 2/22/99		
Task14	15d	Mon 12/7/98	Mon 12/21/98		A-Resource
Task15	12d	Tue 12/22/98	Sat 1/2/99	17	C-Resource
Task16	20d	Sun 1/3/99	Fri 1/22/99	18	D-Resource
Task17	14d	Sat 1/23/99	Fri 2/5/99	19	E-Resource
Task18	7d	Sat 2/6/99	Fri 2/12/99	20	D-Resource
Task19	10d	Sat 2/13/99	Mon 2/22/99	21	C-Resource
Project end	1d	Tue 2/23/99	Tue 2/23/99	8,13,22	

format with the predecessors and required resources identified. When using an integrated project planning system, the data do not need to be entered twice. Different graphical representations are available with single data entry.

Production Phase

The production phase of a project begins with the verification of the product production specifications and the beginning of production of the unit. The final preparation and dissemination of documents is incorporated in this phase including the development of technical and service manuals and other traceability that is required for the product. Many companies are moving to release this information on CD-ROM due to the cost of preparing this essential document in a paper format. The product is tested to ensure that the specifications defined in the definition phase have been achieved. ERP can be used to bridge the transition from the planning to the production phase by supporting the project with detailed capacity and material planning. Timely status feedback is essential during this phase to provide an early warning of any part of the project that may not support the required completion date.

Operational Phase

The operational phase of the project is when the product has been delivered to the customer. This can be a time when the field service personnel may be intimately involved to aid in the installation or training for the product. Field service is further described in Chapter 19. During the operational phase, the realized costs are compared to the quoted costs to determine whether or not the product has been delivered at a profit. The actual cost of the product should not be a surprise at the very end of the project. Effective project management tools provide running feedback on completion status through a process called earned-value analysis or CS^2. This compares cost and schedule through a series of measures like:

1. Budgeted cost of work scheduled (BCWS).
2. Actual cost of work scheduled (ACWS).
3. Budgeted cost of work performed (BCWP).
4. Actual cost of work performed (ACWP).
5. Schedule variance (SV) = BCWP – BCWS or expressed as a percentage (SVP) = SV/BCWS.
6. Cost variance (CV) = BCWP – ACWP or expressed as a percentage(CVP) = CV/BCWP.

No matter what measures are used, it is critically important to evaluate the overall performance of the project to learn what worked well and what could be improved for the next product. Without this "post mortem" on a project, the lessons learned on one project are likely to be learned over and over again. Learning what went well helps the team determine how to repeat the success. Identifying what could be improved provides the opportunity to possibly avoid that situation in the future.

Divestment Phase

The divestment phase of a project manufacturer is the phase where the project team is transitioned from one project to the next. Some companies will dedicate personnel 100% of the time to a particular project. When this project has been completed it is essential to recognize the organizational and cost implications of having another project ready to start. If the project team does not see another product for development available on the horizon there could be a tendency to stretch the current project as long as possible. This can contribute to cost overruns on the current project and adversely impact the profits for this product. The divestment phase is a critical time that must be managed effectively so the organization can take from the lessons learned on the previous product and apply them to the next product. Unfortunately many people experience poor overall project management and the following proverbs have been developed through the years.

Proverbs for Project Management*

- You can con a sucker into committing to an unreasonable deadline, but you can't bully him into meeting it.
- The more ridiculous the deadline, the more it costs to try to meet it.
- The more desperate the situation, the more optimistic the situatee.
- Too few people on a project can't solve the problem — too many create more problems than they solve.
- You can freeze the user's specs but he won't stop expecting.
- Frozen specs and the abominable snowman are alike — they are both myths, and they both melt when sufficient heat is applied.
- What you don't know hurts you.
- A user will tell you anything you ask about — nothing more.
- What is not on paper has not been said.
- Projects progress quickly until they become 90% complete, then they remain at 90% complete forever.
- No major system is ever completely debugged; attempts to debug a system inevitably introduce new bugs that are even harder to find.
- Project teams detest progress reporting because it vividly demonstrates their lack of progress.

---

* Harold Kerzner, *Project Management*, 5th ed.

Projects in ERP

The role of ERP in project management is to provide the common database that supports detailed planning and integration from product design through manufacturing. Product data management (PDM) is frequently used for design cycle control including the initial design release, distribution of the desired design to suppliers and potential multiple manufacturing sites, and managing changes that occur after the design release. The incorporation of the PDM tool has been shown to provide a 15 to 20% improvement in production cost by its linkages to the production engine. A virtual product data manager (VPDM) facilitates tapping into the innovation engine where the improvement to the enterprise can be several orders of magnitude improved. A term PDMII has been coined to capture the holistic integration when PDM is used with VPDM and these are integrated with ERP. PDM and all of its facets were more fully described in Chapter 8. Technology at this writing is still evolving in this area, but this promises to be a major focus for systems development in the next decade.

Project Scheduling

Linking the project management statement of work to ERP can be a challenge. The normal process is to perform a one way download of the project into the ERP system and then begin to manage the project by exception only through ERP. However, a very typical question for this environment is, "How is my project doing?" and "What is the item that is extending the critical path and, if it is reduced, what is the next item?" These questions are very difficult to answer with standard ERP functionality. Utilization of critical chain scheduling for a project provides improved visibility of lead-time and other resource buffers. Tasks are scheduled with realistic expected time duration and the buffers are moved to the appropriate spot in the critical chain. Table 18.2 shows the impact of applying critical chain scheduling to the same project from Table 18.1.

This critical chain schedule can be also visualized graphically in Figure 18.2.

The critical chain scheduling tool has been applied that uses the available resource capacity to provide a more realistic schedule. The critical path (chain) has moved from the bottom row of six activities to the row above with tasks 12, 13, and 9, and the bottom row of activities 17, 18, and 19 as

Table 18.2   Critical Chain Tabular Schedule

Task	Duration	Start	End	Predecessors
Project Part 1	86d	Mon 12/7/98	Tue 3/2/99	
Task1	4d	Mon 12/7/98	Thu12/10/98	
Task2	5d	Fri 12/11/98	Tue 12/15/98	
Task3	1d	Wed 12/16/98	Wed 12/16/98	2, 3
Task4	15d	Thu 12/17/98	Thu 12/31/98	4
Task5	15d	Fri 1/1/99	Fri 1/15/99	5
Task6	20d	Sat 1/16/99	Thu 2/4/99	6
Task7	18d	Fri 2/5/99	Mon 2/22/99	7
FB|Task7-8|				
Project_end-23	8d	Tue 2/23/99	Tue 3/2/99	
Project Part 2	86d	Mon 12/7/98	Tue 3/2/99	
Task8	6d	Mon 12/28/98	Sat 1/2/99	4
Task9	28d	Sun 1/3/99	Sat 1/30/99	17
Task10	9d	Sat 2/6/99	Sun 2/14/99	11,12
Task11	6d	Mon 2/15/99	Sat 2/20/99	13
FB|Task11-13|				
Project_end-23	3d	Sun 2/28/99	Tue 3/2/99	
Task12	9d	Mon 12/7/98	Tue 12/15/98	
Task13	18d	Wed 12/16/98	Sat 1/2/99	16
Project Part 3	83d	Thu 12/10/98	Tue 3/2/99	
Task14	15d	Thu 12/10/98	Thu 12/24/98	
Task15	12d	Fri 12/25/98	Tue 1/5/99	19
Task16	20d	Wed 1/6/99	Mon 1/25/99	20
FB|Task16-19|				
Task17-20	5d	Tue 1/26/99	Sat 1/30/99	
Task17	14d	Sun 1/31/99	Sat 2/13/99	21
Task18	7d	Sun 2/14/99	Sat 2/20/99	23
Task19	10d	Sun 2/21/99	Tue 3/2/99	24
Project_end	1d	Wed 3/3/99	Wed 3/3/99	8,14,25
PB|Project_end-23	9d	Thu 3/4/99	Fri 3/12/99	

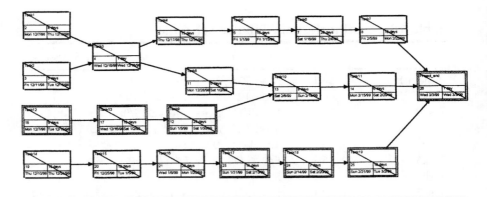

Figure 18.2   PERT chart critical chain schedule.

shown by the thicker borders around the box. This more realistic schedule can then be picked up by the ERP system for use in planning materials.

If traditional project planning is utilized with slack time potential at each step except those on the critical path, then decisions must be made for planning material. The usual strategy is to order the material at lead-time prior to the early start date. The advantage is that if the previous task is completed early, the materials will be ready so the project can continue. The disadvantage is that critical cash resource may be expended before it really needs to be.

Capacity Deployment

Capacity deployment in the project manufacturing environment also can be a challenge. The normal response is to attempt to have all projects in work simultaneously. This allows personnel to easily move from one project to another when a problem arises. The downside of this approach is that typically projects will take much longer. Hal Mather relates a wonderful riddle on how to deploy cranes in a ship unloading exercise. Assume that you have six ships. They will arrive in port at exactly the same time at six different piers. You own six moveable cranes that are each capable of unloading a single ship in 6 days. If you put two cranes on one ship then that ship can be unloaded in 3 days while the other ship must wait. If you are in the shipping business and you make money by having ships on the sea and not in port, how should you deploy your cranes? Assume no interference between the cranes. The traditional approach to project management is to have all six

Table 18.3 Ship Puzzle Solution Options

	Turns Days for Each Ship						Average Days in Port
Cranes/Ship	Ship 1	Ship 2	Ship 3	Ship 4	Ship 5	Ship 6	
1	6	6	6	6	6	6	6
2	3	6	3	6	3	6	4.5
3	2	4	6	2	4	6	4
4	1.5	3	4.5	6	3	6	4
5	1.2	2.4	3.6	4.8	7.2	6	4.2
6	1	2	3	4	5	6	3.5

ships in work at the same time. All projects would have some resource sprinkled on it. This is rather like trying to play poker with 52 people. Each person gets one card and nobody can get a winning hand. The enterprise as a whole loses. Back to the ships. Assuming that you make money by having ships on the water, so your desire is to minimize the amount of time the ships are in port. The options available are shown in Table 18.3.

Clearly the best solution for the enterprise is to have six cranes all dedicated to one ship. The same is true for project management. Rather than attempting to have critical resources multitask across multiple projects it can be shown that dedicating resource to a single project can drastically reduce the project lead-time. Consider that one of the competitive factors for a project manufacturer is overall lead-time. This could provide a competitive edge.

Material Allocation

Material allocation is also more complex in a project manufacturer. Material can be purchased for a specific project and could quite possibly be usable on multiple projects. MRP has an assumption that all materials move into and out of stock. An ERP system that effectively supports project management must have the functionality that material can be purchased directly to the project and not force the identification of a part number and stock transactions. The downside of this approach is when the exact material is desired again and there is no traceability of it ever having been bought. Once again the implementation must weigh the costs and benefits before deciding if and how to implement a part numbering system.

In governmental projects, there are requirements to account in great detail the costs paid for the parts, and to provide assurance that indeed they were used on that project. This is sometimes referred to as tracking the "color of money." A company that does business with the American military, the British military, and the Australian military may find itself in a position of having a part purchased for the British that is needed on an Australian project. The transactions and controls that are required to track the costs and movement of the part could cost more than the part itself. This level of DOD cost accounting can easily lead to high levels of obsolete parts and excess inventory.

Material allocation is dependent on the bill of material. This was the same for standard job shop producers. Bills of material must be 100% accurate to allow the integrated planning systems to work effectively. This is covered in more detail in Chapter 13. The use of PDM systems helps keep the engineering bill of material in alignment with the manufacturing bill of material. Where the project manufacturer differs is the desire or need to track effectivity by serial number. Since the products that are made are typically large capital projects or machines, the effectivity of material usage is desired by the production unit number. Imagine that 12 units will be produced. An engineering change is required on the third unit. The desire would be to have a bill of material with effectivities set by serial number as in the example below.

Parent 185726 Top Assembly

Component	In	Out
136609 SST, housing plates	1	3
142058 Titanium, housing plates	4	12

Although this looks like a great idea, the material planning functionality plans by date. If an ERP system is selected that claims to have this type of effectivity, it is very likely that somewhere else in the system the serial numbers are tied to an expected date schedule. Be very sure when purchasing a system that claims to have serial effectivity to fully understand the requirements of making the material planning function work as desired.

Another challenge for the material planning system is dealing with "as-required" and zero quantity items. "As required" items are typically things like shims, fasteners, lubricants, and hardware. The engineer is reluctant to spend time counting up and specifying all the fasteners required for an assembly. This is further complicated by the ability to substitute fasteners of comparable quality and grip length. In the event of a production problem oversize fasteners may also be used. As anyone who has ever tried to get an assembly put together without all the fasteners knows, the fasteners may look small and inconsequential they can stop a major project from shipping. The most prevalent strategy is to standardize on the fasteners that will be used in all assemblies. These components are then kept on an order point system where the bins are refilled when they get low. This is an excellent area for vendor managed inventory (VMI). Getting a supplier to take care of the fasteners and negotiating so the enterprise only pays for what is actually used from the bins can dramatically reduce the overall cost and improve availability of these critical yet low cost parts.

The same process can be used for "zero per" items. "Zero per" items are things like epoxy, LockTite™, or paint where the amount that is used is so small that it does not bear quantifying on the bill of material. However, similar to fasteners these items can stop an assembly in its tracks. The risk of the vendor managed inventory approach is that future orders may not require what was used in the past. Provided that product mix in the future is similar to that product mix in the past, this approach is very effective. As products change dramatically or require a unique material or configuration, these materials must be controlled through the formal material planning systems.

For consistency, some organizations will attempt to control everything through the formal ERP system and find out the transactions required quickly become too cumbersome to manage. Remember to use the right tool for the right job and the job will be much easier. Understand the process and the desired results before developing and implementing systems to achieve that goal.

Summary

The project manufacturer is a different type of enterprise to manage. Its ability to compete effectively in the market is by designing and building products that are very low in volume and extremely high in variety. One of a kind is not unusual. Project management and project control costing adds a whole level of complexity to the ERP implementation. Projects may span well over a year and the cost collection must continue at the very top project level. Effectively managing scope, time, and resources, including costs, are essential for the enterprise. Part of the basic ERP functionality helps this management process and other parts of the typical ERP system do not support the desired business model. This includes the effectivity on the bill of material, scheduling activities, and allocating material to projects. Since the overall project is controlled through a separate project management system, part status synchronization is desired between the project system and the ERP system. This has become possible only recently through the development of open databases and middleware linkages. Recent developments in project management like critical chain scheduling have also provided new resources and insights into a well-established body of knowledge and toolkit. As customers increasingly demand higher product variety in lower volumes, the pressure is on design and manufacturing to deliver these products in a profitable way. As Heraclitus of Greece said in 513 B.C., "There is nothing permanent except change." Effective integration of ERP, PDM, and project management tools allow the project manufacturer to profitably manage in the face of these increasing changes.

Project Management Resources

ProChain Solutions, Inc. (12910 Harbor Drive, Lake Ridge, VA 22192) provides scheduling software supporting critical chain scheduling, *http://www.prochain.com*. ProChain graciously provided the software and examples used in this chapter.

Project Management: A Systems Approach to Planning, Scheduling and Controlling, Harold Kerzner, Van Nostrand Reinhold, New York, 1997.

Project Management, Strategic Design and Implementation, David I. Cleland, McGraw-Hill, New York, 1995.

Project Management Institute (PMI) establishes project management standards, provides seminars, educational programs, and professional certification that organizations desire for their project leaders. Four Campus Blvd., Newtown Square, PA 19073, 610-356-4600, *http://www.pmi.org*.

Critical Chain, Eli Goldratt, North River Press APICS # 03203, Spanish 03009SP.

Project Management in the Fast Lane: Applying the Theory of Constraints, Robert C. Newbold, St. Lucie Press, APICS # 03650, 1998.

APICS Complex Industry SIG (CI SIG), designed for individuals in complex industries, focusing on the integrated resource tools of project management, configuration control, product data management, regulatory affairs, and systems engineering for products in the aerospace, defense, high-tech communications, and medical equipment industries. 800-444-2742, *http://www.apics.org*.

Note: All resources with an APICS # can be ordered from http://www.apics.org.

19 | Field Service

For a capital goods manufacturer, field service can be either a boon or a bane. Jack Welch, CEO from General Electric has publicly stated that the General Electric of the future will be a service company that also happens to make things. Service will be the main strategy of the company to compete into the future. Service has redefined business strategy for many companies. IBM has embraced quick response service as a critical success factor in the sale of the computers. Getting a laptop serviced takes less than 24 hours and the service facility is centralized in Memphis. IBM has also "call home" functions built into its servers so that when a problem is discovered during routine functions, the field service technician can be called. This sometimes happens even before the user knows there is a problem. Saturn has focused on reducing the overall wait time for service and improving the reliability of the service experience. Overall customer service is a competitive edge for Saturn.

Unfortunately, many companies treat field service as a distant stepchild that must be tolerated rather than a potential success strategy. Parts required to service products in the field are given secondary priority in production scheduling when, in fact, the satisfaction of the installed customer base is essential to retaining that customer for future business. Some companies do not plan for service parts at all and then wonder why they are constantly running out of parts. The customers' ability to secure timely service for a product can be an order winner for the enterprise.

Field Service Inventory Management

If the company has remote field service technicians, managing inventory stored at their locations can be a big challenge. The parts are available to that individual for service, but yet are not easily accessible for the balance of the company. The decision may be made to centralize the entire inventory into one distribution location and deploy the inventory when the call is logged in. Although this minimizes the inventory investment, the problems it can create may be worse than tying dollars up in service inventory.

The enterprise needs to track all inventory assets for their location, use, cost, and configuration. Too frequently these assets are overlooked since they are at remote sites and they can quickly become unusable and obsolete. As deregulation has begun to affect the utilities industries, it has been quickly discovered that real savings could be made with improved management of service parts. The effective planning of field service resources and inventory to support the installed customer base is yet another of the integrated facets of an ERP system.

One of the greatest frustrations for customers and field service technicians alike is not having the right part to complete the service the first time. Customers expect that when their product is brought in for a problem the repair should be complete the first visit. Having to leave their item for an extended period or bring it back increases aggravation for the customer and cost for the company. Having a field service technician return to the job site because of a part's shortage frustrates both the customer and the technician and is more expensive to the enterprise.

A robust design process can go a long way in reducing service inventory. Engineering improvements to a product that are backward effective will significantly reduce the amount of needed service inventory. For example, a new power supply that still fits the footprint and socket holes in an old unit eliminates the need for the technician to carry two power supplies — one for the new unit design and one for the old unit. This also eliminates the need for purchasing and/or manufacturing to build these old units to support product that is still in the field. This low volume production or purchase of old configurations is significantly more expensive than the original production run cost. This design strategy must be specifically stated with performance measures to support it. Designing for serviceability can be a competitive strategy for a company. This includes not only designing parts that can be backwards integrated but also designing products in a modular format.

A modular design format allows the technician to quickly replace the defective module. The defective module can then be sent to the main repair depot for further diagnosis and repair. This design approach minimizes the amount of time the field technician is required at the customer site. It also requires less skill in the field by centralizing the more advanced technical people at the depot. If higher skills are required in the field for service, having the technician adequately trained to work on that equipment is essential for customer satisfaction. Without a focus for serviceability in the design stage, the operations areas face a dizzying array of service parts that are required in very low volumes usually at high cost to the enterprise.

The balance between control and cost is applicable to field service. Some companies will try to control every fuse and fastener. The cost of this control is likely to be several times more expensive than the cost of the parts. From personal experience, a well-known service company once had to send a technician three times to our home to repair a microwave oven. The only part that had to be replaced was a fuse that cost about $1. Keeping the variety of bulbs, fuses, and fasteners to a minimum is part of the overall design for serviceability strategy. Even if there is a wide variety, the cost of sending the technician into the field with an adequate inventory is significantly less than the cost of having the technician return to the site. These items should be expensed at the time they are sent to the technician. Keeping detailed transaction records on these small parts does not add value for the customer or the company.

Field Service Tool Management

In addition to the component parts required for a repair, the field service technician may also require tools. This is another area where having a design for serviceability can help. If the modular design concept is followed then the field service technician should not require unique fixtures or tooling. The service modules should be removable by standard tools like screwdrivers and hex wrenches. If the design requires that alignment or calibration be done in the field, then it is essential for the technician to have these tools. If the tools that are required are more difficult to move than the unit being worked on or having duplicate sets of tools or adjustment fixtures is cost prohibitive, then the repair should be a depot repair.

When a territory is first established for field service, a suggested tool kit should be deployed to the area. Each territory is unique for the installed products and models. This tool kit should reflect the installed units in the region. Sending a technician into the field with tools they will never need adds no value for the technician and increases cost for the company. Once a technician has had some experience in the territory, the tool kit is modified based on the actual performance of equipment in that territory.

The distribution of updated manuals should include the field service technicians. A formalized communication process is required to keep field service personnel aware of changes in the product and service requirements. This communication can be accomplished by sending field service bulletins to the technicians. The downside of this approach is that unless the technician is facing that unit the bulletin may not be read. More recently these bulletin updates are posted on a searchable Intranet Website that can be queried by the technician on demand. The Intranet Website can also include service manuals, engineering drawings, quality control notes, and other manufacturing documentation. This assures that the most up-to-date information is being used. The challenge then becomes how the technician can access it while at the customer site. The development in cellular phone technology that can link to a mobile computing resource has made remote access more accessible.

In addition to service manuals and bulletins, the technician sometimes requires access to a support line for unique problems that cannot be solved from the standard documentation. This support line for a technician should be available during all the hours the technician could be working. While this may seem like common sense, too many companies forget this simple fact. Some companies take an east coast American view on the world and only have their technical support lines open from 7 a.m. to 5 p.m. eastern time. They seem to forget technicians on the west coast are 3 hours behind them. European and Asian technicians can find themselves totally out of time phase and this requires the technicians to call at unusual times in their time zone just to get the needed information.

Field Service and CRM (Customer Relationship Management)

In addition to the tools required to accomplish the repair, the field service technician requires easy access to company systems to communicate customer needs, wants, and desires. The field service technician can provide a wealth of information about the customer's current business state and can quickly identify sales opportunities to be passed to the sales force. This information could include competitive product installations or communication of the customer's intent to purchase new equipment. The customer views the field service technician as an ally and should be an integral part of the complete solution provided by the enterprise. This feedback of the customer's business must be included as part of the overall performance measurement system to positively reinforce this behavior. Some of this information will be collected automatically as products are sold and serviced. However, remember that the ERP system is inwardly focused. The field service technician can provide market focused information that otherwise would never be collected.

Having easy access to the company's systems is a critical tool in the field service technician's toolbox. Personnel who report to work each day to the same location may not consider the challenges faced by the service technician in the field. The technician is face to face with the customer. Having the ability to obtain timely information and quickly solve problems that may arise is paramount. The enterprise system also needs the technician to record activities so the customer can be billed, inventories adjusted, and credit given. Providing tools that make this easy and straightforward go a long way to ensuring these transactions will be accurate. A system that is difficult and complex to use will rarely be used correctly. The process should be easier to complete correctly than incorrectly or it will be ignored altogether. Access to these systems should be available not only during the normal work day for the enterprise but also during off times when it is likely that the service technician will be completing their paperwork. The field service technician is the company's representative in the field. Having the appropriate communication tools goes a long way to help this individual stay integrated with the rest of the enterprise.

Performance measures for the field service technicians include the expected profit and loss measures. In addition to these financial measures, customer satisfaction measures should be equally important. Doing an exceptional job of service may mean that the overall financial performance of the service unit may be less because fewer recalls to the customer site are needed. However, the customer is more satisfied since the equipment requires less repairs and experiences less downtime. The customer will then be more likely to purchase that brand of equipment again.

Mean time between failure, mean time to repair, and the number of calls required to complete a repair are also important service measures. Mean time between failure is the average time between failures. This is a measure that provides feedback on overall product performance. The cause for failure could be an engineering issue, manufacturing defect, or service issue. Mean time to repair is the average time the enterprise takes to return a unit to working order. The definition of working order should be clearly defined when establishing either of these measures. In the computing businesses, the information technology personnel may consider working order as the computer being able to accept commands. To the users, however, their perception of working order is that their application is available. The ERP system can help provide visibility of these measures.

As with all measures in the enterprise, each department cannot be measured in isolation, rather the overall impact to the enterprise must be considered. In one case a company determined the level of service technicians required in the division based on the number of field service calls. At face value this looks like an acceptable way to determine service capacity. However, the reality of the situation was that in one division the service department employed a proactive approach to service that ensured higher equipment availability for the customer. Therefore, they had the smallest number of customer calls. The service manager was forced to reduce the department personnel resource and service inventories based on the corporate direction. The equipment failure in that division quickly rose to the same level as the other divisions. Before the reduction in headcount this division also enjoyed the lowest cost of maintenance because preventive maintenance was proactively planned. Once the department was forced to a reactive model, the overnight shipping cost for parts quickly drove up the expenses for the department. Remember that you will always get what you measure — select your measures wisely.

Field Service and ERP

The ERP system provides the common database from which information can be accessed to support the field service technician. Figure 19.1 shows the linkages from the field service technician into the common enterprise management system.

The arrows in Figure 19.1 represent the linkages provided by the ERP system. ERP provides the product traceability by serial number direct to the technicians so they can be informed of such things as a pending delivery requiring installation or a need to schedule future preventive service. Actual field transactions are accumulated in the ERP database that can determine the mean time between failure and the components that frequently need repair or replacement. This integration provides the required information back to the product data manager so the identified failure points can be improved on the next product update.

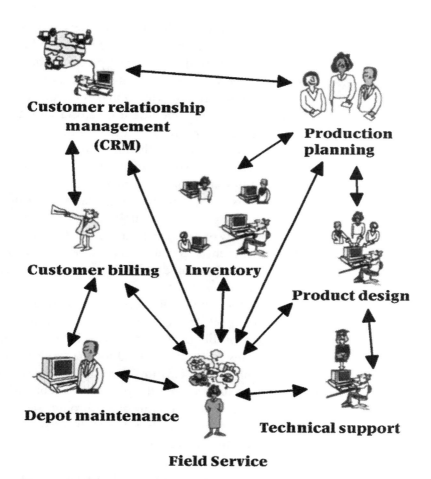

Figure 19.1   Linkages from the field service technician into the enterprise.

The consumption of parts for field service creates additional independent demand that must be included in the overall production plan. Some companies have embraced a policy of keeping an inventory of service part physically separate from the production stores. This is done to hopefully ensure that the parts will not be "stolen" for production use. The reality of this approach is that if production has an urgent requirement for these parts they will somehow find a way to get them. In a similar manner, the service organization will also somehow gain access to production parts. The parts are shared between functions and the enterprise is doubling its stockroom expense. The ERP system can easily track the number of parts that are consumed and distinguish between the demand coming from production and the incremental demand coming from service. The planning tools can then separate and plan for these two very different demands. Keeping service and production parts in the same stockroom location makes the incorporation of engineering changes simpler. Only one inventory stockroom needs to be reviewed and checked during change incorporation. In the event that inventory is stored at remote service locations, the location traceability in the ERP system provides visibility of where old configuration parts may still exist. These remote service locations are usually set up as nonnettable locations to the system since the parts are not readily available to the general enterprise. A nonnettable location is a status that is set for the specific inventory location so that the quantity of parts can be tracked but the material planning system does not consider them as available supply when the material planning explosion is run. Other nonnettable locations in an ERP system include rework and the material review board.

Service delivered at the customer site is linked through the sales order function that provides a means to bill for services rendered in a manner consistent with product billings. This billing function is also integrated with the inventory system so that the inventory that is used for the service call is removed from the appropriate inventory. This inventory reduction is then linked into the overall planning system so that the part can be replenished to the appropriate stocking point. This is accomplished through setting a target inventory level by location within the ERP system. When the balance on hand falls below this target inventory level, the ERP system will automatically replenish this part.

The ERP system can also aid in the forecasting of service parts. Based on the specific product models that are shipped, the ERP system can calculate the expected usage of service parts. If 50 model Xs are shipped and 500 model Ys are shipped, and the service parts have been identified with the expected mean time between failure calculated, the ERP system can then calculate the expected future consumption of these service parts. When this information is linked to the overall shipment information, an inventory stocking strategy by regional location can be developed with a high level of accuracy. All regions are not created equal. One company in the service business made a sweeping decision to consistently stock service parts at all the different repair depots. While this plan looks good on paper, the problem was that parts that were required in one area were not required in another. In this organization 80% of one product's installation was in one region. All regions had service parts for this product regardless of the installed base in their region. An integrated ERP system allows the enterprise to have visibility of real requirements so the inventory strategy can be developed that minimizes cost while maximizing service.

Summary

ERP provides an integrated information and management process that reaches across the enterprise. For companies with a requirement to service products in the field, this integration provides information to effectively manage service inventory and resources. By having this centralized repository of information, insights into overall company performance can be developed including mean time between failure (MTBF), mean time to repair (MTTR), service profit and loss, and overall customer service. In addition, this detailed collection of service information can be tapped through a customer relationship management system (CRM) to provide insights into customer buying habits. This provides the opportunity to develop a custom fit solution or the ability to offer complementary solutions for each customer. The field service technician also can provide insights on the needs, wants, and desires in the market due to their direct relationship with the customer. The effective management of field service is the combination of many diverse processes and tools that can be managed and coordinated through the integration of an effective ERP system.

Field Service Resources and References

Field Service Management: An Integrated Approach to Increasing Customer Satisfaction, Business One Irwin/APICS, 1992, APICS # 03130.

Managing Service As a Strategic Profit Center, Donald F. Blumberg, McGraw-Hill, New York, 1990.

Creating Customer Connections: How to Make Customer Service a Profit Center for Your Company, (Taking Control Series), Jack Burke, Silver Lake Publishing, 1996.

Service Management: Operations, Strategy, and Information Technology, James A. Fitzsimmons, Mona J. Fitzsimmons, 1997, APICS # 03379.

Service Operations Management, Roger Schmenner, 1995, APICS # 03381.

Service Parts Handbook, Joseph D. Patton, Jr. and Herbert C. Feldmann, 1997, APICS # 03156.

The Service Profit Chain, James Heskett, 1997, APICS # 03575.

Breakthrough Customer Service: Best Practices of Leaders in Customer Support, Stanley A. Brown (Ed.), John Wiley & Sons, New York, 1998.

SynchroService, Richard J. Schonberger and Edward M. Knod, Jr., Irwin, 1994, APICS #
  03286.
Note: APICS numbers can be ordered at 800-444-2742 or *http://www.apics.org.*

APPLICATION IV

Eli Schragenheim, MBE Simulations Ltd.

Introduction to the ERP — MICSS Simulator

The ERP–MICSS Simulator is a special addition to this book to allow you to experience managing a small manufacturing company with an integrative information system. Even though the computerized company isn't very large and the information system is not a full-blown ERP system, some of the more challenging issues of management in the ERP era will emerge.

One can relate to the technical side of the ERP package and look for data that are stored, the algorithms it uses, and the output screens and reports it generates. The ERP–MICSS program can allow you to do that. You can look for the information regarding the past performance, like sales graphs, utilization data, and the past performance of the vendors. You also can check how the small MRP module generates work orders and how the information system records the exact state of a work order.

Another point of view is to check the added-value of the ERP system to the performance of the company. In other words, in what ways does the ERP system contribute to the prosperity of the company. Given the availability of all this information, do we know how to make the right decisions? Are the algorithms that are embedded within the information systems the right ones? For instance, does the organization hold the right amount of inventory? That amount is dictated by the algorithms chosen for the purchasing policies and by the parameters set for the MRP planning, like batch sizing and dispatch policy.

The added value of information is dependent on the level of knowledge of the user. ERP packages provide quick access to data and information that were generated in different areas of the company. That means that local managers are exposed to new information. The local manager's decisions have direct impact on all of the system. In the past, these impacts were difficult and sometimes impossible to assess. Under the roof of an integrative information system that uses one big database for the whole organization (with optional connectivity to the intranet and Internet), the availability of integrative information is a reality. Does the availability of the information ensure better business? What upgrades do we need in order to utilize the new technology to make better business decisions?

The enclosed program lets you learn the processes supported by the information system and check their validity. It lets you enhance your understanding of the linkages between the various parts of the organization and identify problematic situations. It also lets you learn to define the type of information that is most relevant to critical decision making. And, above all, MICSS (Management Interactive Case Study Simulator) provides you with a learning platform to enhance your systems thinking for both planning and control. The bottom line of this kind of learning is to enhance the capability to get a complex system under control with the support of the information system.

MICSS was originally designed to be used in a class. Letting management teams, which consist of people from various functions, manage a small manufacturing organization, run the business, make mistakes, and get new insights. This is still the primary use of MICSS. Here, within the scope of a book on ERP, the readers expand their learning by running the scenario, trying different parameters, searching for meaningful data, and getting to know the basic cause and effect within the internal supply chain. This kind of learning is different from reading a book. It lets you learn from experience, by being actively involved throughout the learning process.

The scenario for this book presents a manufacturing organization, Smart Industries Inc., that sells three standard products, based on only four raw materials and produced by only six different machines. Certainly, this is a much simpler environment that any real situation a manager would likely face. However, Smart Industries faces a highly uncertain market demand with a big seasonal peak of demand. How should we set the information system parameters for "optimal" results? What information supports the planning process? What information is needed to support the control process? We let you, the reader, find out yourself by using the knowledge gained from this book and your capability to learn from experience. What a great way to learn from a virtual experience where our mistakes don't cost anything and only trigger our mind to find out why it doesn't work the way we want it to?

Any ERP implementation should include a substantial management education to upgrade all management levels to operate during the times when so much information is available and the problem is to understand what to do with it. Understanding the basic cause and effect in the environment, what information is crucial, and what data are not relevant are of utmost importance to the true success of any ERP implementation. And the success of such implementation is when the company improves its business. Having successfully installed a working ERP system is only one, relatively small, necessary condition. The real success happens only when the bottom line says so. This program is designed to help you learn how to close the gap between having access to information and using it for the benefit of your organization.

WARNING! This type of learning **takes time.** The management issues raised by the program are not easy. In order to take advantage of the learning platform, you have to invest time in going back and forth through this computerized case study. There is no single, optimum solution for it. There is one fairly good solution provided in this section. There are many definite mistakes that good experienced managers might make. Those mistakes are the opportunity to gain new understanding and insight. There is no magic that can do it in an instant. This one certainly needs your undivided attention to be effective.

The Tutorial

It is recommended that you first go through the tutorial. You'll find it at the bottom of the "Open" window. The tutorial takes you on a tour through Smart Industries, Inc. It also shows the main features of the MICSS program. This tutorial is provided so that operating the software should go smoothly and is a tool to get to know the software as soon as possible.

Guided Runs

On top of the regular tutorial, two guided runs are provided with the MICSS program. Using the same technique as the tutorial, the two guided runs accompany you through the simulation, making decisions and reviewing intermediate results. The two runs define a reference point for each subsequent run done by you.

The two guided runs can be accessed after you have called up the ERP-BOOK scenario. Click on the Session menu, then click upon the "Guided runs" entry. You can choose the first or the second guided runs. As the two guided runs reach rather average results, an additional guided run is provided for you — in writing. This is an analysis of the case and a list of the decisions to be made in order to succeed. It is provided in writing rather than on the disk because of the additional explanations needed for it.

The MICSS–ERP Case Study — An Overview

This MICSS scenario provides the reader the opportunity to manage a manufacturing company with four distinct functions:

1. **Marketing and Sales.** This is where the linkage to the customers is maintained. The market of a MICSS scenario is usually noted for the critical importance of maintaining an adequate due-date performance. The market clearly favors faster response time and, of course, reduced prices.
2. **Production.** This is where the transformation of raw materials into finished goods takes place. This is a detailed shop floor. The whole production planning and control is provided by an internal information system which produced work orders based on the actual orders received and the planning parameters as set by the participants.
3. **Purchasing.** Here the raw material control is performed. You have two vendors to choose from. The faster vendor is typically more expensive.
4. **Finance.** Every month you get a profit and loss statement that tells you how good (or bad) you are. You also get the traditional cost accounting analyses of the finished products. You may also look at the earned value analysis (EVA) measurement.

The MICSS case study is a virtual company that badly needs a new management team to show the owners and the world that it can become a profitable enterprise in spite of the losses in the past. Usually, every new management team gets full authority to manage the company for a year.

The MICSS virtual manufacturing company is equipped with a small ERP system that fits the needs of such a small company. However, setting the ERP parameters is far from trivial. Some of the basic parameters are tied to the business strategy. For instance, should you maintain safety stock at the finished products level?

MICSS is a learning tool. It should provoke thinking on the role of information in managing complex organizations. If you wish to know more about MICSS and how to incorporate MICSS in workshops, e-mail us at *mbe@mbe-simulations.com*, or have a look at our Website: *www.mbe-simulations.com*.

License for the Use of the MICSS Program

MBE Simulations Ltd. grants the purchaser of the book, *ERP: Tools, Techniques and Applications for Integrating the Supply Chain,* the license to **one installation** of the enclosed MICSS program on a PC computer or a notebook. Purchaser may not install the MICSS program on a network. You will need a CD drive to work with MICSS.

The use of MICSS is limited to personal learning only. It is strictly forbidden to use the software for any commercial use.

All copyrights in the MICSS program shall at all times remain the property of MBE Simulations Ltd. The user is not allowed to introduce any modifications to the software and to the label on the diskette. The user may not reverse engineer, decompile, list, or print the software.

MBE Simulations Ltd. does not and cannot warrant the performance of or the results that may be obtained by using the software. MBE Simulations Ltd. hereby specifically disclaims any and all express and implied warranties with respect to the software.

Under no circumstances shall MBE Simulations be liable to the user or any other person for any special, incidental, or consequential damages, including, without limitation, lost profit or lost data, loss of other programs, or otherwise, and whether arising out of breach of warranty, breach of contract, tort (including negligence), or otherwise, even if advised of such damage or if such damage could have been reasonably foreseen, except only in case of personal injury where applicable law requires such liability.

Installation of MICSS with the ERPBOOK Scenario

For Windows® 95 and up:

1. Insert the CD into the CD drive.
2. Click on "Start," then click on "Run."
3. Type "X\setup" and click on OK, where the X is the CD drive.
4. Follow the instructions.
5. To call MICSS, put the CD in the drive and click on the MICSS icon.

The ERP–MICSS Case: The Smart Industries Inc. Case Study

A Specific, Nontrivial, MICSS Scenario

The Smart Industries Inc. case study is intended for people who are ready to face a real semicomplex environment with a fairly good integrative information system. To start with, this is a company that sells only three different products, produced by six different workcenters, using only four materials.

In our tour of the Smart Industries company, let's first start with its financial state. The date is January 1, 1999. Presented in Figure A.1 is the profit and loss statement for 1998. A simple glance will be sufficient to know why a new management team is sought.

Just for clarity, these results were achieved by actually running the virtual company by the means of simulation throughout 1998. Obviously, not all the policies and actions taken by the former management were good. In spite of the gloomy financial state, this company has quite a good reputation in the market. The customers value very much the reliability provided by Smart Industries Inc.

The full screen of MICSS, with the view of the marketing and sales department is shown in Figure A.2. The three products have schematic names A1, B1, and C1. Every box contains the firm orders it has to supply, the finished goods (FG) stock that is ready for delivery exactly ontime. The reputation mark, in the product's box, relates to that product market segment. To the left of the reputation mark, an internal management measure

```
Profit and Loss Statement          From:  01/01/98
  ☑ With added value on FG and WIP       To:    12/31/98

Sales...............................................................2,965,500
                                                                   ======
Cost of goods sold:
    Raw materials consumed...........................1,433,414
    Direct labor.............................................276,000
    Production expenses................................168,000
    Depreciation...........................................420,000
Production cost............................................2,297,414
Increase in FG inv...........................................5,257
Increase in WIP............................................-14,468
Gross profit................................................658,875
                                                         ======
Marketing and sales expenses.......................378,000
Management and general expenses.................396,000
Profit before finance...................................-115,125
                                                        ======
Finance expenses...........................................-7,272
Profit before taxes......................................-107,853
                                                        ======
Net profit................................................-107,853
```

Figure A.1   Profit and loss statement for 1998.

for the "on time" deliveries is shown. This measure looks only on the current month percentage of on-time shipments. WIP, showing at the right upper side of the product box, stands for work-in-process. That means the units that are somewhere within the production shop floor. Of course, the full information system lets you access the exact location of the WIP. But, we'll come to that later.

Every view has its own "Information," "Actions," and "Policies" menus. The Policies menu includes those managerial decisions that dictate the behavior of the information system and also the employees.

Figure A.3 is the Policies menu of the Marketing View. It contains the main sales policies. The quoted lead times are expressed in working days. This company works 5 days a week, 8 hours per day throughout the year. Hence, 30 days are equivalent to 6 weeks. This means every order accepted today is given a due date 6 weeks from now. Reduction in the quoted lead-time (QLT) is one of the means to expand the market demand. Similarly the selling price is such a means.

The "Red Line Time" is part of a control mechanism. The assigned 5 days of the "red line time" means when there aren't enough units in the finished

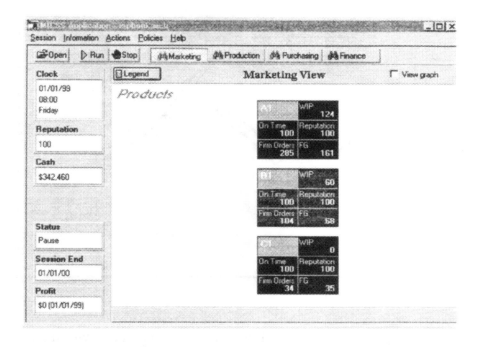

Figure A.2   MICSS sales and marketing view.

goods area to ship within the next 5 days, the product ID will be colored red to signal the management. This concept was covered in more detail in Chapter 2. The work orders that are still on the shop floor that are needed for the next 5 days shipments are acknowledged as "red order." This is one of the most important features of the information system.

	Quoted Lead Time	Price	Safety Stock	Red Line Time
A1		500	0	5
B1	30	1000	0	5
C1	30	1500	0	5

OK   Cancel   Help

Figure A.3   Policies menu of the marketing view.

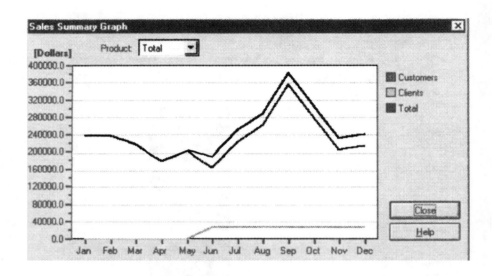

Figure A.4   1998 sales.

Another piece of information is obviously very important. What did last year sales look like? Figure A.4 is a graph that can be found in the Information menu of the Marketing View:

At the bottom of the graph we see a line that the legend displays as "clients." This is a whole market segment that currently the company uses very scarcely. This segment consists of large clients that buy only according to their terms. This segment may provide some additional opportunities next year, but beware, those clients offer low prices. This is one of the crucial decisions you'll have to make.

The top lines represents the main company's market: small customers who come, order, pay the list price and take the merchandise the day it is due. Look at the graph. There is a clear peak in September, while August and October are also higher than normal. There is no need for doubt — there is a seasonal peak of demand. How big is the peak? The information system has real difficulty in telling you that. You can, of course, analyze the graph, but assuming that there is a significant "noise" from the uncertain environment, we cannot tell for certain how big the peak is in relation to the "regular month" or "average month."

Let's now continue our tour into the Production View. The shop floor looks like Figure A.5.

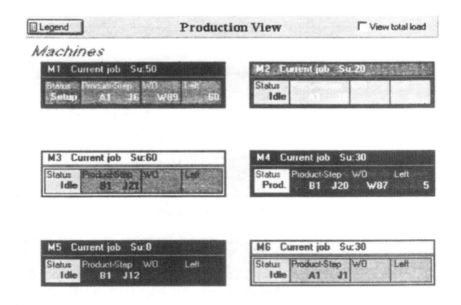

Figure A.5   Production View — shop floor.

Every rectangle represents a work center. All we have in this manufacturing organization are six workcenters. Every workcenter has only one machine.

After reading so much about ERP, you will surely like to know the BOM (bill of material) and the routings. In this small company we have preferred to show a somewhat different representation of both. As a matter of fact, we've combined the BOM and the routing into one. Here is the description of how each of the end products is made.

This is just the combined BOM routings for product A1. In Figure A.6 the flow is from left to right. Product A1 is an assembly of two parts. One is made of materials Z1 and Y1 going into machine M1 for 6 minutes time-per-part (TPP), then M2 for 4 minutes, M3 for 13 minutes, and M4 for another 4 minutes. The other part is built from material Z1, going through M1, M2, and M4. Then the two parts are assembled by M5 and packed by M6. Every operation has its own ID starting with the letter J.

B1 is a somewhat more complicated product to make, but we sell it for a much higher price (Figure A.7).

Operation J12 is a subassembly of two parts. J12 (which also serves as the catalog number of the part) is later assembled by operation J11 with the J20

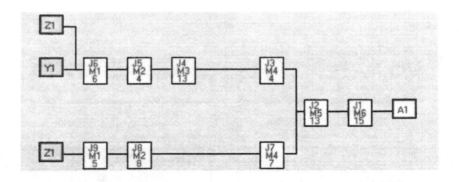

Figure A.6   Combined BOM and routing for product A1.

part. All assemblies in this simple environment are made with a 1:1 ratio. It is that simple.

C1 is certainly the most complicated product (Figure A.8). Two subassemblies are finally assembled with yet another part (J32) at the J24 final assembly operation.

How does the MRP module operate? Every week, on Monday morning, the MRP generates new work orders based on the new market requirements that were received. Work orders are generated, in this variation of the MRP algorithm, for every end product. The work order includes all the materials, quantities, operations, and resources. As no common parts exist in this

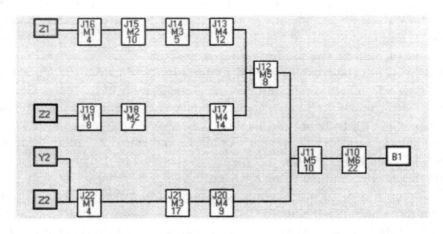

Figure A.7   Combined BOM and routing for product B1.

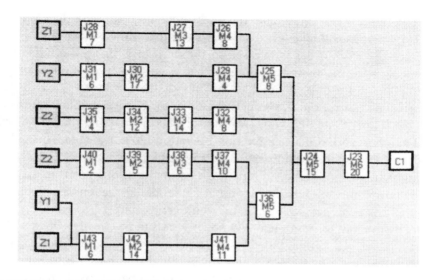

Figure A.8   BOM routing for product C1.

specific environment, there is no need for generating any work orders per part in the BOM.

The minimum batch as currently dictated is for 60 pieces. The minimum batch is dictated for all three products. Surely this is a little bit primitive for an ERP system, but the company is so small that this should not be an obstacle to good overall performance.

Raw materials are released based on a backward scheduling from the order due date. The work order due date is the earliest due-date of the individual customer orders included in it. Each production step (which may be perceived also as a bill of material level) is assigned 4 working days as a lead-time. Therefore, the release is determined as 4 × the number of operations in working days prior to the order due date.

For instance, take the C1 chart. Material Z2 is supposed to enter the J40 operation. The sequence of the operations on that material is: J40, J39, J38, J37, J36 (the subassembly), J24 (final assembly) and J23. All in all, 7 operations, each needing 4 working days to ensure completion. That means Z2 needs 28 working days prior to shipment. In case the work order is planned too late (less than 28 days until shipping), the Z2 materials are released immediately. Right now the company quotes 30 working days for delivery. But, the planning is done once a week and in some cases only 25 days are available until the delivery date. In this case we need to hope that some of the 7 operations will take less than 4 days to process the work order.

Once the work order is released to the floor, it is up to the individual workcenters to process it according to their own priorities. Some management policies are implemented to ensure adequate priorities. A dispatch policy called "current job" instructs the operator to save as many setups as possible. This means that when M4 has finished processing the J20, it will see if another work order that requires operation J20 is available. This policy encourages merging work orders when applicable.

Another policy tries to prevent working on work orders in progress at previous operations. This is the "complete WO" policy that ensures that only when all the parts are available is the work center allowed to work on that order. By the way, the complete WO policy ceases to be effective when a "red order" is available. As mentioned before, a red order means the order is about to be shipped in 5 days. Hence, it is given a higher priority. In this case, a workcenter is requested to start working even on a partial work order.

Achieving good efficiencies is considered to be very important. This is quite a problematic issue in this particular environment. Take a glance at the actual utilization level of the workcenters (Figure A.9). Here is the report for the last 2 months.

This information screen is based on the actual usage of the machines (workcenters) during the last 2 months. The worrying fact is the huge amount of idle time throughout the shop floor. Before you evaluate ways to reduce

Machines Utilization								☒
	December				November			
	Prod.	Setup	Break	Idle	Prod.	Setup	Break	Idle
M1	38.2%	5.9%	5.2%	49.7%	36.0%	4.5%	5.1%	54.5%
M2	43.2%	2.0%	5.9%	48.9%	53.1%	1.8%	2.2%	42.8%
M3	45.9%	3.8%	2.8%	47.5%	56.2%	2.9%	4.1%	36.8%
M4	57.9%	3.5%	13.3%	25.2%	58.9%	3.6%	2.9%	34.6%
M5	37.9%	0.0%	5.4%	56.6%	61.5%	0.0%	9.1%	29.4%
M6	45.0%	0.5%	8.8%	45.7%	74.6%	1.5%	4.4%	19.5%

Figure A.9   Utilization level of the workcenters for 2 months.

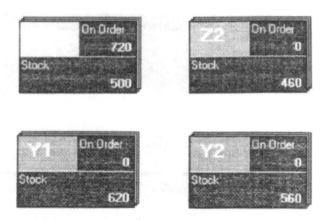

Figure A.10   Purchasing View displays four itemsD

setup time (sorry, in the simulation you can do nothing to reduce the down-time), you will decide how to avoid so much idle time.

By the way, we are lucky here. In the virtual company the depth of the problem is revealed. In so many shop floors people do their best to hide the true amount of idle time (excess capacity). There is much more to see in the Information and Actions of the Production View. Go through the tutorial to discover more.

Let us move to the Purchasing View (department). In this scenario, the task of purchasing is quite simple. There are only four items to look for. These are displayed in the main screen of Purchasing (Figure A.10). The "Stock" field contains the number of units in the stockroom. "On order" shows how many units have been purchased but didn't arrive as of yet.

How does the MRP module function in the Purchasing Department? Surprisingly, the former management of this company has decided not to use it. Instead they use the old algorithm of order point, which is called here "purchase-to-stock." You can activate the MRP module in Purchasing, through the Policies menu. We still recommend that you first run the simu-lation under the "purchase-to-stock" policy, but feel free to change the inven-tory levels.

Figure A.11 shows the current purchasing policy. The order level is the "order point." When the stock drops below the order level, an automatic purchasing order is issued to the default supplier to complement the stock to the max level. The red line level is a warning mechanism that colors the item ID in red when the stock is below that level.

Edit Material Parameters				✕
	Max Level	Order Level	Red Line Level	
Z1	1400	700	100	
Z2	800	400	100	
Y1	800	400	100	
Y2	800	400	100	

Figure A.11 Current purchasing policy.

It is certainly important to know what kind of suppliers the company works with. Figure A.12 shows information about the suppliers. The supplier called "Reg" promises to deliver any purchasing order in 22 working days, which is equivalent to 1 month. The "S.C." column means fixed shipping costs. This means that any order causes this amount of expenses, no matter the size of the order. Then, every item cost is specified. The Fast supplier is much faster, but also more expensive.

We have started the tour with the profit and loss statement. We will now glance at important information that is provided by the Finance (Figure A.13). These are the analyses of the product costs. The allocation was done based on the standard of having 70% of the available time of every machine dedicated to actual processing. The allocation was done according to the net processing time for each product.

Smart Industries Inc. also has one contract with a large client for monthly delivery. You'll find this analysis in the Finance View.

We almost have finished the tour. Not all the information and the policies were covered in this tour, but it should give you a good idea. The one thing

Suppliers							✕
	Name	S.C	QLT	Z1	Z2	Y1	Y2
1	Reg	500	22	(C) 100	(C) 150	(C) 60	(C) 50
2	Fast	650	3	115	175	72	58

Figure A.12 Supplier information.

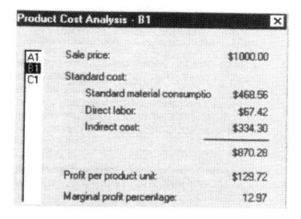

Figure A.13   Product cost analysis for each product.

still left is how to run the simulation, let time proceed, orders come in, and let material and money move. In order to run, you click on the "Run" dialog box, then you face the following screen (Figure A.14).

You can choose to run day by day or "until next month." You can even dictate a specific date. Running longer than 1 month at one time is not recommended. You can stop the run by clicking on the "Stop" dialog box.

Well, the tour is over. Good luck! Please remember that you CAN make this company successful, even without luck.

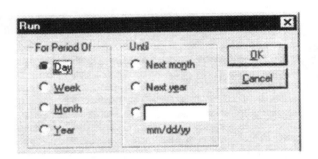

Figure A.14   The "Run" dialog box.

The ERP–MICSS Computerized Case Study Analysis

Developing a Sales and Production Strategy

The Basic Questions and Principles

Smart Industries is a simple manufacturing environment, even though you might not feel that way after playing around with it. Trial and error might lead you to very good results, but the simulator is built upon straightforward rules, which are a reasonable simplification of reality. If this is the case, then a good methodology can be structured so the good results will be generated from a rational analysis. If you can come up with such basic rules for that methodology, then it should apply also to a real world ERP implementation in spite of the huge difference in complexity.

The idea of simultaneously planning the sales and the production is a central idea being openly advocated by Dick Ling. Even though this version of the virtual environment doesn't contain the introduction of new products, there is a lot to plan and execute in the field of sales. The importance of looking at the sales and operation plan in integrative eyes emerges here very clearly.

Handling uncertain market demand is, of course, a dominant factor. In the virtual environment you face highly variable demand and seasonal effects that are not fully known ahead of time. The capacity at hand is certainly limited. Failing to meet the market demand might ruin the company. Hence, there is a huge risk in expanding the market demand beyond the capabilities of the production shop floor.

What can we do, beyond wild guessing? One option that used to be popular in the past is to create huge finished goods stock. You can try this option, but it is not going to work very well here, at least not when you think of "huge" inventories. In the reality of manufacturing organizations, the evils of excess inventory are considerably more than here, as it may happen that certain inventories will turn out to be "dead" — meaning never be sold. What can be evident in this case is the price of producing things that are not needed right now.

The approach that will be used is based on the Theory of Constraints (TOC). This section does not detail how all the steps here are based on the generic TOC philosophy. (Refer to Chapter 2 for more information.) Instead, this section relates to the specifics of the case and comes up with some conclusions. Then we'll try to work it out in the reality (virtual) of the MICSS simulation.

What Blocks the Organization From Achieving More?

The state of the organization for January 1, 1999 is clear — the organization cries for **more sales**. There is no point in looking for reduction of costs. As you cannot reduce management expenses (they don't like that idea), you'll find out that reducing some inventory doesn't bring the organization into big profits. The only valid way is to **get more sales.** This surely does not surprise you. The Reference Run has shown that adding one new contract (Contract No. 3 for a package of A1 and C1) has turned out to be profitable. The problems that were revealed then were lack of materials and lack of capacity at the peak period. Once the purchasing policies were fixed, it seems that lack of capacity was minimal, causing only a small decrease in reputation.

Can We Sell Significantly More?

This question immediately leads us to think what should we sell more of? Should we accept Contract No. 2 (for A1) even though the cost analysis claims it is losing? Should we sell more C1, more B1, and less A1 as the product cost analysis suggests?

Do these questions have anything to do with whatever the situation is in the production shop floor? There is a general tendency to first decide upon the sales planning and then attempt to find a way for production to supply it. Only in cases where there is evident lack of capacity and no simple means to add capacity that the production planning clearly states, "Sorry, not possible." It seems as if the objective of Production is to satisfy the Sales requirements. Isn't it?

Well, in this particular case, there is no short-term way to add capacity. At the start of the year **there is no need to add capacity.** However, if we wish to make money we should **enhance the sales until capacity reaches its limit.** So, in a way Sales must take the challenge to sell all what the shop floor can do. Here we have a problem. There is no definite level of what the shop floor can do. It depends on the product mix. Choosing the "right" product mix can bring in much more money than another product mix that utilizes all the available capacity. So, the key question now becomes:

What is the Most Profitable Product Mix, Given the Current Capacity Profile?

Once we know the answer we can look for alternatives to expand the capacity and calculate the economical value of it. The above question already recognizes the need to look at the combination of the market demand and the operational limits. It leads us to think on the relationship between the two main parameters: market potential and internal capacity.

It looks as if the answer appears in the "Product Cost Analysis" window (at the Finance View, Information). Every unit of product is given a margin. This determines a priority between the products. So, Sales should strive to give more presence to the profitable products — up to the capacity limit.

TOC challenges the traditional cost analysis. It claims that capacity limit of the whole shop floor depends on the identity of one (or very few) resource, which will be the first to turn into a bottleneck. Once a single resource is a bottleneck, the excess capacity on the other resources doesn't help much to produce more (unless you have products that do not need the bottleneck). TOC argues that for an organization to function reasonably the vast majority of the resources need some minimal amount of excess capacity. Therefore, a product mix that succeeds to highly utilize most of the resources may look good on paper, but fails miserably in reality. The MICSS scenario lets you check this claim.

Assuming the TOC claim is right, it is imperative to identify the resource that will become a bottleneck first. The best product mix is one that highly utilizes that particular resource while leaving enough excess capacity on the rest of the resources. There is enough validation that in the case of Smart Industries, the most likely future bottleneck is M4. As a matter of fact we don't want M4 to become a true bottleneck because otherwise we'll miss too many orders, the reputation will go down, and so will the future of this company. We'd look to reach a stage where Sales generates a product mix that utilizes M4 to the point it is flexible enough to face the demand variability and ensures on-time shipments.

An important TOC term is throughput (T), which is similar to the notion of the added value. Throughput, according to TOC, is the rate at which the organization generates money. For a regular business company, T is the revenue from sales minus the truly variable costs (TVC); that is, the costs that vary directly with the number of units sold. This does not usually include direct labor. The main component of TVC is usually material. TOC is very strict in the definition of TVC. Only costs that truly change with every **unit of sale** are considered.

Setting the Sales and Production Strategy

Realizing the role of M4 in the design of strategy, let us gather some crucial information on M4 and the various products. The following table leads us to place our judgment on the right priorities.

Product/Contract	T Per Unit	M4 Minutes	T Per M4 Minute
A1	$232.53	4 + 7 = 11	$21.14
B1	$531.44	12 + 14 + 9 = 35	$15.18
C1	$866.65	8 + 4 + 8 + 10 + 11 = 41	$21.14
Contract 1 (30 B1)	$12,943.09	1050	$12.33
Contract 2 (45 A1)	$9,563.78	495	$19.32
Contract 3 (60 A1 + 15 C1)	$23,194.01	1275	$18.17

The basic idea behind this table to calculate the throughput generated per 1 minute of M4. This corresponds to the T/CU (throughput per constraint's unit) priority criterion. The T per product unit can be found in the Finance View under Product Throughput Summary. The contracts are calculated per shipment. You can easily calculate the T also from the Product Cost analysis and at the Contract Cost Analysis by subtracting the raw material value from the revenue. M4 minutes are based only on the processing times. All the operations done by M4 are included. The last column is simply the division of column 2 by column 3.

The underlying assumption is that M4 is the constraint (the limiting factor to higher profits). If we sell only C1, M2 will become the first bottleneck. Still, under the assumption that we sell all three products, M4 looks as the constraint to the potential increase in sales. The above table shows a tendency to prefer products A1 and C1 to B1. It further prefers Contract 2 (45 units of A1) to both Contract 1 (the existing contract) and the third one (for A1 and C1).

Setup time wasn't included in the table. One can easily argue that for any unit of C1 much more M4 time is needed because the five different operations need more setups than for A1. Setup time depends a lot on the planning batch size. Anyhow, you can validate that considering setups in the above calculation does not change drastically the sequence of priorities, except giving A1 a higher priority than C1.

The above priorities are very different than the one product costing implies. It leads to different strategic and tactical decisions. The Production policies should still be evaluated. The obvious means to enhance sales is to reduce the quoted lead-time. The other choice would be to reduce the price and thus lower the throughput per unit. In order to support the reduction in quoted lead-times and in view of the excess capacity, some changes should be introduced to the production policies, such as reducing the batch size, allowing partial WO to be worked on, and activating the MRP module every day instead of once a week.

In view of the need to enhance sales while keeping the reputation of the company intact, **Purchasing should only seldom choke the production resources.** Either the MRP module should be active at the Purchasing Department, ensuring adequate need dates are specified, or the order levels should be high enough to ensure availability of materials. Both methods should be based on the feedback of the control system.

Initial Decisions

Analyzing the possible actions. As both A1 and C1 are preferable to B1, the reduction of QLT on both to enhance the sales is called for. As A1 is a much higher volume product and we're uncertain how much more sales this move will generate, we should be more careful in reducing the QLT for A1. Note, while C1 is a more complex product than A1, it takes more time to complete a batch of C1 than to complete A1. But, the actual time it takes to process a batch is small relative to the queue time. The queue time depends mainly on the load of the most loaded machine. Hence, we should be more concerned with the possible increase of demand for the higher volume product than for more complex product.

In addition, some buildup of finished goods inventory seems a good idea. This should serve as a protection mechanism against delays in the production floor. Another cause for concern that can be benefited from finished goods inventory is the peak of demand from August through October. If we prepare some inventory when capacity is still available, it would be easier to go through the pressure of the peak.

Some changes in policies should be done in the Production Department. In the Machine Policy entry, all "complete WO" entries should be changed to "partial orders." This change may cause just a few additional setups, but is going to dramatically improve the flow of materials, thus reducing the actual lead-times. Also, there isn't much point in generating new work orders only once a week. This in itself adds 2.5 days to the average lead-time, and 5 days on some of the orders. The latter part causes the more significant damage. So, we should plan every day instead of once a week.

When we come to the Purchasing View, we need to set the parameters anew. We still intend to work with the Regular supplier. However, the Order Level needs to be set to allow at least 2 months for the items that cost more, and more than that for the items that cost less. Then, the Max Level is set so the purchasing orders will be between 200 to 300 units. The "Red Line Levels" are adjusted as well without trying to be too precise.

Actual Run Description

Initial Actions

Please, enter the decision *exactly* as stated here. This is a guided run, with more actions and explanations. After going through this you'll be able to test any other method or decisions.

Actions at the Marketing View

Product A1: Set the Quoted Lead Time to 25 days and the Safety Stock to 40

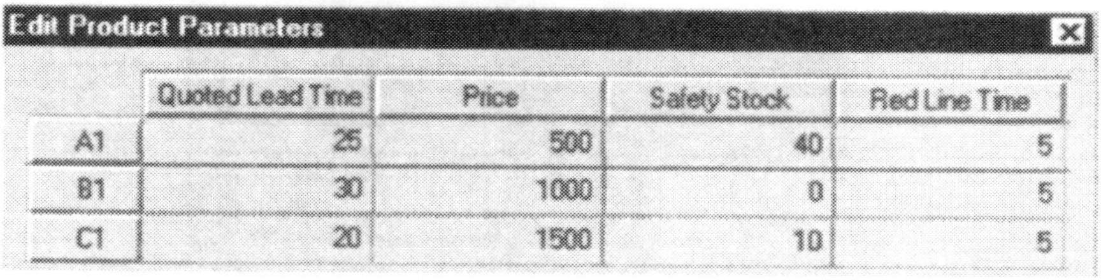

Edit Product Parameters

	Quoted Lead Time	Price	Safety Stock	Red Line Time
A1	25	500	40	5
B1	30	1000	0	5
C1	20	1500	10	5

Figure B.1 Sales Marketing View: end product parameters.

Product C1: Set the Quoted Lead Time to 20 days and the Safety Stock to 10

The rational for the difference in treatment was explained above. The Policies at the Marketing View should be as appears Figure B.1.

In the Production policies (the Set Machine Policy), all "complete WO" policies should be changed to "Partial Policies" (Figure B.2).

Next in the policies of the Production comes the entry of Work Order Planning. The Weekly planning frequency should be changed to Fixed Interval–1 day, which means planning new work orders every day. Also, the batch size should be reduced to 30 units. Figure B.3 is how that screen should look.

The levels in figure B.4 should be entered at the Purchasing View's Policies.

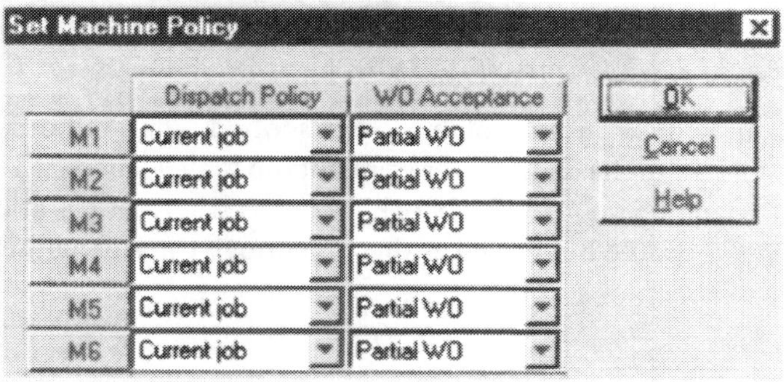

Set Machine Policy

	Dispatch Policy	WO Acceptance
M1	Current job	Partial WO
M2	Current job	Partial WO
M3	Current job	Partial WO
M4	Current job	Partial WO
M5	Current job	Partial WO
M6	Current job	Partial WO

Figure B.2 Set Machine Policy screen.

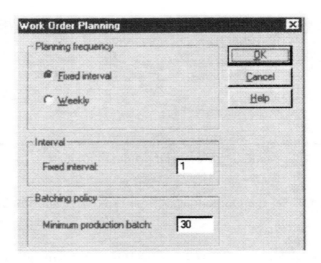

Figure B.3   Production work order planning screen.

The Guided Run Details

Actions (January 1, 1999)

After entering all changes, we recommend you go to the Production View and invoke the View Graph option (upper right of window). Start run for a month (Until Next Month). On 1/11/1999, Contract 2 will be displayed. You may put it into Hold and look at all relevant screens. After that you should click on "Restore Hold" (upper right of screen) and "accept" the contract. The run resumes after you authorize the decision.

Results Review (February 1, 1999)

During the previous run no problems were spotted — no red order viewed, no trouble in the purchasing, queues were not too long. Hence, success should be utilized. Higher level of safety stock for A1 and C1 (preparation for the peak at August) should be entered as there is enough capacity at the moment.

Actions

Reduce the QLT of A1 to 22. Raise the Safety Stock for A1 to 70 and for C1 to 20. Run until next month.

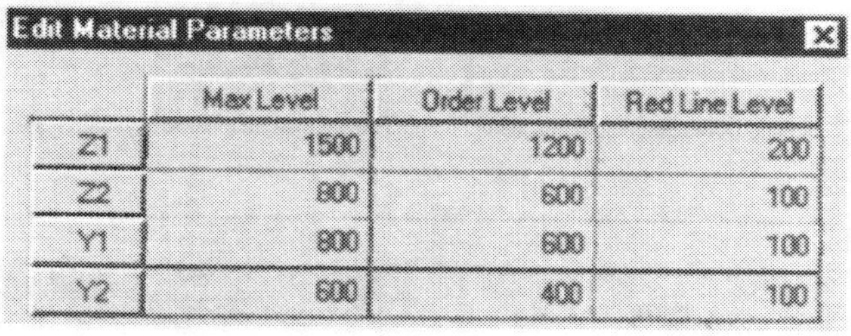

Edit Material Parameters			☒
	Max Level	Order Level	Red Line Level
Z1	1500	1200	200
Z2	800	600	100
Y1	800	600	100
Y2	600	400	100

Figure B.4 Purchasing Edit Material Parameters screen.

Results Review (March 1, 1999)

Just to be certain you've entered all the above decisions, the accumulative profit should be $27,461. During the run, assuming you've run at the Production View, you might have noticed the message of the "Material" with the red box. That means some of the materials were below the Red Line Level. Luckily, it didn't take too long until the supplies arrived. As no end-product has entered the Red Line, the capacity level still supports the load. Hence, we can add more safety stock.

Actions

Change the Safety Stock of A1 to 100 and C1 to 40. Run until next month.

On March 8, 1999, the run is interrupted by the option to extend the contract of B1. According to the analysis above, this contract is the least desirable. *Reject* the offer to extend the contract. The run should resume April 1.

Results Review (April 1)

The accumulative profit now stands on $49,637. Let's view the View Total Load Graph at the Production View (Figure B.5).

While the largest planned work is held at M6 (122 hours, 21 minutes), the most significant load accumulates at M4. M6 does the very last operations, hence all the work orders that are still in the shop are supposed to go through that machine. Right now only 3 hours and 40 minutes of work exist at the site of M6. Unless much more material will come through during the

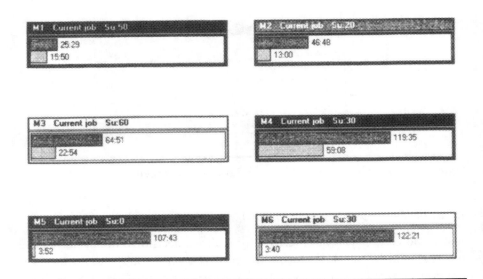

Figure B.5   View Total Load Graph screen.

day, M6 will "starve," meaning it'll be idle. M4 has about half of all the planned work already waiting at the site. The 120 hours planned for M4 means that a new work order should be processed at M4 not earlier than 3 weeks from now. As we now promise A1 and C1 in 4 weeks (A1 a little bit more than that) and the rest, the B1 orders and the contract shipment, later than that, makes the current situation a very reasonable one.

Let's also have a look at the "Rough Cut Capacity" screen (Figure B.6). M4 is clearly the most loaded machine. So, until now we've executed the

	Quantity		Production	Setup	Break	Total
A1	185					
B1	420	M1	54.7%	12.3%	3.5%	70.6%
C1	300	M2	69.2%	3.8%	5.3%	78.3%
		M3	68.4%	6.1%	5.2%	79.7%
		M4	74.9%	4.1%	8.6%	87.6%
		M5	63.8%	0.0%	4.7%	68.6%
		M6	68.1%	1.9%	3.8%	73.8%

Range: 6   day   Months

Rough Cut Capacity

Figure B.6   Rough Cut Capacity screen.

strategy we've decided upon, except that M4 is still far from being a bottleneck. Is 87% load, including setups and downtime, the maximum we can draw from M4?

A1 is our most profitable product. Let's cut its lead time even more. We should not add any more safety stock. We are not too sure we have enough excess capacity for that. The uncertainty in this environment is significant.

Actions

Reduce A1's lead time to 20 days. Run for 1 more month.

On April 15, 1999 the run is interrupted because of yet another new contract. This contract is less desirable than Contract 2 for A1 (see the above analysis). However, it is still better than our product B1. And such a contract does help to smooth the fluctuations in demand and uncertainty. So, should we take it?

Contract Acceptance Review

Do we have enough capacity? Let's view again the "Rough Cut Capacity" screen (Figure B.7).

This is like walking on thin ice. There is not enough protection against the uncertainty that such pressure in capacity causes. Not only is M3 loaded beyond

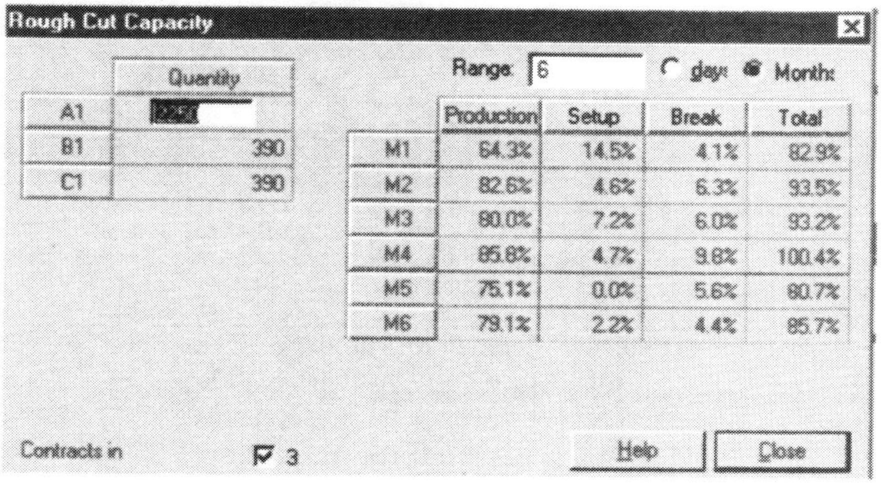
Rough Cut Capacity
Quantity
A1
B1 390
C1 390
Range: 6
days
Months
Production
Setup
Break
Total
M1 64.3% 14.5% 4.1% 82.9%
M2 82.6% 4.6% 6.3% 93.5%
M3 80.0% 7.2% 6.0% 93.2%
M4 85.8% 4.7% 9.8% 100.4%
M5 75.1% 0.0% 5.6% 80.7%
M6 79.1% 2.2% 4.4% 85.7%
Contracts in
3
Help
Close

Figure B.7 Rough Cut Capacity screen.

its limit, but both M2 and M3 don't seem to have enough flexibility; not enough excess capacity to provide flexibility to catch up with incidental delays.

On the other hand, why should we reduce the market demand for B1, our least profitable product? We can raise the price on B1 and thus get less demand and get more money for the demand that will be left. You can try and reduce the forecast for B1 from 390 units (the small table to the left of the screen) to 200 or even to 150 and see the reduced pressure. Let's raise the price in B1 by 10%. This is a mere guess. We'll see in 2 months time whether this was a good guess and, if not, we'll fix it.

Actions for April 15

If the contract is showing, put it on Hold. Raise the selling price of B1 to $1100 (instead of 1000). Then, click on "Resume Hold" and accept the contract!

The above sequence is important. If you first accept the contract, the run will resume and you either need to stop the run or wait until May. As the change in price needs to be introduced on April 15, 1999 to keep the same decisions with that of the guided run — do it in this sequence.

Results Review (May 3, 1999)

The load has even dropped to some degree. That is reasonable enough. No actions are needed.

Actions

Run until next month.

Results Review (June 1, 1999)

The queues look reasonable. Through the run there were considerable fluctuations, but now the situation seems to be under control.

Actions

Run until next month.

Results Review (July 1, 1999)

Previous run was quiet and stable. Maybe we've exaggerated with the raise on B1. Let's not be too greedy. We're facing a peak of demand in August, less than extreme pressure is useful.

Actions

Run for next month.

Results Review (August 2, 1999)

Load is still reasonable, but as we expect more to come, some extra care should be provided. In the Purchasing Department, Y1 is below the Red Line Level (94 units at stock). The next shipment for Y1 is expected on 8/12/99. We'll buy more units from the Fast supplier because we don't want any delay in the peak period. We'll also run week-by-week in the peak time.

Actions

Buy 200 units of Y1 from the Fast supplier. Run for 1 week.

Results Review (August 9, 1999)

The load is significantly increased. M4 has now 150 hours planned and only 12 hours, 15 minutes at the site. PK has 169 hours planned. This length of around 4 weeks of planned load is too much if you have promised to deliver in 4 weeks. As the queues contain some orders with due dates more than 4 weeks from now (the contract shipments and B1), it is certainly tight. As a first measure we'll reduce the safety stocks. This will prevent new orders from adding to the current load because the unassigned stock will be used.

Actions

Reduce the A1 safety stock from 100 to 70. Reduce the C1 safety stock from 40 to 30. Run for another week.

Results Review (August 16, 1999)

The load went down a little bit.

Actions

Run for another week.

Results Review (August 23, 1999)

The load, especially on M5 and M6, is still very high. Z1 just dropped from the Red Line level of 200.

Actions

Reduce the safety stock of A1 to 50 and C1 to 20. Buy 200 units of Z1 from the Fast supplier. Run until the end of the month.

Results Review (September 1, 1999)

The load went down a little. We still need a close watch. We'll run September week-by-week again. Run for 1 week.

Results Review (September 8, 1999)

The load is still around 4 weeks on PK (163 hours). But the load on M4 went down. Meanwhile, we have a red sign for the "Orders." B1 is red. Open the Master Production Schedule (Production View, Information). Work order 206 is colored in red. It is due on 9/14/99, which is 5 working days from now. Click on one of the two lines of work order 206 and then click on the "Show WO" entry. A subassembly operation (J12) is holding the material. M5 is busy on something else. But, M5 has no setup time. So, let's instruct M5 to start working on Operation J12 for Work Order 206. Close the open windows.

Actions

Click on the Actions (at the Production View) and again at "Set Unit Manually." Enter M5 as the machine you would like to address. Click on the third line of the list (WO206, J12) and click OK. Run for another week.

Results Review (September 15, 1999)

Loads are down a bit. We've still the red "Orders" message. This time it is A1 and again it is stuck behind M5. Check the "Shipment List" at the Marketing View. The current stock of finished goods (145) will be enough for the next 4 days. Still, M5 doesn't have setup time, so we'll instruct it to change to WO216, Operation J2.

Actions

Setup M5 to J2/WO216 (third line on the list for M5) through the Actions menu; set Unit Manually entry. Run for another week.

Results Review (September 22, 1999)

Load is down considerably. B1 is shown in red, but if you take off the "View Total Load" for a minute you'll notice that PK actually works on B1. You cannot make it any quicker than that. Click again on the "View Total Load" to see the loads.

Actions

Run until next month.

Results Review (October 1, 1999)

Load is now normal again. The peak is probably over. Right now the red "Materials" box is on.

Actions

Buy 200 units for Z1. Run until next month.

Results Review (November 1, 1999)

During October both red "Materials" and "Orders" were showing for short periods. The load goes down. There is no real pressure anymore. We can try and get more sales by reducing the quoted lead-times of A1 and C1 just a little.

Actions

Reduce the QLT of both A1 and C1 to 18. Run for another month.

Results Review (December 1, 1999)

Load is normal. We can squeeze even more, but we're close to the end of the year. Leave it at that.

Actions

Run for another month.

On December 20, 1999 a request to extend Contract 1 appears. Confirm the extension even though it is for next year. Our period as the management of Smart Industries is ending on January 1, 2000.

Results Review (January 3, 1999)

This is the end of the simulation run. We have a nice profit after taxes of $322,382.

This is NOT the best financial results. If you take more risks you may get more, but you may sometimes lose everything. When you utilize your most loaded resource so that no flexibility is there, you need luck to survive. Take this run as a reference for **good enough and achievable.** Please note that not one shipment was missed! In itself this points out that higher profit is possible, but at the risk of losing a little bit of reputation. The problem is, though, that the difference between losing just a little bit of reputation and losing ALL reputation is very slim.

Drum–Buffer–Rope (DBR) and the Guided Run

In Chapter 2 (The Theory of Constraints and ERP), a description of TOC's planning method is described. In another part of that chapter the control mechanism entitled "Buffer Management" is outlined. The guided run, based on the generic TOC principles are a somewhat simplified form of both Drum–Buffer–Rope and Buffer Management. How does DBR work in the above solution?

The Drum is dictated by the market demand. However, the market demand is controlled by the company according to the capacity of M4. Instead of scheduling M4 in detail and notifying the customers of the promised due date, the company announces a fixed quoted lead-time per project and carefully monitors the queue behind M4. Impacting the market demand by reducing the QLT and raising prices is exactly the meaning of **exploitation** of the constraint. The Drum is the outcome of the considerations of the market demand and the possible impact of certain actions on the market demand vs. the limited capacity on M4.

The "Time Buffer" is directed at shipping. By allowing daily planning and by removing the obstacles to the flow of materials, the quoted lead-time is actually the "buffer" at which the company is committed to ship to customers. This is true when the QLT becomes much shorter than the MRP release calculation. Otherwise, it is the MRP calculation that dictates the length of the time buffer.

The contracts represent here market demand that is known well in advance. The work orders for the contracts are planned 30 days before shipping. Then, the MRP lead-time of 4 days per operation in the combined BOM and routings releases the materials up to 28 days before the due date. These timings are used as a time buffer.

The task of the "Rope" is to ensure that no work is released prior to the date dictated by the Drum. This is fully kept here. The only exception may be the build of finished goods stock. However, this is in line with the assessment that in the peak demand M4 does not have enough capacity to deal with the demand, hence, some well-controlled finished goods stock is provided. The crucial part in implementing a simplified DBR planning is to install Buffer Management as a control mechanism.

Buffer Management is actually implemented here through the Red Line mechanism. What is called in the TOC literature "zone 1" is here "red line," meaning a warning that the protection is almost exhausted. The Buffer Management mechanism is installed here to control the due date performance and the availability of materials.

It is up to you, the reader and the user of the ERP–MICSS simulation case to decide how effective the combination of Drum–Buffer–Rope and Buffer Management actually is. You certainly can try many alternative methods with this simulation.

Index